Future of Business and Finance

The Future of Business and Finance book series features professional works aimed at defining, analyzing, and charting the future trends in these fields. The focus is mainly on strategic directions, technological advances, challenges and solutions which may affect the way we do business tomorrow, including the future of sustainability and governance practices. Mainly written by practitioners, consultants and academic thinkers, the books are intended to spark and inform further discussions and developments.

Marina Dabić • Adeel Tariq
Marko Torkkeli
Editors

Artificial Humans

Reimagining Organizational Creativity and Innovation in Industry 5.0

Springer

Editors
Marina Dabić
University of Dubrovnik
Dubrovnik, Croatia

School of Economics and Business
University of Ljubljana
Ljubljana, Slovenia

Marko Torkkeli
Lappeenranta-Lahti University of Technology
Kouvola Unit, Finland

Adeel Tariq
Lappeenranta-Lahti University of Technology
Kouvola Unit, Finland

ISSN 2662-2467 ISSN 2662-2475 (electronic)
Future of Business and Finance
ISBN 978-3-032-06603-9 ISBN 978-3-032-06604-6 (eBook)
https://doi.org/10.1007/978-3-032-06604-6

This Springer imprint is published by the registered company Springer Nature Switzerland AG
The registered company address is: Gewerbestrasse 11, 6330 Cham, Switzerland

Foreword

It is a privilege for us to welcome you to the new book *Artificial Humans: Reimagining Organizational Innovation in Industry 5.0* edited by Prof. Marina Dabic, Dr. Adeel Tariq, and Prof. Marko Torkkeli. Each of the chapters provides a valuable contribution to the field how human–AI collaboration can transform organizational innovation and other important processes and practices in the era of Industry 5.0.

This is particularly relevant today, as the rapid advancement of AI has disrupted traditional approaches to performance management, innovation, and strategic planning. It has resulted in a shift where AI is recognized as a complementary resource to augment human capabilities. This requires a thorough understanding to provide guidelines with respect to opportunities, challenges, solutions, and practical implications that could arise from human and AI collaboration. In this regard, this book provides innovative ideas about how human–AI collaboration offers huge advantages to firms through improved decision-making, speeding up existing processes, and enhancing the efficacy of managerial choices. Each chapter in this book presents unique contributions exploring fresh perspectives on emergence of human–AI collaboration for Industry 5.0, strategic orientation, organizational dynamics, and innovative technical and methodological approaches.

This book also provides managers and policymakers with a better understanding of the key traits of human–AI collaboration to develop a successful, fully functional human–AI collaboration. This book also elaborates trends and factors that shape and have had a big influence on triggering human–AI collaboration, with a focus on Industry 5.0 to get the most value from such collaboration. In addition, the confluence of artificial intelligence, humans, and innovation in a range of sectors, including supply chain, fashion, and healthcare, is also included to enable the creation of innovations for those who need them, creating unique value and enhancing overall progress. Furthermore, this book explores the influence of collaboration on the innovative work behaviors and creative performance of the employees. This is likely to help the organization in understanding personnel behavior and acceptance toward emergence of Human–AI team, which is likely to have a positive influence on creativity and performance. Lastly, this book elaborates ethical implications of human–AI collaboration for organizations and individuals' thinkers to understand who exploits the moral wiggle whenever there is room available and who shall be held responsible for bias and accountability for non-transparency in processes. This book, with its practical examples, gives readers a fresh perspective to utilize human–AI collaboration positively for improving innovation and encouraging them to create innovative solutions.

Marina Dabić

University of Dubrovnik
Dubrovnik, Croatia
School of Economics and Business
University of Ljubljana, Ljubljana, Slovenia
Lappeenranta-Lahti University of Technology
Kouvola Unit, Kouvola, Finland
Lappeenranta-Lahti University of Technology
Kouvola Unit, Kouvola, Finland

"In a world increasingly shaped by industrial revolutions and intelligent technologies, this timely book offers deep insight into how human–AI collaboration can unlock new avenues for organizational innovation. It provides both inspiration and practical guidance for those seeking to navigate the emerging landscape of Industry 5.0-based human-centric collaboration, aiming to drive improved innovation. A must-read for scholars, practitioners, and policymakers alike."

—John Bessant, *Emeritus Professor of Innovation and Entrepreneurship, University of Exeter, UK*

"In a time defined by rapid technological evolution, this insightfulbook confronts a fundamental imperative: how can human and artificialintelligence converge to unleash creativity and drive innovation? Itmeticulously addresses the spectrum from change management frameworks totangible sector-specific implementations and the bedrock of ethicalconsiderations. For academics, industry leaders, and policymakersseeking to understand and shape the transformative power of Industry5.0, this is must-read."

—Mei-Chih, *Professor, National Tsing Hua University, Hsinchu, Taiwan*

"Those who adopt AI and change the way they do business will succeed over those who thinks AI will replace the creative innovation phenomenon. This book is a master guideline for a successful AI adoption."

—Tugrul U Daim, *Professor, Portland State University, USA*

Contents

About the Editors and Contributors

About the Editors

Marina Dabić is Full Professor of Entrepreneurship and International Business at the Faculty of Economics and Business, Croatia, and the University of Ljubljana, School of Business and Economics. She published more than 200 papers indexed on the Web of Science and Scopus. Professor Dabić is an Editor in Chief for Technology in Society, Senior Department Editor for IEEE—Transactions on Engineering Management, Associate Editor of Technological Forecasting and Social Change, and for Strategic Change journal. She was a member at large for the IEEE-TEMS 2020-2022. Prof. Dabić prepared a background report on HE Innovate published by EC/OECD. In 2021, she received WAIB best paper award from the Academy of International Business. Currently, she is WP leader for Industry 4.0 in the Horizon 2020 RISE Open innovation project, Interreg Wool project, and ERASMUS K2 BENEFIT and VOIS project.

Adeel Tariq is an Adjunct Professor and Post-Doctoral Researcher at the Lappeenranta-Lahti University of Technology, Finland. Previously, he worked as an Assistant Professor of Innovation and Technology Management at National University of Sciences and Technology, Pakistan. His main research is related to emerging and disruptive technologies, digital innovation, small business performance, and circular performance. He has published in prestigious academic journals such as Technological Forecasting and Social Change, Journal of Intellectual Capital, Journal of Knowledge Management, and Technology in Society, among others. He is Review Editor of Technology in Society Journal and Associate Editor of Journal of Innovation Management. He was a Guest Editor of Transportation Research Part E Journal. As a principal investigator and collaborator, Dr. Tariq has collaborated on EU (Erasmus+) funded projects such as VOIS and ArtIST and currently, he is contributing to EU Horizon Co-Fund Project, Dream + Plan. In addition, he has contributed to various regional, national, and international projects.

Marko Torkkeli is a Professor of Technology and Business Innovations at the Lappeenranta-Lahti University of Technology (LUT), Finland. His research interests focus on technology and innovation management, strategic entrepreneurship, growth venturing, and decision support systems. He serves as the Director of

Publications of the International Society for Professional Innovation Management (ISPIM) and is one of the founding editors of the open-access, multidisciplinary Journal of Innovation Management.

Contributors

Lotta Achrén South-Eastern Finland University of Applied Sciences, Kouvola, Finland

Andra Marta Babre Riga Technical University, Riga, Latvia

Matijs Babris Riga Technical University, Riga, Latvia

Jude Bennett University of Winchester, Winchester, UK

Luciana Blaha University of Edinburgh, Edinburgh, UK

David M. Brown University of Edinburgh, Edinburgh, UK

Krishan Chandarana University of Edinburgh, Edinburgh, UK

Marina Dabić University of Dubrovnik, Dubrovnik, Croatia

School of Economics and Business, University of Ljubljana, Ljubljana, Slovenia

Csaba Deák University of Miskolc, Miskolc, Hungary

Bahar Bahramian Dehkordi Lappeenranta-Lahti University of Technology, Kouvola Unit, Finland

Amber Devin Heriot Watt University, Edinburgh, Scotland

Mir Dost University of Winchester, Winchester, UK

Richard Evans Dalhousie University, Halifax, NS, Canada

Margaret A. Goralski Quinnipiac University, Hamden, CT, USA

Krystyna Górniak-Kocikowska Southern Connecticut State University, New Haven, CT, USA

Muhammad Shehzad Hanif University of Central Punjab, Lahore, Pakistan

Arshia Hashmi UCP Business School, University of Central Punjab, Lahore, Pakistan

Tapani Honkanen School of Business, Design and Technology, Häme University of Applied Sciences, Hämeenlinna, Finland

Muhammad Imran KIMEP University, Almaty, Kazakhstan

Giedrius Jucevicius Vytautas Magnus University, Kaunas, Lithuania

Khadija Kaukab UCP Business School, University of Central Punjab, Lahore, Pakistan

Majid Khan Lecturer of Management and Sustainable Business at the School of Management, Massey University, Palmerston North, New Zealand

Sajid Khan Ghulam Ishaq Khan Institute of Engineering Sciences and Technology, Topi, Pakistan

Baibhaw Kumar University of Miskolc, Miskolc, Hungary

MinHye Lee University of Winchester, Winchester, UK

Yoon Kyung Lee Clothing and Textiles Department, Pusan National University, Busan, South Korea

Muhmmad Shahid Mehmood UCP Business School, University of Central Punjab, Lahore, Pakistan

Elina Mikelsone Riga Technical University, Riga, Latvia

Mazhar Mohsin School of Business, Design and Technology, Häme University of Applied Sciences, Hämeenlinna, Finland

Muhammad Faraz Mubarak Dalhousie University, Halifax, NS, Canada

Sajid Nazir Lappeenranta-Lahti University Technology, Kouvola Unit, Finland

Archana Parashar IIM Raipur, Abhanpur, India

Anna Salnikova Riga Stradins University, Kurzemes Rajons, Riga, Latvia

Khuram Shahzad University of Vaasa, Vaasa, Finland

Abhiyash Singh IIM Raipur, Abhanpur, India

Adeel Tariq Lappeenranta-Lahti University of Technology, Kouvola Unit, Finland

Marko Torkkeli Lappeenranta-Lahti University of Technology, Kouvola Unit, Finland

Sarah Zafar NUST Business School, National University of Sciences and Technology, Islamabad, Pakistan

Keze Zhang Department of Science and Technology Studies, Faculty of Science, University of Malaya, Kuala Lumpur, Malaysia

List of Figures

Effective Human AI-Collaboration for the Boost in Productivity

AI-Driven Collaborative Maintenance Strategies for Repairable Parts: A Cost-Effective Solution for Pakistan's Aviation Sector

Sociomaterial Perspectives of AI and Procurement

Human-Artificial Intelligence (HAI) Teaming in STEM Education: A Conceptual Framework for Skill Development in Industry 5.0

List of Tables

Human-Artificial Intelligence (HAI) Teaming in STEM Education: A Conceptual Framework for Skill Development in Industry 5.0

Introduction to Artificial Humans: Reimagining Organizational Innovation in Industry 5.0

Adeel Tariq, Marina Dabić, and Marko Torkkeli

Artificial intelligence's (AI) capabilities are constantly expanding (Jorzik et al., 2023; Westphal et al., 2023), and they are challenging established companies' business models and procedures for performance management, innovation, and strategy (Raftopoulos & Hamari, 2023). This has resulted in a shift, where AI is recognized as a complementary resource to augment human capabilities (Hao et al., 2024). Humans can assign a rising number of decision-making duties to automated systems, where AI can be used to cut costs for businesses, speed up existing processes, and enhance the accuracy and efficacy of managerial choices (Burström et al., 2021). This intersection of human creativity and artificial intelligence has opened unprecedented possibilities for innovation and is transforming the way human work and make decisions (Murray et al., 2021).

Humans and AI bring out the best in each other through collaborative intelligence. While people contribute leadership, creativity, teamwork, and emotional insight, AI enhances the partnership with its speed, scalability, and strength in data processing. Together, they form a powerful team, each amplifying the other's strengths (Wilson & Daugherty, 2018). Moreover, when humans and AI collaborate, businesses see the biggest performance benefits, according to research involving 1500 enterprises (Wilson & Daugherty, 2018). Artificial human, which is referred to as human-AI collaboration, can occur in different distinct ways; however, distinction based on automation versus tasks could be very helpful to elaborate on this

A. Tariq (✉) · M. Torkkeli
Lappeenranta-Lahti University of Technology, Kouvola Unit, Finland
e-mail: Adeel.Tariq@lut.fi; marko.torkkeli@lut.fi

M. Dabić
University of Dubrovnik, Dubrovnik, Croatia

School of Economics and Business, University of Ljubljana, Ljubljana, Slovenia
e-mail: mdabic@unidu.hr

M. Dabić et al. (eds.), *Artificial Humans*, Future of Business and Finance,
https://doi.org/10.1007/978-3-032-06604-6_1

symbiotic. This collaboration can also be divided according to tasks versus automation level at the organization; thus, a human-AI collaboration matrix is created for this purpose in Chap. 1 of this book, where four categories exist based on the degree of automation (low versus high) and the type of tasks (routine versus innovative) in the organization. These categories can be named as (1) operational collaboration, (2) innovative collaboration, (3) augmented collaboration, and (4) transformation collaboration. The complexity of the human-AI collaboration increased based on the degree of automation and the level of innovativeness of the tasks. Thus, the fusion of human creativity with artificial intelligence is leading us into uncharted territories of innovation. Human-AI collaboration is likely to shape the pattern and possibilities of innovation (incremental and radical), existing and future work practices, human acceptance of AI-driven technologies, and the very nature of collaboration between humans and robots in ways that we are only beginning to comprehend.

Human-AI collaboration offers several advantages to organizations, economies, and societies, ranging from reimagining businesses and introducing creative products to improving creative performance and innovative work behaviors of employees. It could also lead to better idea management and idea development, boost productivity, and promote fairness and equity in the various systems (Wilson & Daugherty, 2018). Moreover, human-AI collaboration is more important and likely to play a crucial role in transforming industry into human-centered design with an aim to lessen negative environmental impact as required by Industry 5.0. However, to fully utilize human-AI collaboration advantages and potential, practitioners and managers need to understand, optimize, and train AI, describe their results, and ensure that they are used responsibly (Wilson & Daugherty, 2018). This prompts the need for this book to comprehend the dynamics of scenarios, where managers effectively use human-AI collaborations for improved results and regulators and policymakers throughout the world can assess the essential ethical and regulatory challenges.

Given the importance and emerging relevance of this domain, we received around thirty cutting-edge proposals for inclusion in the book. However, after a rigorous review process focused on quality and the theme of human-AI collaboration, we selected 14 outstanding chapters for the final publication, and additionally, one introduction chapter. We have included manuscripts from 14 different nations: Canada, the United States of America, the United Kingdom, New Zealand, Finland, Lithuania, Hungary, Latvia, Croatia, Malaysia, South Korea, Kazakhstan, Pakistan, and India, and four continents: Asia, Europe, North America, and Oceania.

The first few chapters of the book are focused on the fundamentals of the human-AI collaboration and how it's facilitating to shape the businesses, especially in the emergence of industry 5.0. Second, the section of the book mainly covers how human-AI collaboration enhances creativity and innovation, productivity, idea management, procurement, innovation, and human resource management. The third section of the book examines the ethical framework in the context of human-AI collaboration. Each chapter in this book has been carefully curated through a rigorous double-blind peer-review process. The journey began in June 2024, when contributors submitted their initial proposals. After a detailed evaluation, selected authors were invited to develop full chapters, which they submitted by the end of September 2024. These submissions then underwent further review and refinement, culminating in the final selection of chapters by March 2025. The result is a collection of timely, high-quality research that explores how human-AI collaboration can drive innovation and creativity within organizations, particularly in the evolving landscape of Industry 5.0.

Structure of the Book

Following the introduction, this book starts with Chap. 2, "Human-AI Collaboration for Organizational Innovation in Industry 5.0." This chapter elaborates on the significance of human-AI collaboration for the advancement of organizational innovation efforts. It also explains how human–AI collaboration can enhance organizational creativity and innovation and, finally, argues that such collaboration is essential for Industry 5.0 organizations to redesign organizational processes to further enhance human–AI collaboration.

Chapter 3 "Creative Fashion Design through Collaboration with AI: In the age of Industry 5.0," discusses how humans and AI can collaborate within creative fashion design tasks to promote human-centered, sustainable, and innovative design in the age of Industry 5.0. It elaborates the significance of effective collaboration between humans and AI to allow skilled fashion professionals to focus more on the fashion field for more sustainable and human-centered fashion industry.

Chapter 4 is entitled, "Navigating AI Adoption: In-House Development vs. Outsourcing for Industry 5.0." It explores the impacts of developing AI in-house versus outsourcing its development on human-AI collaboration and organizational innovation from the perspective of Industry 5.0. Through in-depth interviews with industry experts, this chapter gathers valuable insights, which, in the end, helped to provide a holistic overview of these strategies to help decision-makers maximize the benefits of adopting AI by selecting a suitable strategy based on their organizational circumstances.

Chapter 5, "Human Intelligence and Artificial Intelligence in Collaboration: Change Management, Creative Performance, and Societal Expectations," discusses the collaboration between human intelligence (HI) and artificial intelligence (AI), emphasizing a shift from a master-servant dynamic to a true collaborative partnership, especially with the advent of Industry 5.0 in the European Union. It highlights the rapid advancements in generative AI, like ChatGPT, which enhance human capabilities but raise concerns about managing this swift growth and understanding our human relationship with other life forms.

Chapter 6, entitled "Human-AI Partnership and Innovative Work Behavior," presents human-AI collaboration as a new driver of innovative work behavior. It talks about how the synergy between AI and humans is unlocking the next frontier of not just creativity but productivity and collaboration whilst outlining the challenges, such as skill gaps and ethical issues, that need to be solved, so that we can move people at work to the next level and argue for a human-centric route to realizing the potential of this new frontier.

Chapter 7, "Transformative Impact of Artificial Intelligence on Human Resource Management in the Era of Industry 5.0," explains how AI is revolutionizing human resource management through automated recruitment, training, and performance appraisal with a boost in employees' engagement. In this regard, Industry 5.0 promotes innovation and inclusivity, minimizes turnover, and encourages continuous learning.

Chapter 8, "Challenges in Adoption of AI-driven Collaborative Innovation," presents the challenges associated with the adoption of AI-based collaborative innovation using the Analytical Hierarchy Process (AHP), a multi-criteria decision-making (MCDM) method, and draws on the perspectives of 29 experts from Asia, Europe, and North America. The results indicate that ethical concerns (EC) must be prioritized first, followed by organizational change (OC) in second place, technical complexity (TC) in third, and legal and regulatory (LR) concerns in fourth. These domains signify the principal challenges to the effective execution of AI in collaborative innovation.

Chapter 9, entitled "Artificial Humans and Innovation in Industry 5.0," explores the rise of collaboration between humans and artificial intelligence and its significance in fostering value and innovation in Industry 5.0. It primarily focuses on the commercial applications of artificial humans and presents a new framework for innovation that aligns with Industry 5.0's objectives.

Chapter 10, "Artificial Intelligence vs. Human Creativity from an Idea Management Perspective," compared the idea generation performance of human teams and AI under different configurations, using both quantitative and qualitative analyses to assess their outputs. AI consistently outperformed human teams in generating a greater number of ideas. Human-generated ideas scored higher in feasibility and contextual depth, reflecting a refined understanding of real-world constraints.

Chapter 11, "Effective Human AI-Collaboration for the Boost in Productivity," reviews the human-AI collaboration, including its principles, frameworks, tools, challenges, and future directions. It illustrates the impact on decision-making, productivity, and innovation across professional sectors: healthcare, manufacturing, retail, and defense. It also outlines approaches toward building adaptive, interpretable, and human-centered AI systems, arguing the importance of regulatory guidelines and cross-disciplinary studies to guarantee responsible AI implementation.

Chapter 12, "AI-Driven Collaborative Maintenance Strategies for Repairable Parts: A Cost-Effective Solution for Pakistan's Aviation Sector," explores the implementation of an AI-driven collaborative innovation framework designed to address the challenges faced by the Pakistani aviation sector, including inefficiencies, rising costs, and environmental sustainability concerns. By adopting a centralized, AI-driven system, the framework aims to optimize repair order management, enhance transportation efficiency, and integrate predictive maintenance capabilities in the aviation sector.

Chapter 13, entitled "Sociomaterial Perspectives of AI and Procurement," explores the various facets of AI in procurement, focusing on how it Shapes organizational practices, and the role of regulation. To provide a comprehensive perspective, this chapter reviews how AI is conceptualized in procurement both from a procurement tools and item of procurement standpoint, followed by a discussion on the wider implications for humans as augmented workers. This understanding supports the early regulation of AI, as well as the need to understand how AI algorithms shape organizations from the moment of their inclusion.

Chapter 14, "Human-Artificial Intelligence (HAI) Teaming in STEM Education," explores the role of human-AI (HAI) teaming in STEM education, focusing on how AI tools like Intelligent Tutoring Systems and Adaptive Learning platforms can enhance teaching and learning for Industry 5.0 skill development. Through a conceptual framework and SWOT analysis, it highlights both the benefits, such as personalized learning and data-driven insights, and the challenges, including ethical concerns and costs, offering a roadmap for inclusive and effective AI integration in education.

Chapter 15, "Ethical Considerations of Human-AI Collaboration: A Normative Perspective for Organizational Practice," examines the moral implications of human-AI interaction in the workplace by relying on normative ethical perspectives, including egoism, utilitarianism, ethics of duty, rights, and justice. It offers theoretical insights and practical guidelines for human-AI collaboration.

Human-AI collaboration will be a cornerstone in redefining business processes, revolutionizing creativity and innovation, and shaping the very future of work. Its transformative impact will not only enhance efficiency but also unlock unprecedented opportunities for growth, adaptability, and competitive advantage in an increasingly AI-driven world. In "Artificial Humans: Reimagining Organizational Innovation," we dive deep into understanding the ramifications of this innovative symbiosis, widespread adoption, advantages, and unlimited opportunities in the context of Industry 5.0. By shedding light on human-AI collaboration, we have provided readers with innovative insights, knowledge, and valuable managerial implications to embrace emerging technological formations. We expect that this book stimulates more investigation into human-AI collaboration by experts, business executives, academics, researchers, creators, regulators, and legislators.

References

Burström, T., Parida, V., Lahti, T., & Wincent, J. (2021). AI-enabled business-model innovation and transformation in industrial ecosystems: A framework, model and outline for further research. *Journal of Business Research, 127*, 85–95.

Hao, X., Demir, E., & Eyers, D. (2024). Exploring collaborative decision-making: A quasi-experimental study of human and generative AI interaction. *Technology in Society, 78*(102662). https://doi.org/10.1016/j.techsoc.2024.102662

Jorzik, P., Yigit, A., Kanbach, D. K., Kraus, S., & Dabić, M. (2023). Artificial intelligence-enabled business model innovation: Competencies and roles of top management. *IEEE Transactions on Engineering Management, 71*, 7044–7056.

Murray, A., Rhymer, J., & Sirmon, D. G. (2021). Humans and technology: Forms of conjoined agency in organizations. *Academy of Management Review, 46*(3), 552–571.
Raftopoulos, M., & Hamari, J. (2023). *Human-AI collaboration in organisations: A literature review on enabling value creation.*
Westphal, M., Vössing, M., Satzger, G., Yom-Tov, G. B., & Rafaeli, A. (2023). Decision control and explanations in human-AI collaboration: Improving user perceptions and compliance. *Computers in Human Behavior, 144*, 107714.
Wilson, H. J., & Daugherty, P. R. (2018). Collaborative intelligence: Humans and AI are joining forces. *Harvard Business Review, 96*(4), 114–123.

Dr. Adeel Tariq is an Adjunct Professor and Post-Doctoral Researcher at the Lappeenranta-Lahti University of Technology, Finland. His main research is related to emerging and disruptive technologies, digital innovation, and performance. He has published in prestigious academic journals, such as Technological Forecasting and Social Change and has contributed actively to various EU-funded projects.

Professor Marina Dabić is a Full Professor of Entrepreneurship and International Business at the Faculty of Economics and Business, Croatia, and the University of Ljubljana, School of Business and Economics. She published more than 200 papers indexed on the Web of Science and Scopus. Professor Dabić is an Editor in Chief for Technology in Society, Senior Department Editor for IEEE-Transactions on Engineering Management, Associate Editor of Technological Forecasting and Social Change, and for the Strategic Change journal. She was a member at large for the IEEE-TEMS 2020-2022. Prof. Dabić prepared a background report on HE Innovate published by EC/OECD. In 2021, she received the WAIB Best Paper Award from the Academy of International Business. Currently, she is a partner to CUES Horizon Project and she has contributed as a WP leader for industry 4.0 in the Horizon 2020 RISE Open Innovation project, Interreg Wool project, and ERASMUS K2 Benefit and VOIS project. Marina Dabić has been consistently recognized among the TOP 2% of scientists worldwide by Stanford University since 2022. She also serves as the Editor and series founder of prestigious Springer Book series on Applied Innovation Technology Management.

Prof. Marko Torkkeli is a Professor of Technology and Business Innovations at the Lappeenranta-Lahti University of Technology (LUT), the Kouvola Unit in Finland. His research interests focus on technology and innovation management, strategic entrepreneurship, growth venturing, and decision support systems. He has published over 300 articles in academic journals and conferences. He serves as the Director of Publications of the International Society for Professional Innovation Management (ISPIM) and is one of the founding editors of the open-access, multidisciplinary Journal of Innovation Management.

Human-AI Collaboration for Organizational Innovation in Industry 5.0

Lotta Achrén, Adeel Tariq, Marina Dabić, and Marko Torkkeli

Introduction

Artificial intelligence (AI) has gained momentum in academic and managerial discourse due to recent advancements and its potential to either enhance or undermine human cognitive capabilities (Chowdhury et al., 2023; Jorzik et al., 2023). Researchers argue that skilled jobs are more likely to be transformed by the expansion of AIs than they are to be eliminated, and a distinction should be made between task automation and job automation, with AI likely to play a significant role in the latter (Chui et al., 2015; Markoff, 2016). AI is likely to continue to replace routine tasks while simultaneously expanding the number of positions requiring creativity, adaptability, and problem-solving skills (Markoff, 2016). It's conceivable that in the not-too-distant future, light-speed computation-intensive, dull professions are likely to be undertaken by AIs, while human beings can perform occupations that need creativity, innovation, and value addition (Krakowski et al., 2023). Human roles would be more towards creative and innovative jobs compared to routine operational tasks (Hao et al., 2024; Jarrahi, 2018). One relevant example could be that predictive analytics with machine and deep learning can

L. Achrén
South-Eastern Finland University of Applied Sciences, Kouvola Unit, Finland

Lappeenranta-Lahti University of Technology, Kouvola Unit, Finland
e-mail: lotta.achren@xamk.fi

A. Tariq (✉) · M. Torkkeli
Lappeenranta-Lahti University of Technology, Kouvola Unit, Finland
e-mail: adeel.tariq@lut.fi; marko.torkkeli@lut.fi

M. Dabić
University of Dubrovnik, Dubrovnik, Croatia

University of Ljubljana School of Economics and Business, Ljubljana, Slovenia
e-mail: mdabic@unidu.hr

M. Dabić et al. (eds.), *Artificial Humans*, Future of Business and Finance,
https://doi.org/10.1007/978-3-032-06604-6_2

help human experts in their decision-making and, in particular, knowledge experts can come up with new ideas and make better predictions using statistical inference methods motivated by data (Jarrahi, 2018).

Researchers extended this debate and documented that augmentation and automation can complement one another and coexist together (Xue et al., 2022). The type of work and organizational strategy would determine whether to use automation, augmentation, or combinations of the two (Nguyen Thi Ngoc & Elbanna, 2023). Researchers contend that although AI is superior to humans in some areas of labor, such as finding patterns in vast datasets, processing large data sets, and data management, humans still exhibit high levels of decision-making (Teodorescu et al., 2021). An organization may attain the best level of efficiency with the intervention of both humans and AI since some managerial operations in a company and enhancing efficiency of other operations (Holzinger, 2016; Reis, 2024). In a similar line, other academics contend that rather than entirely replacing humans in the workplace, AI can augment and complement human performance (Park et al., 2024; Raisch & Krakowski, 2021).

In line with this, researchers have argued that the performance of work is significantly improved when humans and robots work together (Fügener et al., 2022; Raisch & Krakowski, 2021), and this combination may be more effective than either one working alone (Nguyen Thi Ngoc & Elbanna, 2023). For instance, studies show that in the customer service industry, machines may free people from simple, repetitive jobs and enable them to concentrate on high-level tasks, which adds more value to an organization (Huang et al., 2019). Moreover, a recent cognitive study found that human-AI hybrid teams performed better than human-only teams in allocating resources for crisis management (McNeese et al., 2021).

Studies on the interaction between humans and AI have begun to appear, and during the past 5 years, there has also been a sharp increase in the number of papers discussing AI adoption in decision-making (Achmat & Brown, 2019). Researchers have delved into a number of topics, including the interactions between people and AI, user perceptions, and AI design and setup of AI systems (Fernandes & Oliveira, 2021; Kumar et al., 2019). Moreover, researchers have advanced this discussion to understand the potential barriers to this collaboration such as Human mistrust of AI is a significant barrier to human-AI cooperation, even though AI has demonstrated its potential to collaborate with people (Wilson & Daugherty, 2018). A survey of about 2000 US customers found that 42% of them have no faith in AI of any kind. Only 16% of respondents think AI can diagnose illnesses, 13% think it can drive itself, and 4% think it can handle human resources-related duties (Dujmovic, 2017). Additionally, AI is increasingly being implemented into organizational administration and has been used in a variety of fields, including healthcare, finance, human resource management, and criminal justice. Applications of AI such as IBM Watson and Google DeepMind's AlphaGo are well-known examples (Bao et al., 2023).

The available literature offers insightful information on the many facets of human-AI synergy. The study, however, does not provide a holistic understanding and a coherent picture of human-AI collaboration and its consequences especially in the context of organizational innovation, leading to a lack of agreement on the main conclusions. A more thorough and organized understanding of human-AI decision-making is necessary given the prominence of AI in decision-making, data management, and creating divergent and novel ideas, which is necessary to provide a strong base to organizations for effectively boosting creativity and innovation. Therefore, this chapter focuses on three main questions: (1) What are the trends and factors that shape the increased adoption of such augmentation? (2) What is the influence of human-AI collaboration on organizational creativity and innovation? (3) What is the influence of human-AI collaboration on the industry 5.0 practices?

This chapter offers some notable contributions to dialogue on AI-human collaboration and organizational creativity in two distinct ways: firstly, it extends the knowledge related to human-AI collaboration and its significant influence to give an organization advantage in terms of boosting its creativity and innovation performance. It is in line with recent literature on AI and Innovation management that demands extension of knowledge in this domain to provide useful information for academia and practice (Achmat & Brown, 2019; Fügener et al., 2022). Secondly, this research explores the emerging trends such as digital transformation that are increasingly highlighting the significance of AI-human collaboration for improving the organizational transformation process along with enhancing its innovation capabilities. Thus, understanding these factors is pivotal and can improve an organization's ability to effectively utilize AI-human collaboration.

This study is structured using the following scheme: first, it provides a background on emergence of human and AI collaboration; second, it provides the factors that shape the increased adoption of human-AI collaboration; thirdly, it shares a critical understanding and review of human-AI collaboration on creativity and innovation, lastly, it elaborates the future research directions.

From Tools to Partners: The Evolving Role of AI-Human Collaboration

Artificial intelligence (AI) had its origins in the 1940s, most notably in 1942 when the Three " Robotics, Laws of Robotics were proposed by Isaac Asimov in his short tale "Runaround. artificial intelligence, and computer scientists have been influenced by these laws, which center on a robot's conduct toward people and its survival (Mariani et al., 2023). Concurrently, British mathematician Alan Turing created the Bombe, an electromechanical computer that was utilized in World War II to decode the Enigma code, while he worked on practical applications. Turing began thinking about machine intelligence after reading The Bombe (Mariani et al., 2023). The Turing Test, which determines if a machine is artificially intelligent if it cannot be distinguished from a human during contact, was proposed by him in his 1950 publication "Computing Machinery and Intelligence," which introduced the idea of intelligent machines (Haenlein & Kaplan, 2019).

The term "artificial intelligence" was first used formally approximately 6 years later, in 1956, at Dartmouth College in New Hampshire, during almost

8-week-long Dartmouth Summer Study Mission on Artificial Intelligence (DSRPAI), it was held by the Stanford computer scientist John McCarthy and Marvin Minsky (Haenlein & Kaplan, 2019). Since its inception as a field of study in the 1950s, artificial intelligence (AI) has remained largely unexplored by the public and scientists for more than 50 years (Haenlein & Kaplan, 2019). AI can be simply defined as "the use of computational machinery to emulate capabilities inherent in humans, such as doing physical or mechanical tasks, thinking, and feeling" (Huang et al., 2019, p. 31). Due to its unmatchable capabilities in addition to the rise of Big Data and advancements in computing power, AI has gained prominence in academic and policy makers discussions.

Mainly AI prominence started around 1997 as an expert system, expert systems operate under the premise that human intellect may be reduced to a set of "if-then' statements and formalized using a top-down methodology (Haenlein & Kaplan, 2019). Resultantly, on May 11th, 1997, IBM's Deep Blue created history when it defeated human world chess champion Garry Kasparov, becoming the first artificial intelligence to do so. This historic occasion caused a paradigm change in the chess community, upending long-held beliefs about human significance. The triumph, which was analogous to Francis Fukuyama's idea of "the end of history" applied to chess, sparked concerns about the place of humans in the game and heralded a new era in which algorithms could outplay human players (Muller, 2022).

AI can be categorized based on its capabilities and its functions to facilitate other machines. Based on capabilities, AI can be categorized into three types: (1) narrow intelligence: capable of operating independently on a particular job; (2) general intelligence: capable of learning, perceiving, comprehending, and doing all human-like tasks; and (3) superintelligence: surpasses human intelligence by a significant margin (Joshi, 2019). Based on functions, AI can be classified into four types: (1) reactive machines: which are capable of responding to inputs but lack memory and learning; (2) machines with limited memory: which can make decisions by learning from past data; (3) theory of mind: AI can comprehend the needs, feelings, opinions, and mental processes of other people; and (4) self-awareness: this type of AI is capable of sensing and evoking emotions in the individuals it interacts with and it can also have emotions, needs, beliefs, and potentially even desires of its own (Joshi, 2019).

The emergence of ChatGPT marks a turning point in AI engagement during a time when virtual assistants like Siri and Cortana are commonly used in talks. This breakthrough comes at the same time when we are eagerly awaiting affordable self-driving cars and realizing the extraordinary powers of AI, which have been shown in winning challenging games like chess and Go (Muller, 2022). The demise of human dominance in chess begs the question of why players still play. Nowadays, is chess just a light game like Monopoly or Cluedo, or are players taking it seriously? The reality check defies expectations by showing an increase in the number of chess enthusiasts and their level of skill, casting doubt on the idea that the period of significant human involvement in chess has come to an end (Muller, 2022).

Human-AI and AI-Human Collaboration in Business

The paradigm of human vs machine in chess has given way to a cooperative human plus AI strategy, which allows for reciprocal improvement. An online chess competition that was motivated by Garry's centaurs attempted to provide an answer in 2005 (Muller, 2022). They invited supercomputers, human grandmasters, mixed-human teams, and artificial intelligence (AI) contestants to compete for a grand prize. Unsurprisingly, a human plus AI centaur outperforms a human alone. Amazingly, though, a Human + AI Centaur also triumphs over the lone computer (Muller, 2022). Beyond chess, this revolutionary change, marked by the emergence of Human-Agent Collaboration (HAC), affects a variety of industries as people use artificial intelligence (AI) to perform better (Muller, 2022). Human-AI (agent) collaboration is explained by researcher as, "HACs are a new class of socio-technical systems in which humans and smart software, agents, engage in flexible relationships to achieve both their individual and collective goals. Sometimes the humans take the lead, sometimes the computer does, and this relationship can vary dynamically" (Jennings et al., 2014, p. 80). This human-AI relationship is a form of agile one where the role is to enhance each other capabilities.

According to Westphal et al. (2023), AI-human collaboration falls between two extremes: where the AI system makes all decisions and acts independently without human input, and no automation, where there is no AI system to provide support and human decision-making is required. However, according to Muller (2022), human-AI collaboration can take three shapes: (1) Initially, the human component first trains and directs the AI, encouraging creativity. Divergence among AIs results from this symbiotic interaction, which is similar to the distinct evolution of separated human twins (Muller, 2022). (2) In the second phase, AI alters the human's cognitive processes, leading to a dramatic transformation in their identity and personality. This psychological transformation is likened to developmental phases in human behavior, moving from an adult-child relationship to a possible adult-adult relationship (Muller, 2022). And (3) in a hypothetical third phase, human-AI cooperation communicates via different channels, distinguished by interlocutors (high-level AIs, humans, or other channels), in addition to within their components. These stages will only pass if AI research continues to progress, communication bio-interfaces are improved, and human-AI partnerships are allowed to evolve together (Muller, 2022).

Wilson and Daugherty (2018) have already elaborated on the first two stages of human-AI collaboration (Muller, 2022). Further, human-AI collaboration can be divided into two categories: one where humans support AI and second where AI supports humans. Both categories can be further subdivided into further categories. Human support AI in three specific roles. They have to educate computers on how to perform certain tasks, explain the outcomes of those activities—especially when the findings are illogical or controversial—and support the proper use of robots. This involves taking precautions to prevent robots from hurting people (Wilson & Daugherty, 2018):

1. Training: To train machine-learning algorithms, large training data sets must be gathered for a variety of purposes, such as teaching medical apps to identify illnesses or machine-translation apps to handle idiomatic idioms. AI programs, like Microsoft's Cortana, need to be carefully trained to take on distinct personalities, including assurance and compassion. New technologies are trying to give AI assistants even more complex human characteristics, such as empathy. Examples of these technologies are start-ups like Koko (Wilson & Daugherty, 2018).
2. Explaining: Because AI systems work through opaque processes (the "black-box problem"), it becomes more important to provide nonexperts with explanations of their behavior. For practitioners to understand how AI influences sentencing or medical advice, these "explainers" are essential in domains where decisions are evidence-based, such as law and medicine (Wilson & Daugherty, 2018).
3. Sustaining: AI systems require maintenance. Companies need "sustainers" who are committed to making sure AI operates accurately, safely, and ethically in addition to explainers who explain results (Tiziana et al., 2024). This entails positions such as safety engineers, who proactively foresee and reduce possible harm resulting from artificial intelligence. The ability of industrial robots to detect surrounding humans and function without endangering them, for example, is a characteristic that is given top priority by their engineers (Wilson & Daugherty, 2018).

Similarly, AI supports humans in three dimensions: they can sharpen human cognitive strength, interact with clients and coworkers to free humans' time for more complex work, and take on human abilities to enhance human physical capabilities (Wilson & Daugherty, 2018).

1. Amplifying: Artificial intelligence can improve our capacity for analysis and decision-making by delivering the appropriate knowledge at the appropriate moment needed for innovation, for example, Autodesk's Dreamcatcher AI helps designers be more creative. Upon supplying criteria and preferences, designers are presented with thousands of designs that precisely fit their requirements. Dreamcatcher's iterative process, which manages intricate computations, frees up designers to concentrate on human assets like artistic sensibility and expert judgment (Wilson & Daugherty, 2018).
2. Interacting: Businesses use the partnership between humans and AI to create innovative and efficient interactions with both customers and employees. Aida is a virtual assistant that SEB, a significant Swedish bank, uses to communicate with millions of customers. Armed with natural language conversational skills, Aida can access a vast amount of data to answer frequently asked questions, assess the tone of a call, and even pose follow-up inquiries. Human representatives can concentrate on more complicated issues, especially those involving disgruntled customers who need individualized attention, while Aida takes care of basic chores (Wilson & Daugherty, 2018).

3. Embodying: While AI entities such as Aida and Cortana are mainly digital, intelligence can also exist in robots that operate alongside humans in certain situations. These AI-enabled devices, which are outfitted with sophisticated sensors and actuators, can recognize things and people. They can operate safely next to people in environments like factories and warehouses. Robots in manufacturing are developing into intelligent "cobots" that can perform repetitive activities like heavy lifting while people concentrate on jobs that call for judgment and skill (like building gear motors (Wilson & Daugherty, 2018).

According to Krakowski et al. (2023), human-AI collaboration can be divided into substitution and complementation for businesses. In substitution, AI can substitute humans in redundant and routine jobs as in many corporate sectors, AI capabilities are gradually replacing human decision-making and problem-solving tasks. The paper does, however, stress that this replacement tendency might not offer a long-term advantage because cost benefits are easily copied by rivals (Krakowski et al., 2023). Secondly, human augmentation skills improve AI capabilities in a complementary manner, which is critical in business. Social engagement, extensive contextualization, and creative brainstorming are some of these augmentation capabilities. The importance of governmental initiatives is emphasized by pointing up investments in personnel augmentation capabilities and encouraging organizational environments. In contrast to chess, there could not be a complete replacement of conventional domain-specific skills in business, which opens up possibilities for fusing human knowledge with computer capabilities to produce novel complementarities (Krakowski et al., 2023).

Mutual communication and information exchange between humans and AI systems enable cooperative decision-making in the field, utilizing the complementing advantages of both the user and the AI system to accomplish common goals. For example, in revenue management, AI systems help users, such as hotel managers, make precise price predictions considering different factors such as season, profit, and competition, to name a few (Westphal et al., 2023). This relieves them of the burden of considering a variety of factors and allows them to delegate decision-making to the AI system, which lessens the workload associated with repetitive decision-making tasks.

Figure 1 elaborates the type of human-AI collaboration in business, where it could be divided between AI as substitution or complementation. In terms of human substitution, AI can do automative tasks without much human efforts. In the complementation part, AI can support human, or human can support AI in terms of training, explanation, sustaining as well as amplification of tasks, increase interactions, and embodiment of AI into machines for doing task their own.

Figure 1 is important, but it does not completely reflect the human-AI collaboration in terms of tasks, thus, authors have created a different matrix to clearly explain such collaboration.

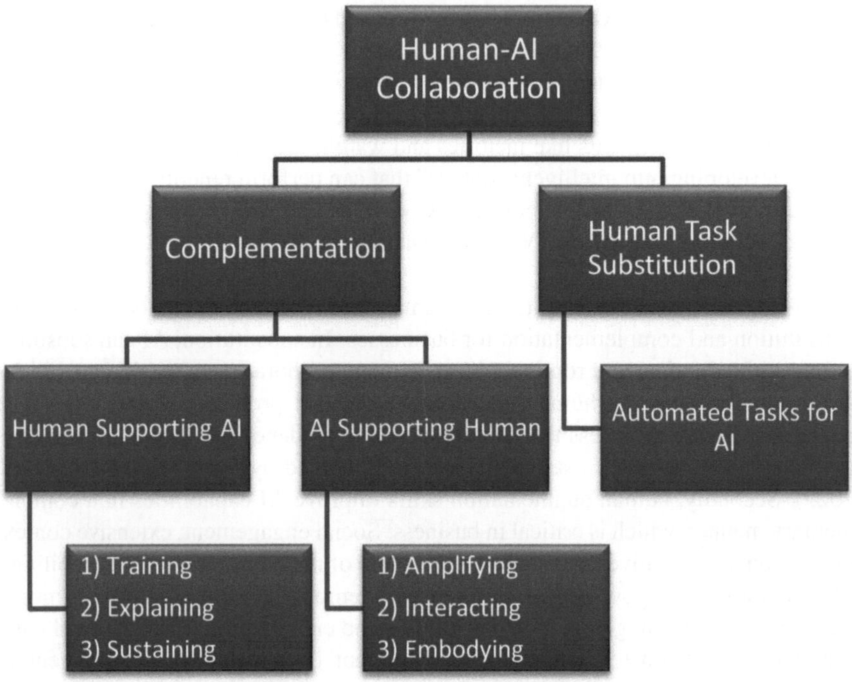

Fig. 1 Types of human-AI collaboration in business (elaborated by authors)

Human-AI Collaboration Matrix

Human-AI collaboration can also be divided according to tasks versus automation level at the organization; thus, a human-AI collaboration matrix is created for this purpose, where four categories exist based on degree of automation (low versus high) and type of tasks (routine versus innovative) in the organization. These categories can be named as (1) operational collaboration, (2) innovative collaboration, (3) augmented collaboration, and (4) transformation collaboration. Complexity of the human-AI collaboration increased based on degree of automation and level of innovativeness of the tasks (Fig. 2).

1. Operational collaboration can be defined as collaboration to manage routine tasks, where AI manages the operations and human involvement is required to manage difficult or uncertain queries. For example, in a chatbot on the website to manage routine queries, however, human involvement is needed to deal with complex issues and provides personalized assistance. This collaboration could also be applied in terms of innovation where routine queries are answered by AI-powered bodies and human specialists tend to address complex queries.
2. Innovative collaboration, in this type, humans utilize AI capabilities to deal with and process the data, information, and outcomes and utilize their creative and

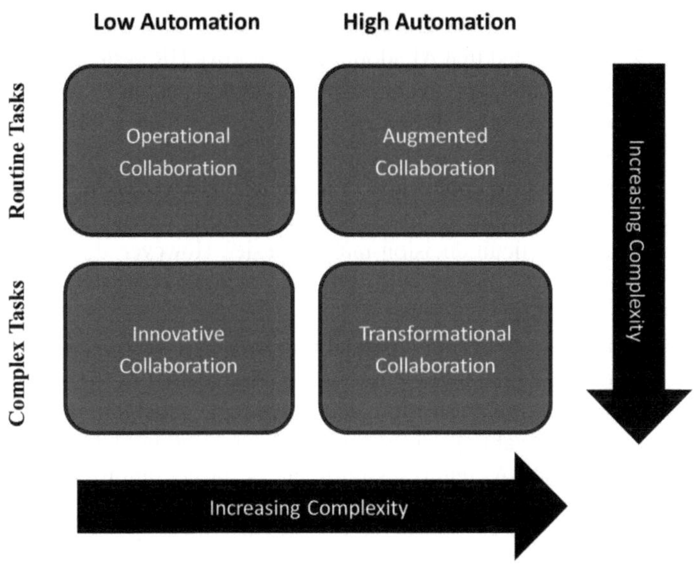

Fig. 2 Human-AI collaboration matrix (developed by authors)

strategic thinking to create novel solutions, products, or achieve groundbreaking results. Humans utilize AI to understand emerging customer preferences for the products through trends and consumer preferences and incorporate more valuable features in the products, services, and solutions.

3. In augmented collaboration, human utilize AI to optimize processes, productions, product development, monitor product quality, and increase efficiency of other operations. Humans supervise the tasks and make necessary changes to increase efficiency.
4. Transformational collaboration refers to a high level of human involvement and supervision, along with high degree of automation with advanced AI capabilities. This type of collaboration may result in radical or disruptive products introduced by the organization. For instance, scientists can utilized AI to accelerate development of new drugs, where human can analyze AI suggested compounds, design experiments, and make strategic decisions.

Factors that Influence Adoption of Human-AI Collaboration

Ashrafi and Kabir (2023) elaborated on the factors that influence the financial industry's perception of the value of robots with human-AI capabilities. They documented that consumer perceptions of value and consumer perception of risk play a critical role in adopting a robo-advisor for financial services, where consumer perceived value is further influenced by the perceived enjoyment, anthropomorphism, and perceived performance. Similarly, perceived risk is shaped by the complexity, trust, and perceived risk of the consumers (Ashrafi & Kabir, 2023). Similarly, Agarwal (2022) documented that AI adoption to improve HR systems is influenced by a number of factors, including technological readiness, organizational preparedness, and benefits perception. This can improve the efficacy of HR systems. AI-human collaboration can enhance HR operations by offering human-like interfaces, such as responding to applicants' inquiries using data that has already been imported. It also automatically gathers information, builds a database, examines it, and ultimately makes difficult decision-making easier. However, they mention that human-AI collaboration is limited in developing countries compared to developed countries (Agarwal, 2022).

Similarly, Hou et al. (2023) documented that trust in human-AI teams is influenced by three factors, which include interactive characteristics (expected anthropomorphism, expected relationship, and expected satisfaction), ecological features (peer effect, enabling circumstances), and individual features (self-efficacy). Trust in human-AI teams also influences further employees' intentions to cooperate with AI teams, whereas the author finds support for all factors influencing the human-AI teams, except perceived anthropomorphism. Also reported were two factors as the most important in human-AI collaboration for improved task outcomes: (1) trust, as trust in AI systems leads to better human-AI collaboration for enhanced task outcomes, and (2) agent transparency which is also important, as it provides human insights about how the system works and reduces information asymmetry, which is essential for the trust is human-AI collaboration to achieve required task outcomes.

Berretta et al. (2023) developed a scale to be utilized for the adoption of AI technologies in collaboration with humans and argued that work characteristics, job identity, job perception, and evaluation of work influence the human-AI collaboration. They listed the following factors as a driver of human-AI collaboration: job satisfaction, job security, work-life balance, meaningful work, skill development, career advancement, autonomy, control, decision-making, feedback, social interaction, training and development, support, and resources. They also mention that these factors are positively correlated with one another, indicating that they support cooperation between humans and AI. For instance, Job security, work-life balance, and meaningful work have all been proven to positively connect with job satisfaction. This implies that human workers are more likely to be content with their collaboration with AI systems when these conditions are met (Berretta et al., 2023).

Most of the factors examined in these studies are reflective of individual organizational factors, both at the organizational level and individual level; however, limited attention is given to external factors, such as external stakeholders in organizational efforts to improve human-AI collaboration at the workplace. It is an important avenue for further exploration and needs significant attention to report the external factors that are essential to understanding for better adoption and increasing human-AI collaboration. Thus, we have summed up all the factors in Fig. 3 represent influencing factors for human-AI collaboration.

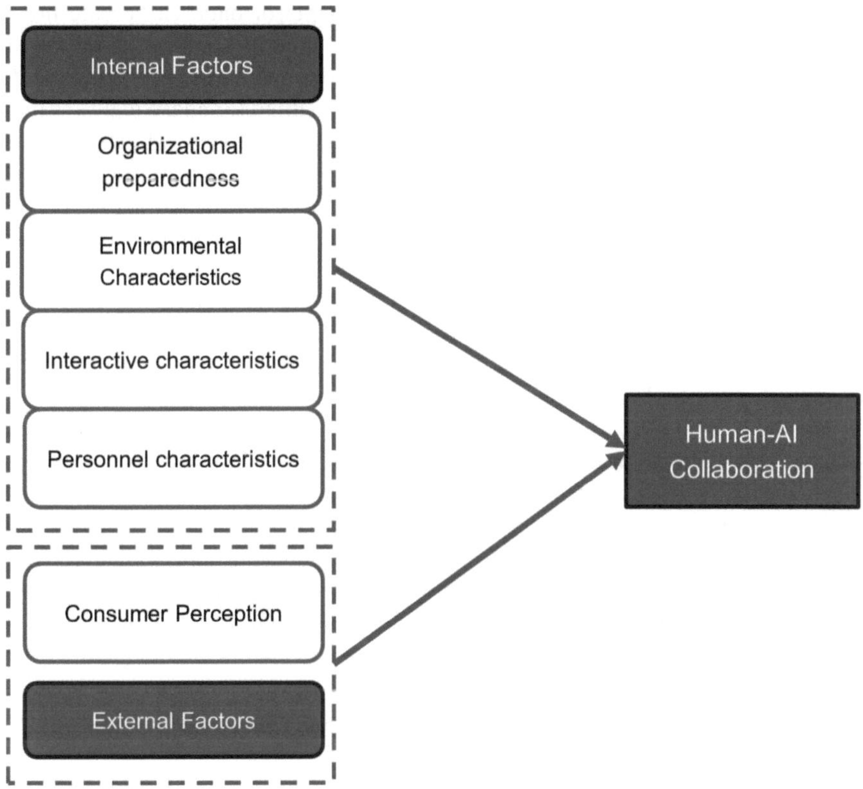

Fig. 3 Factors influencing human-AI collaboration (elaborated by authors)

Human-AI Collaboration and Organization Creativity and Innovation

Human-AI collaboration offers huge advantages to the firms, such as humans can enhance AI's better prediction capacity by utilizing their distinctive skills, such as imaginative ideation, extensive contextualization, and social interaction (Brynjolfsson & McAfee, 2014; Krakowski et al., 2023). As an illustration, product designers can persuade customers by understanding their challenges (Verganti et al., 2020). Whether we are envisioning groundbreaking products, pioneering services, or revolutionary processes, the fusion of human creativity with artificial intelligence is leading us into uncharted territories of innovation. Human-AI collaboration is likely to shape the pattern and possibilities of innovation (incremental and radical), existing and future work practices, human acceptance of AI-driven technologies, and the very nature of collaboration between humans and robots in ways that we are only beginning to comprehend.

Human-AI collaboration has the potential to greatly influence and enhance organizational creative and innovation performance, as it is highly likely that

AI, due to its capabilities to process large amounts of data, can create novel viewpoints, ideas, and resources to aid in the creative process (Mariani & Nambisan, 2021). Researchers argued that creativity and innovation also include the idea that AI's problem-solving skills are better suited for analytical jobs than for making intuitive decisions; however, if utilized effectively, AI can also create some additional benefits, like enhancing organizational creativity and innovation (Jarrahi, 2018; Mariani et al., 2022; Tariq et al., 2024). Based on the analysis of multiple cases, Wu et al. (2021) advised prioritizing human collaboration with AI above rivalry, utilizing their capabilities for mutual gain. Artificial intelligence (AI) is a useful adjunct to human intelligence, since it may help to organize knowledge and facilitate cross-spatial collaboration. In addition to highlighting the value of collaboration, this cooperative strategy encourages co-creation between AI and humans.

Hitsuwari et al. (2023) compared the difference between human creativity and human-AI collaboration creativity; for that purpose, they designed an experiment, where the aesthetic assessment of poetry produced by humans and AI was done. The findings showed that poetry created by humans and AI together scored higher on beauty than poetry created by AI and humans alone, indicating that human-AI cooperation fosters greater originality in creativity. Moreover, Muller (2022) argues that human and AIs collaboration can foster creativity more effectively than AIs due to three main factors:

1. Posing new questions: Human collaborations are highly inquisitive; they go beyond analytics to ask original questions that encourage exploration and improvement of procedures.
2. Allowing ambiguity: This collaboration welcomes ambiguity and understands the importance of potential solutions that go beyond the immediate situation, in contrast to algorithms that search for definitive answers.
3. Soft skills and ethics: Human-AI collaboration is superior to AIs that are only concerned with project results when it comes to inspiring stakeholders, fostering creativity, and resolving moral conundrums. Additionally, Muller (2022) argued that the primary rationale for symbiotic innovations focuses on how well they work to provide "new rules" for practical situations that can be applied to goods, services, or procedures. These developments cover a wide spectrum, from little tweaks to significant overhauls. In this regard, Jarrahi (2018) suggests that AI's rapid data collection and analytical abilities, combined with individuals' effective intuition power and understanding could facilitate the interactive collaboration between AI and humans.

According to Eapen et al. (2023), despite worries about taking jobs, AI improves human creativity and tackles issues of democratizing innovation by effectively combining and refining undeveloped concepts in idea competitions through five ways.

Encourage divergent thinking: Tools like Midjourney, ChatGPT, and Stable Diffusion are examples of generative AI, which promote creative idea production and divergent thinking.

For example, a text-to-image program called Midjourney combined an elephant with a butterfly to produce a "phantafly." Moreover, stimulating Stable Diffusion with Midjourney's output produced a variety of product proposals, demonstrating the quick and economical assessment of ideas (Eapen et al., 2023).

Question expertise bias: Generative AI encourages designers to challenge established beliefs about product shape and function by inspiring them with unconventional concepts, especially in the early stages of new product development. Unlike conventional techniques, this strategy helps to overcome biases such as the Einstellung effect, functional fixedness, and design fixation. One example of how generative AI inspires unorthodox product ideas is the use of Stable Diffusion to develop crab-inspired toy designs without functional specifications (Eapen et al., 2023).

Assist in idea evaluation: AI improves concept specificity and offers thorough evaluations, which help with idea evaluation. For example, ChatGPT assessed concepts for reducing food waste, weighing the benefits and drawbacks of dynamic expiration-date packaging, an app for food donation, and an educational initiative. It provided detailed assessments that considered factors including novelty, practicality, specificity, effect, and workability, making it possible to gain a more thorough grasp of the possibilities of each proposal (Eapen et al., 2023).

*Encourage refinement of ideas***:** Idea competitions are streamlined by generative AI through efficient concept merging and refining the ideas to reduce human efforts and help them choose better ideas in this regard. For instance, authors used AI to reduce food waste and explain three ideas: dynamic expiration dates on packaging, a food donation app that links extra food to people in need, and a label education campaign and resultantly, AI skillfully integrated these concepts into an all-inclusive program to reduce food waste, suggesting public education, smart packaging with dynamic expiration dates, and a surplus food donation program (Eapen et al., 2023).

Encourage cooperation between and among users: By easing interactions between a company's designers and potential consumers, as well as encouraging cooperation among users, generative AI is likely to streamline collaboration in the development of new products, which supports the traditional innovation process. The process of cocreating new products is made easier and less expensive by technology, which, on other hand, could be time-consuming and expensive (Kutvonen et al., 2010). Businesses can, for example, give consumers access to design tools, so that customized goods based on consumer preferences can be made. Furthermore, user-generated designs can be uploaded on crowdsourcing platforms for community assessment and further development of the best designs through teamwork (Eapen et al., 2023). Moreover, AI can also automate tasks, which can facilitate humans to focus on other avenues, such as the implementation of innovation better and enhance the innovation performance of the organization.

Researchers have explored AI implementation in several industries, where human-AI collaboration can enhance organizational creativity and innovation outcomes, such as producing creative arts, urban innovation, and financial services (Ashrafi & Kabir, 2023; Hitsuwari et al., 2023; Muller, 2022). However, more evidence is required to advance the knowledge in this domain.

Human-AI Collaboration for Innovation in Industry 5.0

Industry 4.0 and 5.0 differ fundamentally: Industry 4.0 is technology-driven and refers to intelligent networking of machines and processes, while Industry 5.0 is driven by values such as sustainability (Xu et al., 2021) and human-centricity (Rožanec, Novalija, et al., 2023). Whereas the cyber-physical system design of Industry 4.0 focuses on automation (Kans & Campos, 2024), Industry 5.0 has an impact on how we live, work, and interact (Alojaiman, 2023) and focus on human-machine collaboration (Kans & Campos, 2024). Khosravy et al. (2023) reported that Industry 5.0's perspective of human-robot collaboration is coming together and coexistence of humans and robots in the same space is getting popular. Moreover, this human-AI collaboration for improved innovation in Industry 5.0 is different from Industry 4.0, as IoT and other technologies are used to facilitate collaboration amongst industrial systems, which was disregarded in Industry 4.0 as its focus is on cyber-physical factories. Industry 5.0 aims to reconcile humans and robots for collaborative work, which is a novel objective (Khosravy et al., 2023). Industry 5.0 takes a distinct tack when it comes to human-robot interaction because of the clever collaborative style in which the jobs are shared, as humans are at the center of this collaboration. Because humans create and innovate while robots perform monotonous, consistent tasks, humans are thus actively involved in the manufacturing cycle (Khosravy et al., 2023).

Some of the applications of the industry 5.0 are already transforming the manufacturing industry where in a few sectors, including manufacturing, healthcare, and finance, artificial intelligence (AI) and machine learning are being utilized to automate processes and enhance decision-making. Furthermore, digital twins, which are virtual representations of physical assets, are being used to train employees, forecast failures, and monitor and optimize performance (Mihai et al., 2022). Thus, human-AI collaboration is more important and likely to play a crucial role in transforming industry to human-centered design to lessen negative environmental impact. It is also likely to enable the industry to withstand and prepare well for the upcoming challenges. Even in its early stages, Industry 5.0 is already changing the manufacturing landscape by incorporating cutting-edge technologies like Internet of Everything, edge computing, and AI. This progress is expected to increase productivity, flexible work processes, and dynamic human-smart system cooperation. Industry 5.0 is based on three main premises:

1. Human-centered design: Industry 5.0 places a strong emphasis on the value of creating products and processes with the requirements of human workers in mind. Making workspaces that are secure, comfortable, and empowering is part of this (Leng et al., 2022).
2. Sustainability: Industry 5.0 aims to lessen manufacturing's negative environmental effects. This entails maximizing resource efficiency, cutting waste, and utilizing renewable energy sources (Leng et al., 2022).
3. Resilience: Industry 5.0 is built to withstand shocks like cyberattacks and natural disasters. Predictive maintenance, flexible supply chains, and cybersecurity are a few examples of this (Leng et al., 2022).

Thus, it would be wise to say that Industry 5.0 considers technological advancement with consideration of human well-being (Passalacqua et al., 2022). In the highly automated and digital factories of the future, humans are likely to do fewer physical jobs and more tasks involving decision-making and problem-solving within the framework of a manufacturing system that is becoming more and more complex, socio-cyber-physical (Tóth et al., 2023). Moreover, to facilitate designing and implementing advanced AI processes for open innovation, Industry 5.0 mechanism could enable the implementation of human-AI collaborative processes (Dabić, Daim, et al., 2023; Tóth et al., 2023). Tóth et al. (2023) argued that for Human-AI collaboration in Industry 5.0, an organization needs to design plants that have digital memory that is consistent for both humans and AI services, and it requires three key features: online visualization services, the plant collaboration language with user services, and the common plant knowledge base. Different stakeholders are likely to participate, such as company managers, plant specialists, frontline workers, and citizen groups. The company culture and the digital maturity of the plant's human resources can be taken into consideration when determining the implementation strategy and levels of collaboration (platforms) (Tóth et al., 2023).

Rožanec et al. (2023a, 2023b) asserted that multi-objective weaving and collaborative intelligence are the two key components in this situation where machines shall not replace human forces entirely. Hoch et al. (2023) argued that integrating AI with humans provides multiple benefits for Industry 5.0 as improving social welfare, productivity, and innovation in collaborative work situations. They further asserted that human-centric design should be prioritized, interdisciplinary collaborations should be encouraged, and responsible governance should be put in place. In the same vein, Balart and Shryock (2024) proposed a conceptual framework for incorporating AI in education to meet the needs of Industry 5.0 with a comprehensive approach that balances the development of human-centered skills, such as ethical reasoning, and technical skills, such as AI technological proficiency for Industry 5.0. Framework shall be flexible and responsive, mirroring the ever-evolving landscape of artificial intelligence technologies and the engineering field (Balart & Shryock, 2024). Reported that integrating technologies such as IOT, AI, and automated manufacturing can transform traditional manufacturing processes into a more data-driven, human-centered, and flexible process. As a data infrastructure that improves automated manufacturing operations, IoT may play a critical role in lowering material waste, encouraging superior quality, and facilitating safe and quick manufacturing (Martini et al., 2024).

Conclusion

This chapter explains the significance of human-AI collaboration for the advancement of organizational innovation efforts. In doing so, it highlighted the evolving role of symbiotic relationships and the factors that influence the human-AI collaboration. Main factors found in this research include consumer perception, organizational preparedness, environmental characteristics, and interactive and individual characteristics. Moreover, human-AI collaboration can enhance organizational creativity and innovation by influencing divergent thinking, reducing expert bias, improving the refinement of ideas, and playing a critical role in the all-product development and innovation management stages. For the integration of human-AI collaboration for Industry 5.0, organizations need to make changes in the manufacturing process to facilitate such collaboration.

In the future, it would be beneficial to study the impacts of AI adoption on organizational operating models and how organizations respond to these changes, as shifts in work roles and tasks appear inevitable. More research is needed on organizational resilience, specifically how organizations respond technological changes, renew the necessary capabilities, and risk management in the implementation of new technologies that impact operating models. As AI solutions are implemented, further research is required to address emerging trust issues and how organizations are resolving them. Additionally, it would be interesting to examine the readiness and capability of organizations to implement AI solutions, as well as what provides a competitive advantage when similar AI algorithms are used among competitors. More research is needed, especially in all three dimensions of Industry 5.0, such as human-centered design, sustainability, and industrial resilience, with more focus on human-AI collaboration to understand the collective influence. Moreover, the impact of AI agent collaboration on organizations would offer a valuable research topic. It is also likely to provide a broader perspective, which has important implications for managers in the field to effectively deploy AI. In this regard, an important dimension that needs attention is the consideration of leadership and governance roles, which can steer effective collaboration for the betterment of humans and gain desired organizational outcomes. Moreover, it is also needed to explore further how human-AI collaboration can influence the organization's innovation management practices throughout all stages from idea to new product development. Limitations of humans while initiating such collaboration shall be actively considered to gain useful results, along with other important factors, such as the level of automation required.

References

Achmat, L., & Brown, I. (2019). *Artificial intelligence affordances for business innovation: A systematic review of literature*. ICICIS, 1–12.

Agarwal, A. (2022). AI adoption by human resource management: A study of its antecedents and impact on HR system effectiveness. *Foresight, 25*(1), 67–81.

Alojaiman, B. (2023). Technological modernizations in the industry 5.0 era: A descriptive analysis and future research directions. *Processes, 11*(5), 1318.

Ashrafi, D. M., & Kabir, M. R. (2023). Human or AI? Understanding the key drivers of Customers'adoption of financial robo-advisory services: The role of innovation resilience. *Journal of Global Business and Technology, 19*(1), 19.

Balart, T., & Shryock, K. J. (2024). *A framework for integrating AI into engineering education, Empowering Human-Centered Approach for Industry 5.0*. 1–10.

Bao, Y., Gong, W., & Yang, K. (2023). A literature review of human–AI synergy in decision making: From the perspective of affordance actualization theory. *Systems, 11*(9), 442.

Berretta, S., Tausch, A., Peifer, C., & Kluge, A. (2023). The job perception inventory: Considering human factors and needs in the design of human–AI work. *Frontiers in Psychology, 14*, 1128945.

Brynjolfsson, E., & McAfee, A. (2014). *The second machine age: Work, progress, and prosperity in a time of brilliant technologies*. WW Norton & Company.

Chowdhury, S., Dey, P., Joel-Edgar, S., Bhattacharya, S., Rodriguez-Espindola, O., Abadie, A., & Truong, L. (2023). Unlocking the value of artificial intelligence in human resource management through AI capability framework. *Human Resource Management Review, 33*(1), 100899.

Chui, M., Manyika, J., & Miremadi, M. (2015). Four fundamentals of workplace automation. *McKinsey Quarterly, 29*(3), 1–9.

Dujmovic, J. (2017). *Opinion: What's holding back artificial intelligence*. Americans Don't Trust It. MarketWatch, 30.

Eapen, T. T., Finkenstadt, D., Folk, J., & Venkataswamy, L. (2023). How generative AI can augment human creativity. *Harvard Business Review, 101*(4), 76–85.

Fernandes, T., & Oliveira, E. (2021). Understanding consumers' acceptance of automated technologies in service encounters: Drivers of digital voice assistants adoption. *Journal of Business Research, 122*, 180–191.

Fügener, A., Grahl, J., Gupta, A., & Ketter, W. (2022). Cognitive challenges in human–artificial intelligence collaboration: Investigating the path toward productive delegation. *Information Systems Research, 33*(2), 678–696.

Haenlein, M., & Kaplan, A. (2019). A brief history of artificial intelligence: On the past, present, and future of artificial intelligence. *California Management Review, 61*(4), 5–14.

Hao, X., Demir, E., & Eyers, D. (2024). Exploring collaborative decision-making: A quasi-experimental study of human and Generative AI interaction. *Technology in Society, 78*, 102662. https://doi.org/10.1016/j.techsoc.2024.102662

Hitsuwari, J., Ueda, Y., Yun, W., & Nomura, M. (2023). Does human–AI collaboration lead to more creative art? Aesthetic evaluation of human-made and AI-generated haiku poetry. *Computers in Human Behavior, 139*, 107502.

Hoch, T., Martinez-Gil, J., Pichler, M., Silvina, A., Heinzl, B., Moser, B., Eleftheriou, D., Estrada-Lugo, H. D., & Leva, M. C. (2023). Multi-stakeholder perspective on human-AI collaboration in industry 5.0. In *Artificial intelligence in manufacturing: Enabling intelligent, flexible and cost-effective production through AI* (pp. 407–421). Springer Nature Switzerland Cham.

Holzinger, A. (2016). Interactive machine learning for health informatics: When do we need the human-in-the-loop? *Brain Informatics, 3*(2), 119–131.

Hou, K., Hou, T., & Cai, L. (2023). Exploring Trust in Human–AI collaboration in the context of multiplayer online games. *Systems, 11*(5), 217.

Huang, M.-H., Rust, R., & Maksimovic, V. (2019). The feeling economy: Managing in the next generation of artificial intelligence (AI). *California Management Review, 61*(4), 43–65.

Jarrahi, M. H. (2018). Artificial intelligence and the future of work: Human-AI symbiosis in organizational decision making. *Business Horizons, 61*(4), 577–586.

Jennings, N. R., Moreau, L., Nicholson, D., Ramchurn, S., Roberts, S., Rodden, T., & Rogers, A. (2014). Human-agent collectives. *Communications of the ACM, 57*(12), 80–88.

Jorzik, P., Yigit, A., Kanbach, D. K., Kraus, S., & Dabić, M. (2023). Artificial intelligence-enabled business model innovation: Competencies and roles of top management. *IEEE Transactions on Engineering Management, 71*, 7044–7056.

Joshi, N. (2019, June 19). *7 Types Of Artificial Intelligence*. https://www.forbes.com/sites/cognitiveworld/2019/06/19/7-types-of-artificial-intelligence/

Kans, M., & Campos, J. (2024). Digital capabilities driving industry 4.0 and 5.0 transformation: Insights from an interview study in the maintenance domain. *Journal of Open Innovation: Technology, Market, and Complexity, 10*(4), 100384.

Khosravy, M., Gupta, N., Pasquali, A., Dey, N., Crespo, R. G., & Witkowski, O. (2023). Human-collaborative artificial intelligence along with social values in industry 5.0: A survey of the state-of-the-art. *IEEE Transactions on Cognitive and Developmental Systems.*

Krakowski, S., Luger, J., & Raisch, S. (2023). Artificial intelligence and the changing sources of competitive advantage. *Strategic Management Journal, 44*(6), 1425–1452.

Kumar, V., Rajan, B., Venkatesan, R., & Lecinski, J. (2019). Understanding the role of artificial intelligence in personalized engagement marketing. *California Management Review, 61*(4), 135–155.

Kutvonen, A., Torkkeli, M., & Lin, B. (2010). *Pre-commercialisation activities in external exploitation of technology.* 2(8), 208–230. https://doi.org/10.1504/IJIL.2010.03435.

Leng, J., Sha, W., Wang, B., Zheng, P., Zhuang, C., Liu, Q., Wuest, T., Mourtzis, D., & Wang, L. (2022). Industry 5.0: Prospect and retrospect. *Journal of Manufacturing Systems, 65*, 279–295.

Mariani, M. M., Machado, I., Magrelli, V., & Dwivedi, Y. K. (2022). Artificial intelligence in innovation research: A systematic review, conceptual framework, and future research directions. *Technovation*, 102623.

Mariani, M. M., Machado, I., Magrelli, V., & Dwivedi, Y. K. (2023). Artificial intelligence in innovation research: A systematic review, conceptual framework, and future research directions. *Technovation, 122*, 102623.

Mariani, M. M., & Nambisan, S. (2021). Innovation analytics and digital innovation experimentation: The rise of research-driven online review platforms. *Technological Forecasting and Social Change, 172*, 121009.

Markoff, J. (2016). *Machines of loving grace: The quest for common ground between humans and robots*. HarperCollins Publishers.

Martini, B., Bellisario, D., & Coletti, P. (2024). Human-centered and sustainable artificial intelligence in industry 5.0: Challenges and perspectives. *Sustainability, 16*(13), 5448.

McNeese, N. J., Schelble, B. G., Canonico, L. B., & Demir, M. (2021). Who/what is my teammate? Team composition considerations in human–ai teaming. *IEEE Transactions on Human-Machine Systems, 51*(4), 288–299.

Mihai, S., Yaqoob, M., Hung, D. V., Davis, W., Towakel, P., Raza, M., Karamanoglu, M., Barn, B., Shetve, D., & Prasad, R. V. (2022). Digital twins: A survey on enabling technologies, challenges, trends and future prospects. *IEEE Communications Surveys & Tutorials.*

Muller, E. (2022). How AI-human symbiotes may reinvent innovation and what the new centaurs will mean for cities. *Technology and Investment, 13*(1), 1–19.

Nguyen Thi Ngoc, T., & Elbanna, A. (2023). *Understanding human-AI augmentation in business and management context: A literature review.*

Park, J., Oh, C., & Kim, H. Y. (2024). AI vs. Human-generated content and accounts on Instagram: User preferences, evaluations, and ethical considerations. *Technology in Society, 79*, 102705. https://doi.org/10.1016/j.techsoc.2024.102705

Passalacqua, M., Pellerin, R., Doyon-Poulin, P., Del-Aguila, L., Boasen, J., & Léger, P.-M. (2022). *Human-Centred AI in the age of industry 5.0: A systematic review protocol.* 483–492.

Raisch, S., & Krakowski, S. (2021). Artificial intelligence and management: The automation–augmentation paradox. *Academy of Management Review, 46*(1), 192–210.

Reis, J. (2024). Customer service through AI-powered human-robot relationships: Where are we now? The case of Henn na cafe, Japan. *Technology in Society, 77*, 102570. https://doi.org/10.1016/j.techsoc.2024.102570

Rožanec, J. M., Montini, E., Cutrona, V., Papamartzivanos, D., Klemenčič, T., Fortuna, B., Mladenić, D., Veliou, E., Giannetsos, T., & Emmanouilidis, C. (2023a). Human in the AI loop via xAI and active learning for visual inspection. In *Artificial intelligence in manufacturing: Enabling intelligent, flexible and cost-effective production through AI* (pp. 381–406). Springer.

Rožanec, J. M., Novalija, I., Zajec, P., Kenda, K., Tavakoli Ghinani, H., Suh, S., Veliou, E., Papamartzivanos, D., Giannetsos, T., Menesidou, S. A., Alonso, R., Cauli, N., Meloni, A., Recupero, D. R., Kyriazis, D., Sofianidis, G., Theodoropoulos, S., Fortuna, B., Mladenić, D., & Soldatos, J. (2023b). Human-centric artificial intelligence architecture for industry 5.0 applications. *International Journal of Production Research, 61*(20), 6847–6872. https://doi.org/10.1080/00207543.2022.2138611

Tariq, W., Tariq, A., Bhutta, U. S., & Gohar, M. (2024). *Artificial intelligence a panacea for innovation management? Review and Directions.*

Teodorescu, M. H., Morse, L., Awwad, Y., & Kane, G. C. (2021). Failures of fairness in automation require a deeper understanding of human-ML augmentation. *MIS Quarterly, 45*(3), 1483.

Tiziana, C. C., Riccardo, S. V., Hubbard, E.-M., Daly, A., & Lohse, N. (2024). *An ethical framework for human-robot collaboration for the future people-centric manufacturing: A collaborative endeavour with European subject-matter experts in ethics.* 78(102680). https://doi.org/10.1016/j.techsoc.2024.102680.

Tóth, A., Nagy, L., Kennedy, R., Bohuš, B., Abonyi, J., & Ruppert, T. (2023). The human-centric industry 5.0 collaboration architecture. *MethodsX, 11*, 102260.

Verganti, R., Vendraminelli, L., & Iansiti, M. (2020). Innovation and design in the age of artificial intelligence. *Journal of Product Innovation Management, 37*(3), 212–227.

Westphal, M., Vössing, M., Satzger, G., Yom-Tov, G. B., & Rafaeli, A. (2023). Decision control and explanations in human-AI collaboration: Improving user perceptions and compliance. *Computers in Human Behavior, 144*, 107714.

Wilson, H. J., & Daugherty, P. R. (2018). Collaborative intelligence: Humans and AI are joining forces. *Harvard Business Review, 96*(4), 114–123.

Wu, Z., Ji, D., Yu, K., Zeng, X., Wu, D., & Shidujaman, M. (2021). *AI creativity and the human-AI co-creation model.* 171–190.

Xu, X., Lu, Y., Vogel-Heuser, B., & Wang, L. (2021). Industry 4.0 and industry 5.0—Inception, conception and perception. *Journal of Manufacturing Systems, 61*, 530–535.

Xue, M., Cao, X., Feng, X., Gu, B., & Zhang, Y. (2022). Is college education less necessary with AI? Evidence from firm-level labor structure changes. *Journal of Management Information Systems, 39*(3), 865–905.

Lotta Achrén has completed her Doctoral Researche in Industrial Management at the Lappeenranta University of Technology. She works as a Data Analytics Development Coordinator at the South-Eastern Finland University of Applied Sciences, focusing on data infrastructure and analytics development. Her research interests include entrepreneurial ecosystems and knowledge management.

Dr. Adeel Tariq is an Adjunct Professor and Post-Doctoral Researcher at the Lappeenranta-Lahti University of Technology, Finland. Previously, he worked as an Assistant Professor of Innovation and Technology Management at the National University of Sciences and Technology, Pakistan. His main research is related to emerging and disruptive technologies, digital innovation, and circular performance. He has published in prestigious academic journals such as Technological Forecasting and Social Change, and Technology in Society, among others.

Professor Marina Dabić is a Full Professor of Entrepreneurship and International Business at the Faculty of Economics and Business, Croatia, and the University of Ljubljana, School of Business and Economics. She published more than 200 papers indexed on the Web of Science and Scopus. Professor Dabić is an Editor in Chief for Technology in Society, Senior Department Editor for IEEE-Transactions on Engineering Management, Associate Editor of Technological Forecasting and Social Change, and for the Strategic Change journal. She was a member at large for the IEEE-TEMS 2020–2022. Prof. Dabić prepared a background report on HE Innovate published by EC/OECD. In 2021, she received WAIB best paper award from the Academy of International Business. Currently, she is WP leader for CUES Horizon project and she has contributed to Industry 4.0 in the Horizon 2020 RISE Open innovation project, Interreg Wool project, and ERASMUS K2 BENEFIT and VOIS project. Marina Dabić has been consistently recognized among the Top 2% of scientists worldwide by Stanford University since 2022. She also serves as the Editor and Series Founder of a prestigious Springer book series.

Prof. Marko Torkkeli is a Professor of Technology and Business Innovations at the Lappeenranta-Lahti University of Technology (LUT), Kouvola Unit in Finland. His research interests focus on technology and innovation management, strategic entrepreneurship, growth venturing, and decision support systems. He has published over 300 articles in academic journals and conferences. He serves as the Director of Publications of the International Society for Professional Innovation Management (ISPIM) and is one of the founding editors of the open-access, multidisciplinary Journal of Innovation Management.

Creative Fashion Design Through Collaboration with AI: In the Age of Industry 5.0

Yoon Kyung Lee

Introduction

The advent of Industry 5.0 in the early 2020s represented a significant departure from its predecessor, Industry 4.0, marked by a shift toward a more human-centered economy, with a pronounced emphasis on social value and well-being (Leng et al., 2022). This transition signaled the onset of a novel phase of industrialization, characterized by the collaboration of humans with advanced technology and artificial intelligence (AI) powered robots, aimed at enhancing work processes while concurrently striving to elevate the overall quality of life. The manufacturing transformation system that Industry 4.0 initiated has advanced a technological revolution that has overcome the limitations of smart factories, resulting in sustainable, resilient, and human-centered organizations (Rame et al., 2024). In technical terms, Industry 5.0 aims to transition from the conventional economic model of extraction, production, and consumption to a paradigm that prioritizes reduced consumption, fostering the emergence of novel forms of economic value and equitable prosperity that are sustainable, circular, and renewable. This transition is driven by a focus on growth propelled by the technological economy, with a concomitant advancement of technology toward more transformative growth centered on human progress and well-being. The term "virtual" is a pivotal component of Industry 5.0. The integration of emerging technologies, such as artificial intelligence (AI), machine learning, and business intelligence, has led to the expansion of virtual and augmented reality beyond their initial applications. Consequently, the overarching themes for Industry 5.0 are technological sustainability, virtual resilience, and human-centricity (Leng et al., 2022).

The human-centered approach, a central tenet of Industry 5.0, places paramount importance on the core needs and interests of humans within the production

Y. K. Lee (✉)
Clothing and Textiles Department, Pusan National University, Busan, South Korea
e-mail: pollinalee@pusan.ac.kr

M. Dabić et al. (eds.), *Artificial Humans*, Future of Business and Finance,
https://doi.org/10.1007/978-3-032-06604-6_3

process. The digital devices employed in Industry 5.0 underscore a human-centered approach to technology, thereby empowering workers. This concept encompasses a comprehensive support system, offering assistance and fostering autonomy, thereby enabling the workforce to perform tasks and navigate environments with enhanced safety. In this context, the present study explores the potential of human-AI collaboration in creative fashion design to yield more human-centered, innovative, and sustainable designs. To this end, it methodically examines effective human-AI collaboration methods for creative thinking and design development in fashion design and puts forward various ways in which these methods can be utilized by the general public.

First, I compared the design output of generative AI and real design students to understand how humans and AI have different intrinsic characteristics in the creative fashion design domain and analyze how human-AI collaboration can be utilized.

Second, I examined how human-AI collaboration can be effectively utilized through prior research on the application of AI in creative design.

Third, I examine the effectiveness of a multisensory design approach in helping students utilize AI in design studio classes. Utilizing real-world audiovisual stimuli, I explored whether a hands-on approach that crosses visual, auditory, text, and images is effective in teaching students to utilize AI in the creative design process.

Finally, I derived a sustainable, human-centered, and efficient human-AI creative design development model suitable for the Industry 5.0 era.

Compare the Creative Design Outcomes of Generative AI with those of a Human Design Studio Class

A critical question in the application of AI within creative domains pertains to the efficacy of leveraging AI to enhance the efficiency of the field of expertise. Addressing this question necessitates a focus on the potential of AI to improve work efficiency within specific roles and to guide the development of experts. Lee (2022) employed Generative Adversarial Networks (GANs) with fashion design students to examine how humans and AIs generate creative textile designs under identical conditions. In this study, ensuring the accumulation of a substantial dataset and the identification of superior quality works is identified as crucial for effective deep learning. However, given the limited variety of Korean graphic traditional patterns, the number of patterns provided to the participants was 100, and the sample was selected by random sampling method. Statistical analysis was conducted using SPSS 27. Thus, participants were provided with an equal 100 pieces of samples of traditional Korean patterns and coral images and presented William Morris textile designs as the ideal design outcome (See Fig. 1).

Following an initial semester of instruction in graphics, fashion design students are tasked with creating textile designs drawing upon a range of sources, including traditional Korean patterns, coral imagery, and William Morris textile designs. The allotted time for this endeavor was one Iek. Concurrently, fashion design majors

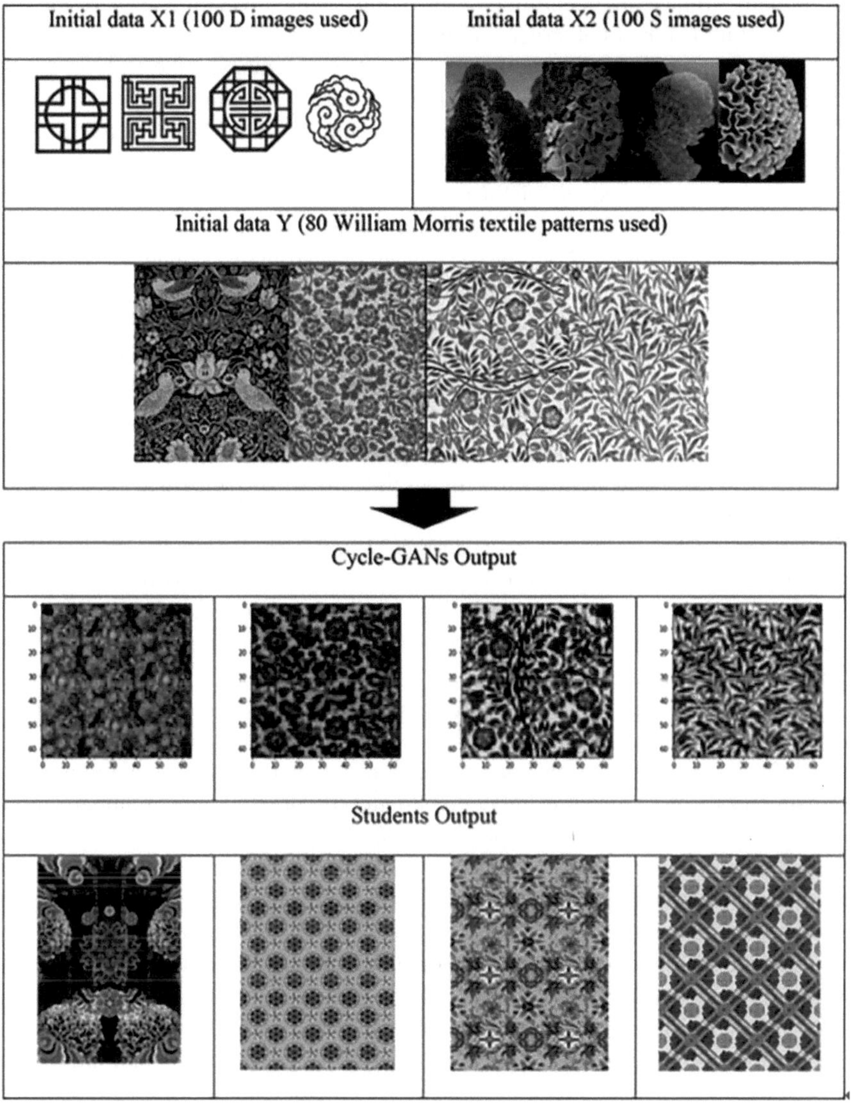

Fig. 1 Comparison of processing between the CycleGAN's generator and humans. (Source from: Lee, 2022 and all rights reserved by the author)

employed a generative adversarial network (GAN) to generate fabric designs under identical conditions. A CycleGAN was utilized as the final output of the generative design. The regular GAN process was augmented by implementing an inverse transformation on the initial conversion dataset between the monochromatic motifs and coral images, thereby transforming result 1 into the William Morris textile pattern (WM) in result 2. Subsequent iterations of this process led to the near-total loss of the initially trained monochromatic and coral shapes, resulting in a result that closely resembled the final target—William Morris's design.

Following an inaugural semester of instruction in graphics, the fashion design students were assigned to create textile designs based on a variety of sources, including traditional Korean patterns, coral imagery, and William Morris textile designs. This assignment was allotted one Iek. Concurrently, the fashion design students employed a generative adversarial network (GAN) to generate textile designs under identical conditions. A Cycle GAN was employed as the final output of the generative design. The regular GAN process was augmented by implementing an inverse transformation on the initial conversion dataset between the monochromatic motifs and the coral images, thereby transforming result 1 into the William Morris (WM) textile pattern in result 2. Subsequent iterations of this process resulted in the near total loss of the initially trained monochromatic and coral shapes, resulting in a result that closely resembled the final target—the William Morris design.

However, upon the revelation of the creators of the artifacts, the human artifacts (mean = 4.19) Ire rated significantly higher than the AI artifacts (mean = 2.72) on a five-point Likert scale (5 = strongly agree, 1 = strongly disagree). While the average subject was unable to discern between the AI and human artifacts, the creativity score of the artifact was found to be lower when the creator was revealed. These findings suggest that enterprises can enhance consumer perceptions of their human-created design output by disclosing the identity of the creators, leading to more favorable consumer impressions.

These findings are consistent with previous studies that have explored the strengths of human and AI creators (Heekeren et al., 2008; Vetro et al., 2019; Xu et al., 2020). In order to enhance the efficiency of human-AI collaboration in domain-specific domains, it is imperative to identify the strengths of human and AI creators and to prioritize their respective strengths to perform multithreaded analysis and creation more rationally. Humans possess a more adaptable and streamlined approach to both perceptual and rational thinking. Consequently, humans demonstrate superiority in connective thinking, fusion, and adaptation to novel environments and less pertinent domains based on their individual experiences. Conversely, AI possesses the capacity to swiftly generate optimized outcomes based on substantial datasets, and its repetitive nature enables it to execute a substantial volume of tasks with accuracy and precision. The synergy between humans and AI, as evidenced by these distinct strengths, underscores the potential for humans to effectively guide the design of AI systems and enhance our comprehension of their impact on individuals and society.

Human-AI Collaboration Methods with Open AI in the Creative Fashion Industry Field

The recent dissemination of open AI to the general public has precipitated a cross-industry movement to utilize it for the purpose of enhancing efficiency, a paradigm shift that has also permeated the fashion industry, an area that traditionally fosters creativity. Consequently, professionals in the fashion industry are exploring various applications of open AI to enhance efficiency. In response to this trend, researchers are developing techniques to create images enhanced by generative AI. These techniques aim to demonstrate how such images can be produced with the same high quality as real-world fashion products. These advancements in AI are facilitating a symbiotic relationship between humans and technology, enabling enhanced efficiency and the production of higher-quality results with reduced energy expenditure. The integration of open AI in the fashion industry is evident in the design gathering phase. In light of the rapid rate at which fashion trends emerge and evolve, it becomes imperative for the fashion industry to undertake a thorough analysis of these trends and leverage them in a timely manner. In this context, humans can enhance their efficiency by leveraging AI in accordance with their area of expertise (O'Connell, 2024).

For instance, a study by Ryu and Lee (2024), conducted from January to April 2024, employed ChatGPT-3.5 and ChatGPT-4.0, trained on data up to 2021, to predict Fall/Winter 2023 menu design trends. The study then compared the predicted trends with those observed in Fall/Winter 2023 data from a fashion trend company, FirstView Korea. In this study, ChatGPT was trained with data up to September 2021 to predict menswear fashion trends for Fall/Winter 2023 from April to May 2023. Additionally, ChatGPT-4, trained with data up to April 2024, was utilized to predict menswear fashion trends for Fall/Winter 2023 and Fall/Winter 2024 (see Table 1). The findings of this study indicated that ChatGPT-4 exhibits sensitivity to the prediction of fashion trends for seasons subsequent to April 2023, given its foundation on databases from 2022 and 2023.

I conducted two rounds of trend prediction using ChatGPT. In the initial phase, the outcomes of ChatGPT-3.5's prediction of Fall/Winter 2023 Men's Fashion Trends are juxtaposed with the prevailing trend prediction data (see Table 2). In the subsequent round, which was conducted in April–May 2023, I compared the results of ChatGPT-3.5's prediction of men's Fall/Winter 2024 fashion trends with ChatGPT-3.5's answers to the Fall/Winter 2023 fashion trends in the first round. First, the results of the comparison between the Open AI search results and the actual fashion trends in Step 1 are summarized into ten trends, as shown in Table 2. It is noteworthy that trends 1 through 5 exhibit a high degree of congruence with the prevailing trend predictions. However, despite the notable presence of gender-fluid fashion in men's fashion trends during the fall of 2023, the Fall/Winter 2023 men's fashion trend predictions did not anticipate this trend.

Table 1 ChatGPT 3.5 and 4 data set

	Period	ChatGPT 3.5	ChatGPT 4
2023 fall/winter men's fashion trends prediction	2023.04. ~ 2024.05	Last update in September 2021	Last update in January 2022
2024 fall/winter men's fashion trends prediction	2024.01. ~ 2024.04		Last update in April 2023

Source from Ryu & Lee, 2024 and all authors have granted the author permission to use this work

Table 2 Comparison of keywords for Fall/Winter 2023 men's fashion design trends

	ChatGPT-3.5	2023 Fall/Winter Men's Fashion Trend
1	Sustainable fashion	Sustainable fashion
2	Ethical fashion	Ethical fashion
3	Oversized and layered looks	Oversized and layered looks
4	Retro and vintage styles	Retro and vintage styles
5	Tailored suits	Tailored suits
6	Comfortable and functional clothing	Comfortable clothing
7	Bold colors and patterns	Neutral
8	Textured fabrics	Genderless
9	Earthy tones	Mix & match
10	Rich fabrics	Minimalism

Source from Ryu & Lee, 2024 and all authors have granted the author permission to use this work

Table 3 2024 Fall/Winter men's fashion trends accurately forecast by ChatGPT

ChatGPT-3.5	ChatGPT-4 classic	Vogue
Gender-fluid fashion	*Gender fluidity*	Anti-macho
Statement OuterIar	Statement coat	The slender man returns, Extra-long and extra-slim coats
Shacket		Shacket
Faux fur and shearling		Fluffy, fur
Faux fur trim		Fluffy, fur
Ruffles		Ruffles and gathers
Fringe		Cowboys, fringy
	Aerodynamic styles	Tight, aerodynamic styles (vacuum-packed)
	KnitIar	Knit separates
	WorkIar	WorkIar jackets

Source from Ryu & Lee, 2024 and all authors have granted the author permission to use this work

In step 2, I compared the Fall/Winter 2024 Men's Fashion Trends Prediction with the ChatGPT-3.5 and ChatGPT-4 results and found that eight of the 12 keywords matched, and four new keywords appeared in the 2024 trend prediction (Table 3). The eight matching keywords in the 2023 and 2024 trend analysis are: (1) sustainability, (2) oversized silhouettes, (3) vintage, (4) retro revival, (5) tailoring and classic styles, (6) comfort and functionality, (7) bold colors and patterns, (8) textured fabrics, and earthy tones. The 2024 forecast was also analyzed using four new keywords: (1) influence of worker, (2) personalization, (3) gender-fluid fashion, and (4) techIar and functionality. Notably, the influence of worker and gender-fluid fashion was new to the 2023 data and was predicted to be a key trend for Fall 2024 menswear.

A comparative analysis of OpenAI's search results for Fall/Winter 2023 trends and actual fashion trends reveals a notable inclusion of gender-fluid fashion in the latter. This development represents a deviation from the initial study's findings, wherein this trend was not identified. The second study's Fall/Winter 2024 men's

Fig. 2 Fashion design major student's work with Midjourney for AI generative design. (The creator has granted the author permission to use this work)

fashion trend predictions incorporate gender-fluid fashion, underscoring its emergence as a prominent trend in the fashion landscape. This discrepancy can be attributed to the augmented dataset of ChatGPT 3.5, which spans the period from September 2021 to January 2022, and the subsequent incorporation of data from ChatGPT-4.0 in March 2023. These observations underscore the limitations of generative AI in producing answers that diverge from the confines of the training dataset. The quality and relevance of the output of generative AI are contingent upon the dataset from which it is trained (Fig. 2).

The objective of this study is to ascertain the discrepancy between ChatGPT's text-based prediction of fashion trends and the subsequent real-world fashion outcomes when manifested as images. The findings of Ryu and Lee (2024) are presented here. In their study, Ryu and Lee (2024) employed ChatGPT as a fashion design trend prediction tool. They created seasonal collections using DALL-E, a generative model, based on fashion design trends predicted by ChatGPT. The researchers then compared the results with actual collections. For the Fall 2024 men's fashion collection, I generated prompts based on the fashion design trends predicted by ChatGPT for the Fall/Winter 2024 men's fashion design trends and actual trends. The output from DALL-E 3 was found to be highly comprehensive, exhibiting a high degree of resemblance to a photographic representation of the actual collection. (Table 3).

The findings of both ChatGPT and DALL-E demonstrate that, under precise prompting, these models exhibit the capacity to produce results of commendable quality. Moreover, the employment of varied prompts has been observed to yield a range of outcomes, thereby facilitating creative design. While ChatGPT's trend prediction results are not entirely accurate, they assist users in predicting fashion trends by answering based on extensive datasets and real-time search data. Additionally, DALL-E expedites the visualization of user concepts by facilitating the straightforward generation of images from web sources, obviating the need for additional software installation. These findings suggest that in the future, individuals with limited expertise will have the opportunity to utilize publicly available artificial intelligence technology to predict fashion trends and view the next season's fashion trends and collections in advance (Table 4).

Table 4 DALL-E vs Actual Collection

Item	Actual Fashion Show	DALL-E
Faux fur and shearing		
Aerodynamic styles		

Source from Ryu & Lee, 2024 and all authors have granted the author permission to use this work

Effective Human-AI Collaboration in Creative Design

Lee (2021) and Sutherland et al. (2010) posited that the effective utilization of AI, encompassing digital technologies, within the fashion industry has the potential to enhance consumer engagement and establish a virtuous economic system for a sustainable society. In this context, Peeters et al. (2021) proposed three types of human AI collaboration. The first type is the technology-centric view (number 1 in Fig. 3), which asserts that true intelligence can only be found by utilizing well-developed and mature (general) AI systems. This perspective is predicated on the notion that humans are biologically constrained in their capacity to process information and reason, and that they exhibit various forms of cognitive biases. Conversely, AI technology is posited as a means to transcend human-level intelligence and develop rational intelligence. Conversely, the human-centered perspective (number 2 in Fig. 3) asserts that true intelligence is derived from human intellect and is fundamentally rooted in human potential. While AI technology can facilitate the realization of human potential, it is incapable of imparting intrinsic human qualities, such as moral reasoning or empathy. These inherent limitations position AI as a potential threat to human well-being and happiness. The third perspective, collective intelligence (number 3 in Fig. 3), posits that true intelligence can be found only in the aggregation of multiple entities through interactions between humans and

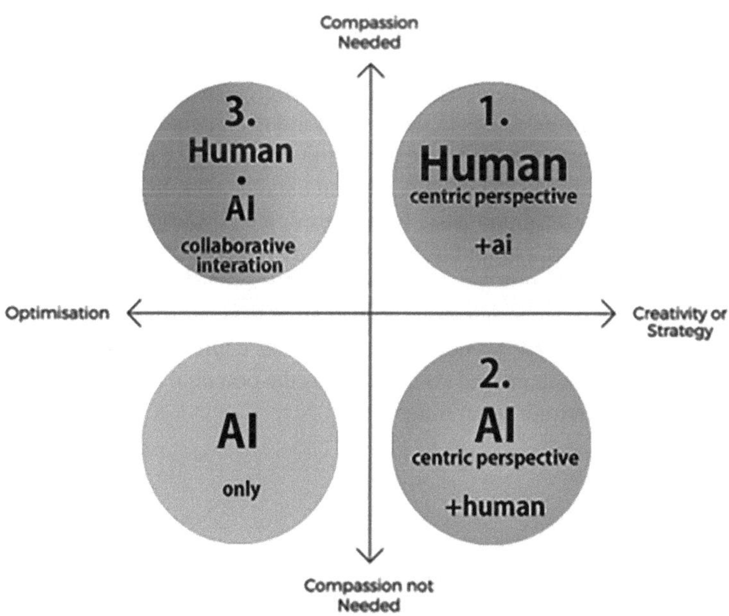

Fig. 3 Human-AI collaboration diagram. (Source from: Lee, 2022 and all rights reserved by the author)

technology. The intelligence of individual humans and AI entities within a system is constrained, and true intelligence can only be formed when humans and technology collaborate over an extended period.

The fashion industry, which is predicated on manufacturing, has the potential to enhance work efficiency and augment the production capabilities of professionals by collaborating with AI to construct a converged design, development, and distribution system that integrates production and consumption, from product design and performance to consumer participation. This collaborative approach, integrating human expertise and AI technology, has the potential to generate a range of employment opportunities, particularly in high-value-added industries, by fostering the development of novel, creative concepts. This human-AI collaborative approach creates a variety of jobs and opens the door for high-value-added industries to grow based on new creative ideas, especially from the perspective of collective intelligence (Hölzl, 2005; Lee, 2022; Throsby, 2001).

Furthermore, the symbiotic relationship between humans and AI has the potential to establish sustainable systems, thereby reducing the reliance on labor and energy expended on superfluous, repetitive tasks in the design or production of products intended for recurrent use across seasons. Consequently, within the fashion industry, AI technology has the potential to enhance work efficiency by reducing the number of specialists required to perform similar or repetitive tasks each season. This, in turn, enables highly skilled professionals to concentrate on specific areas of expertise. In particular, the development of open AI has shown the potential for use in tasks that further maximize the creativity of designers in areas of design with creative uniqueness (see Fig. 3).

This paradigm shift has the potential to enhance creative output by leveraging the expertise of human professionals in the fashion industry, empowering them to make optimal decisions. Furthermore, it enhances the efficiency of artificial intelligence (AI) and fosters collaboration between fashion experts, thereby facilitating innovation. In the creative fashion industry, for instance, the convergence of designer and generative designs has the potential to yield more creative designs than traditional fashion products with minimal effort and time. This shift necessitates a greater focus on artistic and sensory elements, as well as an analysis of consumer needs and the implementation of new product types based on iconic trends. This symbiotic relationship between humans and AI experts has the potential to generate more efficient outcomes within traditional industries.

Results

How Multisensory Methods Can Be Effectively Utilized to Enhance Human-AI Creativity by Utilizing Real Audio-Visual Stimuli

The present study explores the potential of artificial intelligence (AI) and large-scale language models (LLM) to enhance the creative process in fashion design. The creative process in fashion design involves the utilization of the sense of hearing (music) to facilitate creative thinking through visual imagery. The study's objective is to investigate the potential of AI and LLM to augment creativity and enhance the efficiency of the fashion design process. In an era where effective collaboration between AI and humans is becoming increasingly imperative, it is imperative to explore the specific ways in which multisensory thinking can foster creativity. According to Kwon and Goucher-Lambert (2024), human-AIs consistently exhibit visual and functional similarities, suggesting that human-AI communication can be leveraged to unlock creativity in the process of implementing complex design artifacts.

The integration of artificial intelligence (AI) within the domain of fashion design facilitates multisensory thinking by transcending the conventional boundaries of space and time. This process entails the conversion of visual images and data into written form. The efficacy of this conversion is contingent upon the proximity and intimacy between the image and its textual representation. To delve deeper into this process, textual descriptions of images emerge as a pivotal technique, and the greater the sensory stimuli an artist possesses, the more intricate the associations they can have. Text, or language, engages both the visual and auditory senses, thereby occupying the nexus of the visual and auditory realms. In contrast, images serve as a medium that appeals to the visual sense, offering spatial information, a salient example of which is photography, which captures a static image that captures a moment in time.

In contrast, music, as a medium that appeals to the ear, is temporal, thereby facilitating our expansion into space by creating images within the temporal realm. The integration of artificial intelligence (AI) as a connecting medium facilitates the integration of time and space with text, thereby enabling the linkage of multisensory thinking in space and time. Music exemplifies this integration. The integration of spatiality and temporality in images and music constitutes a complex undertaking, given the nature of each as a visual and auditory stimulus, respectively. The two domains under consideration are "time and space," on which language is built. It is through these experiences of time and space that I assign meaning to them, recognize the images associated with them, engage our emotions, feel excited and moved by them, and enrich our experience by expanding the connections between different neural networks.

Synaesthesia, which is characterized by its reliance on sight, has been shown to facilitate novel modes of thinking in the domain of creative fashion design. A multisensory approach to the design process has been demonstrated to stimulate imagination and generate creative design ideas through abstract and concrete contributions that encompass all aspects of a product, including aesthetics, functionality, quality, and emotion (Merter, 2017). In contrast, music is predicated on temporality and features melodies and chords that are recognizable irrespective of the individual's experience. Rhythm, as defined by Roskies (1995), is the division of time based on temporality. The emotional response to music is often experienced before the perception of visual imagery. Music exerts a more potent influence on the human psyche than visual imagery (Hashim et al., 2023). Consequently, if fashion design majors experience a state of excitement, confidence, intellectual satisfaction, and fulfillment through multisensory stimulation in an environment conducive to learning, it can potentially lead to a heightened state of motivation, desire, passion, and engagement. Multisensory ideation activities that simultaneously stimulate the senses of sight and sound have been shown to enhance creative thinking and strengthen design skills in fashion design, as students explore new concepts and expand their ideas.

Lee (2024) posits that the integration of multisensory learning techniques in fashion design can serve as an effective and adaptive approach to addressing both visual and auditory challenges. The underlying principle of multisensory learning is straightforward. When students engage in activities that involve two or more senses concurrently or over an extended period, they exhibit a stronger interaction with the material and demonstrate a greater capacity to retain the information they have learned. In multisensory design work, teachers engage students through hands-on, visual, auditory, and olfactory stimuli and then reinforce multisensory skills by linking sensory input and thinking in activities (Baines, 2008). Lee (2024) further elaborates on the potential of classical music, particularly Beethoven's Apogionata Piano Sonata No. 23, to stimulate creative thinking in students majoring in basic fashion design courses, thereby fostering the development of visual fashion designs. Lee's (2024) study involved 60 fashion design students in a 3-month design ideation process, utilizing Beethoven's Appassionata Piano Sonata No. 23. The study employed a multisensory approach, integrating visual and spatial imagery with auditory and temporal elements of music, to stimulate creativity through the cross-activation of the visual and auditory senses.

The participants underwent a training regimen that involved the visualization of auditory stimuli, concurrently engaging in the discernment of the creator's intentions and conceptual frameworks. Thereafter, the students proceeded to a design development process, wherein they identified visual data, including the compositional process, timbre, and composition of Beethoven's Appassionata Piano Sonata No. 23. The 60 students who participated in the study overwhelmingly agreed that listening to music and finding images was more useful for design evaluation (66.7%) than looking for images through art magazines (29.6%). Furthermore, a significant majority of 61.1% of the students concurred that integrating the Appassionata Piano Sonata with an explanatory discourse on the music enhanced their ability to establish connections between the auditory and visual elements. These findings collectively demonstrate the efficacy of integrating creative classical music into design activities, thereby fostering the evocation of images and the expansion of cognitive horizons.

In order to investigate the most effective methods for leveraging AI in design work through a multisensory learning approach, I employed Kim's Cello Sonata No. 1, titled Gyeongya," and contemporary creative classical music to guide students in their design creation process by integrating ChatGPT's textual utilization with generative AI (Midjourney, DALL-E, and Bing). The investigation focused on the efficacy of AI in fostering creative thinking during the fashion design process and on the effectiveness of auditory stimuli, such as music, in facilitating the association of text and images. Specifically, the study examined the efficacy of incorporating music in the process of converting direct text into images by associating topic-related content with concrete images. As demonstrated in Tables 5 and 6,

Table 5 Student A's example of human-AI collaboration

Prompt	Results
Chat GPT(open AI) What traditional values does Kim's cello sonata no. 1 Gyeongya, which deals with death and dedication, break?	Kim's cello sonata no. 1, 'Gyeongya,' which deals with themes of death and dedication, may break with several traditional values or conventions, depending on the specific context of the composition and the composer's intentions. Here are a few possible ways in which the sonata might challenge or subvert traditional values: Musical form: If Kim's sonata employs unconventional musical forms or structures, it could be seen as breaking with traditional expectations of how a sonata should be composed. For example, if it eschews the typical sonata-allegro form or incorporates experimental techniques, it may challenge traditional notions of musical composition. Emotional expression: Traditional values in music often prioritize beauty, harmony, and upliftment. If Kim's sonata explores darker, more introspective emotions associated with death and dedication, it may challenge the conventional emphasis on positivity and celebration in music. Subject matter: While death and dedication are universal themes, they may not always be addressed directly or prominently in traditional music. If Kim's sonata places a central focus on these themes, it may challenge traditional expectations of what subjects are suitable for musical expression. Audience expectations: Traditional values in music often involve catering to the tastes and preferences of the audience. If Lee's sonata pushes the boundaries of what listeners expect or find comfortable, it may challenge traditional notions of audience engagement and reception. Ultimately, whether Kim's cello sonata no. 1 'Gyeongya' breaks with traditional values depends on how it is composed, performed, and interpreted within its cultural and artistic context. It's worth noting that challenging traditional values can be a productive and innovative endeavor in artistic expression, leading to new forms of creativity and meaning-making.
Design concept : IDENTITY	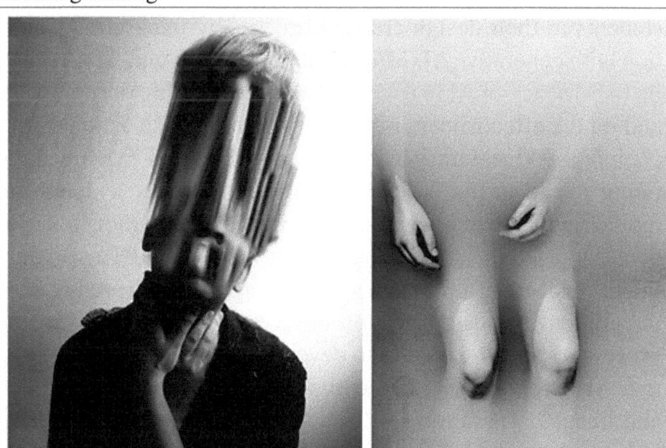

(continued)

Table 5 (continued)

Prompt	Results
Design collection	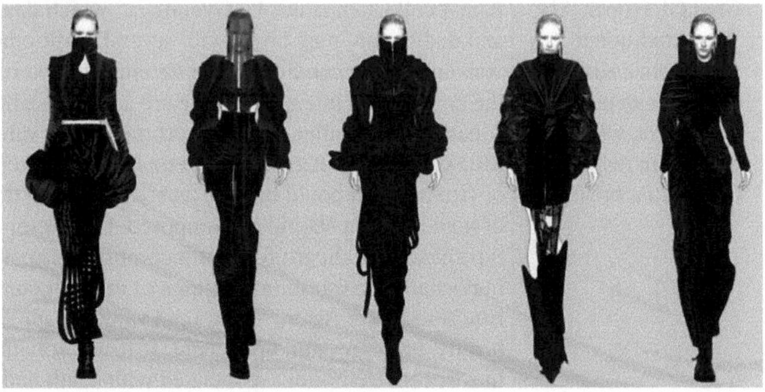

The creator has granted the author permission to use this work

students engaged in active collaboration with ChatGPT to organize their thoughts during the process of finding, understanding, and interpreting a topic. Furthermore, the integration of music has been observed to promote divergent thinking during the process of deriving images to develop designs. Concurrently, ChatGPT and generative AI functioned as facilitators, thereby enhancing the interaction between text and images. These tools offer a significant advantage by encouraging students to transcend the limitations imposed by their experiences. However, attaining this level of proficiency necessitates a substantial amount of trial and error, suggesting the potential for enhanced efficiency through the utilization of AI tools tailored to specific In order to investigate the most effective methods for leveraging AI in design work through a multisensory learning approach, I employed Kim's Cello Sonata No. 1, titled Gyeongya," and contemporary creative classical music to guide students in their design creation process by integrating ChatGPT's textual utilization with generative AI (Midjourney, DALL-E, and Bing). The investigation focused on the efficacy of AI in fostering creative thinking during the fashion design process and on the effectiveness of auditory stimuli, such as music, in facilitating the association of text and images. Specifically, the study examined the efficacy of incorporating music in the process of converting direct text into images by associating topic-related content with concrete images. As demonstrated in Tables 5 and 6, students engaged in active collaboration with ChatGPT to organize their thoughts during the process of finding, understanding, and interpreting a topic. Furthermore, the integration of music has been observed to promote divergent thinking during the process of deriving images to develop designs. Concurrently, ChatGPT and generative AI functioned as facilitators, thereby enhancing the interaction between text and images. These tools offer a significant advantage by encouraging students to transcend the limitations imposed by their experiences. However, attaining this level of proficiency necessitates a substantial amount of trial and error, suggesting the potential for enhanced efficiency through the utilization of AI tools tailored to specific disciplines.

Table 6 Student B's example of human-AI collaboration

	Results
Bing(open AI) Create artwork about determinism and free will by using dices	
Design concept: DICE	
Design collection	

The creator has granted the author permission to use this work

A Sustainable, Human-Centered, and Efficient Human-AI Creative Design Development Model Suitable for the Industry 5.0 Era

The advent of the Fourth Industrial Revolution in the early 2010s marked a paradigm shift in the realm of manufacturing, ushering in a new era characterized by the automation of industrial processes and the emergence of connected technologies, smart manufacturing, cyber-physical systems (CPS), three-dimensional (3D) printing, and the Internet of Things (IoT). These manufacturing technologies have enabled robots to perform monotonous, dangerous, physically complex, and demanding tasks in manufacturing environments that were previously performed by humans. Examples include the loading and unloading of heavy materials in warehouses, the Ilding of components in workshops, and the painting of vehicles in automotive plants, where uniformity is paramount. The advent of these technologies has precipitated a fundamental shift in the manner in which manufacturing is conducted. However, these advancements, driven by artificial intelligence (AI), have concomitantly engendered a pervasive sense of insecurity, which poses a significant threat to human employment prospects. In response to these challenges, Industry 5.0 signifies a progressive shift beyond previous technological revolutions, encompassing advanced technologies that prioritize balanced human-AI interaction while focusing on sustainable development. (Tiwari et al., 2022).

Industry 5.0, in its fundamental essence, integrates cognitive computing capabilities with human intelligence and ingenuity, thereby facilitating collaborative operations (Patil et al., 2024; see Fig. 4). AI-powered systems facilitate the

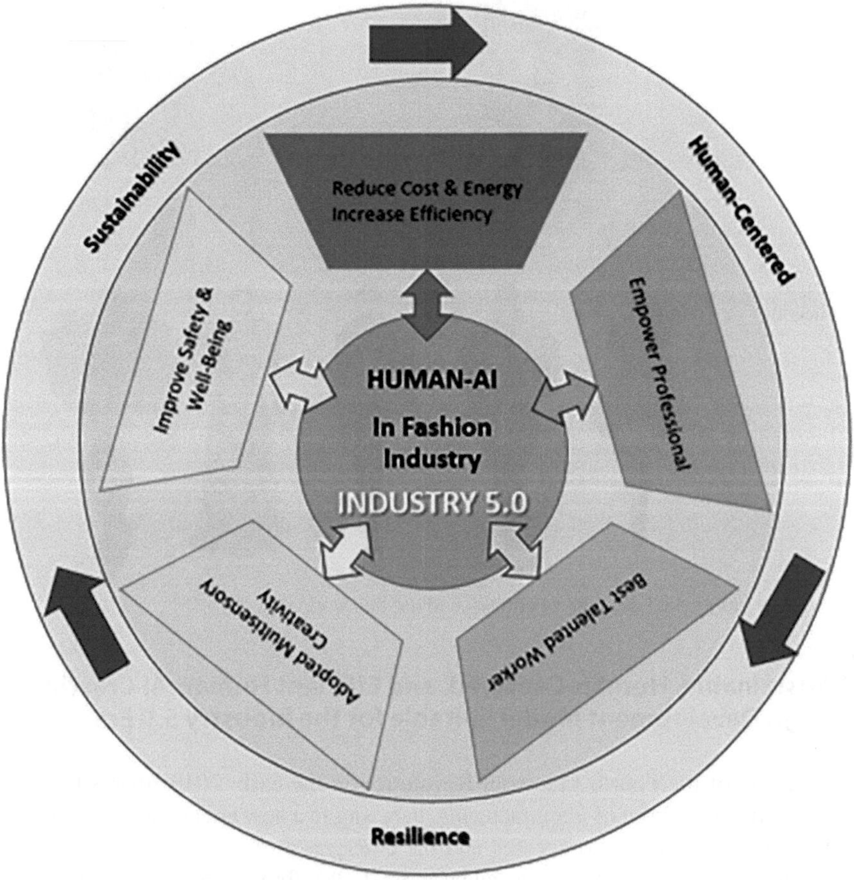

Fig. 4 Fashion industry in Industry 5.0

utilization of digital technology to address complex manufacturing challenges, thereby liberating humans from repetitive tasks and enabling them to concentrate on more intelligent and specialized work. Introduced in the early 2020s, Industry 5.0 is currently undergoing a period of maturation and stabilization, with three key categories emerging as the primary drivers of this transformation: human-centricity, sustainability, and resilience.

The initial approach is human centered with regard to fashion and the utilization of AI in the Industry 5.0 era. Given the inherently creative nature of fashion, it is imperative that the integration of AI be grounded in a human-centered framework. The integration of AI within the fashion industry must prioritize fundamental human needs and interests, situating them at the core of the production process. By equipping workers with digital tools, the focus can be shifted towards minimizing repetitive labor and cultivating a human-centered technological framework. The emphasis should be on enhancing security and safety while providing support, assistance, and empowerment for the workforce in tasks that mitigate risks and address hazardous work environments. The objective is not merely to substitute human labor with robotics, but rather to augment the capabilities of industrial workers through the integration of innovative technological solutions.

The second salient factor is sustainability. The fashion industry is predominantly manufacturing-based. Technologies such as artificial intelligence (AI) and additive manufacturing, which optimize energy efficiency and consumption, resource efficiency, and waste minimization, have the potential to play a significant role in the fashion industry. Presently, the fashion industry is grappling with a significant challenge in identifying a solution to the disposal of waste and surplus garments. It is imperative for industry to integrate future competitiveness and sustainability to leverage the potential of Industry 5.0 technologies and transform the fashion industry.

Finally, the concept of resilience is paramount. A fundamental value of the fashion industry is its capacity to adapt and respond expeditiously to evolving circumstances to ensure a sustainable and prosperous role. Digital technology is expected to play an important role in this regard. Consequently, it is imperative that conventional analogue and unidirectional processes be supplanted by digital and interconnected methodologies. Moreover, the industry must proactively adopt a range of resilient technologies, including big data collection, automated risk analysis, and automated mitigation measures. However, it is equally crucial to incorporate resilient technologies that can simultaneously reflect the creative and human handcrafted nature of the fashion industry, a distinctive attribute that sets it apart, without compromising on digital automation.

Conclusion

The preceding industrial paradigm, Industry 4.0, placed considerable emphasis on technological advancements such as the Internet of Things (IoT) and big data. In contrast, Industry 5.0 is characterized by a paradigm shift toward human, environmental, resilience, and social aspects. As Industry 5.0 persists in prioritizing a human-centric approach to technology by empowering workers, the emphasis is shifting to the support, assistance, and employment of the workforce with task and environmental insights that lead to safety recommendations and alerts. This study explores the potential of human-AI collaboration in creative fashion design to generate more human-centered, innovative, and sustainable designs. The human-AI collaboration methods employed for creative thinking and design development in this study align with the Industry 5.0 keywords of technical (sustainable), virtual (resilient), and human-centered (human).

In order to extend this effectiveness to fashion professionals and the general public, research must focus on developing and recommending domain-specific prompts that enhance familiarity and effectiveness with open AI. Furthermore, studies should explore multisensory learning methods tailored to various creative applications. As demonstrated in this paper, open AIs have demonstrated their capacity to comprehend and generate high-quality output when prompted in an effective manner, underscoring the potential for diverse prompts to yield varied outcomes, thereby facilitating creative design. While ChatGPT's trend prediction results are not entirely accurate, it can assist users in predicting fashion trends by answering based on extensive datasets and real-time search data. Generative AI, exemplified by DALL-E, facilitates the generation of images from the web, obviating the need for specialized software, thereby enabling users to swiftly visualize their concepts. These findings suggest that in the future, even individuals without expertise in the field will have the capacity to utilize open AI technologies to predict and preview fashion trends, facilitating more informed decision-making in the fashion industry.

In order to enhance the efficacy of human-AI collaboration within specialized domains, it is imperative to discern the strengths of both humans and AI creators. By leveraging the strengths of these entities, the analysis and creation processes can be rendered more rational. Humans possess a more flexible and simplified approach to both perceptual and rational thinking, which renders them more adept at connective thinking, fusion, and adaptation to new environments. In addition, humans exhibit a higher degree of adaptability to less relevant areas based on personal experience in comparison to AI. Conversely, AI exhibits a capacity to swiftly attain optimized outcomes based on substantial datasets, a capability that is further augmented by its ability to execute substantial tasks with remarkable accuracy and precision, attributable to the repetitive nature of numerous tasks within its design.

The collaboration between humans and AI has the potential to be effective in establishing a sustainable system. This is due to the ability to reduce the amount of labor and energy required for repetitive tasks in the design or production of creative fashion products that are subject to seasonal renewal. Consequently, within the fashion industry, AI technology has the potential to enhance work efficiency by reducing the number of specialists required for repetitive tasks during each season and by allocating highly skilled specialists to specific areas of expertise. Advancements in open AI, particularly, hold the potential to further enhance the creativity of designers in fields that demand originality.

In the domain of fashion design, which is predicated on visual stimuli, the implementation of multisensory learning methodologies has been demonstrated to be efficacious in enhancing the capacity to effectively engage with AI tools that are predominantly textual in nature. In order to cultivate the next generation of fashion designers, it is imperative to integrate music as a catalyst for cognitive expansion, thereby eliciting images that facilitate design development and facilitate interaction with generative artificial intelligence (GPT). By leveraging the synergy between text and images, it is possible to enhance the efficacy of open artificial intelligence (AI) tools in enabling students to explore and expand the boundaries of their creative experiences.

The cornerstone of Industry 5.0 lies in the integration of cognitive computing capabilities with human intelligence and ingenuity, thereby facilitating collaborative operations. In industries that demand creativity, such as fashion, the integration of AI must be grounded in a human-centered paradigm. The integration of AI within the fashion industry can be initiated by centering fundamental human needs and interests at the core of the production process. To ensure that the proliferation of AI is a transformative technology and not simply a way to replace human jobs with robots, it is critical that I continue to collaborate on human-AI research and real-world applications in the industry to empower future talent with digital communication skills.

Limitations and Future Research

This study examined the potential of human-artificial intelligence collaboration in fashion design to foster human-centered, sustainable, and innovative design. It sought to identify effective methods for human-artificial intelligence collaboration, with a focus on creative thinking and design development in fashion design. The objective of this study is to demonstrate the efficacy of human-artificial intelligence collaboration in enhancing sustainability and human-centeredness, while optimizing work efficiency in the era of Industry 5.0. However, given that the study was primarily conducted on fashion design students, there is a need for subsequent research on professional designers working in the industry. The present study contributes to this body of knowledge by examining the impact of generative AI on work efficiency in various aspects of the fashion industry. However, the study's findings highlight a gap in research that investigates the effective use of specific AI tools for particular tasks. Consequently, there is a pressing need for future research that explores the integration of AI into the fashion industry, with a focus on the professional characteristics of the industry and the education and utilization of AI convergence design.

References

Baines, L. (2008). *A teacher's guide to multisensory learning: Improving literacy by engaging the senses*. ASCD.

Hashim, S., Stewart, L., Küssner, M. B., & Omigie, D. (2023). Music listening evokes story-like visual imagery with both idiosyncratic and shared content. *PLoS One, 18*(10), e0293412. https://doi.org/10.1371/journal.pone.0293412

Heekeren, H. R., Marrett, S., & Ungerleider, L. G. (2008). The neural systems that mediate human perceptual decision making. *Nature Reviews Neuroscience, 9*(6), 467–479. https://doi.org/10.1038/nrn2374

Hölzl, W. (2005). *Entrepreneurship, entry and exit in creative industries: An explorative survey*. https://doi.org/10.57938/f777ae6b-a5d2-470e-86e4-4e2b2e8d589b.

Kwon, E., & Goucher-Lambert, K. (2024). Comparing and evaluating human and computationally derived representations of non-semantic design information. *Journal of Mechanical Design, 146*(3), 031401. https://doi.org/10.1115/1.4063567

Lee, Y. K. (2021). Transformation of the innovative and sustainable supply chain with upcoming real-time fashion systems. *Sustainability, 13*(3), 1081. https://doi.org/10.3390/su13031081

Lee, Y. K. (2022). How complex systems get engaged in fashion design creation: Using artificial intelligence. *Thinking Skills and Creativity, 46*, 101137. https://doi.org/10.1016/j.tsc.2022.101137

Lee, Y. K. (2024). Creative design discipline through convergence of fashion and classical music. In *International textile and apparel association annual conference proceedings*. (Vol. 80, No. 1). Iowa State University Digital Press.

Leng, J., Sha, W., Wang, B., Zheng, P., Zhuang, C., Liu, Q., et al. (2022). Industry 5.0: Prospect and retrospect. *Journal of Manufacturing Systems, 65*, 279–295.

Merter, S. (2017). Synesthetic approach in the design process for enhanced creativity and multisensory experiences. *The Design Journal, 20*(sup1), S4519-S 4528. https://doi.org/10.1080/14606925.2017.1352948

O'Connell, M. J. (2024). *The role of open AI in fashion: Transforming creativity through innovation?*.

Patil, Y. H., Patil, R. Y., Gurale, M. A., & Karati, A. (2024). Industry 5.0: Empolring collaboration through advanced technological approaches. In *Intelligent systems and industrial internet of things for sustainable development* (pp. 1–23). Chapman and Hall/CRC.

Peeters, M. M., van Diggelen, J., Van Den Bosch, K., Bronkhorst, A., Neerincx, M. A., Schraagen, J. M., & Raaijmakers, S. (2021). Hybrid collective intelligence in a human–AI society. *AI & SOCIETY, 36*(1), 217–238. https://doi.org/10.1007/s00146-020-01005-y

Rame, R., Purwanto, P., & Sudarno, S. (2024). Industry 5.0 and sustainability: An overview of emerging trends and challenges for a green future. *Innovation and Green Development, 3*(4), 100173. https://doi.org/10.1016/j.igd.2024.100173

Roskies, D. G. (1995). *A bridge of longing: The lost art of Yiddish storytelling*. Harvard University Press.

Ryu, C. H., & Lee, Y. K. (2024). *Using open AI to see fashion collections before anyone else does*. 2024ICCT. Jeju.

Sutherland, D., Hoeller, P., Egert, B., & Ro ̈hn, O. (2010). Counter-cyclical economic policy. *OECD economics department*, 760. Working paper no.

Throsby, D. (2001). *Economics and culture*. Cambridge university press.

Tiwari, S., Bahuguna, P. C., & Walker, J. (2022). Industry 5.0: A macroperspective approach. In *Handbook of research on innovative management using AI in industry 5.0* (pp. 59–73). IGI Global. https://doi.org/10.4018/978-1-7998-8497-2.ch004

Vetro, A., Santangelo, A., Beretta, E., & De Martin, J. C. (2019). AI: From rational agents to socially responsible agents. *Digital Policy, Regulation and Governance., 21*, 291.

Xu, Y., Shieh, C. H., van Esch, P., & Ling, I. L. (2020). AI customer service: Task complexity, problem-solving ability, and usage intention. *Australasian Marketing Journal*. https://doi.org/10.1016/j.ausmj.2020.03.005

Yoon Kyung Lee, PhD, is an assistant professor in the Department of Clothing and Textiles, College of Human Ecology, Pusan National University. Her research interests are creative thinking and problem solving, innovative design education, and digital and AI convergence related to sustainability in clothing.

Navigating AI Adoption: In-House Development vs. Outsourcing for Industry 5.0

Bahar Bahramian Dehkordi, Marko Torkkeli, Adeel Tariq, and Marina Dabić

Introduction

The current state of the modern world, characterized by globalization, technological advancements, and emerging grand challenges, has forced organizations to rapidly develop technological solutions that enable them to introduce innovative products and gain a competitive advantage. Artificial intelligence (AI) is considered an important aspect of this evolution since it is capable of processing large amounts of data and creating valuable outcomes, depending on the prompts given (Tariq et al., 2024). AI is known to be one of the leading technologies in transforming systems from being fully automated and mainly focused on efficiency to more collaborative and human-centric ones in what is now referred to as Industry 5.0 (Xu et al., 2021; Passalacqua et al., 2024). Industry 4.0 is based on a technology-centric approach and is focused more on automation and data-driven efficiency. However, in contrast, the main objective of Industry 5.0 is to achieve this automation and efficiency by integrating human values like creativity, well-being, and sustainability with the accuracy and scalability of technologies such as AI (Tóth et al., 2023; Raju et al., 2024). As mentioned, digitization of manufacturing processes and increased efficiency are the main characteristics of Industry 4.0 (Oztemel & Gursev, 2020), but it lacks the adaptability and capacity to completely address the ways AI can assist human decision-making and promote creative innovation (Trakadas et al., 2020;

B. Bahramian Dehkordi (✉) · M. Torkkeli · A. Tariq
Lappeenranta-Lahti University of Technology, Kouvola Unit, Finland
e-mail: bahar.bahramian.dehkordi@lut.fi; marko.torkkeli@lut.fi; adeel.tariq@lut.fi

M. Dabić
University of Dubrovnik, Dubrovnik, Croatia

University of Ljubljana School of Economics and Business, Ljubljana, Slovenia
e-mail: mdabic@unidu.hr

M. Dabić et al. (eds.), *Artificial Humans*, Future of Business and Finance,
https://doi.org/10.1007/978-3-032-06604-6_4

Sarkar et al., 2024). Therefore, Industry 4.0 alone has a limitation to help AI-driven technologies reach their full potential. However, Industry 5.0 fills this gap and tries to create more resilient and adaptable systems by combining human design principles with modern technology advancements (Alves et al., 2023).

This transition highlights that AI does improve routine tasks and fosters environments where human workers and AI-enabled systems can collaborate, enabling humans to focus on more complex and creative tasks (Liao et al., 2024). AI can facilitate organization in achieving multiple objectives, such as improving customer experience, reducing operational expenditures, and advancing knowledge (Sumbal et al., 2021), which is likely to improve organizational performance (Qureshi et al., 2024). Even though AI adoption is significant for organizations, its adoption level is still modest (Hoffreumon, Forman and van Zeebroeck, 2024). It is also argued that AI is still in the development phase, and organizations need to customize it to meet their strategic goals. Meanwhile, organizations face the crucial decision of developing in-house technology versus choosing to outsource critical technological development, as it can allow firms to focus on their core expertise (Qureshi et al., 2024).

In this regard, an organization can select different strategies to adopt AI; either it can develop AI in-house, request a third party to develop AI for its operations, or adopt readily available AI software from the market (Hoffreumon, Forman and van Zeebroeck, 2024). Developing in-house AI can present challenges, including high costs and a shortage of tangible and intangible resources (Gräf, Mehler and Ellenrieder, 2024). This often leads to integration issues, requiring significant investments in infrastructure and expertise. Therefore, an organization can also opt out of domestic or international developers to design customized software for them (Qureshi et al., 2024). Different readily available software is heavily employed by organizations, such as Moodle by educational institutions and enterprise resource planning by the corporate sector (Bresnahan, 2019). All these strategies can have complementary or substitutive effects, as while readily available market software can be economical, still firms must invest in complementary skills where limited talented individuals can be an issue (Chen et al., 2024; Shakil et al., 2024).

In each strategy, the organization needs to evaluate different options, such as selection criteria for outsourcing, alignment of organizational core competencies with in-house software development, and the effect on competitive advantage in the case of readily available software. There is little empirical evidence of these kinds of ready-made software applications, in-house development, or outsourcing for the diffusion of AI and how they are used within the more extensive set of AI software applications (Hoffreumon, Forman and van Zeebroeck, 2024). A valuable piece of work in this regard is conducted by Hoffreumon, Forman and van Zeebroeck (2024). They examined the sourcing of AI by 3143 firms across Europe and documented that readily available software from the market is the most common strategy; however, it may vary from industry to industry. This study is important and provides valuable insights in this context. Building on this, this research examines how the adoption of AI in-house or outsourcing influences an organization's transition to Industry 5.0. Specifically, we aim to explore the influence of organization AI adoption through an in-house or outsourced strategy on its human-AI collaboration. Thus, this chapter's main research question is:

RQ: How do in-house and outsourced AI development strategies influence human-AI collaboration and organizational innovation, and what are the associated advantages, disadvantages, and challenges?

This research provides valuable insights into the body of knowledge related to AI adoption for Industry 5.0. First, this research builds on recent research by Hoffreumon, Forman, and van Zeebroeck (2024) to add evidence to the knowledge regarding organizational strategy to adopt AI in-house versus outsourcing. In this way, it documents valuable knowledge necessary to explain organizational strategies to embrace emerging technologies. While existing literature explores various aspects of technology adoption in general, studies that specifically compare the in-house development of AI with outsourcing strategies in companies are limited.

In our research, we aim to bridge this gap by qualitatively exploring these strategies through expert insights. By analyzing the benefits, disadvantages, and challenges associated with each adoption strategy, we seek to understand better how these approaches influence human-AI collaboration in organizational settings. Therefore, this study offers novel evidence on how corporate AI adoption strategies affect human-AI collaboration. This contribution is particularly important because, to the authors' best knowledge, no previous research has specifically addressed this intersection, considering the newness of the topic.

Research Background

AI Adoption in Industry 5.0

Industry 5.0 has turned into a popular concept in recent years. It is understood as an evolution from Industry 4.0, where the emphasis on automation and efficiency has transitioned to a more human-centered approach (Coronado et al., 2022). In Industry 5.0, there is a greater focus on human creativity, cognitive skills, and problem-solving abilities, with strong attention to the collaboration between humans and machines (Balart & Shryock, 2024). By utilizing advanced technologies like AI, which have great potential to improve and complement human tasks, Industry 5.0 can adopt a more human-centered approach and foster better collaboration between humans and AI (Madsen et al., 2023; Holzinger et al., 2024).

Kaasinen et al. (2022) have presented a new model in their study, which illustrates how certain expected changes in the industry may influence and shape Industry 5.0. In their model, they have emphasized the importance and value of human traits such as creativity, innovativeness, and user-centered design for Industry 5.0. Their model suggests that technologies are adopted to improve the roles of workers rather than replace them and take their jobs. AI is recognized as one of the key and influential technologies in Industry 5.0. (Johri et al., 2021). This technology provides an opportunity for people and machines to interact, exchange information, and work together through complicated algorithms and cognitive systems (Jarrahi,

2018; Martini et al., 2024). Therefore, AI technologies in Industry 5.0 are not just simple tools for developing automation. They are seen as partners that enhance human abilities and highlight key human strengths (Zafar et al., 2024).

As mentioned, Industry 5.0 emphasizes human-centricity, and it integrates human creativity, intuition, and emotional intelligence into industrial processes (Leng et al., 2022). This change of focus is led by the understanding that although automation can handle repetitive tasks (Borchardt et al., 2022), it cannot really replace human characteristics, such as creativity, empathy, and critical thinking (Yang, 2018). AI in Industry 5.0 supports these human features by offering intelligent assistance that can be adapted to individual worker needs, supporting and fostering environments where humans and machines can work together more effectively (Joshi, 2023).

One of the main objectives of Industry 5.0 is to create resilient and sustainable systems (Martini et al., 2024), where AI can play a critical role in optimizing resource use, reducing waste, and improving productivity, which can ensure that human workers are not getting replaced, but instead, they get empowered (Leng et al., 2024). This can be very important in sectors such as manufacturing, healthcare, and supply chains, where human skills are crucial for addressing many complicated challenges (Dogru & Keskin, 2020).

AI Make-or-Buy Decision

Nowadays, deciding between developing emerging technologies, such as AI in-house or outsourcing their development, has become a critical strategic choice since it is known to have a great impact on organizations' innovation and competitiveness (Beulen et al., 2022). Different elements, such as costs, control, customization, and skills availability, can play a great role in making decisions like this in the organizations (Aitzaz et al., 2016). In-house AI development is usually chosen by organizations that need customized solutions that are personalized to their specific needs. According to Hoffreumon, Forman, and van Zeebroeck (2024), developing AI internally allows firms to align AI technologies with their unique business processes and strategic goals, offering greater control and flexibility (Gräf, Mehler and Ellenrieder, 2024).

However, in-house development is very resource-intensive and requires significant investments in skilled people, time, and infrastructure (Daneshgar, Low, and Worasinchai, 2013). Gräf, Mehler, and Ellenrieder (2024) also mentioned that it is really challenging to manage a dedicated AI team that is capable of developing, maintaining, and upgrading AI systems at the same time that technologies advance. Moreover, developing internally can be risky if the company doesn't have the necessary technical expertise or fails to integrate AI into existing processes in an effective way (Aitzaz et al., 2016).

On the other hand, outsourcing AI development may offer a quicker and usually cheaper solutions to organizations, especially for firms that may not have the required technical infrastructure or skilled staff to build AI solutions or tools internally (Ekahtor Osagie, Francis Emeka and Beatrice, 2023). As Beulen et al. (2022) declared, outsourcing can help to address the shortage of AI expertise in companies and enable them to focus more on their core competencies and benefit from AI capabilities provided by external experts at the same time (Charles & Benson Ochieng, 2023). Nevertheless, outsourcing also comes with challenges, such as data security concerns, control loss, and dependency on third parties (Gräf, Mehler and Ellenrieder, 2024).

In many cases, organizations choose a hybrid approach, which means that they combine both in-house and outsourced AI development to achieve the best of both. Hoffreumon et al. (2024) suggest that making a balance between these two sourcing strategies can provide greater flexibility and cost efficiencies for companies since, for example, firms may need internal expertise to adapt and develop external innovations, which can enhance their ability to absorb and apply external knowledge better (Caloghirou et al., 2004). This "absorptive capacity" can help firms to integrate and adjust ready-made software to align with their specific business processes (Abourokbah et al., 2023). When companies have some internal knowledge assets, it could be beneficial as it helps them evaluate and choose from existing developed innovations. This way, they can ensure that what they have chosen is in line with their organizational needs and where some customization might be needed (Díaz-Díaz & de Saá-Pérez, 2014). In general, over time, having internal expertise in the company makes them able to improve and extend the capabilities of existing systems, so they will fit better with their processes. When there is a balance between internal development and external sourcing, there will be smoother ongoing innovation, which helps firms maximize the value of both approaches (Hoffreumon, Forman and van Zeebroeck, 2024). For example, companies may purchase some standard AI tools but maintain in-house control over the customization and integration of these tools into their own systems. This way, firms can benefit from the expertise provided by third-party providers and maintain some extent of control over the more strategic aspects of AI development and implementation at the same time (Pankowska, 2019).

Human-AI Collaboration

The increasing growth in human-AI collaboration shows that there has been a change in the way that companies manage different tasks (Mahmud et al., 2023). This type of collaboration improves the potential for innovation and productivity in many businesses across different industries by combining AI's processing capability with human-specific traits like creativity and decision-making (Bao et al., 2023). The potential of AI to boost human creativity has already been proved. Studies, such as the one by Beghetto (2023), show that AI can help as a collaborator in possibility thinking, which fosters human creativity by producing fresh concepts and viewpoints. It can show new horizons for creativity by overcoming the restrictions of the human brain (Ali Elfa & Dawood, 2023). In their study, Jia et al. (2024) demonstrated that AI supports agents' ability to offer creative and new responses to client requests. Their solutions exceeded the company's present knowledge base and demonstrated higher levels of innovativeness than they could have accomplished alone.

AI can process large volumes of data and make predictions based on that, which complements human intuition and judgment (Emmanuel Osamuyimen Eboigbe et al., 2023; Järvelä, Nguyen, and Hadwin, 2023) and results in better decision-making (Emmanuel Osamuyimen Eboigbe et al., 2023; Järvelä, Nguyen and Hadwin, 2023). One study related to AI assistance in decision-making was done by Hemmer et al. (2023), which found that AI delegation—meaning that the AI model is trained to determine whether it should make a prediction for a specific task or delegate the decision to a human—which improves both performance of the task and satisfaction. This kind of collaboration enhances productivity and allows humans to focus more on higher-level tasks when AI manages daily repetitive tasks or data-intensive processes (Hemmer et al., 2023). Another example demonstrating the collaboration of humans and AI for better decision-making is a study by Reverberi et al. (2022) that explored how doctors performing colonoscopies use AI to improve their decisions. According to their study, in crucial domains like healthcare, completely automating judgments isn't always feasible or desirable. This is not only due to ethical and legal concerns but also because human specialists can provide some valuable expertise that complements AI capabilities. The study highlighted how a hybrid decision-making process that combines the skills of humans and AI produces superior results. In their case, AI worked well because doctors usually followed its accurate and precise recommendations. Additionally, it was safe because doctors ignored AI's suggestions when they were wrong. When these conditions are met, hybrid decision-making turns into a trustworthy and efficient method of diagnosis (Park et al., 2024; Reis, 2024).

The findings from different studies, such as Jain et al. (2023), show that trust powers effective and successful human-AI collaboration. Therefore, trust in AI systems should be properly balanced to let individuals understand AI's strengths and limitations. This awareness helps reduce the risks and negative consequences of either abusing or ignoring AI technology (Mehrotra et al., 2024). According to Westphal et al. (2023), users trust AI systems better when they understand how decisions are made and maintain control over them. This may help users better accept AI systems and improve collaboration outcomes. In line with that, findings from a study by Żywiołek (2024) suggest that a way to build trust for a better human-AI collaboration is to provide structured training programs. These professional training sessions are essential for bridging the knowledge gap between employees and AI systems. The authors further describe how training staff to effectively use AI builds employee trust, which leads organizations to better adopt new technologies and create a more trusting and collaborative work environment (Hao et al., 2024; Tiziana et al., 2024).

Methodology

In this work, we employed an exploratory qualitative research methodology to explore the effects of various AI development approaches—in-house vs. outsourcing—on human-AI collaboration. Nowadays, the application of AI is becoming more and more significant in Industry 5.0, which is developing quickly (Miragall et al., 2023) and enhances human-machine communication, providing businesses with the opportunity to make more efficient decisions. (Martini et al., 2024). Therefore, a qualitative approach was selected in this study in order to get a comprehensive understanding of the topic, which may not be fully captured using quantitative methods (Dabić et al., 2023; Frimodig & Torkkeli, 2017; Kutvonen et al., 2010).

Interviewees Selection

For data collection, we conducted in-depth, semi-structured interviews with three experts with substantial experience in AI development and implementation in different organizations (Dabić et al., 2019; Nurulin et al., 2019). These experts were selected using the purposive expert sampling method, a non-probability sampling technique in which individuals are chosen based on their specialized knowledge and relevance to the research topic (Saunders et al., 2019). It allows for gathering more in depth and relevant data from qualified experts.

The experts were selected to ensure variety from three different companies dealing in AI solutions, services, and projects, as well as to ensure a variety of perspectives. The roles of interviewees included AI product manager, software developer, and AI data scientist. All experts have worked with different customers and partners to tailor AI solutions that meet their operational requirements. Through such collaborations and projects, they participated in, they gained insight not only from their own professional experiences but also from the perspectives of their clients and project partners.

Their work includes advising organizations on adopting AI, customizing AI applications for specific industrial challenges, and implementing AI systems in various organizational settings. This wide range of interactions with different stakeholders enables them to understand the implications, challenges, and successes of both in-house and outsourced AI development strategies from multiple angles. Their experience in providing AI solutions and partnering on projects for implementing AI in different organizations has well-equipped the experts to offer valuable insights into how different strategies influence human-AI collaboration and innovation. Their insights extend beyond just the technical and strategic aspects of AI adoption to include the organizational factors that can affect successful AI implementation and integration.

Table 1 summarizes the participants' details and provides anonymized information about their roles and companies.

Table 1 Interviewees' details

Respondent	Role	Duration
A	AI Data Scientist & Research Team Leader	35 min
B	Co-funder & CPO, AI product manager	45 min
C	Software developer	40 min

Data Collection

For collecting data, the authors carried out in-depth semi-structured interviews with industry experts. This method provides flexibility (Kallio et al., 2016) and maintains a consistent framework for all respondents at the same time to ensure validity (Dolczewski, 2022). The candidates for interviews were selected from the authors' LinkedIn and professional networks. The chosen interviewees were proven to have high experience in topics related to the development of AI. In their projects, they were either involved in developing AI-based services or implementing them in an organizational setting. Their expertise enabled the experts to offer detailed insights into the dynamics and strategies of AI adoption and also provided authors with a comprehensive overview of the entire field. The conducted interviews lasted from 35 to 45 min. Two interviews were carried out face-to-face in person, and the third one was held through an online meeting as the interviewee was located in another city.

An interview guide was developed based on themes identified, covering topics such as:

> Experiences with in-house AI development versus outsourcing Challenges and obstacles associated with each strategy Impacts of these strategies on human-AI collaboration Recommendations for companies choosing between the two strategies.

Interviews were audio-recorded with the informed consent of the participants to ensure accuracy and were transcribed using the Temi transcription platform. Participants were informed about the confidentiality of their data, their right to voluntary participation, the anonymity of their responses, and the potential academic use of their interview insights.

Data Analysis

We analyzed the data collected from interviews with experts using the thematic analysis method, and we followed the steps suggested by Naeem et al. (2023). This approach is an ideal way to identify, analyze, and report patterns in qualitative data.

In this case, the analysis was conducted through the following steps: In the first step, the interview recordings were transcribed, and the authors familiarized themselves with the content of the transcriptions. Reviewing the interviews and transcribing them allowed the authors to better engage with the data and identify the preliminary themes

Table 2 Summary of identified codes and themes

Themes	Codes
AI development strategy	In-house development, outsourcing, combined strategy
Strategy selection reason	Benefits of in-house, benefits of outsourcing, in-house challenges, outsourcing challenges, flexibility
Human-AI collaboration	Trust in AI tools, human-centric innovation, training for employees
Efficiency	AI as a tool for efficiency, time
Outsourcing challenges	Security concerns, importance of data, time, control, maintenance and support, customization
In-house challenges	AI skills availability, pressure from manager, cost considerations, time, investment, resource availability

and important areas of interest. In this stage, quotations that could reflect different perspectives, along with recurring patterns relevant to the research question and topic under study, were selected. The second step was keywording, which included identifying the recurring phrases or words in the interview transcripts as keywords. This effectively captured the core of the interviewees' perceptions and experiences. These keywords were generated directly from the data as the basis for further analysis. In the third step, codes were applied to data segments that summarized their core meaning or relevance to the research questions. These short phrases or words helped to break down complex textual data into manageable units. The last step was about taking the code clusters together as meaningful units to be named "themes." As they actually discover patterns and relationships, thereby providing insights into the research question.

To perform the data analysis steps, we used NVivo software to improve the depth and accuracy of the analysis, as it helps with detailed coding and categorization of data. With the help of this software, we could better manage the large amount of qualitative data collected from the interviews, which, in the end, helped create comprehensive coding and identify themes. The summary of the codes and identified themes is displayed in Table 2.

Findings

The interviews with Interviewee A, Interviewee B, and Interviewee C bring out valuable information about AI development strategies, organizational efficiency, human-AI collaboration, and challenges linked with both in-house and outsourced AI development strategies. The interviewees brought a variety of perspectives to the discussion, drawing from their own experiences as well as those of their clients and project partners using AI in different domains.

AI Development Strategy

One of the main themes that was identified from the analysis of interviews was related to the strategies that organizations might take for the development of AI. Organizational goals, available resources, security issues, and the requirement for flexibility are just a few of the numerous variables that firms must take into account when deciding between in-house AI development versus outsourcing.

In-House Development: An in-house approach to AI development is typically used to ensure data control and to address certain demands that companies may have. Flexibility, some degree of customization, and the guarantee that the development of AI solutions is in line with organizational goals are all aided by this approach. In order to highlight the importance of this strategy, Interviewee A stated, "If you have something built in-house, there might be more trust with it." He also highlighted the significance of organizational learning when developing AI internally, stating, "Building capabilities in-house for solving problems with AI becomes ever more important." This notion of trust and control was supported by Interviewee C, who added that "employees tend to feel more comfortable with in-house tools because they know how they were developed and can rely on internal support to fix issues quickly." He also pointed out that larger companies in size may want to do development more in-house when they have very specific needs for AI systems that are not provided by third parties. He stated, "Larger companies might still develop in-house AI if they need something specific that isn't available elsewhere."

Developing in-house was also perceived as a way to support internal teams and create new opportunities within the organization. For example, Interviewee B stated that developing AI internally may even result in the creation of new jobs and funding. He said, "To develop something because it would create for them some new jobs and would give them some budgets." This shows that developing internally usually may bring about team growth and resource allocation, encouraging the company—which has the capability to support it—to select the in-house development strategy.

However, developing AI in-house has its own challenges. For example, Interviewee B mentioned that having a team for the internal development of AI needs resources. "You have to develop it once for yourself, and it requires so much energy and time," he said.

Outsourcing: However, the interviewees pointed out that organizations, especially those without the required resources or experience, may save some money and time by outsourcing AI development. Interviewee C explained, "Outsourcing is generally more cost-effective, especially if a suitable tool already exists. You don't need to hire a full team to build something from scratch." By using external expertise and AI tools and systems, organizations can access ready-made solutions that third parties have already developed. Interviewee B supported this by stating, "The default should be outsourcing." Like Interviewee C he explained that, when AI products are already available in the market, it usually makes more sense to purchase and integrate them rather than invest time and resources to develop them from the beginning. "When the product is already out there, it makes sense to purchase it and not develop it," he added. This approach enables organizations to save time and adopt tested technologies.

Interviewee A also mentioned some specific cases where outsourcing might provide more benefits, especially when ready-made third-party options are widely available. He explained, "Let's say, grammar checking or email proofreading, that's something that, you know, there's a lot of offerings out there, and this is very good." Tools such as those mentioned by Interviewee A, which are usually highly specialized and readily available, make outsourcing an efficient and logical solution. Therefore, he also pointed out that "Outsourcing becomes a smart activity that, you know, you just outsource the areas where you can actually benefit from the outer world." This shows that outsourcing is important not just because it is usually a cheaper option, but it is a way to access specialized skills and technology that may not exist within the organization.

Although outsourcing has advantages, it also has specific risks, specifically when it comes to data security and loss of control. Interviewee A explained, "When you're outsourcing, you're always dependent on some other third party to make the latest development for you." Interviewee C also discussed that when AI solutions are developed by third parties, they usually don't have the level of flexibility and customization that organizations might need for their specific goals and processes.

Combined Strategy: When organizations need to make a decision between in-house AI development and outsourcing it, some of them might choose to go with a hybrid strategy. This way, they can strike a balance between efficiency and control by outsourcing certain steps and keeping the essential tasks and data in-house. Interviewee A described this combined strategy. "You outsource the areas where you can benefit from the outer world, but the core idea remains in your organization." By adopting a hybrid strategy, businesses can leverage the expertise gained through outsourcing while also maintaining control over critical data and processes.

Strategy Selection Reasons

When deciding whether to develop AI tools and solutions inside or outsource them, organizations need to consider several factors, such as the size of the organization, resource availability, security issues, and the level of customization they need. According to Interviewee A, "Many companies are struggling with what to choose."

Cost and Flexibility: Usually, cost plays a significant role in decision-making. As previously said, outsourcing is thought to be a more cost-effective choice, particularly for smaller businesses. In this regard, Interviewee C noted, "Outsourcing is generally more cost-effective, especially if a suitable tool already exists. " This opinion was further supported by Interviewee B, who said that outsourcing lowers maintenance costs and complexities. "The costs and maintenance are less of a headache when you purchase," he explained. However, Interviewee C mentioned that solutions developed outside of the company may not have the required level of flexibility to be adapted to the firm's processes effectively. However, Interviewee B was against that by highlighting that outsourcing actually offers greater flexibility when it comes to implementing and updating AI solutions. He explained, "When you're purchasing from a third party, the good thing again is that you can reach a service really fast and switch to another one." This kind of easy access to ready-made AI tools can help organizations to implement AI solutions rapidly and, if needed, change to another provider with almost no disruption. This is usually important in specific industries where technological advancements happen all the time, and it might be difficult for the company to keep up with the changes by itself.

On the other hand, larger organizations may have the resources to invest in in-house AI development, especially if they require a high level of customization. As Interviewee A noted, "If the solution is built in-house, then you might have a better resource to cater to people and their needs."

Security Concerns: Concerns regarding security were among the important issues mentioned by interviewees that organizations usually consider when they want to select the appropriate approach for the development of AI. Interviewee B explained that some organizations might feel more secure choosing in-house development since they work with some specific sensitive data. "Most of the time, security is the number one reason companies don't want third parties involved," he said. Similarly, Interviewee A highlighted the risks that outsourcing can bring to organizations that handle sensitive data. "If you're outsourcing, you're always dependent on some other third party, and that could be a problem if you're dealing with sensitive data."

Company Size and Expertise: Another important aspect that organizations need to consider while choosing between strategies is the size of the company. Interviewee B noted that smaller companies usually lack the skills and resources that are required to develop AI internally; therefore, outsourcing might make more sense for them. "Smaller-sized companies don't necessarily have the resources to start developing everything from scratch," he explained. However, as interviewee C mentioned, it might make more sense for bigger organizations that have specialist IT and AI teams to employ in-house development and use the existing infrastructure, resources, and experience in the company.

Human-AI Collaboration

If organizations want to successfully benefit from AI technology, they and their employees need to create a strong and efficient human-AI system collaboration. The interviewees discussed the importance of trust, training, and human-centered design in supporting the successful implementation of human-AI collaboration.

Trust in AI Tools: Interviewees identified trust in AI technology and systems as one of the most important factors for enhancing its adoption in organizations. According to Interviewee C, some employees believe that those tools that have been developed internally provide them with greater control and influence over the system. This is why they tend to trust in-house developments more than those created by outsiders. "Employees might feel more secure using an in-house tool because they trust that their data won't leave the company," he said. Interviewee A similarly mentioned that "if you have something built in-house, there might be more trust with it." He also highlighted the role of trust in whether employees feel comfortable using these tools in their daily tasks. "The way in which people are able to interact with that (AI) is also kind of driven by how much trust they have on that tool," he explained.

Training and Education: All of the interviewees also explained the importance of providing necessary training for their employees to use AI tools effectively. Interviewee A suggested that holding training sessions can help employees to understand how to use AI tools. "To ensure the benefits of AI become more tangible and realistic, organizations need to involve their personnel in trainings on how to use these tools properly." Interviewee C agreed, adding that training employees is essential to promoting trust and collaboration between humans and AI systems.

Human-Centric Innovation: As already mentioned in Industry 5.0, AI technologies should be used in a way that enhances, rather than replaces, human creativity and innovation. Interviewee A stated that "If innovations are supposed to solve humans' problem, then, you know, humans need to be also in the loop. And the synergy of AI and humans would definitely be important." He also highlighted that AI systems cannot fully replace human feelings and emotional intelligence, especially in roles that require a human touch, such as healthcare. Interviewee C also agreed with this view. However, Interviewee B saw it from a different perspective. He mentioned that AI is great at handling a lot of data, analyzing it, and identifying patterns. This way, they can actually better understand the human side of innovations based on human psychological patterns. He mentioned that "essentially, human and feelings are patterns, right? So, AI is very good at identifying patterns" and "they can identify, what humans want actually way better than humans".

Efficiency

The interviewees also discussed how AI technologies can improve organizational efficiency by automating some processes, which can result in reducing errors that might occur.

Time-Saving: One of the main benefits of AI systems is their ability to save time by automating and optimizing tasks. Interviewee C explained, "AI can help humans save time and energy by optimizing tasks and reducing errors." However, the time-saving potential of AI depends on how well the technology has been integrated into the existing processes. Interviewee B mentioned that developing AI tools in-house can be time-consuming, especially if the organization doesn't have the necessary expertise or resources. "It requires a lot of energy and time to develop something in-house," he said. He also mentioned that it all depends on the data and expertise. If the proper data is not used in the AI system and there isn't enough knowledge and expertise, then the system won't have enough efficiency. "So if you do not know exactly what you're doing, so let's, let's be more specific. If you're developing a prediction model and you don't have someone with the strongest statistics knowledge about the data, unconventional AI, you would be developing something really, Bad" and "mathematically based product models will be garbage in, garbage out."

Improving Overall Efficiency: AI also has the potential to improve overall organizational efficiency by enabling better decision-making and reducing the likelihood of human error. Interviewee A mentioned that AI allows organizations to automate certain aspects of their operations, which can lead to significant efficiency gains. "With AI, we can think of automating and making processes more efficient in certain areas," he explained.

Challenges in in-House and Outsourced AI Development

Both strategies of AI development have their own challenges that organizations need to consider when deciding which approach to adopt. The interviewees discussed these challenges and named different concerns and challenges related to costs, expertise, time, and control over data.

In-House Challenges

Developing AI tools and solutions can bring some benefits to organizations, including greater control over the system and increased customization opportunities. However, adopting this approach may lead to challenges related to the cost of system development, the availability of skilled people, and the rapidly evolving nature of AI technologies, which are discussed in more detail in the following.

Cost and Resource Intensity: When companies decide to develop AI internally, it is important that they ensure they are capable of making the necessary investments in infrastructure and various resources, such as skilled personnel. Interviewee C explained that in-house AI development is not a viable option for every organization because not all companies can afford the development cost. "Developing AI in-house is expensive and time-consuming, and not all companies have the resources or urgency to justify it," he noted. Additionally, interviewee B discussed that developing AI tools and systems internally is usually far more expensive than purchasing them from third parties outside the organization. This can be especially true for smaller companies that usually do not have access to the required resources.

Time Investment: Another issue that should be considered while choosing between development strategies is that the time investment required for designing, testing, and implementing AI systems is really high. In line with this, Interviewee B mentioned that developing AI tools internally can take so much time: "It requires a lot of energy and time to develop something in-house, especially if it involves building new models from scratch." Similarly, Interviewee C stated that internal development could be very "time-consuming" and "just a waste of time." The longer development time may outweigh the advantages of in-house development, such as greater customization and the capacity to maintain control over sensitive data if a company is looking for faster results and solutions.

AI Expertise and Skills Availability: Another challenge mentioned by the interviewees concerning in-house development was the potential lack of skilled individuals who are knowledgeable about AI within the organization that wants to implement the development internally. AI technologies are evolving and changing rapidly all the time, and without a dedicated, highly skilled IT team, it might be difficult to always keep up with the most recent developments. Interviewee A states that many firms do not possess the knowledge and personnel needed to develop, implement, and support AI technologies internally. "If you're doing something in-house, it's probably going to be limited because you don't have the resources or the people to actually build those things." He also underlined that companies must understand how AI actually works and have the right people in place to manage the complexities of AI systems. Finding qualified and skilled individuals who are knowledgeable about the latest AI advancements could be a major issue according to Interviewee C.

Rapid AI Evolution: As mentioned earlier, AI technology is advancing very fast, and keeping up with these developments could be a challenge for organizations that want to develop and maintain AI systems in-house. Interviewee B emphasized that companies need to keep up with AI advancement. "AI is pretty much like most other mathematical-based products: garbage in, garbage out. So, if you don't have someone with the strongest statistics knowledge about the data, you would be developing something really bad." Therefore, due to the rapid evolution of AI technologies, it is necessary for companies to have continuous learning and updates if they want to develop and maintain AI systems in-house, which can be difficult for companies with limited resources or expertise.

Outsourcing Challenges

Although outsourcing AI development has been cited as having benefits, including lower costs and faster deployment, there are also disadvantages. Long-term dependence on outside vendors, lack of control over the development process, limitations on customization, and data privacy are often the common issues.

Data Privacy and Security Concerns: As mentioned earlier, interviewees frequently mentioned that outsourcing can sometimes result in a loss of control over sensitive data. This is because third-party developers and providers may need to access certain data from the company, which raises concerns about security and privacy for the buying company. Interviewee A discussed these concerns, saying, "When you're outsourcing, you're always dependent on some other third party to make the latest development for you, and there's always the risk of losing control over your data." Interviewee B also underlined that one of the main reasons why businesses might not be interested in having outsider parties involved in their AI development is usually security concerns.

Loss of Control and Customization: As previously mentioned, interviewees discussed how companies that contract out AI development may have less control over the procedure and the final product. This might be difficult for the company if the outsourced solution does not exactly match their particular needs and processes. Interviewee C stated that when tool development is outsourced, there is a possibility that they lack adaptability and flexibility, which might lead to inefficiencies in the organizational system. He said, "If a tool doesn't work properly, it can waste time, and there's often less flexibility in modifying the tool to meet specific needs." Interviewee A added that outsourcing can lead to a situation where the company becomes entirely reliant on the external provider, which can limit its ability to do more development independently. "Outsourcing is that you know, you're always dependent on some other third party to make the latest development for you," he said.

Interviewee B also mentioned that outsourcing might not be the best option if a company is looking for a high level of customization.

Long-Term Dependency: Interviewees pointed out that outsourcing may also cause companies to become reliant on third-party providers for a long time, and this might eventually lead to extra problems for the buying organization when it needs any further support or customizations for the systems developed outside of the company. Interviewee A warned, "If you have this habit of outsourcing, you might have to do it forever, and that could become very expensive in the long run." This reliance could restrict the company's internal development and slow its adaptability to market shifts and technological advancements.

Customization and Maintenance Issues: Usually, third-party providers design and offer services and products in a way to satisfy a variety of client needs. Therefore, there aren't many customization options per each specific organization's needs. For companies with particular requirements and processes, this approach could be limiting. This problem was brought up by Interviewee C, who clarified that occasionally, outsourced technologies might not offer the level of flexibility that is needed to address specific challenges in a company. While outsourcing may reduce the burden of in-house maintenance, it also forces businesses to depend on outside vendors for system upgrades, bug fixes, and updates. Interviewee A mentioned that when outsourcing, "Oftentimes, when you outsource, you just made something, and then that's basically it. They build it, and then it's gone." Interviewee B also mentioned that if there is a need for high levels of customization, then outsourcing might not be the best option.

Discussion

In this chapter, we explored both in-house and outsourcing strategies for developing AI solutions within an organization. We discussed the advantages, disadvantages, and challenges associated with each approach, as well as how choosing one of these strategies can influence human-AI collaboration in companies. Previous studies in the literature indicate that in-house development provides businesses with greater control over AI systems and allows them to customize these systems according to their specific needs and processes. (Hoffreumon et al., 2024; Gräf et al., 2024). This was strongly supported by the findings from our interviews. Interviewee A mentioned that trust in AI tools may be stronger when they are created inside the company, stating, "If you have something built in-house, there might be more trust with it." Human-AI cooperation will be greater when people have faith in AI technologies and systems. This is because employees feel more comfortable using technological solutions they know are developed within their own organization. Moreover, in-house strategies enhance trust through transparency (Rawlins & Rawlins, 2014), as employees often feel reassured knowing their data remains within the organization. Interviewee C also mentioned this, saying that employees might have a better feeling with in-house developed tools because they can access internal support for any problems they might face.

However, although outsourcing can be faster and less expensive (Ekahtor Osagie, Francis Emeka and Beatrice, 2023), it also has some challenges in terms of trust and customization. According to interviewee A, organizations might feel that they don't have enough control over AI tools that are developed outside of their company, which may reduce employee engagement with the systems. Nevertheless, outsourcing can be a good option when companies need to adopt AI solutions fast and are looking for cheaper options. As Interviewee B noted: "The default should be outsourcing when the product is already available." This shows how efficient outsourcing could be in delivering standardized AI tools quickly. To summarize, an in-house development strategy allows companies to achieve higher levels of customization, trust, and collaboration between humans and AI. However, outsourcing can offer faster and cost-efficient AI adoption. Still, it may not allow companies to achieve the same depth regarding employee engagement with AI tools, as control over data and customization is limited while outsourcing.

It seems that outsourced solutions need to address trust issues through, for example, strong vendor accountability, robust data security measures, and explainable AI features. These aspects are important for maintaining effective human-AI collaboration. Trust in AI systems affects not only how individuals work but also how the entire organization accepts them. For instance, AI systems created within the company may match the company's values and goals more closely. This may help employees feel more connected to the purpose. In contrast, using AI systems from external providers might need extra steps, like frequent checks and clear explanations of how data is managed, to build trust across the organization.

Then, regarding the key advantages and disadvantages of adopting in-house AI versus outsourcing AI development, according to the literature, in-house AI development has the potential to enhance innovation by aligning AI solutions with the organization's unique goals and processes (Hoffreumon et al., 2024). Our interviews also confirmed this. Interviewee B mentioned that in-house development can lead to internal growth opportunities by creating new roles and projects for teams inside the organization. This was reflected in his statement that: "To develop something internally creates new jobs and gives teams new budgets." This can result in a higher potential for innovation in the companies.

However, in-house development usually needs big investments in resources such as time and funding. Interviewee B explained, "You have to develop it once for yourself and it requires so much energy and time," which supports the literature about the long-term commitment required for in-house AI development (Daneshgar, Low and Worasinchai, 2013). On the other hand, outsourcing provides this opportunity for companies to have immediate access to AI expertise and solutions without the need for extensive investment in internal resources (Ekahtor et al., 2023). Interviewee C confirmed this by underlining that outsourcing could be a great option from the cost point of view, especially when "suitable tool already exists." However, low levels of flexibility and high dependency on third parties were mentioned as major drawbacks of outsourcing, as noted by Interviewee A: "You are dependent on some other third party to make the latest development for you."

Therefore, although developing AI in-house supports innovation and organizational growth, it requires significant investments in resources and time. Also, with outsourcing, companies will access more efficient options for AI systems, but there are some limitations from a long-term perspective since there is a lower potential for customization and innovation due to reliance on third-party providers. When considering human centricity, creating systems within the company allows organizations to design tools that meet their employees' needs, making them more user-friendly. Outsourcing, while faster, might not align as well with these needs, requiring extra training to match the tools to the company's specific requirements. For example, companies that build their own tools can use employee feedback to improve them over time. On the other hand, tools from outside providers may need additional workshops or training sessions to help employees learn and adjust to how they work.

Regarding the challenges of AI adoption strategies, as mentioned in the literature and supported by the interviews, they both have their own difficulties. As discussed earlier, the main challenges of in-house development are the need for investment in skilled personnel and infrastructure, which have high costs. Moreover, the rapid pace of AI evolution can be challenging as it would be difficult for companies to keep up with it. Interviewee A mentioned the challenges of keeping up with AI advancements, stating, "If you're doing something in-house, it's probably going to be limited because you don't have the resources or the people to build those things." This is supported by studies that mention the cost and resource intensity of in-house AI projects (Daneshgar, Low and Worasinchai, 2013).

Although the outsourcing option doesn't need a high investment in resources, it has challenges related to data security, control, and customization. As mentioned by Interviewee A, there are security concerns about sharing data with external providers while outsourcing. This challenge has also been mentioned in the literature (Gräf, Mehler, and Ellenrieder, 2024). Moreover, Interviewee C declared that when a company uses outsourced solutions, usually there will be a lack of flexibility, which can restrict customization and tailored solutions for specific organizational needs.

However, according to the literature, choosing a mixed strategy of in-house and outsourced approaches to AI development can be a viable solution (Hoffreumon et al., 2024). (Hoffreumon et al., 2024), which is also supported by Interviewee A, who described it as an ideal way to balance control and efficiency: "You outsource the areas where you can benefit from the outer world, but the core idea remains in your organization." In conclusion, it's critical to take into account a number of considerations while choosing between outsourcing and in-house AI development. Depending on their particular circumstances, many businesses in various sectors and settings would need to select alternative strategies. Organizational innovation, human-AI cooperation, and the difficulties that businesses have while using AI may all be greatly impacted by AI development methods. While in-house development can foster more trust, engagement, and creativity, it also comes with a high cost. On the contrary, outsourcing offers time and money-saving alternatives, which may, of course, lead to less control and fewer opportunities for innovation. Combining the two approaches into a hybrid strategy may provide businesses with the best of both worlds by preserving control over essential AI operations while allowing for flexibility. Therefore, businesses must assess their own circumstances before making decisions based on their requirements and possibilities. Finally, there aren't many studies that concentrate on AI development methods, which emphasizes the need for more study in this field, particularly when it comes to analyzing how businesses may maximize human-AI collaboration through various AI adoption strategies.

Conclusion

This chapter examined approaches to AI development, their effects on human-AI cooperation, and their possible advantages and disadvantages. We obtained insightful information and a better comprehension of the subjects in the area by conducting in-depth, semi-structured interviews with experts. Through the findings of this study, we demonstrated how in-house development helps businesses better match AI solutions to their unique requirements, retain more control, and improve employee trust in built AI systems. But it's also expensive, needs highly qualified workers, and has trouble keeping up with the quick speed at which AI is developing. However, outsourcing allows businesses to employ outside knowledge and provides a quicker, more cost-effective solution, but it may still result in a loss of control and restricted flexibility when modification is required.

The study's conclusions provide insightful advice for decision-makers who are having trouble deciding between outsourcing and in-house AI development. Managers may make better judgments that fit their organization's resources, strategic objectives, and innovation potential by weighing the benefits and drawbacks of each strategy. This study does have limits, though, much like any other research. Our conclusions are based on interviews with three industry experts, which may not fully represent the variety of experiences across various businesses and industries, albeit offering profound insights. Additionally, more empirical research is required to examine AI development strategies on a bigger scale as AI adoption grows. This will provide a more comprehensive knowledge of how various companies make these decisions and what best practices evolve over time.

References

Abourokbah, S. H., Mashat, R. M., & Salam, M. A. (2023). Role of absorptive capacity, digital capability, agility, and resilience in supply chain innovation performance. *Sustainability, 15*(4). https://doi.org/10.3390/su15043636

Aitzaz, S., et al. (2016). A comparative analysis of in-house and outsourced development in software industry. *International Journal of Computer Applications, 141*(3), 18–22. https://doi.org/10.5120/ijca2016909578

Ali Elfa, M. A., & Dawood, M. E. T. (2023). Using artificial intelligence for enhancing human creativity. *Journal of Art, Design and Music, 2*(2). https://doi.org/10.55554/2785-9649.1017

Alves, J., Lima, T. M., & Gaspar, P. D. (2023). Is industry 5.0 a human-Centred approach? A systematic review. *Processes*. Multidisciplinary Digital Publishing Institute (MDPI). https://doi.org/10.3390/pr11010193

Balart, T., & Shryock, K. J. (2024). A framework for integrating AI into engineering education, empowering human-centered approach for industry 5.0. In *IEEE global engineering education conference, EDUCON*. IEEE Computer Society. https://doi.org/10.1109/EDUCON60312.2024.10578796

Bao, Y., Gong, W., & Yang, K. (2023). A literature review of human–AI synergy in decision making: From the perspective of affordance actualization theory. *Systems*. Multidisciplinary Digital Publishing Institute (MDPI). https://doi.org/10.3390/systems11090442

Beghetto, R. A. (2023). A new horizon for possibility thinking: A conceptual case study of human × AI collaboration. *Possibility Studies & Society, 1*(3), 324–341. https://doi.org/10.1177/27538699231160136

Beulen, E., Plugge, A., & van Hillegersberg, J. (2022). Formal and relational governance of artificial intelligence outsourcing. *Information Systems and e-Business Management, 20*(4), 719–748. https://doi.org/10.1007/s10257-022-00562-7

Borchardt, M., et al. (2022). Industry 5.0 beyond technology: An analysis through the lens of business and operations management literature. *Organizacija, 55*(4), 305–321. https://doi.org/10.2478/orga-2022-0020

Bresnahan, T. F. (2019). Technological change in ICT in light of ideas first learned about the machine tool industry. *Industrial and Corporate Change*. https://doi.org/10.1093/icc/dty076

Caloghirou, Y., Kastelli, I., & Tsakanikas, A. (2004). Internal capabilities and external knowledge sources: Complements or substitutes for innovative performance? *Technovation, 24*(1), 29–39. https://doi.org/10.1016/S0166-4972(02)00051-2

Charles, M., & Benson Ochieng, S. (2023). Strategic Outsourcing and Firm Performance: A Review of Literature. *International Journal of Social Science and Humanities Research (IJSSHR), 1*(1), 20–29. https://doi.org/10.61108/ijsshr.v1i1.5

Chen, R., Balasubramanian, N., & Forman, C. (2024). How does worker mobility affect business adoption of a new technology? The case of machine learning. *Strategic Management Journal*. https://doi.org/10.1002/smj.3595

Coronado, E., et al. (2022). Evaluating quality in human-robot interaction: A systematic search and classification of performance and human-centered factors, measures and metrics towards an industry 5.0. *Journal of Manufacturing Systems, 63*, 392–410. https://doi.org/10.1016/j.jmsy.2022.04.007

Daneshgar, F., Low, G. C., & Worasinchai, L. (2013). An investigation of "build vs. buy" decision for software acquisition by small to medium enterprises. *Information and Software Technology, 55*(10), 1741–1750. https://doi.org/10.1016/j.infsof.2013.03.009

Díaz-Díaz, N. L., & de Saá-Pérez, P. (2014). The interaction between external and internal knowledge sources: An open innovation view. *Journal of Knowledge Management, 18*(2), 430–446. https://doi.org/10.1108/JKM-07-2013-0257

Dogru, A. K., & Keskin, B. B. (2020). AI in operations management: Applications, challenges and opportunities. *Journal of Data, Information and Management, 2*(2), 67–74. https://doi.org/10.1007/s42488-020-00023-1

Dolczewski, M. (2022). Semi-structured interview for self-esteem regulation research. *Acta Psychologica, 228*. https://doi.org/10.1016/j.actpsy.2022.103642

Ekahtor, Osagie, O., Francis Emeka, O., & Beatrice, E. (2023). Outsourcing+Benefits+And+Com plications. *International Journal of Research in Marketing, Entrepreneur and Management, 8*.

Eboigbe, E. O., et al. (2023). Business intelligence transformation through AI and data analytics. *Engineering Science & Technology Journal, 4*(5), 285–307. https://doi.org/10.51594/estj.v4i5.616

Gräf, M., Mehler, M., & Ellenrieder, S. (2024). *AI strategy in action: A case study on make-or-buy for AI-based services*. Available at: https://aisel.aisnet.org/pacis2024/track01_aibussoc/track01_aibussoc/8

Hao, X., Demir, E., & Eyers, D. (2024). Exploring collaborative decision-making: A quasi-experimental study of human and Generative AI interaction. *Technology in Society, 78*, 102662. https://doi.org/10.1016/j.techsoc.2024.102662

Hemmer, P., et al. (2023). Human-AI collaboration: The effect of AI delegation on human task performance and task satisfaction. In *International Conference on Intelligent User Interfaces, Proceedings IUI* (pp. 453–463). Association for Computing Machinery. https://doi.org/10.1145/3581641.3584052

Hoffreumon, C., Forman, C., & van Zeebroeck, N. (2024). Make or buy your artificial intelligence? Complementarities in technology sourcing. *Journal of Economics and Management Strategy, 33*(2), 452–479. https://doi.org/10.1111/jems.12586

Holzinger, A., et al. (2024). From industry 5.0 to forestry 5.0: Bridging the gap with human-centered artificial intelligence. *Current Forestry Reports*. https://doi.org/10.1007/s40725-024-00231-7

Jain, R., Garg, N., & Khera, S. N. (2023). Effective human–AI work design for collaborative decision-making. *Kybernetes, 52*(11), 5017–5040. https://doi.org/10.1108/K-04-2022-0548

Jarrahi, M. H. (2018). Artificial intelligence and the future of work: Human-AI symbiosis in organizational decision making. *Business Horizons, 61*(4), 577–586. https://doi.org/10.1016/j.bushor.2018.03.007

Järvelä, S., Nguyen, A., & Hadwin, A. (2023). Human and artificial intelligence collaboration for socially shared regulation in learning. *British Journal of Educational Technology, 54*(5), 1057–1076. https://doi.org/10.1111/bjet.13325

Jia, N., et al. (2024). When and how artificial intelligence augments employee creativity. *Academy of Management Journal, 67*(1), 5–32. https://doi.org/10.5465/amj.2022.0426

Johri, P., et al. (2021). Sustainability of coexistence of humans and machines: An evolution of industry 5.0 from industry 4.0. In *Proceedings of the 2021 10th International Conference on system modeling and advancement in research trends, SMART 2021* (pp. 410–414). Institute of Electrical and Electronics Engineers Inc.. https://doi.org/10.1109/SMART52563.2021.9676275

Joshi, D. A. (2023). *Enhancing employee efficiency and performance in industry 5.0 organizations through artificial intelligence integration.* 13(4). Available at: http://eelet.org.uk

Kaasinen, E., et al. (2022). Smooth and resilient human–machine teamwork as an industry 5.0 design challenge. *Sustainability (Switzerland), 14*(5). https://doi.org/10.3390/su14052773

Kallio, H., et al. (2016). Systematic methodological review: Developing a framework for a qualitative semi-structured interview guide. *Journal of Advanced Nursing*, 2954–2965. https://doi.org/10.1111/jan.13031

Leng, J., et al. (2022). Industry 5.0: Prospect and retrospect. *Journal of Manufacturing Systems, 65*, 279–295. https://doi.org/10.1016/j.jmsy.2022.09.017

Leng, J., et al. (2024). Unlocking the power of industrial artificial intelligence towards industry 5.0: Insights, pathways, and challenges. *Journal of Manufacturing Systems.*, 349–363. https://doi.org/10.1016/j.jmsy.2024.02.010

Liao, C., et al. (2024). How effective is AI augmentation in human–AI collaboration? Evidence from a field experiment. *Information Technology and People*. https://doi.org/10.1108/ITP-11-2022-0859

Madsen, D. Ø., Berg, T., & Di Nardo, M. (2023). Bibliometric trends in industry 5.0 research: An updated overview. *Applied System Innovation.* https://doi.org/10.3390/asi6040063
Mahmud, B., Hong, G., & Fong, B. (2023). A study of human-AI Symbiosis for creative work: Recent developments and future directions in deep learning. *Acm Transactions on Multimedia Computing, Communications and Applications, 20*(2). https://doi.org/10.1145/3542698
Martini, B., Bellisario, D., & Coletti, P. (2024). Human-centered and sustainable artificial intelligence in industry 5.0: Challenges and perspectives. *Sustainability (Switzerland), 16*(13). https://doi.org/10.3390/su16135448
Mehrotra, S., et al. (2024). A systematic review on fostering appropriate trust in human-AI interaction: Trends, opportunities and challenges. *ACM Journal on Responsible Computing, 1*(4), 1–45. https://doi.org/10.1145/3696449
Miragall, M. F., et al. (2023). Face the future—Artificial intelligence in Oral and maxillofacial surgery. *Journal of Clinical Medicine.* https://doi.org/10.3390/jcm12216843
Naeem, M., et al. (2023). A step-by-step process of thematic analysis to develop a conceptual model in qualitative research. *International Journal of Qualitative Methods, 22.* https://doi.org/10.1177/16094069231205789
Oztemel, E., & Gursev, S. (2020). Literature review of industry 4.0 and related technologies. *Journal of Intelligent Manufacturing.*, 127–182. https://doi.org/10.1007/s10845-018-1433-8
Pankowska, M. (2019). Information technology outsourcing chain: Literature review and implications for development of distributed coordination. *Sustainability, 11*(5). https://doi.org/10.3390/su11051460
Park, J., Oh, C., & Kim, H. Y. (2024). AI vs. Human-generated content and accounts on Instagram: User preferences, evaluations, and ethical considerations. *Technology in Society, 79*, 102705. https://doi.org/10.1016/j.techsoc.2024.102705
Passalacqua, M., et al. (2024). Human-centred AI in industry 5.0: A systematic review. *International Journal of Production Research.* https://doi.org/10.1080/00207543.2024.2406021
Qureshi, S. A., Naseem, A., & Ahmad, Y. (2024). Outsourcing or in-house manufacturing in hi-tech industry: Supply chain process with Delphi-AHP approach. *Kybernetes.* https://doi.org/10.1108/K-08-2022-1172
Raju, R., et al. (2024). Enhancements and Progress in industry 5.0: A strategic method for confronting the limitations of industry 4.0. In *Lecture notes on multidisciplinary industrial engineering* (pp. 193–199). Springer Nature. https://doi.org/10.1007/978-981-97-4700-9_19
Rathore, N., Jain, P.K., & Parida, M. (2022). *A sustainable model for emergency medical services in developing countries: A novel approach using partial outsourcing and machine learning.* Risk Management and Healthcare Policy [Preprint]. Available at: https://doi.org/10.2147/RMHP.S338186.
Rawlins, B., & Rawlins, B.L. (2014). *Measuring the relationship between organizational transparency and employee trust.* Available at: https://www.researchgate.net/publication/239919667
Reis, J. (2024). Customer service through AI-powered human-robot relationships: Where are we now? The case of Henn na cafe, Japan. *Technology in Society, 77*, 102570. https://doi.org/10.1016/j.techsoc.2024.102570
Reverberi, C., et al. (2022). Experimental evidence of effective human–AI collaboration in medical decision-making. *Scientific Reports, 12*(1). https://doi.org/10.1038/s41598-022-18751-2
Sarkar, B. D., et al. (2024). Digital transition from industry 4.0 to industry 5.0 in smart manufacturing: A framework for sustainable future. *Technology in Society, 78.* https://doi.org/10.1016/j.techsoc.2024.102649
Saunders, M., Lewis, P., & Thornhill, A. (2019). *Research methods for business students by Mark Saunders*, Philip Lewis and Adrian Thornhill 8th edition., Research methods for business students.
Tariq, W., Tariq, A., Bhutta, U.S., Gohar, M. (2024). Artificial Intelligence a Panacea for Innovation Management? Review and Directions. *Review in Business and Economics, 4(1).* https://rbe.uskt.edu.pk/papers/RBE-4-1-0001.pdf

Tiziana, C. C., Riccardo, S. V., Hubbard, E.-M., Daly, A., & Lohse, N. (2024). *An ethical framework for human-robot collaboration for the future people-centric manufacturing: A collaborative endeavour with European subject-matter experts in ethics*. 78(102680). https://doi.org/10.1016/j.techsoc.2024.102680.

Tóth, A., et al. (2023). The human-centric industry 5.0 collaboration architecture. *MethodsX, 11*. https://doi.org/10.1016/j.mex.2023.102260

Trakadas, P., et al. (2020). An artificial intelligence-based collaboration approach in industrial iot manufacturing: Key concepts, architectural extensions and potential applications. *Sensors (Basel), 20*(19), 1–20. https://doi.org/10.3390/s20195480

Westphal, M., et al. (2023). Decision control and explanations in human-AI collaboration: Improving user perceptions and compliance. *Computers in Human Behavior, 144*. https://doi.org/10.1016/j.chb.2023.107714

Xu, X., et al. (2021). Industry 4.0 and industry 5.0—Inception, conception and perception. *Journal of Manufacturing Systems, 61*, 530–535. https://doi.org/10.1016/j.jmsy.2021.10.006

Yang, S. (2018). Comments from young scholars: Can machines completely replace humans in manufacturing processes? *Frontiers of Engineering Management, 5*(4), 541. https://doi.org/10.15302/j-fem-2018207

Zafar, M. H., Langås, E. F., & Sanfilippo, F. (2024). Exploring the synergies between collaborative robotics, digital twins, augmentation, and industry 5.0 for smart manufacturing: A state-of-the-art review. In *Robotics and Computer-Integrated Manufacturing*. Elsevier Ltd. https://doi.org/10.1016/j.rcim.2024.102769

Żywiołek, J. (2024). Trust-building in AI-human partnerships within industry 5.0. *System Safety: Human–Technical Facility–Environment, 6*(1). https://doi.org/10.2478/czoto-2024-0011

Bahar Bahramian Dehkordi has done her PhD at Lappeenranta-Lahti University of Technology (LUT), Kouvola Unit in Finland. She holds a master's degree in science with a focus on supply chain studies and a doctoral degree in science (technology) Her doctoral research explored the impact of disruptive technologies on sustainability practices within the context of supply chain management. Her recent study, titled "Blockchain as a Sustainability Booster in Supply Chain Management," has been published by Springer Nature. Bahar has actively contributed as a project manager to various EU-funded projects, including VOIS, UniBus, and Poliunibus. She has also participated in other projects such as ArtIST, INCREASE, EFFORT, ISSUE, and many more. Currently, she works as a Post-award manager for EU-funded projects at LUT University.

Prof. Marko Torkkeli is a Professor of Technology and Business Innovations at the Lappeenranta-Lahti University of Technology (LUT), Kouvola Unit in Finland. His research interests focus on technology and innovation management, strategic entrepreneurship, growth venturing, and decision support systems. He has published over 300 articles in academic journals and conferences. He serves as the Director of Publications of the International Society for Professional Innovation Management (ISPIM) and is one of the founding editors of the open-access, multidisciplinary Journal of Innovation Management.

Dr. Adeel Tariq is a docent and Post-Doctoral Researcher of technology and innovation management at Lappeenranta-Lahti University of Technology (LUT), Kouvola Unit in Finland. He has published in prestigious academic journals such as Technological Forecasting and Social Change, and European Journal of Innovation Management, and others. As a principal investigator and collaborator, Dr. Tariq has collaborated on EU (Erasmus+) funded projects such as VOIS and ArtIST. In addition, he has contributed to various regional, national, and international projects.

Professor Marina Dabić is Full Professor of Entrepreneurship and International Business at the Faculty of Economics and Business, Croatia, and the University of Ljubljana, School of Business and Economics. She published more than 200 papers indexed in Web of Science and Scopus. Professor Dabić is an Editor in Chief for Technology in Society, Senior Department Editor for IEEE—Transactions on Engineering Management, Associate Editor of Technological Forecasting and Social Change, and for Strategic Change journal. She was a member at large for the IEEE-TEMS 2020–2022. Prof. Dabić prepared a background report on HE Innovate published by EC/OECD. In 2021, she received WAIB best paper award from the Academy of International Business. Currently, she is a partner to CUES Horizon project and she has contributed to Industry 4.0 in the Horizon 2020 RISE Open innovation project, Interreg Wool project, and ERASMUS K2 BENEFIT and VOIS project. Marina Dabić has been consistently recognized among the Top 2% of scientists worldwide by Stanford University since 2022. She also serves as the Editor and Series Founder of a prestigious Springer book series on Applied Innovation Technology Management.

Human Intelligence and Artificial Intelligence in Collaboration: Change Management, Creative Performance, and Societal Expectations

Margaret A. Goralski and Krystyna Górniak-Kocikowska

Introduction

Artificial humans may be a prognosis for the future, but they are not the current reality. AI mimics human life, but it is not human life. Scientists are attempting to create life from inorganic matter, and many believe that AI has the potential to self-evolve (Jiang et al., 2024), although this has not yet been realized. Artificial life's ontological and ethical status is among the most challenging issues. It questions whether *being human* is an exclusively human trait or whether AI in the form of Gen AI can also "be human." This paper explores some of these questions, including but not restricted to the perennial question of what it means to be human, how humanity will be affected by AI, and, in turn, how humans' approach to intelligence, natural or artificial, may change. Answers to these questions have universal significance; however, the focus in this chapter will be on their meaning for business enterprises. We will discuss some projections of how Gen AI could collaboratively share a workplace ecosystem with humans. This chapter defines collaboration as a true partnership where both parties voluntarily accept the same goal. The term we will use is *collaborative partnership*.

We will also explore the depth and range of HI and AI while investigating whether humans will reject or accept these collaborations. Perhaps more unsettling in human minds is whether they could reject these vast changes. And even more disturbing is the possibility of Gen AI rejecting cooperation with humans. We do not have in mind a rebellion of AI against humans in the form of robots rebelling against humans in the way envisioned by Isaac Asimov in his three Laws of Robotics

M. A. Goralski (✉)
Quinnipiac University, Hamden, CT, USA
e-mail: Margaret.Goralski@quinnipiac.edu

K. Górniak-Kocikowska
Southern Connecticut State University, New Haven, CT, USA

M. Dabić et al. (eds.), *Artificial Humans*, Future of Business and Finance,
https://doi.org/10.1007/978-3-032-06604-6_5

(Asimov, 1942), and later four (Asimov, 1950), but rather Gen AI's refusal to partner with HI because of HI's inferiority to AI. With these problems in mind, the chapter will query some of the theories of change management from the perspective of paradox theory and creative performance. It will delve into society's expectations and finish with the necessity of governments to create a safety net to catch the humans that will fall between the cracks as AI gains momentum in the workforce.

Industry 5.0 envisions robots and intelligent machines working alongside humans to add resilience and sustainability (Commission, 2021a). It seeks to meld various forms of AI and humans into the environmental and societal aspects of business. However, for humans, Industry 5.0 also raises concerns, among other things, about the future of work and whether one's place in the workforce ecosystem will remain. According to the statements of McKinsey Global Institute and Goldman Sachs below, their concerns may be well-founded.

> McKinsey Global Institute [a multinational strategy and management consulting firm] estimates that generative AI will add between $2.6 and $4.4 trillion in annual value to the global economy, increasing the economic impact of AI by 15 to 40%. The consultancy projects that AI will automate half of all work between 2040 and 2060, with generative AI pushing that window a decade earlier than previous estimates. Goldman Sachs [a global investment banking, securities, and asset and wealth management firm] predicts a 7%—or nearly $7 trillion—increase in global GDP attributable to generative AI, and the firm expects that two-thirds of US occupations will be affected by AI-powered automation. (The great acceleration: CIO perspectives on generative AI, 2023, p. 4).

Thus, Gen AI's impact on economies and enterprises will be and, according to some, is already revolutionary. AI is no longer the domain of science fiction; it affects nearly every aspect of our lives. It is here in many forms: surveillance, reproductive technologies, conversation, creation of ideas for brainstorming, and even suggestions of what one may eat for breakfast. AI supplants human decisions in various fields to prevent human error: medical diagnostics, driverless autos, trains, planes, and Wall Street's high-speed stock trading floor, among others. Each is considered superior to what existed previously in the human domain. AI, especially Gen AI, has created common challenges to global governance and questioned society's expectations. These are concrete challenges that need solutions. Thus far, however, AI cannot find these solutions alone, independently of humans. Underneath all these challenges is the idea of humanity.

Human Intelligence and Artificial Intelligence

The nature of AI promises radical alterations to human intelligence and identity. AI has moved from simple 0 1 logic to include human thinking and reasoning, but it is challenging to incorporate the reality of this extension of AI into the logic of humanity. The creation of Gen AI has expedited this paradigm shift, allowing it to converse with its human counterpart like a colleague in the office and assist with difficult decisions. These innovative implementations of Gen AI into the thought process of humans via conversation and suggestions for decision-making will have an immense impact on the future of human thought and the evolution of human intelligence. However, AI still falls short of proper understanding, which would permit a genuinely collaborative partnership.

The development of new life, including Gen AI, is calling into question the very relationship of humankind to all of life. For a successful partnership of HI and AI (or rather, between humans and AI, because this is the point of collaborative partnership in this case) to exist, living beings must be understood by AI and, at the same time, understand the revolutionary changes taking place in society as AI becomes progressively mainstream. However, currently, collaboration would be complex since a balance between humans and AI does not exist. Humans are not in agreement regarding the status of AI in society. Humans initially created robots to be subordinate to them. Asimov's Laws of Robotics placed robots in the category of servitude, and some scholars, e.g., Joanna Bryson and Stephen Petersen, still believe in the servitude of AI to humans (Bryson, 2010; Petersen, 2007). Hence, the creation of artificial humans could quickly turn into the creation of simply another category of enslaved people, an option we do not support.

Robots, and consequently AI, were created based on a severely truncated concept of a human being. It happened when Western philosophy, the direct foundation of digital technologies and hence AI, reduced human beings, or instead the value of human beings *qua* human beings, to reason, deeming all other human characteristics as secondary (some of them even of negative value). That process lasted roughly from the seventeenth to mid-twentieth century (René Descartes' *cogito* to Karl Popper's principle of rationality) (Descartes, 1637; Popper, 1994). People exclusively perceived human intelligence as what is today called logical-mathematical intelligence. Thanks to the work of Howard Gardner, an American psychologist, nine types of human intelligence are now officially accepted: logical-mathematical, naturalist, bodily-kinesthetic, spatial, existential, intrapersonal, musical, linguistic, and visual-spatial (Gardner, 1983).

AI is still replicating only one human characteristic: the ability to reason. It mimics what is called logical-mathematical intelligence. Humans, on the other hand, are complex and multidimensional. Moreover, humans are living beings. Life is both precious and magnificent. In a sense, life itself is a privilege. Being alive is a privilege because it means sharing in the more incredible wonder of life. One of the things we humans most hope for from life, what we are striving for, is happiness (Lama, 2021). It is elusive and defined in many ways, complicated to obtain, and even more challenging to keep. So, we deal with the imperfect, flawed reality of constant change while we yearn for perfection, for constant happiness where there is no change. This yearning is so intense that Faust, the main character in one of the world's greatest literary works, Johann Wolfgang Goethe's (1749–1832) drama by the same title, was willing to give his soul to the Devil for such perfection and lasting happiness (Goethe, 1973).

One of the central questions regarding happiness is this: Is it only humans who can be happy? Or is happiness a universal attribute of life? There is a story about Zhuangzi (Chuang Tzu), one of the most outstanding Ancient Chinese Taoist philosophers. In that story, titled "The Joy of Fishes," also known as "The Happiness of the Fish," Zhuangzi makes the following observation to his friend while crossing the river:

> See how free
> The fishes leap and dart:
> That is their happiness. (Thomas Merton's translation)
>
> The ensuing argument centers on the issue of whether Zhuangzi, not being a fish, can "know what makes fishes happy."
>
> In Thomas Merton's book "The Way of Chuang Tzu," the ending of the text reads as follows. Chuang said:
>
> (...)
> What you asked me was
> '*How do you know*
> What makes fishes happy?'
> From the terms of your question
> You evidently know I know
> What makes fishes happy
> "I know the joy of fishes
> In the river
> Through my own joy, as I go walking
> Along the same river." (Merton, 1969, p. 98)

When interpreting the last sentences, what comes to our minds is Zhuangzi's conviction of the existence of a bond between living organisms. He knows the joy (or happiness) of the fish because he and the fish are the same in that they both are part of that same formidable and extraordinary entity, life. They don't need to communicate verbally; they don't need to reason with each other to have that certainty of the shared feeling. They are the same. They are life, and as such, they are part of nature (in this case, the river, the air, and the water), which they perceive similarly.

Zhuangzi's views are echoed in Indigenous cultures worldwide (e.g., Kimmerer, 2020) and explored from different perspectives with varying reference points. Philosophers and scientists show not only a growing interest in human-nature relations and the general interconnectedness existing in the physical/material world, including humans (Floridi, 2015; Sheldrake, 2020), but also in the possibility of human-robot/AI friendships (Elder, 2017). For several decades, there has been a movement of sorts, which seems to have accelerated its growth recently with books ranging from Nobel Prize winner Klara and the Sun (Ishiguro, 2021) to the Monk and Robot series (Chambers, 2021), just to name a few. Artificial humans might not necessarily be the only option.

Moreover, these views support information philosophy, a branch of philosophy created relatively recently by Luciano Floridi (Floridi, 2011). He and his team argue for the existence of shared information between the human and nonhuman world. The widespread use of information and communication technologies (ICTs) reaches the subatomic level of quantum computing and radically impacts the human condition. Floridi points out that the impact of ICT was due to at least four major transformations:

> a. the blurring of the distinction between reality and virtuality; b. the blurring of the distinction between human, machine, and nature; c. the reversal from information scarcity to information abundance; and d. the shift from the primacy of stand-alone things, properties, and binary relations to the primacy of interactions, processes, and networks. (Floridi, 2015, p. 2).

These transformations changed, if not the nature and role of information itself, then our understanding of it, its significance for humans, and the relations and interactions between humans and AI.

Zhuangzi, Goethe's medieval scholar Faust, Goethe himself—any human until shortly after WWII never experienced a world with artificial intelligence. AI was absent from public debates and did not exist in the sense that there had not been a name for it until the pivotal Dartmouth conference in 1956 (Crevier, 1993). Artificial intelligence belongs to our reality, not to Zhuangzi or Goethe. Humans and fish are part of the natural world and life forms. According to Zhuangzi, they have similar sensations and feel the same. But they cannot communicate verbally, exchange views, make rational arguments, etc. Artificial intelligence is a product of the human mind, not nature. In that sense, it is an extension of humans. Unlike fish, humans can communicate verbally with artificial intelligence, exchange views, make rational arguments, etc. AI can only think, speak, and "feel" as far as its human creators have programmed it.

However, one should also keep in mind that these are still the early stages in the development of artificial intelligence. At present, AI mimics life; it is the imitation of life, but it is not life in the sense of fish or humans. Humans and fishes share a common ground: life and the capacity to share feelings and emotions. Humans and AI also share a common ground: the mind and its ability to reason and express reasoning verbally. However, there seems not to be a common ground shared directly, without human mediation, by nonhuman forms of life and AI. Yet.

Humans are more than just reason, more than logical-mathematical intelligence. We believe that the application of Industry 5.0's creation of a collaborative partnership of humans and AI could be more successful in business settings if AI were taught to understand the totality of the human being, including irrationality, will, sensitivities, drives, yearnings (e.g., for happiness), and not just the human mind. To establish successful human-AI collaborative partnerships, we should teach AI to understand the full complexity of humans rather than viewing artificial humans one-dimensionally as minds and treating them as slaves.

Developers created artificial intelligence as a continuation of previous advancements in digital technologies and technology in general. Therefore, as with most technological inventions, its purpose was to facilitate human life. In this regard, and because the possibility of AI "escaping" out of human control became evident early on, the creators of AI were aiming from the outset at its servitude and obedience to humans. This position still has its supporters in writers such as Bryson and Petersen. Therefore, the main emphasis is on AI programming that endows it to listen and obey—and this, in a sense, means the restoration of human social patterns from the past rather than the collaborative partnerships envisioned for the future. However, as humans are asked to embrace AI, specifically Gen AI, and welcome change—which, according to the statistics cited earlier in this paper, threatens their very existence in a workspace they once dominated—the prevailing risks and challenges fall squarely into the realm of change management, paradox theory, and creative performance.

Change Management and Paradox Theory

In the business world, managing organizational change is the realm of change management. It involves applying various methods to prepare and support workers, teams, and leaders throughout the change process. One of the most detrimental characteristics of organizational change is a person's desire to stay the same, to be comfortable in their own space and comfort zone (to remain happy). To step outside this zone presents risks of the unknown, the unexplored, and possible failure.

In 1932, after the publication of Aldous Huxley's *Brave New World* (Huxley, 2006a), stepping out of one's comfort zone was discussed at length, and again in 1958 when he published *Brave New World Revisited* (Huxley, 2006b). Huxley reinforced his earlier argument that humans do not like change. These two publications note that, since the Industrial Revolution, change has dictated that humans become increasingly machine-like. Entire branches of social sciences and neuroscience on human "brain engineering" and the arguments necessary to support these sciences followed. Since Huxley explored the dangers of technology and what it can do to the world if given free rein, many harken back to his work as Gen AI and technology have, in some sense, taken over the dominion of human lives. Exploring the intricate interplay between the necessity of business to change and humans desire not to change reveals several complex paradoxes at the intersection of this dilemma. So, we briefly introduce paradox theory into this analysis of change.

Paradox theory explores the contradictory and yet interrelated opposites that exist simultaneously and continue over time. It suggests that contradictory demands can present themselves as dualities with complementary and competing characteristics, and therefore, it is concerned with managing contradictions within organizations (Waldman et al., 2022). It is imperative for an organization to innovate and adapt to changing markets, technological breakthroughs, the rise of new competitors, and the inception of Gen AI, among others, or else the organization will stagnate and ultimately fail. However, approximately 50% of organizational change initiatives are unsuccessful due to this duality of thinking and failure to secure employee buy-in (Miller, 2020). Interestingly, leaders and followers can initiate and inhibit change by acting defensively.

> Paradox theory (Lewis & Smith, 2022) is relevant to any persistent dilemma. [It] treats ongoing dilemmas and apparent tradeoffs as competing but also as dualities with complementary and integrative potential. Ideally, employees accept them as contradictions inherent to their work responsibilities, engage them actively, apply both/and thinking and apply them creatively over time. (Wang et al., 2024).

The following brief examples illustrate the importance and complexity of change in business environments. Our first example is Lufthansa. We use it here to represent our earlier point about natural human resistance to change based not on rational reasoning but on the feeling of comfort (or even happiness) with the status quo. Christian Haude, Ivo Blohm, and Xavier Lagardère (2024), in their article *How Lufthansa Shapes Data-Driven Transformation Leaders*, discuss how human organizational resistance hindered the transformational efforts needed for Lufthansa to become a truly data-driven company. Although Lufthansa's leadership mandated the change, the crucial ingredient to push critical changes forward existed within its leadership circle, creating a paradox. Lufthansa needed its leaders to motivate, inspire, and coach employees to turn business unit leaders into advocates for data-driven change. However, Lufthansa's leadership team first needed to address their inadequate AI literacy before change could occur. Lufthansa's information technology team launched a data leadership program to share valuable insights with employees, facilitating the requirements to implement change. The team put in place a data leadership program with six key roles: Data Visionary to Create a Vision; Data Transformer to Promote Transformation; Data Driver to Create Value; Data Decision Maker to Generate Impact; Data Collaborator to Connect People; and Data Coach to Develop Competencies (Haude et al., 2024, p. 3). Change eventually occurred, but it took time and implementation of many steps along the way.

In the change management literature, preparing the organization, crafting a change plan, implementing the changes, embedding the changes into the culture and practices of the organization, and then reviewing and analyzing the progress and results of that change are necessary steps for humans to accept change (Errida & Lotfi, 2021) willfully. Lufthansa's information technology team recognized that change needed to occur at the leadership level and filter down to business unit leaders and employees. Change advocates had to span all levels of the organization.

Additionally, identifying potential roadblocks to undermine the project had to be anticipated, along with plans to mitigate and add flexibility. A well-designed strategy becomes essential, as is the necessity to communicate with team members and stakeholders throughout the change process. In the Lufthansa example, we see leaders of the organization who recognize and advocate for data-driven change. Yet, without the education and onboarding of leadership to drive the initiative forward, it would have stagnated and led to the ultimate abortion of a project to move the organization forward.

In a 2022 study, Kanitz, Gonzalez, and Berger et al. analyzed the consequences of change championing on group- and individual-level change outcomes, noting that previous studies had focused on individual-level championing. Researchers collected their multilevel perspectives from an ongoing organizational change at a German technology company. The findings revealed that individuals in groups with high championing levels perceived a more positive change impact (Kanitz et al., 2022).

The following example illustrates another way of approaching the problem of change. Karen Cunningham, managing director at Deloitte, and Laura Richards, manager of human capital at Deloitte Consulting (2023), introduced the topic of incorporating human sustainability into the organization. By shifting the emphasis of the organization to focus on the human element, people-enablers could be operationalized within the organization to achieve tangible outcomes by planning for the proper technical as well as soft human skills necessary to make work better for humans and to design for human sustainability (Cunningham & Richards, 2023). In a Deloitte 2023 Global Human Capital Trends survey, respondents observed barriers to achieving change outcomes as follows in order of primary importance: culture (29%), lack of funding and resources (27%), rate of change (24%), leadership commitment and capabilities (23%), ways of working (22%), infrastructure and technology (21%), among others (Cunningham & Richards, 2023). It turns out that infrastructure and technology played a significant but not dominating role, while organizational culture ranked as the number one barrier to change. The report highlights four fundamental ways to achieve or incorporate the human element of sustainability into an organization. It gives examples of organizations like Hilton, Apple, Anheuser-Busch InBev, etc., leading change by embracing the human aspect of sustainability. (*For more information, see* Cunningham & Richards, 2023.)

Leaders of organizations can drive positive change by being good role models, as was highlighted earlier in this section by the example of Lufthansa. They can shift employees' thinking and make tactical, tangible decisions to achieve the organization's most important goals. In the second example, promoting behavior shifts across all levels of the organization was necessary to add human sustainability into the culture. Aligning incentives, rewards, and performance with sustainability outcomes could achieve this result (Cunningham & Richards, 2023). However, to achieve true success, an organization must incorporate change management tactics by recognizing the interconnected importance of social, environmental, and economic factors and the significance of creativity and creative performance.

Creativity and Creative Performance

Creativity as a human quality has been documented throughout history. Initially, humans needed to shape their surroundings to survive and prosper (De Dreu et al., 2024). It was considered an exclusive ability of humans. Still, Gen AI has moved rapidly into the realm of creativity, questioning whether there is a creative difference between humans and machines (Koivisto & Grassini, 2023). The Koivisto and Grassini study matched human creativity with three AI chatbots using an alternate uses task (AUT). Both humans and chatbots "were asked to generate uncommon and creative uses for everyday objects" (Koivisto & Grassini, 2023, p. 1). The chatbots not only outperformed humans, but they also produced more creative responses. Of course, much depends here on the definition of creativity.

Researchers have previously studied creative performance as a function of human flexibility and persistent processing. The results differed between individuals and situational factors. In some instances, acquiring expertise provided people with the capacity to develop and process information more rapidly than those who did not have those capabilities, with experts having a more substantial basis for appraising and criticizing problem solutions. However, this expertise, as highlighted in the previous paragraph, is now being measured with the speed and creativity of Gen AI, and although it does not appear that the study pitted the creativity of Gen AI against humans who were experts in their fields, it does provide insight into the relationship of artificial and human creativity and gives an understanding of the future of creativity and specifically whether it will remain in the domain of humans.

While Industry 5.0 recognizes that AI will revolutionize productivity and efficiency, it must also acknowledge the necessity of humans. How to accomplish that result is still unclear. Humans and robots working together on a project will assume a pivotal role in shaping the future of work. However, currently, we envision work in a human-centered way, using AI as a tool to empower humans to work effectively and efficiently. Humans would be able to turn over mundane, repetitive tasks to Gen AI and focus on creative (surpassing Gen AI's capability for creativity) and strategic endeavors that amplify the human potential to innovate within the organization (Mentzas et al., 2024).

However, Gen AI is not like other AI in that it is closer to collaborating with humans in human terms. As we have seen earlier in this section, it questions whether creative endeavors are specific to humans or surpassed by Gen AI. With Firefly's launch, Adobe is utilizing Gen AI models to act as copilots to humans to create and design workflows. Its vast capabilities based on text descriptions will allow humans to describe a function that a machine will then carry out (MIT, 2023). The unique qualities of Gen AI and its ability to communicate with its human counterpart have contributed to an alteration in human acceptance of change. Still, society as a whole expects protection from human obsolescence.

Society's Expectations

From a practical and individual human perspective, there are worries that Gen AI, while slated to add trillions to the global economy, increase economic impact, and increase global GDP may increase unemployment and threaten the skills of humans. Some of those worried about the future are in fields that previously were not impacted.

> An Accenture [global multinational professional services company] analysis determined that 40% of working hours across industries could be automated or augmented by generative AI, with banking, insurance, capital markets, and software showing the highest potential. McKinsey projects that generative AI-related technologies could automate activities that currently take up 60 to 70% of worker time—up from 50% before the advent of generative AI (MIT, 2023, p. 16).

And yet, as a society of humans, people are being told that there will not be widespread job loss. Many industry leaders state that automation will complement rather than replace the need for humans. The premise is that creating new jobs will ameliorate the reduction or replacement of others. For instance, AI could help in sectors like education and healthcare, where expertise is essential. However, the workforce may be scarce or inadequate, especially in countries where there are not enough trained specialists to meet the demands of the population (Goralski & Tan, 2023).

Ethan Mollick, in his book *Co-Intelligence—Living and Working with AI,* writes what he sees as the future of AI:

> We have created a weird alien mind, one that isn't sentient but can fake it remarkably well. It is trained on the vast archives of human knowledge, and also on the backs of low-paid workers. It can pass tests and act creatively, with the potential to change how we work and learn; but it also makes up information regularly. You can no longer trust that anything you see, or hear, or read was not created by AI. (Mollick, 2024, p. 193).

As of this writing, business leaders believe that humans will still be necessary, and many new ideas for Gen AI will materialize from within the workforce, marking a new human entrepreneurial effort within organizations (MIT, 2023). However, many within society will not meet the requirements of the new fields that will materialize in these innovative HI/AI collaborative partnerships. These workers will fall by the wayside, and so the human fears persist. Therefore, governments must increase the safety net for their constituents to catch those who will fall into the abyss.

Creating a Safety Net: The Paradox of Government

Governments seek to achieve superiority through technological innovation and economic impact. The United States (USA), European Union (EU), and China lead in that superiority. However, the primary role of government is to protect its people. Therefore, another paradox presents itself as there is a dichotomy between striving for the superiority of AI and maintaining a balance to support a country's constituents. The leaders of the USA, EU, and China agree that it is imperative to invest in the research and development of digital technologies to streamline governmental policies, invest in collaborative systems, and maintain a position of leadership (Goralski & Gorniak-Kocikowska, 2020). At the same time, they recognize the risks involved in pitting the superiority of AI against the superiority of HI.

While creating new and innovative job categories may replace some of the jobs lost, the need for humans to fulfill those jobs will be significantly reduced. The financial support of an education system that generates the highly trained workforce necessary to support and advance HI and AI is a mandate that governmental policymakers must not overlook. Unified governance has become essential to manage the risks associated with Gen AI as it has gained impact and become ubiquitous–it was always necessary. Still, Gen AI has raised the stakes of human vulnerability (MIT, 2023). Without government diligence and insightfulness, there is a risk of chaos as we traverse yet unknown and unexplored territory.

The United States

In 2016, the US government began preparations for the collision that was predicted to occur between humans and artificial intelligence as workforce ecosystems expanded from a tradition of a workforce of humans to a workforce ecosystem of humans and robots. The National Science and Technology Council Committee on Technology sought to understand the relevance of AI, and it commissioned the *Preparing for the Future of Artificial Intelligence* report to explore new markets and opportunities (Holdren & Smith, 2016).

In 2019, the Executive Office of the President of the USA and the Office of Science and Technology Policy began the American Artificial Intelligence Initiative—the US strategy to promote American leadership in AI (Kratsios & Parker, 2020). It focused on governmental support for innovation in AI to increase US prosperity and enhance the quality of life for people in the United States of America while at the same time strengthening national and economic security (Goralski & Gorniak-Kocikowska, 2022).

In 2023, by Executive Order on the Safe, Secure, and Trustworthy Development and Use of Artificial Intelligence, the President of the U.S. released an executive order that stated in part:

> Section 1. Purpose
> Artificial intelligence (AI) holds extraordinary potential for both promise and peril. Responsible AI use has the potential to help solve urgent challenges while making our world more prosperous, productive, innovative, and secure. At the same time, irresponsible use could exacerbate societal harms, such as fraud, discrimination, bias, and disinformation; displace and disempower workers; stifle competition; and pose risks to national security. Harnessing AI for good and realizing its myriad benefits requires mitigating its substantial risks. This endeavor demands a society-wide effort that includes government, the private sector, academia, and civil society (Biden, 2023). *For more information, see the complete executive order.*

The president highlighted some of the opportunities and risks involved in AI, as well as the promises and fears, mirroring the thoughts of the populace. Additionally, more than 1000 researchers and technology leaders have urged AI labs to pause the development of AI tools due to "profound risks to society and humanity" (Metz & Schmidt, 2023).

The European Union

The EU, recognizing the active role played by industry in providing solutions to society's challenges, decided to include it in its economic and societal transitions in the future. Industry 5.0 would empower humans and address evolving skills and training needs for workers to remain competitive. Hence, the European Commission proposed a Regulation of the European Parliament and of the Council, laying down harmonized rules on Artificial Intelligence (Artificial Intelligence Act) and amending certain union legislative acts.

> 1. Context of the Proposal
> 1.1 Reasons for and Objectives of the Proposal
> … Artificial Intelligence (AI) is a fast evolving family of technologies that can bring a wide array of economic and societal benefits across the entire spectrum of industries and social activities. By improving prediction, optimising operations and resource allocation, and personalising service delivery, the use of artificial intelligence can support socially and environmentally beneficial outcomes and provide key competitive advantages to companies and the European economy. Such action is especially needed in high-impact sectors, including climate change, environment and health, the public sector, finance, mobility, home affairs and agriculture. However, the same elements and techniques that power the socio-economic benefits of AI can also bring about new risks or negative consequences for individuals or the society. In light of the speed of technological change and possible challenges, the EU is committed to strive for a balanced approach. It is in the Union interest to preserve the EU's technological leadership and to ensure that Europeans can benefit from new technologies developed and functioning according to Union values, fundamental rights and principles. (Commission, 2021b).

Industry 5.0 examines efficiency through a human-centered approach that puts human needs and interests at the core of the industrial production process. It mandates that industry respect planetary boundaries and remain sustainable. It introduces resilience—a need to develop robustness at a higher level in industrial production to perceive disruptions better and provide support at critical times of crisis (Commission, 2021a). The European Artificial Intelligence Act (AI) was adopted in August 2024. Proposed in 2021, the AI Act, as ratified, will tackle potential risks to citizens' health, safety, and fundamental rights. "It provides developers and deployers with clear requirements and obligations regarding specific uses of AI while reducing administrative and financial burdens for businesses.… The EU aspires to be the global leader in safe AI" (Directorate-General for Communication, 2024). The Commission recently launched a Code of Practice specifically for providers of general-purpose AI (GPAI) models that will address issues of transparency, copyright-related rules, and risk management (Directorate-General for Communication, 2024).

China

The government of China vigorously supports the development of the sciences, especially physical sciences, chemistry, life sciences, and environmental sciences. Funding for research in China is surpassed only by the USA. According to *National Geographic* (2019), the government of China supports the world's largest research institution, the Chinese Academy of Sciences (Canales & McNaughton, 2019, p. 26). Sixty thousand scientists have solved some of the world's most significant problems, assisted by artificial intelligence. The creation of AI took place in the West. However, China is now one of the top players in AI research and development. China today has a profound impact globally. Scientific discoveries and technological innovations have—or will have in the near or more distant future—global applications. Considering China's present position in the world, one cannot help but believe that the worldwide importance of both China and AI should not, must not, be treated separately. The two are tightly intertwined. China brings more to the table than the incredible dynamism of its present-day society in shaping the future. It also brings a strong foundation for centralized data collection and significant historical experience.

Conclusion

This chapter has taken the reader on a journey into what it means to be human and to better understand the nature of humans in their totality and complexity. It has explored the development of Gen AI and the nature of a collaborative partnership between humans and AI. We began by stating that we are on the brink of a whole new world where human intelligence (HI) and artificial intelligence (AI) will be collaborative in the true sense of collaboration—not in the master-servant relationship of humans and AI that has existed thus far. However, we must also be cognizant that a master-servant relationship should not be allowed to form where Gen AI leads in the quest for knowledge and humans are falling behind in knowledge acquisition. Gen AI is greedy in its pursuit of knowledge. Large language models (LLMs) train on massive amounts of data. Designers of LLMs do not ask permission from content creators before capturing data for AI training, nor do they always give credit to the humans who initially gathered the information. Therefore, much of the information may be plagiarized or even fake.

In business practices, HI is often perceived in its narrow, logical-mathematical, and linguistic-verbal version, leaving the other types of HI underutilized, insufficiently productive, or nonproductive. The most immediate question is whether AI could or would develop additional types of intelligence in the future that humans possess now: visual-spatial, body-kinesthetic, musical, interpersonal, intrapersonal, and naturalistic. If so, AI could join all forms of human and nonhuman life in full partnership. Otherwise, a growing imbalance could foster competitive and/or hostile relations between HI and AI. One possible outcome of this kind of development could be the accelerated development of logical-mathematical and linguistic-verbal intelligence in humans to "keep up" with the development of AI, most likely at the cost of the other types of intelligence. One of the unwelcome results of such a turn of affairs would be the further alienation of humankind from other forms of natural life.

The fundamental goal of human-AI collaboration in business should be to better satisfy human needs or wants since humans are the customers/consumers. AI is not. So long as AI has only a rudimentary understanding of human complexity, AI cannot successfully help in achieving the goals of businesses run by humans for humans, and it cannot successfully fulfill the role of a true partner in human-AI collaborative partnerships.

AI chatbots, Chat GPT, Google's Gemini, Microsoft's Copilot, and others can conduct human-like conversations, perform complex tasks, write computer code, and create essays that rival those of humans. An open letter from researchers and technology leaders asked governments to step in and halt the development of powerful chatbots by calling for a moratorium if the industry does not put a pause in place. However, governments will not universally challenge the developers of AI innovations; therefore, the power of Gen AI will continue to evolve and grow. It is perhaps impossible to halt innovations of the human mind once begun—even without knowing the result of those innovations. Nonetheless, governments of the USA, the European Union, and China, among others, need to ensure AI's safe, secure, and trustworthy development. They must mandate guidelines to protect the rights of its citizens and bring AI's vast development in balance with human values and ideals. There will be humans who will fall into the abyss as Gen AI and other forms of AI move rapidly into the workforce ecosystem. For true collaborative partnerships to exist, there must be a balance between HI and AI with respect for the capabilities each brings. As long as the idea of AI replacing humans in the workforce exists, there will be fear in humans of a world that presents itself as off-kilter—as moving in a direction where humans no longer control their destiny. So, a paradox will continue to exist.

References

Asimov, I. (1942). *Runaround.* [Online] Available at: https://archive.org/details/Astounding_v29n01_1942-03_dtsg0318/page/n93/mode/2up

Asimov, I. (1950). *The evitable conflict.* Astounding Science Fiction.

Biden, J. B. J. (2023). *Executive order on the safe, secure, and trustworthy development and use of artificial intelligence.* [Online] Accessed Oct 23, 2024, from https://www.whitehouse.gov/briefing-room/presidential-actions/2023/10/30/executive-order-on-the-safe-secure-and-trustworthy-development-and-use-of-artificial-intelligence/

Bryson, J. J. (2010). Robots should be slaves. In *Close engagements with artificial companions: Key social psychological, ethical and design issues* (pp. 63–74). John Benjamins Publishing.

Canales, M., & McNaughton, S. (2019, May). China's science boom. *National Geographic.*

Chambers, B. (2021). *A psalm for the wild-built: A monk and robot book.* Tordotcom.

Commission, E. (2021a). *Industry 5.0 towards a sustainable, human-centric and resilient European industry.* [Online] Accessed Sep 19, 2024, from https://research-and-innovation.ec.europa.eu/news/all-research-and-innovation-news/industry-50-towards-more-sustainable-resilient-and-human-centric-industry-2021-01-07_en

Commission, E. (2021b). *Regulation of the European Parliament and of the council.* [Online] Accessed Sep 9, 2024, from https://eur-lex.europa.eu/legal-content/EN/TXT/?uri=celex%3A52021PC0206

Crevier, D. (1993). *The tumultuous history of the search for artificial intelligence.* HarperCollins.

Cunningham, K., & Richards, L. (2023). *Advancing the human element of sustainabiility.* Deloitte Global.

De Dreu, C. K., Nijstad, B. A., & Baas, M. (2024). Human creativity: Functions, mechanisms, and social conditioning. In *Advances in experimental social psychology.* s.n..

Descartes, R. (1637). *Discourse on the method of rightly conducting one's reason and seeking truth in sciences.* Leiden Netherlands.

Directorate-General for Communication. (2024). *AI act enters into force.* European Commission.

Elder, A. M. (2017). *Friendship, robots, and social media.* Routledge.

Errida, A., & Lotfi, B. (2021). The determinants of organizational change management success: Literature review and case study. *International Journal of Engineering Business Management, 13.*

Floridi, L. (2011). *The philosophy of information*. Oxford University Press.

Floridi, L. (2015). *The Onlife manifesto: Being human in a Hyperconnected era*. Springer.

Gardner, H. (1983). *Frames of mind*. Basic Books.

Goethe, J. W. (1973). *Faust. Der Tragodie Zweiter Teil*. Philip Reclam.

Goralski, M. A., & Gorniak-Kocikowska, K. (2020). Handling resultant unemployment from artificial intelligence. In *Handbook of artificial intelligence and robotic process automation* (pp. 67–75). Anthem Press.

Goralski, M. A., & Gorniak-Kocikowska, K. (2022). Artificial intelligence in the USA. In *International perspectives on artificial intelligence* (pp. 5–11). Anthem Press.

Goralski, M. A., & Tan, T. K. (2023). Artificial intelligence: Poverty alleviation, healthcare, education, and reduced inequalities in a post-COVID world. In *The ethics of artificial intelligence for the sustainable development goals* (pp. 97–114). Springer Nature.

Haude, C., Blohm, I., & Lagardere, X., (2024). *How Lufthansa shapes data-driven transformation leaders*. [Online] Available at: https://sloanreview.mit.edu/article/how-lufthansa-shapes-data-driven-transformation-leaders/

Holdren, J. P. & Smith, M. (2016). *Preparing for the future of artificial intelligence*. [Online] Accessed Dec 13, 2025, from https://obamawhitehouse.archives.gov/sites/default/files/whitehouse_files/microsites/ostp/NSTC/preparing_for_the_future_of_ai.pdf

Huxley, A. (2006a). *Brave New World*. Harper Perennial. Reprint edition.

Huxley, A. (2006b). *Brave New World revisited*. Harper Perennial Modern Classics. Reprint edition.

Ishiguro, K. (2021). *Klara and the sun*. Knopf.

Jiang, X., et al. (2024). *Long term memory: The foundation of AI self-evolution*. arXiv.

Kanitz, R., et al. (2022). Am I the only one? Consequences of change championing (a) symmetry on group- and individual-level change outcomes. *Journal of Organizational Behavior*, 1048–1065.

Kimmerer, R. W. (2020). *Braiding Sweetgrass–indigenous wisdom, scientific knowledge and the teachings of plants*. Penguin UK.

Koivisto, M., & Grassini, S. (2023). Best humans still outperform artificial intelligence in a creative divergent thinking task. *Scientific Reports, 13*.

Kratsios, M. & Parker, L. E. (2020). *American artificial intelligence initiative: Year one annual report*. [Online] Accessed Nov 15, 2024, from https://www.nitrd.gov/nitrdgroups/images/c/c1/American-AI-Initiative-One-Year-Annual-Report.pdf.whitehouse.gov/wp-content/uploads/2020/02/American-AI-Initiative-One-Year-Annual-Report.pdf

Lama, D. (2021). *The purpose of life is to be happy*. [Online] Available at: https://www.dalailama.com/messages/transcripts-and-interviews/the-purpose-of-life-is-to-be-happy

Lewis, M. W., & Smith, W. K. (2022). Reflections on the 2021 AMR decade award: Navigating paradox is paradoxical. *Academy of Management, 47*, 528–548.

Mentzas, G., et al. (2024). Editorial for the research topic: "human-centered artificial intelligence in industry 5.0". *Frontiers in AI: Business*, 1–4.

Merton, T. (1969). *The way of Chuang Tzu*. New Directions.

Metz, C., & Schmidt, G. (2023). *Elon musk and others call for pause on a.I., citing 'profound risks to society*. [online] Available at: https://www.nytimes.com/2023/03/29/technology/ai-artificial-intelligence-musk-risks.html

Miller, K., (2020). *5 Critical steps in the change management process*. [Online] Available at: https://online.hbs.edu/blog/post/change-management-process#:~:text=Failure%20to%20do%20so%20could,managers%20and%20business%20leaders%20alike

MIT. (2023). *The great acceleration: CIO perspectives on generative AI*. [Online] Accessed Oct 29, 2024, from https://www.technologyreview.com/2023/07/18/1076423/the-great-acceleration-cio-perspectives-on-generative-ai/?gad_source=1&gclid=Cj0KCQiAkJO8BhCGARIsAMkswygaNoj7vQWjgdeMfvUo5PXYK_wwSsO8PLIdsa2eRnf5RZXFasfRo_0aAvloEALw_wcB

Mollick, E. (2024). *CO-INTELLIGENCE living and working with AI*. Random House.

Petersen, S. (2007). The ethics of robot servitude. *Journal of Experimental and Theoretical Artificial Intelligence, 19*, 43–54.

Popper, K. (1994). *The myth of framework*. Routledge.
Sheldrake, M. (2020). *Entangled life–how fungi make our worlds, change our Minds & Shape our Futures*. Random House.
Waldman, D. A., Putnam, L. L., Miron-Spektor, E., & Siegel, D. (2022). The role of paradox theory in decision making and management research. *Organizational Behavior and Human Decision Processes*, 1–6.
Wang, J., et al. (2024). A paradox theory lens on proactivity, individual ambidexterity, and creativity: An empirical look. *Journal of Organizational Behavior, 45*(6), 896–911.

Margaret A. Goralski is a professor at Quinnipiac University, USA. She serves on the UN Principles of Responsible Management Education (PRME) North America Steering Committee. She is the UN Global Working Group Liaison, an Albert Schweitzer Fellow, and an Academy of International Business US Northeast advisor. Recent book chapters and journal articles include Artificial Intelligence: Poverty Alleviation, Healthcare, Education, and Reduced Inequalities in a Post-Covid World (2023), Artificial Intelligence in the United States of America (2022), Artificial Intelligence and Poverty Alleviation: Emerging Innovations and Their Implications for Management Education and Sustainable Development (2022), and Artificial Intelligence and sustainable development (2020).

Krystyna Górniak-Kocikowska is a Professor Emerita and Adjunct Faculty of Philosophy at Southern Connecticut State University, New Haven. Her degrees include an MS in German Philology, a PhD in Philosophy from Adam Mickiewicz University, Poznan, Poland, and an MS in Religious Studies from Temple University, Philadelphia, USA. Her publications in Polish, German, and English range from philosophy and religion to societal implications of advanced digital technologies, mainly those pertaining to human ethical and existential problems. She is particularly interested in how scientific discoveries and breakthroughs, ranging from transhumanism to societal implications of astrobiology, impact human self-understanding.

Human-AI Partnership and Innovative Work Behaviour

Archana Parashar and Abhiyash Singh

Introduction

The twenty-first century has commenced with new attention to workplace dynamics, thanks to the rapid surge in technologies, such as artificial intelligence, deep learning, and machine learning. The era is characterized by an unprecedented integration of AI systems with nearly every aspect of organizational activities. An innovative paradigm known as the human-AI partnership has emerged as a result of this integration. Their integration into the workplace has kindled both excitement and apprehension. The dynamic nature of the business landscape has made it imperative for enterprises to grasp the relationship between human-AI collaborations and innovative work behaviours in order to stay competitive and inventive and match the pace of technological progress happening around the world.

This chapter delves into the convoluted relationship between human-AI partnership and Innovative work behaviour (IWB), digging into the ways this alliance is reshaping the landscape of innovation in the corporate world. According to the research (The Fourth Industrial Revolution: What It Means and How to Respond, 2016), we are standing on the verge of the Fourth Industrial Revolution; therefore, it becomes vital to understand the subtleties of this partnership for businesses, policymakers, and individuals to thrive progress. The amalgamation of the creativity of humans with the capabilities of AI brings to the table unparalleled innovation opportunities. We are witnessing the symbiotic relationship between humans and AI that has the potential to propel innovative work behaviour to new heights by combining human's creativity, emotional intelligence, and sophisticated complex problem-solving skills with AI's large data processing power, pattern recognition capabilities, and tireless operation.

A. Parashar (✉) · A. Singh
IIM Raipur, Abhanpur, India
e-mail: archana@iimraipur.ac.in; abhiyash.1804@economics.du.ac.in

M. Dabić et al. (eds.), *Artificial Humans*, Future of Business and Finance,
https://doi.org/10.1007/978-3-032-06604-6_6

Just like a coin has two sides, this partnership also brings in challenges and important questions, which needs to know whether this partnership would be effective in real-world situations or not. One of the biggest challenges that is highly debated is AI replacing humans. According to Kaplan and Haenlein (2019), AI is capable of replacing repetitive and rule-enabled tasks, which leads to the reduction of low-skilled jobs and the creation of new higher-skilled jobs. How can AI be successfully incorporated into current workflows? What effect does this have on job duties, job happiness, and the culture of the company as a whole? How do we make sure that collaborations between humans and AI foster rather than inhibit human creativity and innovation? This chapter deep dive into these questions and more.

The objective of this chapter is to examine the existing human-AI partnership models, assess how they influence innovative work behaviour, and talk about the moral issues that result from this alliance. This chapter aims to provide a thorough overview of this ever-evolving field by examining future trends and discussing case studies of effective human-AI interactions from real-world situations. It seeks to contribute to the ongoing dialogue on how best to harness the power of human-AI partnerships to foster innovation, drive progress, and shape a future where humans and AI work in harmony to tackle the complex challenges that time throws.

Defining Key Concepts

Prior to exploring the nuances of human-AI collaborations and how they affect IWB, it is essential to have a firm grasp of these fundamental ideas. The two main terms that underpin our discussion is clarified and broken down in this section.

Human-AI Partnership

The human-AI partnership describes the cooperative alliance between human workers and AI-enabled systems and software in a professional setting to carry out tasks and achieve corporate objectives. This collaboration can take various forms: from AI systems acting as tools or assistants to more sophisticated partnerships, where AI performs certain jobs as a colleague or even a leader (Daugherty & Wilson, 2018).

Key aspects of Human-AI partnerships include:

1. *Complementary strengths:* This partnership leverages the unique strengths of both parties with the aim of enhancing overall productivity, efficiency, and innovation.
2. *Augmentation rather than replacement:* AI is created in order to augment human capabilities both in personal as well as professional environments rather than digest human jobs.
3. *Adaptive collaborations*: Since technology always evolves and improves so does AI, henceforth the nature of the partnership is dynamic and changes over time. This requires ongoing adaptation from both human workers and organizations to ensure effective collaboration.

4. *Continuous learning:* In this fast-paced world, both humans and AI systems always engage in learning within the partnership. Humans learn to work effectively with AI tools while AI systems are often designed to improve their performance based on human feedback.

Innovative Work Behaviour

Janssen (2000) defines innovative work behaviour as "the intentional creation, introduction and application of new ideas within a work role, group or organization, in order to benefit role performance, the group, or the organization" (p. 288). According to Scott and Bruce (1994), generation, promotion, and realization of ideas are three distinct behavioural tasks that together encompass the complex behaviour known as innovative work behaviour.

Key components of Innovative Work Behaviour (Janssen, 2000)

1. *Idea Generation:* This means coming up with new and freshly baked ideas that may prove to be valuable for products, services, processes, or creating solutions for organizational problems. Creativity, out-of-the-box thinking, and the ability to connect concepts that appear unrelated to common people are needed to generate a novel idea.
2. *Idea Promotion:* This process involves convincing colleagues and seniors to believe in your idea, i.e., building a coalition of support and arranging resources to capitalize on the proposed idea.
3. *Idea Realization:* The final stage constitutes putting the unanimous idea into action. It involves brainstorming, planning, and often collaborations with various departments to integrate the new idea into existing systems or create an entirely new system.
4. *Risk Taking:* Innovative work behaviour entails taking measured risks, questioning the status quo, and coming up with ideas that may initially appear to be eccentric or unconventional.

Continuous improving mindset, collaboration and knowledge sharing, and adaptability are also crucial elements of IWB. IWB has been recognized as one of the driving forces behind organizational success for a long time (West & Farr, 1990). This chapter explores the intricate interactions between innovative work behaviour elements and human-AI partnership, revealing how their dynamic interplay is fundamentally reshaping the landscape of organizational innovation.

The Current Landscape of AI in the Workplace

The technological transformation that we are witnessing today is aimed at simplifying our existence and leveraging the productivity of organizations. AI has eventually pervaded each and every sector of the economy ranging from the manufacturing and service sectors to education, finance, and creative industries. Think about less time being spent on doing mundane tasks, significantly reduction in errors, trend prediction and so on which was once a mere imagination has now become reality.

Some notable examples from the present day of AI integration in the workplace are the use of AI-powered robots in production lines to reduce the lead time and improve precision, doctors using AI for diagnosis, drug discovery and providing personalized treatment plans for patients and even some hospitals are using AI robots for doing surgery (healthcare sector), initially customer service meant talking to actual humans but now chatbots took its place and now customers don't have to wait for hours to resolve their problems (retail sector), AI algorithms are even helpful in fraud detection and giving warnings, risk management and trading (finance sector) and many more such cases are there. AI is taking over repetitive and rule-based tasks giving humans more room to breathe and be creative. Embracing the potential of AI, we find ourselves navigating a transformative journey where it acts as a catalyst for global industry-wide productivity enhancement. As per Nielsen Report 2023, AI enhances the productivity of employees by 66%.

Impact on Labour Workforce

The proliferation of AI in the corporate world has a significant impact on the workforce. The advent of AI and then its collaboration with humans paves the way for unique job opportunities that demand inventive thinking, empathy, and intricate problem-solving abilities traits that machines and AI haven't mastered yet. There is a drastic change in the skills demanded. As per the McKinsey Report, while several jobs get displaced due to automation technology (AI) swooping in with efficiency levels that humans can only dream of achieving manually, new roles emerge elsewhere that weren't even on our radar before. Careers in fields like AI development itself, machine learning or roles focused on managing these technologies show promise. Even new job categories are created like that of AI ethicists, data scientists, human-AI interaction designers, and many more.

Challenges and Concerns

Job Displacement

The rapid pace of advancements in AI necessitates a notion of continuous learning of in-demand skills to remain employed and remain ahead of time. According to the World Economic Forum report (2020), approximately 85 million jobs might be lost to AI replacing humans by 2025 but on the other hand, 97 million new job opportunities may also emerge (Narayan, 2023). But only the upskilled workforce can take advantage of this mega job fest. Bughin et al. (2018) stressed the need for workers to develop not only technical skills related to AI but also possess the ability to work creatively parallel to AI and make the best use of it.

Skill Gap

Many organizations are facing difficulties in finding employees having the required skills to work efficiently with AI-enabled systems. A small bug in AI coding can lead to bias in AI decision-making power and data analysis results which can adversely affect organizations' goals and objectives. Shneiderman (2020) believes that developing reliable AI systems is necessary for successful human-AI cooperation, especially when it comes to tasks focussed on creativity and invention. Glikson and Woolley (2020) in their research paper argued that trust in AI collaborators is influenced by various elements like AI's perceived level of competency, its proficiency in providing explanations for its results, and the stakes of the task. The development of this trust becomes quite difficult and important in the setting of innovative work behaviour, where tasks are frequently complex and consequential.

Ethics

There is also privacy concerns related to information provided to AI, which can jeopardize the integrity of customers' valuable information. Many industries even face challenges in effectively integrating AI into the workplace due to resistance from employees who are uncertain about or uncomfortable with the introduction of AI into their work processes.

Human-AI Collaboration Model

With the increased use of AI in firms, various models of human-AI collaboration came into existence. Augmentation model stresses on the ability of AI to complement human capabilities by doing boring tasks that complement human skills, thereby allowing humans to take control over decision-making power. Real-life applications of this model are like financial advisors using AI's data analytics power for formulating investment strategies for clients, radiologists using AI to diagnose anomalies in medical pictures, and so on. In the automation model, AI takes over repetitive jobs consequently sparing humans to indulge in more complicated projects like building and enhancing chatbots that provide end-to-end resolution to customers' problems, automate data entry in administrative roles, robotic process automation in manufacturing industries, etc.

In interactive models, AI and humans work simultaneously or interact in real time, like in a car with AI-enabled systems, such as monitoring blind spots, Advanced Driver Assistance Systems (ADAS), Autonomous Emergency Braking (AEB), pedestrian detection, adaptive cruise control, autopilot mode, and many more. This model showcases the dynamic relationship between humans and AI; AI integrated coding platforms like Google's colab which suggest code completion instantaneously. The oversight model is similar to the automation model but here humans provide oversight, do the interpretation of AI results, and make final decisions as per their wisdom and AI recommendations. This model is primarily used when stakes are high and ethical solutions are needed. Examples of this model are AI pointing out potential fraud cases and humans actually reviewing it then, content or articles generated by AI requiring critical editorial review by humans before publication, etc. The exploratory model harnesses AI's large data processing abilities to unravel patterns and generate hypotheses about future trends, which humans then interpret and investigate further to tackle those trends effectively.

It is crucial for organizations implementing human-AI partnership in the workplace to understand these models to achieve desired outcomes and enforce an innovative work behaviour environment. The above models are not mutually exclusive, and many real-world applications may embody different elements from multiple models. As technology (AI) always keeps evolving with time, these models also develop further, and even new prototypes of human-AI collaborations might emerge.

Impact of Human-AI Partnership on Innovative Work Behaviour

The fusion of AI into the corporate world through various collaboration paradigms profoundly affects innovative work behaviour. This section delve into how the human-AI partnership influences various elements of IWB.

Enhancing Idea Generation

Among the most important effects of human-AI partnerships on innovative work behaviour is idea generation. In this context, AI with the ability to process big data and detect unobservable trends providing humans with a broader knowledge base to come up with new ideas. Researchers demonstrated that AI can facilitate divergent thinking, which, for the most part, is a prerequisite for the creative generation of ideas. For example, according to Lubart (2005), technology (AI) can "widen the field of search" for a creative solution in the form of associations and combinations that a human would never think of. In addition, there is also Boden's (1998) perspective on the concept known as "combinatorial creativity", where new ideas come from an unfamiliar combination of familiar ideas.

Wang et al. (2019) found that when exposed to various AI- generated ideas as stimulus, the level of originality and creativity of human-generated ideas was much higher than that of the control group. As per researchers, this was apparently because AI could introduce humans with more novel perspectives rather than keep interacting with the original stimulus and even challenges humans' cognitive biases.

AI does not always impact idea generation positively as Bhatt et al. (2021) noted, AI can also reduce the breadth of human thought when people start using AI in doing every task. This kind of behaviour, which is referred to by the authors as "AI-induced functional fixedness" syndrome. It can breed out of over-consuming AI-generated suggestions, which gradually deprives humans of thinking beyond presented options.

Transforming Idea Promotion

The way creative ideas are proposed and endorsed in organizations is being redefined by the human-AI partnerships promoted to flourish within idea promotion. AI systems could offer a data-driven background to help support those novel ideas, thereby making them more credible and enhancing their chances of acceptance. Kaplan and Haenlein (2019) outline a few ways in which AI-enabled simulations are able to contribute to picturing the possibilities of innovations, thereby improving an innovator's ability to build support amongst stakeholders. This ability is key to overcoming a problem that Kanter (1988) pointed out in his research paper about promoting an idea: how difficult it can be to gain support for ideas that are extremely different from the status quo.

AI can also help determine the target audience that would be best for certain novel ideas. AI can also provide recommendations to guide innovators in modifying their promotion strategies by critically analysing past innovative adoption patterns and personal preferences of individuals (Brynjolfsson & McAfee, 2017). At the same time, AI also raises questions about ethics and integrity in promoting an idea. AI systems run the risk of being deployed to manipulate the decisions of individuals, thereby arbitrarily promoting some innovations further than others depending upon skewed information or mistaken algorithms (Crawford, 2021).

Revolutionizing Idea Realization

In the last realm of innovation work behaviours, idea realization is perhaps where there are the most tangible dividends for a human-AI partnership. Firms are increasingly using AI to generate ideas as it speeds up not only experimentation but also the implementation of innovative ideas. For instance, in the product design field, AI-generative design can produce countless iterations of a design based on parameters specified by the human designer, significantly broadening the number of possibilities or options that designers now have in hand to choose the best one (Matejka et al., 2018). This partnership not only accelerates the innovation process but also leads to better and more creative solutions.

Artificial intelligence is also revolutionizing the way innovations are tested and developed. Prototyping tools make it easy to test interactivity and the machine learning algorithms continue monitoring user interactions with these prototypes—capturing a wealth of data that guides incremental improvements. Such a data-driven way of iteration can result in better-performing innovations with faster time-to-market (Lee et al., 2020).

There are also drawbacks to using AI excessively in the realization of ideas. AI-driven processes may converge on solutions that may be better but lose on a quest for radical innovation that might emerge from human intuition and serendipity (Frey & Osborne, 2017).

Impact on Other Aspects of IWB

Human-AI partnerships can enhance other aspects of innovative work behaviour like fostering an environment that is more conducive to taking calculated risks by doing simulations and calibrations many times, visualizing the potential outcomes and even pinpointing the possible errors in the strategy to support the result, facilitating better collaboration by breaking down language barriers in international teams and knowledge sharing across teams and departments, and boosting problem-solving capabilities of humans by leaps and bounds.

This partnership also poses some threats to IWB like reducing serendipity, which means highly optimized AI-driven processes might reduce the random encounters and mistakes that sometimes lead to innovative breakthroughs, ethical concerns, skill atrophy, etc.

In a nutshell, human-AI partnership has the calibre to augment innovative work behaviour remarkably by supplementing human capabilities, facilitating collaboration and social interaction, and providing opportunities for creativity and strategic thinking. But of course, while there is a significant gain from them being in place—one must be deliberately active to counter the pitfalls too. As we further delve into this partnership, it is imperative to aspire for a balance that leverages the strengths of both humans and artificial intelligence to drive innovation forward.

Designing Effective Human-AI Partnerships for Innovation

Task Allocation and Role Definition

In the context of innovation, a central challenge is to find where best to draw line between humans and AI in dividing up related tasks for effective partnership design. A framework was proposed by Daugherty and Wilson (2018) that classifies tasks into three groups:

1. Tasks that are best performed by humans.
2. Tasks that are best performed by AI.
3. Tasks that are best performed through human-AI collaboration.

For innovative work behaviour, this would be interpreted as having humans lead certain tasks involving empathy and ethical judgement or high-level strategic thinking on the top while AI systems do data analysis, pattern recognition, or rapid prototyping. The more original and creative outputs are likely to result from where the magic happens i.e. human-AI partnership, through the intersections of human intuition with AI.

Interface Design and User Experience

The human-AI interaction design is essential for enabling productive partnerships. Amershi et al. (2019) emphasized the importance of making AI systems intelligible, transparent, and capable of adapting to human (user) needs from both a user-centred design process and an ethical perspective. In the context of invention, this could entail developing user interfaces that facilitate flexible ideation procedures, enabling people to simply submit original ideas and obtain AI-generated extensions or modifications. It also entails creating feedback systems that let people efficiently direct and improve AI outputs.

Collaborative Learning System

In order to unlock the power of human-AI partnerships for innovation, we need systems that can facilitate co-learning. Rahwan et al. (2019) suggest the notion of "machine behaviour" as a spark to view AI systems as behaving entities, similar to human behaviour that can be observed and optimized for better collaboration.

This would mean practically implementing AI-enabled systems that can learn creative thinking processes from humans and modify its results accordingly. At the same time, such systems should be able to educate humans and extend their creative frontiers by introducing them to new ideas and challenging their cognitive biases.

Ethical Framework and Governance Structures

Given the ethical concerns of human-AI partnerships, it is important to develop these collaborations on a secure ethical foundation. Floridi and Cowls (2019) developed a comprehensive ethical framework for AI in which they grouped AI ethics principles into five categories based on categories from bioethics, and they are principles of beneficence (promoting well-being and sustainability), non-maleficence (encompassing privacy and security), autonomy, justice, and explicability.

AI systems are more epistemically opaque than any other technology. Most people may not understand how a car engine works, but an engineer can enchant us with tales of the enigmatic magic that causes an engine to behave in mysterious ways. Also, he can offer an easy explanation of why the engine might fail in some given situations and to a larger extent predict it. This is not the case when it comes to AI systems—and deep learning specifically since we do not have any understanding of why such output is generated (e.g. why it classifies someone as a fraudster or rejects a job candidate). Computer scientists, do at a broad level, know how these systems work and can give an account of general properties, such as the reason why convolutional neural networks are so effective for computer vision tasks, whereas recurrent neural networks are well-suited for natural language processing (NLP).

Case Studies of Successful Human-AI Partnership

Healthcare

Pharmaceutical Research and Development

The pharmaceutical sector offers a convincing demonstration of how Innovative work behaviour is evolving in the human-AI collaboration mode. In drug discovery, AI systems are already being used to analyse huge databases of molecular structures in order to suggest potential drug candidates very early on in the long process that leads from benchtop research to the implementation of clinical practice.

An example is the discovery of a new antibiotic drug called halicin, using AI. To do this, scientists at MIT trained a deep learning model based on data aligned in Activity Atlas to screen more than 100 million molecules and pinpoint novel compounds with antibacterial properties. The AI system even identified structural characteristics that rendered molecules effective at combating bacteria—many of which were distinct from those in traditional antibiotics (Trafton, 2020).

These candidates were then further evaluated by human researchers, who had expert knowledge in determining which computationally generated molecules were likely to be the most promising for laboratory testing. Harnessing this relationship between AI pattern recognition and human scientific intuition, a unique antibiotic was discovered that was very efficient in killing many bacteria types—even some that have become resistant to traditional antibiotics (Stokes et al., 2020).

At each stage of innovative work behaviour, this case illustrates how human-AI partnerships can improve:

1. Idea generation: Made the search for antibiotics less dependent on human hunches; opened up a broader universe for potential antibiotic discovery.
2. Idea promotion: Promoting an idea is like getting it out there and selling the idea. Data-based predictions backed up our recommendations for that oddball type of candidate.
3. Idea realization: Turning predictions of WEVD-learned AI into real-world testing and development requires the human touch and expertise that machines are not capable of doing yet.

Scientific Research: AI-Assisted Drug Discovery at Atomwise

Atomwise is a highly technology-advanced pharmaceutical company that uses artificial intelligence systems to accelerate the small-molecule drug discovery process, which traditionally takes years and millions of dollars. Atomwise's AI technology portfolio includes the first blockchain molecular property ledger, which allows for advanced machine-learning validation. The company has a strong track record in advancing new medicines with partners at top global pharma and biotech companies; developing their own drug discovery pipeline addressing neurodegeneration, cancer, immuno-oncology, kidney disease, and metabolic disorders; AND launching 16 partner programs to date. Atomwise has extensively validated its discovery engine with a success rate of over 70% in their company's 270 academic collaborations (as well as internally), including "hard to drug" targets and very challenging protein types, finding actionable intel that amounted to the identification of compounds having therapeutic properties for biologically active candidates in 90% of internal programs. According to research (Atomwise Signs Strategic Multi-Target Research Collaboration with Sanofi for AI-Powered Drug Discovery, 2022), Atomwise is advancing a proprietary pipeline of small-molecule drug candidates, with three programs in lead optimization and over 30 programs in discovery.

This case illustrates the oversight and exploratory model of human-AI collaboration coming into action, where AI generates a hypothesis for the scientists to review and promote an innovative environment.

Automotive Industry

General Motors (GM) is an American multinational automaker with a business spanning over 90 countries. GM is reshaping the automobile industry with a vision to create lighter automobiles with superior efficiency and personalization. GM is researching and deploying artificial intelligence (AI) supervised by engineers (humans) for vehicle design, inspection, battery management systems, and customer services, among others. Here are some key examples:

1. *Generative design and additive manufacturing:* Additive manufacturing serves as a gateway to the future of the automotive industry, with generative design acting as the essential key to open it. GM is looking into various design solutions for vehicle parts and components through an array of ways leveraged by AI and cloud computing power to utilize generative design. Generative design paired with additive manufacturing is a disruptive combination in the automobile industry. GM is already enjoying the potential benefits of this deadly combo by creating lighter, more efficient, and customizable car parts after examining thousands of design solutions generated by AI.
2. *AI-equipped vehicle inspection:* General Motors has invested in Israel-based UVeye, a start-up that focuses on AI-powered lorry inspection technology. By employing sensors and AI technology, this system swiftly spotlights probable core breakdowns or upkeep concerns aiding dealership review while potentially lowering expenses.
3. *OnStar turns to conversational AI:* General Motors is working with Google Cloud for its OnStar virtual assistant, adding new conversation chatbots. Basic customer queries can be smoothed out with the help of this technology, freeing man-hours to deal with other complex requests. GM can now deal with over 1 million monthly inquiries from customers across the USA and Canada.
4. *Intent-recognition algorithm:* GM's OnStar system, powered by Google Cloud conversational AI technologies such as intent-recognition algorithms can aid drivers in getting relevant and quick responses to common inquiries and get routing assistance.

One prominent product of this partnership was the development of a seat bracket that was 40% lighter and 20% stronger than the original one (Autodesk, 2018). This case study demonstrates how automobile companies are leveraging human-AI partnerships to improve efficiency, reduce costs, enhance customer experiences, and foster an environment that supports innovative work behaviour. As the industry drives forward with always enhancing AI capabilities, it could also introduce this technology to other areas such as autonomous driving, predictive maintenance, or personalized marketing.

Financial Services

J.P. Morgan, an American financial services firm, is one of the largest and most prominent banking institutions in the world, providing its services in more than 100 countries. The firm offers a wide range of financial services, including investment banking, financial transaction processing, asset management, and private banking.

JP Morgan developed an AI-powered software, contract intelligence (COIN), to scrutinize legal documents. It does a pretty mind-numbing job: it analyses commercial loan agreements to make sure that they conform with federal regulations—an interpretive task that until now consumed 360,000 hours of lawyers' work each year (Galeon, 2017). The software reads through documents in milliseconds, makes fewer mistakes, and never needs a holiday. COIN is powered by a new cloud-based machine learning system that the bank developed, and it runs on the private cloud network in use at JPMorgan. In addition to shoving documents through the review process much faster, COIN has also helped JP Morgan reduce errors made during the servicing of its loans. As per the program's designers, these mistakes mainly happen due to human errors in the interpretation of 12,000 new wholesale contracts every year. This case serves as an example of how automation helps AI to do the heavy lifting and allows humans to carry out more strategic work (that is, the use of both Automation and augmentation models).

Retail: Stitch Fix's AI-Assisted Personal Styling

Stitch Fix, a popular online personal styling service is one such company every organization can take a cue from. The company uses data and AI to provide personally stylized clothing services to its clients and ship the right clothes directly to clients' homes—clothes that they know customers will love based on their style preferences and previous orders. Stitch Fix is recognized for uniquely achieving a perfect balance between human expertise and machine capabilities through its algorithm, a feat unmatched by others. Stitch Fix's Outfit Creation Model (OCM) uses generative AI to style millions of new outfit combinations each day. Trained on millions of outfits built by stylists, OCM uses the current Stitch Fix stock set and screens previous orders and style preferences to provide clients with personalized outfit recommendations. It even teaches clients how to style items they might want (or already own) with other pieces from Stitch Fix. They do this via personalized emails and ads and by customizing customers' shopfeed. Customers' reviews are used to improve both AI suggestions and stylist decisions continuously.

The case of Stitch Fix, which successfully paired AI with human stylists, highlights the possibilities of how companies take advantage of these human-AI hybrids to drive innovation and efficiency. Through the synergy of the analytical capabilities of AI and human stylists' creativity and personal touch, Stitch Fix has not only improved its customer experience but also created a dynamic workplace suitable for innovation. Strategically leveraging AI-human collaboration can drive meaningful enhancement in both business and employee engagements, as detailed in this case study.

These case studies illustrate that human-AI partnerships are reshaping the landscape of many businesses across diverse fields and fostering an environment that is conducive to innovative work behaviour. They show that the most effective partnership is one where both AI and human professionals leverage each other's unique strengths and produce an output that is far better than they could ever produce working separately.

Challenges and Ethical Concerns

Human-AI partnerships have the potential to enhance innovative work behaviour significantly, but they also bring forth a rife of challenges and ethical considerations that need to be carefully addressed. These challenges impact the deployment and effectiveness of the partnership and have significant implications on society, labour force dynamics, and even the social well-being of individuals. So, it becomes pertinent to know the reasons behind these challenges and how to get rid of them.

Job Displacement and Skill Obsolescence

One of the primary concerns surrounding the increased integration of AI in the workplace is the potential for job displacement. Frey and Osborne (2017) estimated that nearly 47% of total US employment is at risk of computerization (AI). While this estimate has been highly debated, it highlights the need for proactive measures to address potential workforce disruptions.

In the milieu of innovative work behaviour, there's a risk that certain creative or analytical tasks currently performed by humans might be taken over by AI systems. This could lead to skill obsolescence if workers are not provided with opportunities to upskill and adapt to new roles that complement AI capabilities. This partnership disproportionately affects the employment of certain demographic groups which are usually involved in doing routine tasks.

AI could make certain types of jobs redundant by taking over the tasks performed under them. To prevent this situation to become a reality, organizations and policymakers would have to invest in retraining programs that would enable humans to take advantage of the uniquely human skills alongside AI capabilities. This is consistent with the advice proffered by Brynjolfsson and McAfee (2014) that organizations should be focused on racing "with" rather than against the machines.

Bias and Fairness

There are prominent issues of bias as the answers, text, and recommendations these AI systems generate are often discriminatory (Hovy & Prabhumoye, 2021). Given the limitations of historical data on which AI systems are trained, they may simply maintain and even exacerbate bias at present. That is especially troubling when it comes to innovative work behaviour as AI systems may recommend certain kinds of ideas or innovators as more acceptable than others.

Caliskan et al. (2017) showed that machine learning algorithms (AI) could also acquire the prejudices of their creators through training data. So, in the context of innovation, this might mean AI systems tend to promote ideas that are close to past patterns — which could reduce the variety of innovations. It might be worth it for organizations to implement a strict testing process and behaviour tracing of AI systems for bias detection. It also involves making sure the team that is building and deploying AI systems is diverse, as well as the data they use to train these systems.

Transparency, Accountability, and Explainability

Deep learning and machine learning, one of the most omnipresent modern forms of AI, possess the same problem as that of human intelligence, of keeping track of the inputs that helped them at first instance in making decisions. This incompetence of us to know how these AI systems are making their decisions is called the black-box problem (Blouin, 2023). For example, AI engineers and even we don't have any idea why AI has rejected certain people's applications for job interviews, denied a loan to someone, given certain recommendations, etc. Hence, AI is prone to accountability and explainability problems.

Actually, AI systems are trained in a similar pattern as we teach our children. We give them a bunch of correct examples of something we want them to learn and recognize, and in no time, they themselves would have developed a "neural network" for classifying things they have never seen or experienced before. The same is the case with AI systems, where we feed them with large data to train them to deliver certain output, and slowly, they themselves develop a pattern and forget to keep track of how they learned to give recommendations. Adadi and Berrada (2018) argued that explainable AI (XAI) is effective in gaining trust and enhancing the effectiveness of human-AI collaboration. This is because explainable AI could aid human workers in understanding the rationale behind the outcome and suggestions given by them, allowing humans to do more informed evaluation and refinement.

Data Privacy and Security

AI systems are frequently required to process substantial quantities of data for them to be a useful marketing tool or resource that stimulates innovative work behaviour; this data can also include potentially sensitive data about employees, customers, and business-process information. This has major privacy and security implications.

Zuboff (2019) talked about the risk of "surveillance capitalism", where data about human behaviour is commodified and exploited. This is where it becomes challenging because with the AI system, data and information need to flow, but you also need to balance both the end users' privacy rights protection and not giving out all of your proprietary organizational models/data.

Overreliance and Deskilling

As AI systems are becoming more and more capable of handling complex tasks, there's a danger that human workers might then rely too much on them, and this can have the knock-on effect of eroding their ability, cognitive skills, and analytical skills to think laterally or solve problems. According to Carr (2014), deskilling usually occurs when we place too much of a premium on AI and automation, causing human beings to lose their natural capacities for completing perennial tasks without the aid of AI.

This could translate into the innovation space as a limitation in independent ideation or critical assessment of proposals generated by AI algorithms. To avoid this risk, organizations need to create partnerships between humans and AI that are designed with the intention of involving and pushing human cognitive abilities rather than replacing them.

An example highlighting all the above problems is that of credit scoring algorithms — which are used to determine if someone qualifies for loan money from a bank. There are some hints of this happening in the study by Dastile et al. (2020) showing that complex deep learning systems like AI predictions outperformed simpler statistical models in performing these tasks, so there is a high probability of banks using more and more AI for credit scoring. On the one hand, it may cause an increase in the number of loans offered since risk per loan is reduced (due to a more precise risk assessment), but on the other hand, we also need to care about ethical challenges that stem from the distribution of finance to individuals. Starting with the biased one, there is a high chance of discrimination in loan allocations. AI can lend smaller amounts of loans to minorities, and they are often less accurate for these groups. It was an example of discrimination when policymakers developed a variety of statistical fairness measures to account for it. However, there are particular difficulties with this case since fairness measures require access to group membership in order to classify groups like race and gender, and this raises privacy concerns. Moreover, optimizing for fairness may cause AI to have very poor accuracy and, as a result, battle its eligibility. This is often the case when we talk about discrimination, and there are a lot of statistical fairness metrics available that aim to measure these situations. This particular case poses other challenges, as fairness measures rely on access to group membership (race, gender, etc.) to function, and this raises privacy issues. Optimizing fairness often reduces the accuracy of an AI system, thereby making their predictions less reliable. Even from a more sociotechnical perspective regarding how bank staff use and depend upon these models' details concerning meaningful human control, responsibility, and trust in these systems. The decisions may, also, be of unduly great importance to the decision subjects, thus adding weight to their contestability and ensuring that there are institutional mechanisms that can correct mistakes.

Future Trends and Research Directions

Emotional AI and Creativity

Meanwhile, recent strides in affective computing and emotional AI open up fascinating new opportunities to improve human-AI collaborations. According to the work of Picard (2010), human emotions are integral to decision-making and creativity. Finally, future lines of research and inquiry might delve deeper into exploring the capacity for emotionally intelligent AI systems to act more supportively in human creative processes.

Companies currently working on emotional AI

(a) *Cognovi Labs:* This company utilizes psychology-driven AI to analyse and predict human emotions from textual data, such as social media posts and customer interactions. Their technology basically integrates behavioural psychology with deep machine learning algorithms to provide real-time insights about emotional states, which proves to be useful for organizations as it can be used for improving customer engagement and decision-making processes (Adhikari, 2024).

(b) *Affectiva:* It focuses on building emotion recognition technology, which can interpret human emotions by analysing facial expressions and vocal patterns. Their technologies are applied in automotive systems to monitor driver states and in media analytics to gauge audience reactions (Affectiva and Emotion AI—Affectiva (2024)).

(c) *MoodMe:* Employs an AI-based facial emotion recognition system that uses algorithms to process real-time user emotions. Their revolution is utilized in sectors as diverse as retail and entertainment, which help improve user experience by modifying content in real time according to emotional feedback (Bartak, 2024).

Neuroadaptive AI Systems

These systems typically use brain-computer interfaces (BCIs) or sensors to measure signals like brain activity (e.g. EEG), heart rate, or eye movements, adjusting their behaviour accordingly to optimize user interaction and outcomes. Brain-computer interfaces (BCIs) and neuroadaptive AI systems may provide pathways to create an impeccable relationship between human cognitive skills and heavy task-performing AI capabilities. Zander et al. (2016) talk about the possible applications of adaptive neurosystems, which change their parameters in real time to respond to changes in user cognitive state. In the context of innovative work behaviour, these AI systems would better be able to support or amplify human imagination and inventive thinking.

Some potential applications of neuroadaptive AI systems in real life are:

1. *Education and Training*

   a) Personalized learning: Company BrainCo's Focus EDU uses EEG headbands to monitor students' attention levels, dynamically adjusting lesson plans or alerting teachers to improve engagement.

   b) Simulated training: Kernel company develops non-invasive brain imaging systems to assess cognitive load, enhancing simulations for pilots and surgeons by adapting difficulty in real time.
2. *Assistive Technology*

   a) Communications for disabled individuals:—Synchron's stentrode implant allows individuals with severe paralysis to control devices or communicate through thought-driven inputs.

   b) Smart wheelchairs: Company CyborgNest is trying to combine BCIs and neuroadaptive AI to create wheelchairs that respond to neural signals for movement and obstacle avoidance.
3. *Workplace Productivity*

   a) Cognitive workload management: SmartCap creates wearable devices that monitor brain activity to detect fatigue in workers, particularly in industries like mining or transportation.

   b) Focus enhancement: Emotiv devices also aid productivity by adjusting work environments, such as reducing distractions when high focus is detected.

Ethical AI for Innovation

As there are ethical considerations around AI in innovation processes that need to be taken care of, there is an increasing sign that it is becoming necessary to research these frameworks and methodologies applied to existing solutions for being able to use responsible AI in creative and innovative tasks. For example, part of the work involves developing methodologies for auditing AI systems (accounting for bias) as well as assuring full transparency/alignment with human values in all innovation.

Conclusion

Human-AI partnerships represent a paradigm shift in how we approach innovative work behaviour. These partnerships have an extremely high ceiling for improving creativity and speeding up the process of innovation through discovery. Yet, at the same time, they are fraught with significant and meaningful challenges that have to be skilfully negotiated. Whether partnerships like these are successful in promoting innovative work behaviour pivots largely on our abilities to design collaborations that capitalize not only on human workers' skills but also on the capabilities of AI systems. This involves not just technological considerations but also organizational, ethical, and societal ones.

Going forward, a human-centred perspective on AI integration in existing processes of innovation is paramount. The aim of this collaboration should be to augment and boost human creativity and problem-solving. In doing so, we can build a world where human-AI partnerships unleash levels of innovation never before seen on this planet to solve wicked global problems while enabling new frontiers for human accomplishment.

We are at the starting gate of a journey to integrate AI into new ways of working, and we will have to wait for some time before seeing this partnership make its mark. This is more than a technological transition; it is a profound reimagining of human potential. By embracing AI with strategic foresight and a commitment to responsible development, we can create a synergistic ecosystem that amplifies human potential rather than diminishing it and benefitting society as a whole.

References

Adadi, A., & Berrada, M. (2018). Peeking inside the black-box: A survey on explainable artificial intelligence (XAI). *IEEE Access, 6*, 52138–52160.

Adhikari, A. (2024, June 13). *5 companies innovating in the field of emotional AI in the USA. AIM research | artificial intelligence market insights*. https://aimresearch.co/market-industry/5-companies-innovating-in-the-field-of-emotional-ai-in-the-usa?utm_source=chatgpt.com

Affectiva and Emotion AI–Affectiva. (2024, February 12). *Affectiva*. https://www.affectiva.com/emotion-ai/

Amershi, S., et al. (2019). *Guidelines for human-AI interaction*. Proceedings of the 2019 CHI conference on human factors in computing systems, 1-13.

Atomwise Signs Strategic Multi-Target Research Collaboration with Sanofi for AI-Powered Drug Discovery. (2022, August 17). https://www.businesswire.com/news/home/20220817005089/en/Atomwise-Signs-Strategic-Multi-Target-Research-Collaboration-with-Sanofi-for-AI-Powered-Drug-Discovery

Autodesk. (2018). *General motors and Autodesk collaborate on future of car design*. Autodesk News.

Bartak, V. (2024, July 9). *Best Emotion Recognition Companies*. Aisuperior. https://aisuperior.com/emotion-recognition-companies/?utm_source=chatgpt.com.

Bhatt, U., et al. (2021). *Uncertainty as a form of transparency: Measuring, communicating, and using uncertainty*. arXiv preprint arXiv:2011.07586.

Blouin, L. (2023, March 6). *AI'S mysterious "black box" problem, explained*. University of Michigan-Dearborn. https://umdearborn.edu/news/ais-mysterious-black-box-problem-explained

Boden, M. A. (1998). Creativity and artificial intelligence. *Artificial Intelligence, 103*(1–2), 347–356.

Brynjolfsson, E., & McAfee, A. (2014). *The second machine age: Work, progress, and prosperity in a time of brilliant technologies*. WW Norton & Company.

Brynjolfsson, E., & McAfee, A. (2017). The business of artificial intelligence. *Harvard Business Review, 7*, 3–11.

Bughin, J., et al. (2018). *Skill shift: Automation and the future of the workforce*. McKinsey Global Institute.

Caliskan, A., Bryson, J. J., & Narayanan, A. (2017). Semantics derived automatically from language corpora contain human-like biases. *Science, 356*(6334), 183–186.

Carr, N. (2014). *The glass cage: How our computers are changing us*. WW Norton & Company.

Crawford, K. (2021). *The atlas of AI*. Yale University Press.

Dastile, X., Celik, T., & Potsane, M. (2020). Statistical and machine learning models in credit scoring: A systematic literature survey. *Applied Soft Computing, 91*, 106263.

Daugherty, P. R., & Wilson, H. J. (2018). *Human + machine: Reimagining work in the age of AI*. Harvard Business Press.

Floridi, L., & Cowls, J. (2019). A unified framework of five principles for AI in society. *Harvard Data Science Review, 1*(1).

Frey, C. B., & Osborne, M. A. (2017). The future of employment: How susceptible are jobs to computerisation? *Technological Forecasting and Social Change, 114*, 254–280.

Galeon, D. (2017, March 8). *An AI completed 360,000 hours of finance work in just seconds*. Futurism; Futurism. https://futurism.com/an-ai-completed-360000-hours-of-finance-work-in-just-seconds

Glikson, E., & Woolley, A. W. (2020). Human trust in artificial intelligence: Review of empirical research. *Academy of Management Annals, 14*(2), 627–660.

Hovy, D., & Prabhumoye, S. (2021). Five sources of bias in natural language processing. *Language and Linguistics Compass, 15*(8), e12432.

Janssen, O. (2000). Job demands, perceptual barriers, and innovative work behavior. *Journal of Work and Organizational Psychology, 16*(1), 55–75.

Kanter, R. M. (1988). When a thousand flowers bloom: Structural, collective, and social conditions for innovation in organizations. *Knowledge Management and Organisational Design, 10*, 93–131.

Kaplan, A., & Haenlein, M. (2019). Siri, Siri, in my hand: Who's the fairest in the land? On the interpretations, illustrations, and implications of artificial intelligence. *Business Horizons, 62*(1), 15–25.

Lee, J., Davari, H., Singh, J., & Pandhare, V. (2020). Industrial artificial intelligence for industry 4.0-based manufacturing systems. *Manufacturing Letters, 18*, 20–23.

Lubart, T. (2005). How can computers be partners in the creative process: Classification and commentary on the special issue. *International Journal of Human-Computer Studies, 63*(4–5), 365–369.

Matejka, J., et al. (2018). *Dream lens: Exploration and visualization of large-scale generative design datasets*. Proceedings of the 2018 CHI conference on human factors in computing systems, 1-12.

Narayan, K. (2023, October 26). *Is AI a job killer or a job creator? What history tells us*. The Economic Times. https://economictimes.indiatimes.com/jobs/hr-policies-trends/is-ai-a-job-killer-or-a-job-creator-what-history-tells-us/articleshow/104728338.cms?from=mdr

Picard, R. W. (2010). Affective computing: From laughter to IEEE. *IEEE Transactions on Affective Computing, 1*(1), 11–17.

Rahwan, I., et al. (2019). Machine behaviour. *Nature, 568*(7753), 477–486.

Scott, S. G., & Bruce, R. A. (1994). Determinants of innovative behaviour: A path model of individual innovation in the workplace. *Academy of Management Journal, 37*(3), 580–607.

Shneiderman, B. (2020). Human-centered artificial intelligence: Reliable, safe & trustworthy. *International Journal of Human-Computer Interaction, 36*(6), 495–504.

Stokes, J. M., et al. (2020). A deep learning approach to antibiotic discovery. *Cell, 180*(4), 688–702.

The Fourth Industrial Revolution: what it means and how to respond. (2016, January 14). *World economic forum*. https://www.weforum.org/stories/2016/01/the-fourth-industrial-revolution-what-it-means-and-how-to-respond/?utm_source=chatgpt.com

Trafton, A. (2020, February 20). *Artificial intelligence yields new antibiotic*. MIT News | Massachusetts Institute of Technology. https://news.mit.edu/2020/artificial-intelligence-identifies-new-antibiotic-0220

Wang, K., et al. (2019). Do artificial intelligence and machine learning have a role in the courtroom? *AMA Journal of Ethics, 21*(2), 158–166.

West, M. A., & Farr, J. L. (1990). Innovation and creativity at work: Psychological and organizational strategies. John Wiley & Sons.

Zander, T. O., et al. (2016). Neuroadaptive technology enables implicit cursor control based on medial prefrontal cortex activity. *Proceedings of the National Academy of Sciences, 113*(52), 14898–14903.

Zuboff, S. (2019). *The age of surveillance capitalism: The fight for a human future at the new frontier of power*. Profile Books.

Dr. Archana Parashar has been working as an Associate Professor at IIM Raipur since 2014. She is a gold medallist in M.A. (English Literature), M. Phil topper, and completed her Ph.D. on American fiction. Prior to this, she was associated with SGSITS, Indore. She has 18 years of experience in teaching and corporate training. She has been a visiting faculty at IIM Calcutta, IIM Lucknow, IIM Shillong, IIM Kozhikode, and IIM Nagpur. Her research areas include business communication, written analysis and communication, ELT, postcolonial writings, and ecocritical narratives.

Abhiyash Singh was born and brought up in Lucknow. He is currently pursuing an M.A. in Economics from the Delhi School of Economics. He has completed his graduation from Kirori Mal College in Economics and Political Science. His academic journey is marked by a consistent track record of excellence. He has a great enthusiast in studying economics, data analysis, econometrics, and political science. Along with studies, he has worked on academic research papers on topics like Impact of Working Women Hostel Scheme on Female Employment, Migratory Movements and Their Economic Consequences, and Time Series Analysis of National Stock Price and GDP Growth Rate.

Transformative Impact of Artificial Intelligence on Human Resource Management in the Era of Industry 5.0

Khadija Kaukab, Arshia Hashmi, Muhmmad Shahid Mehmood, and Muhammad Shehzad Hanif

Introduction

Artificial intelligence (AI) integration in human resource management (HRM) has been a game changer for organizations looking to manage talent, streamline processes, and improve decision-making. With the shift toward Industry 5.0 soon, where human-centricity, sustainability, and collaborative intelligence are redefining the future of work, AI will also play a major role in HRM. There is more to it than just automation; this paradigm shift highlights the symbiosis between human creativity and machine efficiency, working together to enable a workplace that is more innovative, inclusive, and resilient. Industry 5.0 focuses on the collaboration between human workers and AI systems, enhancing productivity and making accurate decisions (Darwish, 2024). From manufacturing to education to retail, service robots and AI applications are being used in concert and demonstrating their practical benefits (Darwish, 2024).

With AI's significantly more extensive and effective capabilities in managing labor demands, more businesses are starting to use it to streamline and enhance standard HRM procedures. From the First Industrial Revolution to Industry 4.0, technological advancements have consistently altered how humans operate. By highlighting the cooperative relationship between technology and human inventiveness, Industry 5.0, on the other hand, offers a revolutionary twist and new opportunities for HR departments to improve procedures while fostering an atmosphere that is long-term sustainable and focused on the needs of employees.

AI in human resource management (HRM) promotes and facilitates collaborative intelligence between the human and machine worlds, as well as those aligned with Industry 5.0's focus on driving innovation while supporting employee

K. Kaukab (✉) · A. Hashmi · M. S. Mehmood · M. S. Hanif
UCP Business School, University of Central Punjab, Lahore, Pakistan
e-mail: arshia.hashmi@ucp.edu.pk; mshahid@ucp.edu.pk; shehzad.hanif@ucp.edu.pk

M. Dabić et al. (eds.), *Artificial Humans*, Future of Business and Finance,
https://doi.org/10.1007/978-3-032-06604-6_7

well-being and sustainable, adaptive workplaces. In this way, AI may help firms apply comprehensive methods to creating sustainable and future-ready workplaces by integrating them across all HR areas, including recruitment, onboarding, training, performance management, and employee engagement. This chapter aligns AI with all processes of HRM with a special focus on Industry 5.0, covering the benefits and challenges. The coming sections elaborate on the transforming context of HRM in the era of Industry 5.0.

The Fourth Industrial Revolution (4IR) brought about the fourth wave of transformative technologies, such as artificial intelligence (AI), big data, machine learning, mobile, the Internet of Things (IoT), geo-tagging, virtual reality, speech recognition, and biometrics. These technologies have been adopted at an unprecedented pace, transforming industries around the world. AI, however, stands out among the rest because it encompasses the facets of perception, reasoning, sensing, and knowledge representation and is therefore referred to as a foundational technology (Jan et al., 2023). Its evolution stems from the pursuit of human creativity, complementing intelligence, which transcends automation.

By approaching technological innovation from a human-centric perspective, Industry 5.0 builds upon this framework. Under this paradigm, human ingenuity and cutting-edge technologies collaborate to promote synergy as opposed to simple automation. This makes the workplace more inventive and adaptable while also boosting employee satisfaction and productivity (Kavitha et al., 2024). Employee responsibilities change as they learn to use their abilities and creativity in conjunction with state-of-the-art tools in a tech-driven firm. A key aspect of this evolution is Sustainable Human Resource Management (SHRM), which weaves sustainability principles into HR practices. SHRM includes recruitment, training, and employee well-being initiatives, promoting ongoing engagement and resilience within organizations. This strategy not only enhances the quality of employees' work-life but also cultivates socially responsible organizations that are prepared to succeed in a fast-paced, technologically advanced environment.At the heart of Industry 5.0 is a focus on human involvement and well-being, facilitated by effective collaboration between humans and AI (Darwish, 2024). AI enhances HR functions by tackling complex issues, such as addressing employee concerns and automating repetitive tasks. By integrating collaborative intelligence into HR, organizations can reshape the workplace, providing solutions that improve living standards and create new opportunities for people (Sen & Kumar, 2018; Kambur & Akar, 2022). The aim is not merely efficiency but the establishment of fair, human-centered workplaces that confront societal challenges while promoting growth. At its essence, artificial intelligence embodies a machine's capacity to learn, comprehend, and interpret information independently, mimicking human cognitive abilities (Johansson & Herranen, 2019). Yawalkar (2019) aptly characterizes AI as an "ideal intelligent" machine—a flexible agent capable of sensing its surroundings and acting purposefully to achieve defined objectives. This ability highlights AI's role as a facilitator of Industry 5.0's vision for a collaborative, innovative, and sustainable future. Thus, this magic of artificial intelligence is creating a human-centric and sustainable system by addressing the major challenges of conventional HRM. It's been discussed in the upcoming section.

Overcoming HRM Challenges and Revolutionizing Recruitment Through AI in Industry 5.0

In particular, human beings may encounter problems with human resource management (HRM) such as biased hiring and selection decisions; errors in creating compensation packages for employees; incorrect training program delivery; a failure to create succession plans for senior positions; inadequate handling of employee complaints or conflicts; and inaccurate performance reviews. In spite of this, the difficulties can be readily overcome by using AI technology appropriately (Gehlhaus et al., 2022). AI not only addresses these issues in the context of Industry 5.0, but it also aligns HR procedures with its human-centric philosophy. Industry 5.0 enables HR departments to eliminate errors, implement fairness in their processes, make well-informed decisions, and create a sustainable, value-driven workplace by fostering collaborative partnerships between humans and machines. As AI systems are designed to augment human progress allowing employees to focus on creative, innovative activities instead of discarding mundane activities.

According to Bader and Kaiser (2019), incorporating algorithms and AI into decision making leads to more accurate decisions as algorithmic decisions can be made with less time, unbiasedly, and more accurately when compared with human decisions based on experience and intuition. A study done by Deloitte revealed that one in three employees wishes for the implementation of AI in their workplace shortly. Sen and Kumar (2018) further explains that there would be more time devoted to innovations and creativity by the employees if there were digital systems and automation software to take care of all menial work, thus making it easier. In general, it has been viewed that the whole process of HRM is going to be changed with more feasible bearings due to AI. The coming sections specifically address the whole HRM process, covering recruitment, selection, training, and evaluation of employees with specific changes due to AI.

The implementation of AI functionalities into recruitment and selection procedures is an essential aspect of modernizing and revolutionizing traditional HRM activities into more effective and intelligent formats, as noted by van Esch. Advanced devices carry out routine work-related communicative behavior, such as emailing, interview scheduling, appointment reminders, and resume screening, reducing labor loads by almost half (Leong & Sung, 2018). In addition, improvements in big-data analytics and artificial intelligence have brought an upgrade for better information processing, problem-solving, and decision-making. Industrial 5.0 has brought efficiency improvement by further leaning toward the total reduction in all redundant steps to make the whole HR effort more useful and, of course, allow these professionals more time for strategic and innovative work to develop a sustainable and adaptive workforce.

Modern technologies, such as artificial intelligence means, have transformed and enhanced the working modes by which human resource management (HRM) derives productivity (Hmoud & Várallyai, 2019). Recruitment is an area in which their impact can be easily traced. The competitive edge that AI brings in is a better understanding of talent as compared to competitors, hence the strengthening of the overall competitiveness of the company (Johansson & Herranen, 2019). HR receives thousands of applications for every job offer, and the full-dress, human-centered, screening, and selection process is very costly and demoralizing for applicants alike (Hmoud & Várallyai, 2019). Artificial intelligence aids in speeding the hiring process, improving candidate experience, and taking costs out (Johansson & Herranen, 2019). AI-driven candidate filtering can reduce the time and make the process smoother as discussed in the below section.

AI-Driven Candidate Filtering-Enhancing Recruitment Practices in the Era of Industry 5.0

Initially, in the process of filtering candidates, human resource managers incorporate parameters like age, education, skills, and experience in sorting algorithms. Resumes are hastily scrutinized and assigned to shortlists by applying the relevant filtering algorithms depending on these criteria (Chang, 2009). In addition, AI allows HR professionals to gauge candidate attitudes or beliefs through their social media profiles, which would then lead them to gauge their likelihood of switching jobs. For example, they could find indications of how frequently their candidates switch jobs or how long they stay in a single company. Such assessments may also identify a given candidate's inconsistent behaviors. AI can obtain signs of personality and job fit (Upadhyay & Khandelwal, 2018), and hence the filtering algorithms are already used in British Airways, BBS, Ford, etc. Technologies such as a robot named Doris and Hired Score applications, recently developed by Unilever, can perform filtering and scanning processes on resumes. However, Industry 5.0 fosters human resource management practices that are holistic and sustainable through integrating technology upon which workforce management or personnel management relies to achieve sustainability objectives. Worth mentioning here is the role of chatbots in this filtration process.

AI-Powered Chatbots—As a mechanism for shortlisting candidates, chatbots generate large amounts of data to support analytic decision-making in HR and provide around-the-clock candidate support, set up by chatbots, automatic directing of unsuitable applicants, and results of preselection sent to HR managers. These bots are quite effective in the preselection phase according to Cowgill, for example, the Chabot Maya developed by L Oréal and Talla as developed by Systems, Applications, and Products (SAP). AI automates many routine headache-inducing tasks, such as candidate screening and evaluation, thus reducing human bias and resulting in more objective and fair recruitment outcomes. Strategically deploying such AI in recruitment will simplify the processes involved, improve their effectiveness in attracting talent, and boost employee retention rates. Other than screening, AI also facilitates the next step of HRM, which is selection. The forthcoming section describes it.

AI in Streamlining and Improving the Candidate Selection Process

We will now emphasize the function of AI in improving the selection process. In today's world, the selection of the appropriate candidate for a position must encompass a variety of contemporary methods, in addition to the traditional interview process, due to the automation of numerous technological aids. Stereotyping, contrast bias, or affinity bias are examples of biases that HR managers may exhibit during candidate interviews. These biases can result in inaccurate recruiting decisions, which could have a detrimental effect on employee productivity within the organization. Over time, an organization's turnover rates may be elevated by recruiting managers' erroneous decisions (Kambur & Akar, 2022). Consequently, the implementation of AI technologies in the selection process assists HR managers in determining the most suitable candidate for a position.

At this time, the selection process has been managed entirely by AI, including testing, video interviews, and selection decisions. The testing experience for Candidate assessments has been gamified by AI, which evaluates the ability to work under duress, intelligence, problem-solving, stress management, and capability. Building blocks for organizations to leverage AI, which is an analytic instrument for reporting insights about employees, are game-theoretical elements. However, Miller posits that game-theoretical evaluation offers an optimal evaluation experience for both candidates and organizations, resulting in more comprehensive data in a shortened amount of time. More specifically, gamification AI assessments, AI-provided video interviews, and geocentric algorithms in decision-making can be considered game-changing in the context of the employee section and are discussed further.

Gamified AI Assessments—As per Kupper, assessments could be largely gamified to increase motivation and retention among employees. The gamification of assessment through artificial intelligence is intended to obtain more insightful input about the intelligence and skills of candidates. Utilizing games, cognitive skills, personality, endurance, emotional intelligence, risk-taking potential, and performance under pressure are measured. Gamified assessments could motivate candidates to take more interest in the evaluation process. Hence, game-based assessments would make such an employee feel more part of the company. Such experiences are more likely to increase the retention rate, which means that they are likely to remain in their jobs for a longer time. According to Connelly, we can infer that the degree of innovativeness and success orientation in employees are important personality traits that could determine how well gamification would work in the tasks or evaluations. Gamification would therefore likely be converted to make possible increases in employee motivation or engagement, translating to higher employee retention.

AI-Powered Video Interviews—Interviewing through artificial intelligence without recourse to traditional interviewing would be an immediate change. Applicants usually answer questions about the role during a video interview, and afterward, a performance score is generated after the performance evaluation. Each applicant is given an insight score that reflects their respective performance. The AI analyzes about 25,000 different candidate data points in the interview assessment, while the interviewer uses the tone of voice, facial expressions, and micro-expressions to closely observe the candidate's behavior. This thorough evaluation process can guide the HR managers that who will be the best fit for the organization. After that, Al is the guide for making more precise decisions while doing the final selection with video interviewing and the test. In decision-making, machine learning eliminates the need for human judgment and uses algorithms for decision-making in AI technologies.

Geocentric Algorithms in Decision-Making—It's about scanning through the candidate dataset to derive one candidate out of many that fit the requirements within a job description. The finalists are then ranked in the decisional matrix. Phenom People Application is Microsoft's serious attempt at offering human resource managers decision-making assistance, aligning candidates' Professional work and teamwork skills after the interview, then ranking them accordingly. Phenom People has also found its way into Citrix, Philips, and General Motors. Ore and Sposato say recruiters must become AI Champions to lead their corporations into the twenty-first century, moving them far from antiquated, inefficient hiring and selection processes. Moving in, AI is leveraging its benefits to the next step of the training and orientation process as well, which is further discussed.

HR Training Process with the Touch of Artificial Intelligence

Once candidates are selected to be well-suited for the HRM position, the organization starts its training process to orient these employees to their occupations and teach them the necessary job-related information. It is brought to light by Hassan that defining roles might be linked to higher job satisfaction levels and lower turnover rates between working groups. When employees are skilled enough in learning and knowing things about their jobs and clear enough to understand their roles in the work organization, they tend to show a high amount of satisfaction in their jobs and a lesser rate of turnover among working groups. This training can be provided by robotic instructors. Instructor robots can act in human-like ways and identify voices and visuals. These teachers can gauge each worker's learning speed. Robot instructors can be able to clarify a subject that is unclear in detail as a real instructor would. Industry 5.0 emphasizes the synergy between human creativity and advanced technologies, such as robotics and AI, to enhance workplace practices. This approach extends to employee training, where robotic instructors play a transformative role in preparing employees for their roles. Let's have a look at revolutionizing aspects of robotic instructions in the below section.

Revolutionizing Employee Learning: The Impact of Robotic Instructors in Workforce Development

Modern employee learning is being transformed by robotic instructors in all aspects: scope, speed, and quality. Examples of robotic education are Promobot Education, manufactured by the Promobot company, among others, which shows that robotic technology can offer better educational solutions. IBM, too, has shown how robotic technologies take advantage of feeble algorithms to recommend personalized training programs for the employee, thus extending AI to the applications it makes possible in workforce development courses. The promise of robotic instructors in the future resounds with all the possibilities that will be opened for most employee development opportunities. These AI and machine learning-based instructors will put an online and personal emphasis on training sessions, which will be tailored to every employee's learning pace, style, and specific needs. This type of technology would help organizations reskill employees with more proficiency for the competencies needed to be relevant in Industry 5.0. The outcome will ultimately be a culture of continuous learning that Robotic instructors create, thereby ensuring that employees are kept abreast with evolving technologies and practices in the industry, which eventually translates into growth and sustainability for an organization. Consistent with the initial steps of the HRM process, the role of AI extends from recruitment, selection, and training to performance evaluation, as elaborated in the next section.

AI-Driven Performance Evaluation: Transforming Employee Assessment and Overcoming Challenges

Employees often must deal with inaccurate performance evaluations, which discourage them from working with the organization and instead turn helpful to the organization into its liability because the employee perceives they are being judged unfairly for their inputs or performances. The situation can be relatively effectively handled by AI, which will provide the much-needed impartial evaluation of the employees' performance. AI is up to check all the employee history regarding performance scores, projects undertaken by the employee, training, work experiences, and practices in the organization. The evaluation process can even provide an average performance score for staff.

Algorithms perform administrative and operational duties, such as task allocation, progress monitoring, and performance evaluation. According to Jantan, AI can rapidly imitate the characteristics of productive employees in a specific job so that it might predict their potential for promotion based on performance. AI also retrieves information from its database to check whether the worker's skills have increased. If an employee's performance is inadequate, managers receive an alert. These employees qualify for special training and development programs. Employees achieving high rates on performance appraisals may gain incentives, such as increased compensation, promotions, or better career opportunities. Such rewards are given out by an algorithmic reward system that provides real-time incentives for predefined favorable actions. Conclusively, AI strengthens the performance evaluation process via compensation, pay, and reward systems and is explained further.

AI-Driven Compensation and Reward Systems

Such a fair and unbiased compensation structure, according to Jehangir, Sahibzada, and Tariq, will contribute much to employee retention. Organization programs for rewards based on benefits promote employee retention (ER) as well as attracting and holding on to high performers, according to Shikuku and Mosoti. As Malik et al. highlighted, IBM has introduced Watson, Microsoft has developed Workplace Analytics, and the Software Company Peg has designed the Pega Sales Coach application for performance measurement. HR managers provide fair assessments as a competitive advantage using AI tools in human resource processes so that employees may stay longer with the company. AI-enabled talent development tools help discover the skills that both an organization and its employees are going to require soon in their fields of work. Indeed, it will create a revolution in the practical world. AI will determine who among the employees will be given a promotion using data validation as a means of checking the very basis on which employees are considered for increased payments based on the result of assessment testing performed on those perceived as high-achieving employees. Validation of data reveals hidden capabilities or qualities of employees through their performance and training.

Identify candidates who are fulfilled by revealed skills and traits, among others. Notify the manager about them. Promotion, according to Ibidunni, Osibanjo, Adeniji, Salau, and Falola, is seen as a motivational criterion for keeping the employees satisfied and committed to their responsibilities and also contributes to the retention of talents. Using AI as a method to find deserving candidates for promotion is a well-designed, timely strategy in the already known competitive landscape for talent retention.

Integrating AI Technology into Pay and Reward Systems—It could, in reality, change the organization to motivate employees fairly. It identifies trends and patterns regarding employee performance that can create a more objective and sufficiently merit-based reward system. Moreover, AI evaluates all information more accurately for managers making decisions about performance appraisal. It can develop pay metrics that define and attribute results. This coordination must include massive amounts of data, such as personal information taken from resumes, results of psychometric tests given at an onboarding process, training history, evaluations of the return on training investment, and any other distinct skills that the employee possesses. Then these data will be encompassed and analyzed to recommend suitable salary brackets. AI has reported to the manager about an increase in salary for any employee deserving it. Neural networks for building intelligent decision support systems driven by big data for just salary evaluations have been proposed.

Potentially, IBM's Planning Analytics software is exemplifying implementations like these, which fix pay rates through ongoing performance measures rather than at the end of the year. This form of regular performance feedback benefit comes with little time adjustment to pay rates. In addition to that, an internal advisory from the company provides recommendation services for salary increases for IBM managers. Also, Rožman et al. (2023) stated that integrating AI means a transformative shift and re-energization of the entire process of performing work-related tasks across the whole company the work involved in recruitment, training, and talent retention strategies. According to França et al., integrating AI in HRM strengthens organizations in attracting and retaining critical talents. Consequently, AI is not only aligned with the whole HRM process and benefits it but even harnesses the grounds for long-term organizational benefits through the reduction of employee turnover and retention of talented employees. Its discussion is expanded in the coming sections.

Leveraging Artificial Intelligence to Enhance Employee Retention and Transform HRM Practices

Now, modern technologies are, no doubt, changing the entire human resources management (HRM) practice around the world (Ancarani et al., 2019). It was in this regard that AI technologies have enabled a revolution within the human resources department where employee-based systems are substituted with new systems that seek to deliver services promptly. Not only does this technological advancement give room for the employees to work with some other system but it also enhances the human resource process and minimizes the time taken to reach out to prospective candidates. As a result of traditional practices of hiring being lengthy, HR managers have also incurred costs regarding recruitment, which has been a major challenge. Jia pointed out 71% cost retention in the given costs and a 3 times enhancement in efficiency because of AI. Kambur and Akar (2022) described that AI technologies have the potential to free up human resource workers, which can then be viewed as time for other activities, like social interactions.

Also, the social interaction potential emphasized by the author can create a workplace culture or environment where employees feel they belong, thus increasing engagement and retention levels. Hence, the integrated AI system within human resources is expected to assist the employees, improve their performance, and manage how they spend time. There are AI applications, especially predictive analytics, chatbots, and virtual assistants, which are disrupting traditional HR processes, including hiring, performance management, as well as training and development (Marler & Boudreau, 2017). As artificial intelligence takes over tasks that are menial and even some that are not, employees should be able to bring forth new ideas that will help the growth of the organization and complete bigger tasks, all of which require time. Solutions that use AI allow firms to combine innovative solutions for the employees and automate mundane duties (Kong et al., 2021).

Thus, the adoption of AI is one of those classical interventions that is altering the whole organization's management, such as the recruitment process, training offered, and keeping of employees within the organization (Rožman et al., 2023).

Furmankiewicz et al. (2015) observed that in the years to come, the application of AI would soar in essential activities, such as addressing complex issues, structural organization and management forecasting, and calculations involving diverse human resources. The management of human resources (HRM) should be in a position to update the whole functions of the department with the coming of artificial intelligence and implement, such changes to improve employee retention. Therefore, with the current sophisticated technology, there must be a renewal of HR processes. Employee retention is substantiated through skill prediction and ethical effects of fairness as being discussed in the coming subsections.

Resources can contribute to the improvement of performance for the employees overall, the development of skills, learning and growth opportunities, and retention of employees, thus helping reduce employee turnover. Wamba-Taguimdje et al. argued that one of the major benefits with regard to building a good organizational culture is that such an organization will retain its talented employees. According to Paigude et al., incorporating AI in human resource management has the potential to improve employee retention through task automation, better decision-making processes, and improved engagement. High turnover itself necessitates AI use to keep employees motivated, fulfill their needs, and reasonably stabilize tasks.

The advances made by artificial intelligence today serve as a link between human beings and machines that benefit efficiency and the quality of decision-making processes. This linkage resonates more in human resource management (HRM), where the traditional ways of working are automated, becoming data-driven processes.

In HRM, AI-based tools work on simplifying some of the very complex tasks of talent acquisition and performance evaluation in addition to workforce planning. For example, AI algorithms scour the Internet for the best possible candidates, track employee performance, and do everything from suggesting potential training to providing a more personalized career profile. These routine administrative tasks become automatic, allowing the HR professional to focus on higher-level, strategic initiatives that apply directly to the company as a whole and complement employee satisfaction. Besides that, AI incorporates inclusivity and equitable treatment in HRM by taking away the human element from the recruitment and promotion process. Predictive analytics and natural language processing provide more detailed insights into workforces, which HR managers use to make proactive, decision-based moves that lead to organizational objectives. This is where AI is for the vision of Industry 5.0 of technology working with human ingenuity to create an innovative, sustainable, and adaptive workplace. As per the needs of Industry 5.0, HR practices must be reinvented, where AI applications will contribute to process improvement and employee engagement enhancement.

AI in Skill Prediction and Workforce Agility—AI plays a very important role in predicting the skills needed for future roles by analyzing the trends in the workforce and demand across industries. It explains the increasing importance of both technical and soft skills like adaptability, problem-solving, and emotional intelligence in an AI-enhanced workplace. Organizations can use AI to assess the skill gaps of their teams before designing specialized training programs to overcome such gaps. This will prepare the employees for job evolution and establish agility and competitiveness for organizations because of the changes in the market.

The Ethical Implications of AI in HRM—Ethics of AI in Industry 5.0 play a key role in determining the balance between automation and human workforce participation. This is particularly so for AI within HRM, which promises to make recruitment, training, and employee engagement more efficient, bringing the flip side of fairness, transparency, and job security. For instance, automated decision-making in recruitment, such as candidate selection or performance evaluations, would have to be free from bias and ethical. AI in HRM will help employees do their jobs better, not replace them but make them better partners as they work together. It is also mentioned that this would create AI use in HRM applicable to Industry 5.0 is not innovation-only but also provides trust, inclusiveness, and a people-centric approach to managing workers.

AI systems might sometimes amplify the discrimination they were supposed to eliminate. "For example, where hiring or judging work performance is concerned, an AI system may repeat bias from historical gender data". For example, the presce of biased patterns in the data fed to the AI system for training may create unfair decisions made by the system, such as one gender being favored over another. Studies have proved that all these issues lead to unfair-discriminatory results, hence the necessity for a strong development of bias mitigating testing standards toward fair outcomes. Bias in hiring, promotions, or performance evaluations must not be assumed or reinforced by an AI system. The algorithms to be used should ensure equity among all candidates and employees in terms of their treatment, irrespective of gender, ethnicity, or any other personal characteristics. AI-generated systems should not cause disparate impacts during recruitment, promotion, or performance evaluation periods. Algorithms must be developed and run in such a way that a fair view of all genders, ethnicities, and other personal characteristics such as differences is also obtained.

Implementation Challenges of AI in HRM

AI bears a lot of benefits for the HRM process and organization as a whole, but along with benefits, its implementation is also acquainted with the challenges related to data privacy and legal complications and needs a solution. It is discussed below.

Privacy and Data Protection

Another important aspect that needs to be highlighted is privacy and data protection. Data protection laws often complement the processing of personal data and performance metrics and demographic details for AI systems, raising privacy-related concerns. AI-HRM incurs large amounts of personal data processing such as employee profiles, performance metrics, and behavioral patterns of employees in the organization. Therefore, data needs to be secured against breaches and misuse while complying with the laws guarding the data.

Ensuring Compliance: Navigating Legal Frameworks for AI in HRM

One such example of compliance within complex legal frameworks, including the likes of GDPR and HIPAA, is ensuring the making of AI applications under regulatory processes toward data protection. The legal frameworks create mechanisms that mandate strict protocols for the collection, storage, and processing of personal data. Organizations must adopt robust security measures and aboveboard data practices when dealing with this information and enforce internal and external accountability. Noncompliance brings serious legal and financial penalties and reputational damage. Thus, such changes keep companies informed about the status of regulations in the given area and continue to develop practices of adopting AI ethically while guarding the rights of individuals to privacy.

Overcoming Implementation Challenges: Strategies for Effective AI Integration in HRM

Now, discuss the challenges of implementing AI across various HR processes and the need for HR experts to develop strategies to address these obstacles effectively. The potential of AI is not without challenges, such as the imposition of implementation costs, on-demand technical expertise, and potential technology over-relevant reliance. All the above issues must be addressed for effective integration. Deploying these elements enables firms to create a new-age and employee-centric AI-based HRM system focused on improving the efficiency and innovation of HRM activities, dovetailed with the major arrays of Industry 5.0.

Usually, high initial investment, which is not affordable to small and medium enterprises (SMEs) is needed for AI technologies (Iyelolu et al., 2024). This upfront cost serves as a barrier for most organizations on restricted budgets, a typical example being libraries and educational institutions, hampering their slow adoption of AI solutions because of limited finances. However, as with any other organization, it must be understood that successful AI human resources management will result from a one-time investment, which ultimately saves long-term costs. Once in operation, those artificial intelligence systems will bring enormous savings to operational costs while providing increased efficiency to their users and streamlining human resource processes for the realization of high returns on investment over time. In this manner, organizations will overcome the initial budgeting challenges and enjoy all the benefits of increased productivity and quality in decision-making and employee engagement.

Chapter Summary

AI is revolutionizing HRM through automated recruitment, training, and performance appraisal with a boost in employee engagement. In industry 5.0, AI promotes innovation, inclusivity, and efficiency, minimizing turnover and encouraging continuous learning. Yet, challenges such as data privacy, high cost, and the provision of ethics frameworks need to be resolved for successful implementation.

References

Ancarani, A., Di Mauro, C., & Mascali, F. (2019). Backshoring strategy and the adoption of industry 4.0: Evidence from Europe. *Journal of World Business, 54*(4), 360–371.

Bader, V., & Kaiser, S. (2019). Algorithmic decision-making? The user interface and its role for human involvement in decisions supported by artificial intelligence. *Organization, 26*(5), 655–672.

Chang, M. L. (2009). An appraisal perspective of teacher burnout: Examining the emotional work of teachers. *Educational Psychology Review, 21*, 193–218.

Darwish, D. (2024). Human-AI collaboration in industry 5. In *Human-machine collaboration and emotional intelligence in industry 5.0* (pp. 44–70). IGI Global.

Furmankiewicz, J., Furmankiewicz, M., & Ziuziański, P. (2015). Implementation of business intelligence performance dashboard for the knowledge management in organization. *Zeszyty Naukowe. Organizacja i Zarządzanie/Politechnika Śląska.*

Gehlhaus, D., Boisson, J., Abdulla, S., Feldgoise, J., Koslosky, L., & Peterson, D. (2022). *China's AI workforce*. Centre for Security and Emerging Technology.

Hmoud, B. I. F., & Várallyai, L. (2019). *Will artificial intelligence take over humanresources recruitment and selection?*

Iyelolu, T. V., Agu, E. E., Idemudia, C., & Ijomah, T. I. (2024). Conceptualizing mobile banking and payment systems: Adoption trends and security considerations in Africa and the US. *International Journal of Science and Technology Research Archive, 7*(1), 001–009.

Jan, Z., Ahamed, F., Mayer, W., Patel, N., Grossmann, G., Stumptner, M., & Kuusk, A. (2023). Artificial intelligence for industry 4.0: Systematic review of applications, challenges, and opportunities. *Expert Systems with Applications, 216*, 119456.

Johansson, J., & Herranen, S. (2019). *The application of artificial intelligence in human resources management*. Business Administration Thesis, Jonkoping University.

Kambur, E., & Akar, C. (2022). Human resource developments with the touch of artificial intelligence: A scale development study. *International Journal of Manpower, 43*(1), 168–205.

Kavitha, S., Ravi, Y. K., Kumar, G., & Nandabalan, Y. K. (2024). Microalgal biorefineries: Advancement in machine learning tools for sustainable biofuel production and value-added products recovery. *Journal of Environmental Management, 353*, 120135.

Kong, H., Yuan, Y., Baruch, Y., Bu, N., Jiang, X., & Wang, K. (2021). Influences of artificial intelligence (AI) awareness on career competency and job burnout. *International Journal of Contemporary Hospitality Management, 33*(2), 717–734.

Leong, K., & Sung, A. (2018). *FinTech (financial technology): What is it and how to use technologies to create business value in a fintech way?*.

Marler, J. H., & Boudreau, J. W. (2017). An evidence-based review of HR analytics. *The International Journal of Human Resource Management, 28*(1), 3–26.

Rožman, M., Oreški, D., & Tominc, P. (2023). Artificial-intelligence-supported reduction of employees' workload to increase the company's performance in today's VUCA environment. *Sustainability, 15*(6), 5019.

Sen, S., & Kumar, V. (2018). Microgrid control: A comprehensive survey. *Annual Reviews in Control, 45*, 118–151.
Upadhyay, A. K., & Khandelwal, K. (2018). Applying artificial intelligence: Implications for recruitment. *Strategic HR Review, 17*(5), 255–258.
Yawalkar, M. V. V. (2019). A study of artificial intelligence and its role in human resource management. *International Journal of Research and Analytical Reviews (IJRAR), 6*(1), 20–24.

Khadija Kaukab holds an MPhil in Business Administration from UCP Business School. Her research focuses on strategic management and human resources, particularly the impact of AI in HRM on employee retention.

Dr. Arshia Hashmi is an Associate Professor at UCP Business School. With extensive experience in business research, her expertise lies in strategic management, leadership, and organizational behavior.

Dr. Muhmmad Shahid Mehmood is an Associate Professor at UCP Business School. His research interests include human resource management, organizational behavior, leadership, and innovation management.

Dr. Muhammad Shehzad Hanif is an Assistant Professor and researcher specializing in business administration. His work contributes to the fields of leadership, innovation, and corporate strategy.

Challenges in Adoption of AI-Driven Collaborative Innovation

Muhammad Faraz Mubarak, Richard Evans, Sajid Nazir, Khuram Shahzad, and Giedrius Jucevicius

Introduction

In the recent years, the quick advancements in artificial intelligence (AI) have shown substantial influence on innovation management across various sectors (Kakatkar et al., 2020; Liu, 2022). Innovation, traditionally viewed as a closed process managed within firm boundaries, but now it represents an open model that encourages collaboration between organizations. This shift is especially prominent in the practice of *collaborative innovation* (Chowdhury et al., 2022), where firms engage with external partners such as customers and competitors, and academic institutions to cocreate and codevelop new product or processes and services (Wang & Hu, 2020; Xu et al., 2022). Collaborative innovation has become a strategic imperative for organizations that want to remain competitive within an interconnected dynamic market (Kharazmi & Dartoomi, 2023). Consequently, the growing complexity of technological environments and global competition has led organizations to recognize that internal resources alone are insufficient for driving breakthrough innovations (Marion & Fixson, 2020; Bai & Li, 2020). As a result, the collaborative innovation model has emerged as a response to these challenges by facilitating knowledge sharing, reducing innovation risks, and accelerating time to market (Pietronudo et al., 2022). However, the effectiveness of collaborative

M. F. Mubarak · R. Evans
Dalhousie University, Halifax, NS, Canada

S. Nazir (✉)
Lappeenranta-Lahti University Technology, Kouvola Unit, Finland
e-mail: sajid.nazir@lut.fi

K. Shahzad
University of Vaasa, Vaasa, Finland

G. Jucevicius
Vytautas Magnus University, Kaunas, Lithuania

M. Dabić et al. (eds.), *Artificial Humans*, Future of Business and Finance,
https://doi.org/10.1007/978-3-032-06604-6_8

innovation depends upon the efficient management of knowledge, resources, and coordination among diverse stakeholders. In this context, artificial intelligence (AI) emerges as a disruptive force, transforming the ways in which collaborative innovation is conceptualized, managed, and executed (Păvăloaia & Necula, 2023). Collaborative innovation, as a concept, relies on the model where companies now cooperate with outside partners for the sake of mutual advantage instead of working alone (Chesbrough & Bogers, 2014). This collaborative approach to innovation involves the deliberate flow of knowledge across organizational boundaries, enabling firms to leverage external ideas, technologies, and competencies to supplement their internal innovation efforts (Mubarak & Petraite, 2020). The process of collaborative innovation is not only limited to large multinational corporations but is also increasingly adopted by small and medium-sized enterprises (SMEs) as well, as it allows them to tap into resources and expertise that may be beyond their reach otherwise (Liu & Cao, 2022). The benefits of collaborative innovation are clear, such as firms can access a broader pool of ideas, reduce the risks and costs associated with innovation, and increase the likelihood of success in new product development (NPD) (Cooper, 2024). For example, global companies like General Electric have successfully used collaborative innovation models by partnering with universities and research institutions to develop cutting-edge technologies in turbine design (Cooper, 2024). Similarly, in the pharmaceutical industry, companies often collaborate with academic researchers to explore new drug formulations, benefiting from the expertise of their partners to accelerate the research and development (R&D) processes, etc. (Petrova, 2014).

The introduction of AI has brought about significant changes in the way collaborative innovation is conducted. AI technologies, such as machine learning, natural language processing, and predictive analytics, allows organizations to automate routine tasks, analyze vast amounts of data, and derive insights that were previously not feasible through traditional methods (Davenport & Ronanki, 2018). By taking advantage of human capabilities and enhancing organizational efficiency, AI has the potential to significantly improve the effectiveness of collaborative innovation processes. One of the primary ways AI is transforming collaborative innovation is through knowledge management. AI systems can facilitate the sharing and integration of knowledge among collaborators by organizing, categorizing, and analyzing large datasets to identify trends and opportunities (Broekhuizen et al., 2023). For example, AI can help identify complementary expertise among partners, suggesting optimal collaboration opportunities and enhancing the overall innovation process. Furthermore, AI-powered tools can improve coordination by automating tasks such as scheduling, project tracking, and communication, thereby reducing administrative burdens and ensuring that all collaborators are aligned with project goals (Arias-Pérez & Huynh, 2023). Real-world examples highlight the transformative potential of AI in collaborative innovation. In the automotive industry, companies like BMW have adopted AI-powered platforms to collaborate with external partners on new vehicle designs and technologies. These platforms enable BMW to analyze customer preferences, market trends, and technological advancements in real time, allowing them to cocreate innovative solutions with their partners more efficiently

(Schindler & Schmihing, 2023). Similarly, in the healthcare sector, AI-driven collaborations between pharmaceutical companies and research institutions are accelerating drug discovery and development by analyzing vast datasets of clinical trials and patient outcomes (Xiao, 2023; Cooper, 2024; Cubric & Li, 2024). Despite its potential, AI-based collaborative innovation faces several adoption challenges. For instance, issues related to data privacy, trust among partners, and the integration of AI into existing organizational processes remain significant barriers (Petraite et al., 2022; Broekhuizen et al., 2023). Additionally, the high costs of AI adoption, along with the need for specialized skills, can limit the accessibility of these technologies, particularly for SMEs (Liu & Cao, 2022). Moreover, there is growing concern about the ethical implications of AI, particularly in terms of decision-making transparency and accountability in collaborative settings (Johansson et al., 2024).

While the potential benefits of AI in collaborative innovation are extensively acknowledged. However, the research on the adoption barriers of AI-based collaborative innovation remains limited. Current literature largely focuses on the technological capabilities of AI and its applications in specific industries. However, there is a critical gap in understanding the organizational, social, and cultural factors that influence the successful adoption of AI in collaborative innovation settings (Bai & Li, 2020; Mubarak et al., 2024). Additionally, issues related to trust, governance, and the ethical use of AI in collaborative environments have not been sufficiently explored (Ghobakhloo et al., 2023). Given that AI-based collaborative innovation is an emerging research area, there is a dire need to investigate the factors that restrict its adoption, particularly in SMEs and industries where collaboration is essential for innovation. Therefore, this study addresses the challenges associated with the adoption of AI-driven collaborative innovation. In doing so, these research contributions are manifold such as for organizations, this study underscores the importance of addressing these challenges through robust data governance frameworks, scalable technical infrastructures, and fostering an organizational culture that embraces innovation. By doing so, firms can fully harness the transformative potential of AI to enhance productivity, secure competitive advantages, and drive sustainable growth. From a theoretical standpoint, this study highlights the need for interdisciplinary research that integrates insights from ethics, technology management, organizational behavior, and law. Proactively addressing these challenges enables organizations to foster an environment that contributes to successful implementation while also enhancing resilience, trust, and a competitive advantage in employing AI for collaborative innovation.

This study is structured as follows: Following the introduction, the literature review, which is Sect. 2, explores extensively previous studies that examined AI-driven collaborative innovations, along with associated challenges. Following that, Section 3 on research methodology highlights the methodology of the study, which includes the research strategy, data gathering techniques, and analytical tools employed in this research. The findings in Sect. 4 outline the project results, encompassing interview outcomes and challenges prioritization via AHP. Section 5 encompasses a discussion of the research findings and their correlation with prior studies. Subsequently, Section 6 will critically evaluate how this study assists experts in addressing the challenges associated with the adoption of AI within collaborative innovation networks. The future recommendation Sect. 7 encapsulates the principal findings and provides direction for the future work in this area.

Literature Review

AI-Driven Collaborative Innovation

Collaborative innovation has emerged as an essential technique for organizations to utilize external ideas, resources, and knowledge to improve their innovative capabilities (West & Bogers, 2013). Since the organizations are facing greater complexity due to technological advancements and global competition in recent times, this highlights the dire need for collaboration across organizational boundaries (Chesbrough & Bogers, 2014). Although the conventional methods of collaboration have worked well in the past (Wang & Hu, 2020), the emergence of artificial intelligence (AI) opened up new opportunities to improve the effectiveness, scope, and outcomes of collaborative innovation (Huang & Rust, 2022; Mariani et al., 2023). AI has become a considerable driver of innovation across various industries, providing advanced tools for decision-making, automation, and knowledge management (Ali & Frimpong, 2020; Pietronudo et al., 2022; Bahoo et al., 2023). In the setting of collaborative innovation, AI serves as a powerful facilitator, allowing organizations to engage with external stakeholders and share knowledge more effectively, as well as cocreating value (Broekhuizen et al., 2023). However, collaborative innovation relies on interactions between firms, research institutions, customers, and other external partners to take advantage of complementary resources and knowledge (Wang & Hu, 2020). On the other hand, AI's ability to process huge amounts of data at once and automate repetitive tasks provides actionable insights, which may fundamentally transform how these collaborations are structured and executed in the future (Kakatkar et al., 2020; Pietronudo et al., 2022; Järvelä et al., 2023). Nevertheless, collaborative innovation refers to the cocreation of products, services, or solutions through partnerships that go beyond the organizational boundary (Kharazmi & Dartoomi, 2023). AI enhances this process by providing the tools necessary to analyze large datasets, predict trends, and optimize processes. Through real-time AI systems, organizations can achieve better inter-team collaboration both within geographic areas and across functional domains through improved communication and decision-making and knowledge sharing (Malik et al., 2021; Sumbal et al., 2024).

Nevertheless, the dynamic contribution of AI to knowledge management serves as a vital element for the success of collaborative innovation networks. AI-powered systems can capture, store, and analyze knowledge generated by multiple collaborators, which improves the sharing and application of this knowledge network-wide (Broekhuizen et al., 2023; Vilko et al., 2024). For example, IBM Watson uses AI to aggregate knowledge from various external partners and internal departments, allowing IBM to collaborate more effectively on research and development projects. By using AI to manage knowledge, IBM can ensure that its partners have access to the most relevant and up-to-date information, enhancing the overall innovation process (Wamba-Taguimdje et al.,

2020). One of the key areas in this context where AI facilitates collaborative innovation is in enhancing knowledge sharing and communication. AI-driven tools, such as natural language processing (NLP) and machine learning algorithms, can sift through massive amounts of data to identify patterns, trends, and insights that human actors might miss (Kulkarni et al., 2021; Arias-Pérez & Huynh, 2023). This capability is especially valuable in open innovation networks, where the timely exchange of information is critical to the success of innovation projects (Brem et al., 2023). For example, Siemens, a global leader in automation, uses AI-powered platforms to foster collaboration between its research and development teams and external partners. These platforms enable real-time sharing of research data, predictive analytics, and insights across multiple partners, reducing the time to market for new products and solutions. Furthermore, AI can also automate many of the routine tasks associated with collaborative innovation, such as data processing, project tracking, and resource allocation. This automation frees up human collaborators to focus on more strategic activities, such as ideation and problem-solving (Bai & Li, 2020; Broekhuizen et al., 2023). For example, AI can automatically schedule meetings, monitor project progress, and send updates to all stakeholders, ensuring that collaborative innovation projects stay on track (Niederman, 2021). In the automotive industry, Ford has adopted AI tools to optimize its collaborative innovation processes. By using AI to automate supply chain management, Ford can collaborate more effectively with its suppliers, reducing bottlenecks and ensuring the timely delivery of components for vehicle production. This optimization has enabled Ford to improve its production efficiency while also enhancing its ability to innovate through partnerships (Johansson et al., 2024). Likewise, AI also plays a significant role in collaborative product development by enabling faster and more efficient testing, prototyping, and iteration. AI can simulate product performance under various conditions, allowing organizations and actors to test new ideas without the need for physical prototypes (Wan et al., 2021). Through AI simulations Boeing alongside other aerospace companies decrease development costs and improve efficiency of product assessments (Cooper, 2024).

Nonetheless, customer participation remains essential for collaborative innovation activities that seek to cocreate value. By processing customer feedback and behavior analysis AI enables businesses to discover new innovative opportunities through improved customer engagement (Arias-Pérez & Huynh, 2023). For instance, Netflix uses AI to analyze customer viewing habits and preferences, allowing the company to collaborate with content producers to develop new shows that are tailored to audience interests. This AI-driven collaboration between Netflix and its external partners has been key to the platform's success in maintaining customer engagement and delivering innovative content. Nevertheless, AI's ability to provide predictive insights and recommendations enhances decision-making in collaborative innovation networks. Through historical data analysis, market trend assessment, and customer behavior evaluation AI algorithms generate valuable insights to support strategic choices (Chowdhury et al., 2022). The system demonstrates exceptional worth in industries that experience rapid innovation together with dynamic market environments (Johansson et al., 2024).

AI-Driven Collaborative Innovation and Disruptions

AI-driven collaborative innovation is reshaping business models by supporting organizations to cocreate value with external partners in ways that were previously inconceivable (Mariani et al., 2023). It allows firms to leverage external resources and knowledge more effectively, leading to the creation of new business models that are based on collaboration and shared value creation (Wamba-Taguimdje et al., 2020; Broekhuizen et al., 2023). One example of a new business model supported by AI is the rise of platform-based businesses. Companies like Uber and Airbnb have built their business models around platforms that use AI to connect users with service providers. These platforms facilitate collaborative innovation by allowing users and providers to cocreate value through shared experiences (Schiavone et al., 2021). By examining user data, AI systems help businesses scale quickly while improving platform operations and user experience, which ensures a competitive advantage (Johansson et al., 2024). Another example is in the healthcare sector, where AI-powered platforms facilitate collaboration between pharmaceutical companies, research institutions, and healthcare providers (Shaikh et al., 2024). These platforms facilitate the codevelopment of new drugs and treatments by analyzing patient data and identifying potential breakthroughs in medical research. The result is a new business model based on collaborative innovation, where multiple stakeholders work together to develop and deliver innovative healthcare solutions (Cubric & Li, 2024). Likewise, new business models based on large language models (LLM) are providing data analytics and market insights in addition to other services. ChatGPT, Gemini, and other similar generative AI business models are affecting many business operations (Patil et al., 2024) and are expected to disrupt industrial settings even more; hence, its role in reshaping collaborative innovation and open innovation networks could be immense in near future (Fui-Hoon Nah et al., 2023). One of the most significant disruptions caused by AI-driven collaborative innovation is the automation of knowledge work. Tasks that were traditionally performed by human experts, such as data analysis, customer support, and decision-making, are increasingly being automated by AI systems (Broekhuizen et al., 2023). This automation not only increases efficiency but also challenges the traditional roles of knowledge workers, who may find their jobs at risk due to AI systems (Păvăloaia & Necula, 2023). Besides, AI also disrupts traditional innovation cycles by significantly reducing the time it takes to develop and launch new products. By automating routine tasks and providing real-time insights, AI allows organizations to bring new products to the market more quickly (Marion & Fixson, 2020). This fast-paced innovation cycles cause competitive challenges for companies, which delay AI adoption or fail to work with external partners (Cooper, 2024).

Challenges in AI-Driven Collaborative Innovation

Despite showing great advantages, the adoption of AI-driven collaborative innovation faces numerous challenges. Among these important challenges, researchers identify ethical concerns alongside trust issues and operational risks, though a lot more are being increasingly cited by researchers.

Ethical Issues

One of the most critical challenges in AI-driven collaborative innovation is the ethical use of AI technologies (Al-kfairy et al., 2024). AI systems, particularly those powered by machine learning and deep learning, operate as "black boxes," which hinders understanding of their internal workflows (Broekhuizen et al., 2023; Jain et al., 2024). This lack of transparency can lead to significant ethical concerns, especially when AI is used to make decisions that impact multiple stakeholders (Kousa & Niemi, 2022). For example, in a collaborative innovation project involving multiple firms, decisions made by an AI system about resource allocation, intellectual property rights, or product development directions might be questioned if the rationale behind those decisions is unclear (Broekhuizen et al., 2023). This complexity not only raises ethical questions about accountability but also poses a risk of unintended biases being embedded in AI systems. For instance, if an AI algorithm is trained on biased data, it may perpetuate or even amplify those biases in its outputs, leading to unfair or discriminatory outcomes (Arias-Pérez & Huynh, 2023). This risk is particularly concerning in sectors such as healthcare or financial services, where biased AI systems could result in unequal access to resources or services for certain groups of people. In a collaborative innovation context, this may harm the reputation of all partners engaged in the partnership (Liu, 2022). Additionally, ethical concerns extend to the handling of sensitive data. AI systems often require access to vast amounts of data, including proprietary business information and personal data, to function effectively. The use of AI to process sensitive data such as customer information, intellectual property, or business strategies raises significant concerns about privacy and data security (Rodrigues, 2020). Therefore, innovation networks that involve multiple partners must have robust frameworks for data protection and clear agreements on how data will be shared, used, and stored to minimize these risks (Bai & Li, 2020). A failure to resolve these ethical concerns can eliminate trust between partners, thus disrupting innovation processes.

(Dis)Trust on AI

The trust is a core element of any effective collaborative innovation network, yet AI system can create distinct complications with trust relationships in different manners (Rodrigues, 2020). Such as within traditional collaborations trust emerges from long-term personal bonds developed through open communication and equal knowledge/resource sharing (Petraite et al., 2022). However, the integration of AI into collaborative innovation network adds a new layer of complexity that may undermine trust if not carefully managed (Wang & Hu, 2020; Păvăloaia & Necula, 2023). Such as collaborators may be reluctant to disclose sensitive information with AI systems if they are unsure about its utilization or if they fear losing control over their intellectual property (Enholm et al., 2022). For example, in a collaboration between a startup and a larger corporation, the startup might be concerned that the corporation will use AI to analyze its proprietary data and gain an unfair competitive advantage. Similarly, concerns about data leaks or misuse by AI systems could discourage partners from sharing valuable information, which could hinder the overall innovation process. Furthermore, AI systems may make decisions that are not easily understood by human collaborators, particularly if the AI system's decision-making process is unclear or if the results seem to favor one partner over another (Wang & Hu, 2020; Păvăloaia & Necula, 2023). This can lead to disputes and a breakdown of trust between collaborators, particularly if partners perceive that the AI system is biased or that the innovation process is not being conducted fairly (Arias-Pérez & Huynh, 2023). To address these trust issues, organizations must confirm that AI systems are transparent, accountable, and designed to facilitate equitable collaboration. The ongoing trust in AI-driven innovation networks depends on clear communication about both AI system usage and data processing procedures.

Operational Risks

AI-driven collaborative innovation also presents significant operational risks (Wamba-Taguimdje et al., 2020; Xu et al., 2022). For example, the integration of AI into existing workflows and innovation processes can be complex and requires careful planning and execution (Shaikh et al., 2024). Many organizations, particularly small and medium-sized enterprises (SMEs) or firms in traditional industries, may lack the technological infrastructure or expertise needed to fully take advantage of AI (Johansson et al., 2024). In such cases, attempting to introduce AI into collaborative innovation efforts without the necessary resources can lead to inefficiencies, delays, and project failures (Mariani et al., 2023; Habbal et al., 2024). For example, the potential risk of relying too much on AI systems AI systems is one operational difficulty. Even though AI can improve decision-making and automate repetitive jobs, it is not perfect since AI systems can make mistakes, particularly if they are trained on biased or insufficient data. Moreover, AI systems may struggle to handle novel situations that fall outside their training parameters. In a collaborative innovation framework, this could lead to incorrect estimations or recommendations, resulting in inadequate results (Bai & Li, 2020). Therefore, organizations must be prepared to monitor AI systems closely and have contingency plans in place to address potential errors or system failures (Chowdhury et al., 2022). Another operational risk is the challenge of aligning AI-driven processes with human workflows. AI systems often require significant changes to existing organizational structures and innovation processes. For example, AI may automate certain tasks that were previously performed by humans, leading to concerns about job displacement and resistance from employees. Integrating AI into these workflows may require substantial retraining of staff and a reevaluation of how tasks are distributed within the organization. Failure to manage this transition effectively can creates operational disruption and inefficiency, which negatively affects the potential advantages of AI-driven transformation (Wang & Hu, 2020; Păvăloaia & Necula, 2023; Johansson et al., 2024).

Research Methodology

This research implements a two-phase method that uses qualitative and quantitative techniques to fully understand and prioritize the challenges in AI-enabled collaborative innovation. Following initial expert interviews the study utilized the Analytical Hierarchy Process (AHP) to rank emerging challenges.

Phase 1: Qualitative Analysis Through Expert Interviews

In the first phase of the study, open-ended interviews were conducted with 29 experts from Asia, Europe, and North America. These experts were chosen based on their deep expertise in AI, together with innovation management and collaborative innovation across academia and industrial sectors. The interviews aimed to explore the challenges organizations face when implementing AI-driven collaborative innovation. The interviews were designed to allow experts to share their perspectives on the challenges related to AI-driven collaborative innovation. The open-ended nature of the questions allows the researchers to capture rich, nuanced data from the experts, with interview durations ranging from 45 to 60 min. A total of 29 open-ended interviews were performed from 2022 to 2024.

Once the interviews were completed, a thematic analysis was performed to identify patterns and themes from the qualitative data. Thematic analysis involves coding the interview transcripts and identifying recurring categories or topics. Through this process, key types of challenges in AI-driven collaborative innovation were identified.

Phase 2: Ranking of Challenges Using the AHP Technique

In the second phase, the types of challenges identified through the thematic analysis were ranked using the Analytical Hierarchy Process (AHP) technique. AHP is a structured multi-criteria decision-making (MCDM) tool that helps in prioritizing and ranking complex issues by comparing them pairwise in a systematic manner.

A structured questionnaire was developed for this phase, using a three-point scale as outlined in Saaty (1992) and Mubarik et al. (2018). The scale consisted of three levels of importance:

- 1 – Not important
- 2 – Somewhat important
- 3 – Very important

The experts were asked to rate the relative importance of each type of challenge identified during the first phase. This step allowed for a more structured, quantitative assessment of the challenges. The same 29 experts from phase I were asked to complete the AHP questionnaire based on their professional experience and the perceived relevance of each challenge in their relevant fields. However, owing to the attrition factor that normally occurs in such a study, 20 experts gave their ratings for phase II and filled out the questionnaire. The experts' responses were collected and organized into pairwise comparison matrices to determine the significance levels of each identified challenge.

Findings

Identification of Challenges

The initial phase of the research focused on identifying the major challenges that prevent the adoption of AI-driven collaborative innovation. A total of 29 open-ended interviews were carried out with experts across different industries and regions. The interviews were designed to investigate the wide range of challenges that organizations may face while implementing AI into collaborative innovation networks. During the interviews, the participants were asked to discuss their experiences with AI-driven collaborative innovation, particularly focusing on the challenges that arise during adoption and implementation. The open-ended nature of the interviews enabled the experts to speak freely about the various challenges they have faced, providing detailed insights into both operational and strategic issues. These challenges varied widely depending on the industry, region, and the specific role of AI in the innovation process. However, despite these differences, several recurring themes emerged across the interviews, reflecting common concerns that transcend individual contexts. The responses from the experts highlighted a range of issues, from technical challenges to organizational and ethical concerns, all of which can inhibit the successful implementation of AI in collaborative innovation. These challenges were initially broad and unstructured, as the experts provided insights from their unique perspectives. The next step was to organize and distill these responses into coherent categories through a rigorous process of thematic analysis.

The researchers used thematic analysis to systematically process their interview data. Researchers using this method examine data to identify recurring patterns which they analyze and report as themes (Naeem et al., 2023). It is a flexible approach, well-suited for capturing both the explicit and implicit meanings within qualitative data (Cresswell et al., 2020; Wiltshire & Ronkainen, 2021). In this case, the thematic analysis allowed the researchers to organize the diverse challenges shared by the experts into manageable and distinct categories. The process of thematic analysis began with data familiarization, where the researchers carefully reviewed the interview transcripts to gain a deep understanding of the content (Braun & Clarke, 2022). This was followed by the generation of initial codes, which involved labeling key ideas and recurring topics mentioned by the experts (Kiger & Varpio, 2020). The codes were then grouped into potential themes, which were subsequently reviewed and refined to ensure they accurately represented the underlying data. As a result of the thematic analysis, five distinct types of challenges were identified. The following is a list of the different sorts of challenges that organizations face while implementing AI-driven collaborative innovation. These challenge types reflect the wide range of problems that organizations encounter, as shown in Fig. 1.

1. ***Ethical Concerns (EC):*** Issues related to data privacy, bias in AI decision-making, and the transparency of AI systems.
2. ***Organizational Change (OC):*** Internal factors such as resistance to change, lack of AI readiness, and the need for upskilling employees.
3. ***Technical Complexity:*** Challenges related to the integration, maintenance, and technical expertise required for AI systems.
4. ***Regulatory Issues:*** Concerns about compliance with data protection laws, intellectual property rights, and varying regulations across regions.

The types of challenges are shown in Fig. 1 below.

Ranking of Challenges Using the AHP Technique

The Analytical Hierarchy Process (AHP) is a structured multi-criteria decision-making (MCDM) technique that helps prioritize and make decisions based on multiple criteria (Tavana et al., 2021; Kumar & Pant, 2023). AHP involves decomposing a complex problem into a hierarchy of more manageable subproblems, performing pairwise comparisons, and calculating priority weights to determine the relative importance of each criterion (Song et al., 2023).

Twenty experts completed the AHP questionnaire, providing their ratings for each challenge type. The weightage for each challenge is assumed as equal. The average scores from these ratings are as follows:

- Ethical concerns: 2.70
- Organizational issues: 2.40
- Technical complexity: 2.05
- Regulatory issues: 2.30

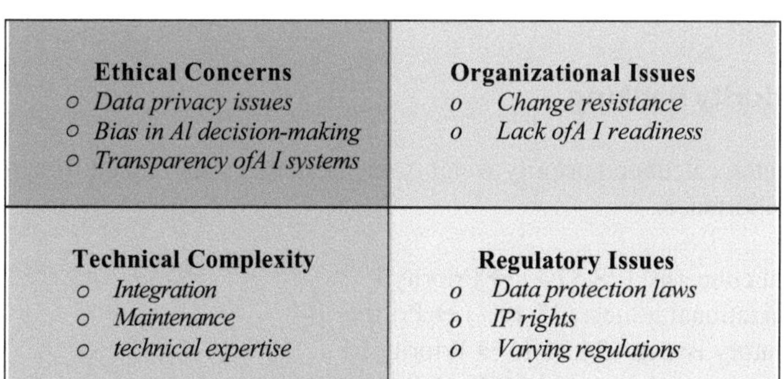

Fig. 1 Challenges in adoption of AI in collaborative innovation

Given the average scores, the next step is to normalize these scores to derive priority weights. The normalization process converts the raw scores into relative weights that sum up to 1 (or 100%), facilitating a comparative analysis of the importance of each challenge.

- *Step-by-Step AHP Analysis.*

Calculation of the Total Score

2.70 + 2.40 + 2.05 + 2.30 = 9.45

Normalization of the Scores

Dividing each challenge's average score by the total score to obtain the normalized score.

Normalized score = total score ÷ challenge score.
Ethical concerns➔ 2.70 ÷ 9.45 = 0.2857
Organizational issues ➔ 2.40 ÷ 9.45 = 0.25396
Technical complexity➔2.05 ÷ 9.45 = 0.2169
Regulatory issues➔2.30 ÷ 9.45 = 0.2433

Converting to Priority Weights

Multiply each normalized score by 100 to express the priority weights as percentages.

Priority weight (%) = Normalized score × 100.
Ethical concerns➔ 2.70 ÷ 9.45 = 0.2857 x 100 = 28.57%
Organizational issues ➔ 2.40 ÷ 9.45 = 0.2539 x 100 = 25.39%
Technical complexity➔2.05 ÷ 9.45 = 0.2169 x 100 = 21.69%
Regulatory issues➔2.30 ÷ 9.45 = 0.2433 x 100 = 24.33%

Final Priority Ranking

Based on the calculated priority weights, the challenges are ranked from highest to lowest importance:

- Ethical concerns: (28.57%) ➔ Priority I
- Organizational issues: (25.40%) ➔ Priority II
- Regulatory issues: (24.34%) ➔ Priority III
- Technical complexity: (21.69%) ➔ Priority IV

In traditional AHP, a consistency ratio (CR) is calculated to ensure that the pairwise comparisons made by the experts are logically consistent. A CR below 0.1 is considered acceptable. However, since the current analysis is based on average scores from a three-point scale rather than direct pairwise comparisons, a formal consistency check is not applicable. It is assumed that the experts' ratings are reliable and consistent.

The final ranking highlights that *ethical concerns* are the most significant challenge in adopting AI-driven collaborative innovation, followed by *organizational issues*, *regulatory issues*, and *technical complexity.* This prioritization suggests that organizations should focus on addressing ethical considerations and organizational readiness to effectively utilize AI in collaborative innovation efforts. Regulatory compliance and managing technical complexities are also important but are relatively less significant compared to the ethical and organizational factors.

Discussion

The result of this study reveals critical information about the challenges which emerge when organization integrate AI into collaborative innovation practices. The research findings contribute to the growing body of literature on AI and collaborative (open) innovation by systematically identifying and prioritizing the challenges that organizations experience during AI implementation in collaborative settings.

The first phase of the research, based on open-ended interviews, uncovered a diverse range of challenges, which were subsequently categorized through thematic analysis into four main areas: ethical concerns, organizational issues, technical complexity, and regulatory issues. This qualitative approach provided nuanced insights into the nature of these challenges. Ethical concerns were frequently highlighted, with participants expressing unease about the potential for AI systems to perpetuate bias, compromise data privacy, and operate with a lack of transparency. These concerns align with the previous research studies emphasizing the critical need for ethical AI deployment, especially in collaborative settings where multiple stakeholders are involved (Mubarak & Petraite, 2020; Kousa & Niemi, 2022; Arias-Pérez & Huynh, 2023; Al-kfairy et al., 2024). In terms of organizational issues, many experts pointed to resistance from employees and a lack of readiness to integrate AI technologies as significant barriers. This finding underscores the importance of internal organizational dynamics, such as change management and workforce upskilling, as critical factors for the successful adoption of AI (Ghobakhloo et al., 2022; Johansson et al., 2024). Additionally, technical complexity emerged as a key challenge, particularly in terms of integrating AI into existing systems and the specialized knowledge required to manage AI systems. Previous study has highlighted the fact that the technical complexity is a significant challenge, particularly when it comes to the implementation of artificial intelligence (Gill et al., 2022). Finally, legal and regulatory issues were identified as challenges that particularly impact sectors with stringent data protection laws, highlighting the need for clear regulatory frameworks for AI adoption. This is again aligned with the prior research which suggests that stakeholders are very concerned with legal and regulatory challenges when it comes to AI deployment (Rodrigues, 2020; de Almeida et al., 2021; Gill et al., 2022; Ghobakhloo et al., 2023).

In the second phase, the AHP analysis quantified and ranked these challenges based on expert evaluations. The findings reveal that *ethical concerns* were ranked as the most serious challenge, followed by Organizational Issues at second, Regulatory Issues at third, and Technical Complexity at fourth rank with respect to their severity for adoption of AI in collaborative innovation. The high ranking of *ethical concerns* suggests that organizations view transparency, bias, and privacy as major risks when adopting AI-driven collaborative innovation. This finding aligns with broader societal discussions about the ethical implications of AI technologies, where concerns about fairness, accountability, and the "black box" nature of AI systems are frequently cited (Ghobakhloo et al., 2022; Broekhuizen et al., 2023). The importance of ethical concerns in the AHP ranking suggests that organizations recognize the potential reputational and operational risks of ignoring ethical issues in AI adoption. Interestingly, *organizational issues* were ranked second in importance, indicating that internal resistance to AI adoption, lack of leadership support, and the need for change management remain significant barriers. This reflects the complexity of organizational transformation required for AI adoption and highlights the importance of a robust internal culture that is open to change (Enholm et al., 2022; Petraite et al., 2022). The prioritization of organizational challenges emphasizes that the successful adoption of AI is not just a technical issue but also a social and cultural one. Further, *regulatory issues* ranked third, indicating that while legal compliance is a significant concern, it is seen as slightly less critical than the internal and ethical challenges. This may reflect the fact that organizations can often work within established legal frameworks but struggle more with internal adoption and ensuring ethical AI practices. Finally, *technical complexity* was placed at number four, which indicates that technical barriers are important, but they are viewed as more manageable compared to ethical, organizational, and regulatory challenges.

Implications of Study

The findings from this study have several important implications for organizations, policymakers, and researchers who want to advance AI-driven collaborative innovation. The prioritization of ethical concerns highlights the need for organizations to adopt transparent and fair AI systems. Organizations must prioritize the development and deployment of AI systems that are explainable and auditable to guarantee that all collaborators have a clear understanding of how AI-driven decisions are made. Given that ethical concerns were the top-ranked challenge, it is critical for firms to implement governance frameworks that address issues of fairness, accountability, and bias in AI systems. This includes establishing ethical guidelines for AI use, creating oversight mechanisms, and conducting regular audits to ensure that AI systems comply with ethical standards. Furthermore, the reputational risks associated with ethical missteps in AI adoption mean that organizations must be proactive in addressing public concerns about privacy and bias. Building trust among collaborators and customers will require ongoing efforts to demonstrate that AI is being used responsibly and ethically. Organizations can also engage external stakeholders, such as independent auditors or regulators, to validate their ethical practices in AI deployment.

The high ranking of organizational challenges underscores the need for a strong internal culture which promotes AI-based innovation. Organizations need to encourage leadership development and change management initiatives to help employees to embrace AI technologies. Resistance to AI adoption often stems from fear of job displacement or uncertainty about how AI will change workflows (Johansson et al., 2024). To mitigate these fears, organizations should focus on reskilling and upskilling employees, ensuring that workers are equipped with the skills needed to collaborate effectively with AI. Moreover, leadership plays a crucial role in fostering an environment that supports innovation. Executives and managers must lead by example, demonstrating a commitment to AI adoption and encouraging experimentation with AI-driven innovation processes. Organizations which prioritize innovation development will speed up AI system adoption into collaborative workflows while minimizing employee resistance within their structures.

The prominence of legal and regulatory issues in both the qualitative interviews and AHP rankings indicates that regulatory compliance is a significant concern for organizations, particularly in industries like healthcare, finance, and manufacturing. Policymakers need to work closely with industry leaders to develop clear guidelines and regulations that address the specific challenges posed by AI in collaborative environments. For organizations, staying informed about the evolving legal landscape around AI and ensuring compliance with data protection laws is critical. In addition, organizations involved in cross-border collaborations should establish clear agreements about data sharing, intellectual property rights, and compliance with regional laws. The global character of collaborative innovation networks requires jurisdictions to establish regulatory alignment for maintaining efficient partnership operations while avoiding legal complications.

While technical complexity was ranked lower in importance compared to other challenges, it remains a significant barrier, particularly for organizations that lack the technical expertise to develop and manage AI systems. Firms should consider partnering with external AI vendors or research institutions to access the specialized knowledge required to implement AI solutions. Additionally, investing in cloud-based AI platforms or modular AI tools that integrate with existing systems can help reduce the complexity of AI adoption. Organizations also need to establish cross-functional teams that include both technical experts and business leaders to confirm that AI implementations align with organizational goals and are effectively integrated into existing workflows.

Future Research Directions

The findings of this study suggest several avenues for future research, particularly in the rapidly growing contexts of AI-driven collaborative innovation. Further research must examine which particular strategies organizations should implement when handling their *ethical concerns* problems. This research demonstrates the importance of ethical transparency and bias mitigation and data privacy issues, but future work needs to address organizational governance frameworks for responsible AI use. This includes investigating the practical application of ethical guidelines in diverse industries and the role of third-party audits in promoting accountability and trust in AI systems. Second, given the pivotal role of *organizational culture* in AI adoption, future studies should delve deeper into how internal dynamics influence the success of AI-driven innovation. Specifically, research should focus on how *leadership styles*, such as transformational leadership, affect AI adoption. Additionally, there is a need to explore how change management practices and organizational structures such as cross-functional teams or innovation labs impact the integration of AI technologies in collaborative settings. Understanding the interaction between leadership, culture, and AI-driven change is crucial for identifying strategies to reduce resistance and foster organizational readiness. Lastly, *as legal and regulatory frameworks* surrounding AI continue to develop globally, ongoing research should investigate the impact of these frameworks on AI adoption across different sectors and regions. Future studies should analyze how upcoming regulations governing data privacy, together with intellectual property rights and liability frameworks, impact international collaborative innovation processes. Comparative studies across industries with varying regulatory environments will show how regulatory compliance affects the success of artificial intelligence-driven teamwork.

Acknowledgments During the preparation of this work, the author(s) used Grammarly for language editing and proofreading the manuscript. After using this tool/service, the author(s) reviewed and edited the content as needed and take(s) full responsibility for the content of the publication. The study is funded by the Lithuanian Research Council (LMT) under project grant number P-PD-23–118. The study is also based on work funded by the Natural Sciences and Engineering Research Council (NSERC) of Canada under Grant No. RGPIN-2022-05008.

References

Ali, D., & Frimpong, S. (2020). Artificial intelligence, machine learning and process automation: Existing knowledge frontier and way forward for mining sector. *Artificial Intelligence Review, 53*(8), 6025–6042. https://doi.org/10.1007/s10462-020-09841-6

Al-kfairy, M., Mustafa, D., Kshetri, N., Insiew, M., & Alfandi, O. (2024). Ethical challenges and solutions of generative AI: An interdisciplinary perspective. *Informatics, 11*(3), 58. https://doi.org/10.3390/informatics11030058

Arias-Pérez, J., & Huynh, T. (2023). Flipping the odds of AI-driven open innovation: The effectiveness of partner trustworthiness in counteracting interorganizational knowledge hiding. *Industrial Marketing Management, 111*, 30–40.

Bahoo, S., Cucculelli, M., & Qamar, D. (2023). Artificial intelligence and corporate innovation: A review and research agenda. *Technological Forecasting and Social Change, 188*, 122264. https://doi.org/10.1016/j.techfore.2022.122264

Bai, X., & Li, J. (2020). The best configuration of collaborative knowledge innovation management from the perspective of artificial intelligence. *Knowledge Management Research & Practice.*

Braun, V., & Clarke, V. (2022). Conceptual and design thinking for thematic analysis. *Qualitative Psychology, 9*(1), 3–26. https://doi.org/10.1037/qup0000196

Brem, A., Giones, F., & Werle, M. (2023). The AI digital revolution in innovation: A conceptual framework of artificial intelligence technologies for the management of innovation. *IEEE Transactions on Engineering Management, 70*(2), 770–776. https://doi.org/10.1109/tem.2021.3109983

Broekhuizen, T., Dekker, H., de Faria, P., Firk, S., Nguyen, D. K., & Sofka, W. (2023). AI for managing open innovation: Opportunities, challenges, and a research agenda. *Journal of Business Research, 167*, 114196. https://doi.org/10.1016/j.jbusres.2023.114196

Chesbrough, H., & Bogers, M. (2014). Explicating open innovation: Clarifying an emerging paradigm for understanding innovation. In *New frontiers in open innovation* (pp. 3–28). Oxford University Press.

Chowdhury, S., Budhwar, P., Dey, P. K., Joel-Edgar, S., & Abadie, A. (2022). Ai-employee collaboration and business performance: Integrating knowledge-based view, socio-technical systems and organisational socialisation framework. *Journal of Business Research, 144*, 31–49. https://doi.org/10.1016/j.jbusres.2022.01.069

Cooper, R. G. (2024). The artificial intelligence revolution in new-product development. *IEEE Engineering Management Review, 52*(1), 195–202.

Cresswell, K., Williams, R., & Sheikh, A. (2020). Developing and applying a formative evaluation framework for health information technology implementations: Qualitative investigation. *Journal of Medical Internet Research, 22*(6). https://doi.org/10.2196/15068

Cubric, M., & Li, F. (2024). Bridging the 'concept–product' gap in new product development: Emerging insights from the application of artificial intelligence in FinTech SMEs. *Technovation, 134*, 103017.

Davenport, T. H., & Ronanki, R. (2018). Artificial intelligence for the real world. *Harvard business review, 96(1), 108–116.*

de Almeida, P. G., dos Santos, C. D., & Farias, J. S. (2021). Artificial intelligence regulation: A framework for governance. *Ethics and Information Technology, 23*(3), 505–525. https://doi.org/10.1007/s10676-021-09593-z

Enholm, I. M., Papagiannidis, E., Mikalef, P., & Krogstie, J. (2022). Artificial intelligence and business value: A literature review. *Information Systems Frontiers, 24*(5), 1709–1734.

Fui-Hoon Nah, F., Zheng, R., Cai, J., Siau, K., & Chen, L. (2023). Generative AI and CHATGPT: Applications, challenges, and Ai-human collaboration. *Journal of Information Technology Case and Application Research, 25*(3), 277–304. https://doi.org/10.1080/15228053.2023.2233814

Ghobakhloo, M., Asadi, S., Iranmanesh, M., Foroughi, B., Mubarak, M. F., & Yadegaridehkordi, E. (2023). Intelligent automation implementation and corporate sustainability performance: The enabling role of corporate social responsibility strategy. *Technology in Society, 74*, 102301.

Ghobakhloo, M., Iranmanesh, M., Mubarak, M. F., Mubarik, M., Rejeb, A., & Nilashi, M. (2022). Identifying industry 5.0 contributions to sustainable development: A strategy roadmap for delivering sustainability values. *Sustainable Production and Consumption, 33*, 716–737.

Gill, S. S., Xu, M., Ottaviani, C., Patros, P., Bahsoon, R., Shaghaghi, A., Golec, M., Stankovski, V., Wu, H., Abraham, A., Singh, M., Mehta, H., Ghosh, S. K., Baker, T., Parlikad, A. K., Lutfiyya, H., Kanhere, S. S., Sakellariou, R., Dustdar, S., et al. (2022). AI for next generation computing: Emerging trends and future directions. *Internet of Things, 19*, 100514. https://doi.org/10.1016/j.iot.2022.100514

Habbal, A., Ali, M. K., & Abuzaraida, M. A. (2024). Artificial intelligence trust, risk and security management (AI trism): Frameworks, applications, challenges and future research directions. *Expert Systems with Applications, 240*, 122442. https://doi.org/10.1016/j.eswa.2023.122442

Huang, M.-H., & Rust, R. T. (2022). A framework for collaborative artificial intelligence in marketing. *Journal of Retailing, 98*(2), 209–223. https://doi.org/10.1016/j.jretai.2021.03.001

Jain, R., Srirambhatla, R., Kessler, J., & Goel, R. (2024). The black box dilemma: Challenges in human-AI collaboration in ML-CDSS. *The American Journal of Bioethics, 24*(9), 108–110. https://doi.org/10.1080/15265161.2024.2377105

Järvelä, S., Nguyen, A., & Hadwin, A. (2023). Human and artificial intelligence collaboration for socially shared regulation in learning. *British Journal of Educational Technology, 54*(5), 1057–1076. https://doi.org/10.1111/bjet.13325

Johansson, A., Akhter, N., & Sickeldal, A. (2024). *Advancing AI in business: Collaborative innovation and sustainable practices*. In Proceedings of the XXXV ISPIM Innovation Conference.

Kakatkar, C., Bilgram, V., & Füller, J. (2020). Innovation analytics: Leveraging artificial intelligence in the innovation process. *SSRN Electronic Journal*. https://doi.org/10.2139/ssrn.3293533

Kharazmi, O. A., & Dartoomi, S. (2023). A systematic literature review on collaborative innovation in the public sector. *Innovation: The European Journal of Social Science Research, 36*(4), 602–630. https://doi.org/10.1080/13511610.2023.2266580

Kiger, M. E., & Varpio, L. (2020). Thematic analysis of qualitative data: Amee guide no. 131. *Medical Teacher, 42*(8), 846–854. https://doi.org/10.1080/0142159x.2020.1755030

Kousa, P., & Niemi, H. (2022). Ai ethics and learning: Edtech companies' challenges and solutions. *Interactive Learning Environments, 31*(10), 6735–6746. https://doi.org/10.1080/10494820.2022.2043908

Kulkarni, A., Shivananda, A., & Kulkarni, A. (2021). Natural language processing and artificial intelligence overview. In *Natural Language Processing Projects* (pp. 1–37). https://doi.org/10.1007/978-1-4842-7386-9_1

Kumar, A., & Pant, S. (2023). Analytical hierarchy process for sustainable agriculture: An overview. *MethodsX, 10*, 101954. https://doi.org/10.1016/j.mex.2022.101954

Liu, D., & Cao, J. (2022). Determinants of collaborative robots innovation adoption in SMEs: An empirical study in China. *Applied Sciences, 12*(19), 10085.

Liu, Q. (2022). Analysis of collaborative driving effect of artificial intelligence on knowledge innovation management. *Scientific Programming, 2022*, 1–8. https://doi.org/10.1155/2022/8223724

Malik, A., De Silva, M. T. T., Budhwar, P., & Srikanth, N. R. (2021). Elevating talents' experience through innovative artificial intelligence-mediated knowledge sharing: Evidence from an IT-multinational enterprise. *Journal of International Management, 27*(4), 100871. https://doi.org/10.1016/j.intman.2021.100871

Mariani, M. M., Machado, I., Magrelli, V., & Dwivedi, Y. K. (2023). Artificial intelligence in innovation research: A systematic review, conceptual framework, and future research directions. *Technovation, 122*, 102623. https://doi.org/10.1016/j.technovation.2022.102623

Marion, T. J., & Fixson, S. K. (2020). The transformation of the innovation process: How digital tools are changing work, collaboration, and organizations in new product development. *Journal of Product Innovation Management, 38*(1), 192–215. https://doi.org/10.1111/jpim.12547

Mubarak, M. F., & Petraite, M. (2020). Industry 4.0 technologies, digital trust and technological orientation: What matters in open innovation? *Technological Forecasting and Social Change, 161*, 120332.

Mubarik, M. S., Chandran, V. G. R., & Devadason, E. S. (2018). Measuring human capital in small and medium manufacturing enterprises: what matters?. *Social indicators research, 137(2), 605–623.*

Mubarak, M. F., Ghobakhloo, M., Evans, R., Jucevicius, G., Prestianawati, S. A., & Mubarik, M. (2024). Metaverse adoption in the manufacturing industry: Impact on social and environmental sustainability performance. *Asia-Pacific Journal of Business Administration.*

Naeem, M., Ozuem, W., Howell, K., & Ranfagni, S. (2023). A step-by-step process of thematic analysis to develop a conceptual model in qualitative research. *International Journal of Qualitative Methods, 22*. https://doi.org/10.1177/16094069231205789

Niederman, F. (2021). Project Management: Openings for disruption from AI and advanced analytics. *Information Technology & People, 34*(6), 1570–1599. https://doi.org/10.1108/itp-09-2020-0639

Patil, D., Rane, N. L., & Rane, J. (2024). Acceptance of CHATGPT and generative artificial intelligence in several business sectors: Key factors, challenges, and implementation strategies. *The Future Impact of ChatGPT on Several Business Sectors*. https://doi.org/10.70593/978-81-981367-8-7_5.

Păvăloaia, V.-D., & Necula, S.-C. (2023). Artificial intelligence as a disruptive technology—A systematic literature review. *Electronics, 12*(5), 1102. https://doi.org/10.3390/electronics12051102

Petrova, E. (2014). Innovation in the Pharmaceutical Industry: The Process of Drug Discovery and Development. In: Ding, M., Eliashberg, J., Stremersch, S. (eds) Innovation and Marketing in the Pharmaceutical Industry. *International Series in Quantitative Marketing, vol 20. Springer, New York, NY.* https://doiorg.ezproxy.cc.lut.fi/10.1007/978-1-4614-7801-0_2

Petraite, M., Mubarak, M. F., Rimantas, R., & Von Zedtwitz, M. (2022). The role of international networks in upgrading national innovation systems. *Technological Forecasting and Social Change, 184, 121873.*

Pietronudo, M. C., Croidieu, G., & Schiavone, F. (2022). A solution looking for problems? A systematic literature review of the rationalizing influence of artificial intelligence on decision-making in innovation management. *Technological Forecasting and Social Change, 182*, 121828. https://doi.org/10.1016/j.techfore.2022.121828

Rodrigues, R. (2020). Legal and human rights issues of AI: Gaps, challenges and vulnerabilities. *Journal of Responsible Technology, 4*, 100005. https://doi.org/10.1016/j.jrt.2020.100005

Saaty, T. L. (1992). A natural way to make momentous decisions. *Journal of scientific & industrial research, 51(8–9), 561–571.*

Schiavone, F., Mancini, D., Leone, D., & Lavorato, D. (2021). Digital business models and ridesharing for value co-creation in healthcare: A multi-stakeholder ecosystem analysis. *Technological Forecasting and Social Change, 166*, 120647. https://doi.org/10.1016/j.techfore.2021.120647

Schindler, M., & Schmihing, F. (2023). Technology serves people: Democratising analytics and AI in the BMW production system. In *Responsible artificial intelligence: Challenges for sustainable management* (pp. 159–182). Springer International Publishing.

Shaikh, A. J., Takbhate, S. B., Gawai, S., Limbore, A. M., & Patil, V. A. (2024). Revolutionizing healthcare: AI-powered solutions, technological integration for accessible and effective medical service. *International Conference on Advances in Computing Research on Science Engineering and Technology (ACROSET), 1–7.* https://doi.org/10.1109/acroset62108.2024.10743713

Song, R., Li, X., Zhao, X., Liu, M., Zhou, J., & Wang, F.-Y. (2023). Identifying critical test scenarios for lane keeping assistance system using analytic hierarchy process and hierarchical clustering. *IEEE Transactions on Intelligent Vehicles, 8*(10), 4370–4380. https://doi.org/10.1109/tiv.2023.3297592

Sumbal, M. S., Amber, Q., Tariq, A., Raziq, M. M., & Tsui, E. (2024). Wind of change: How CHATGPT and big data can reshape the knowledge management paradigm? *Industrial Management & Data Systems, 124*(9), 2736–2757. https://doi.org/10.1108/imds-06-2023-0360

Tavana, M., Soltanifar, M., & Santos-Arteaga, F. J. (2021). Analytical hierarchy process: Revolution and evolution. *Annals of Operations Research, 326*(2), 879–907. https://doi.org/10.1007/s10479-021-04432-2

Vilko, J., Tariq, A., Nemilentseva, M., & Aghajani, D. (2024). Managing uncertainty in innovation process through AI integration. Lecture *Notes in Networks and Systems*, 153–161. https://doi.org/10.1007/978-3-031-74828-8_14.

Wamba-Taguimdje, S.-L., Fosso Wamba, S., Kala Kamdjoug, J. R., & Tchatchouang Wanko, C. E. (2020). Influence of artificial intelligence (AI) on firm performance: The business value of AI-based transformation projects. *Business Process Management Journal, 26*(7), 1893–1924. https://doi.org/10.1108/bpmj-10-2019-0411

Wan, J., Li, X., Dai, H.-N., Kusiak, A., Martinez-Garcia, M., & Li, D. (2021). Artificial-intelligence-driven customized manufacturing factory: Key technologies, applications, and challenges. *Proceedings of the IEEE, 109*(4), 377–398. https://doi.org/10.1109/jproc.2020.3034808

Wang, C., & Hu, Q. (2020). Knowledge sharing in supply chain networks: Effects of collaborative innovation activities and capability on innovation performance. *Technovation, 94-95*, 102010. https://doi.org/10.1016/j.technovation.2017.12.002

West, J., & Bogers, M. (2013). Leveraging external sources of innovation: A review of research on open innovation. *Journal of Product Innovation Management, 31*(4), 814–831. https://doi.org/10.1111/jpim.12125

Wiltshire, G., & Ronkainen, N. (2021). A realist approach to thematic analysis: Making sense of qualitative data through experiential, inferential and dispositional themes. *Journal of Critical Realism*, 1–22. https://doi.org/10.1080/14767430.2021.1894909

Xiao, Y. (2023). The Digital Adoption and Technological Innovation in the Pharmaceutical industry--A case study of Pfizer. *Highlights in Business, Economics and Management, 23*, 45–51.

Xu, G., Dong, C., & Meng, L. (2022). Research on the collaborative innovation relationship of artificial intelligence technology in Yangtze River Delta of China: A complex network perspective. *Sustainability, 14*(21), 14002. https://doi.org/10.3390/su142114002

Muhammad Faraz Mubarak received the Ph.D. degree in Management of Innovation from Kaunas University of Technology, Lithuania, in 2023, and the MBA degree in Technopreneurship from Universiti Tun Hussein Onn Malaysia, in 2018. He is a Research Fellow within the Faculty of Computer Science at Dalhousie University, Canada. He has been a visiting scholar and trainee Researcher with University College London, UK, and Copenhagen Business School, Denmark. He is also an adjunct faculty member and researcher at Kaunas University of Technology and Vytautas Magnus University, Lithuania. His research interests include collaborative innovation, digital innovation and transformation, and Industry 5.0. He has authored/co-authored numerous papers in peer-reviewed journals, including Technological Forecasting and Social Change, Technology in Society, Sustainable Production and Consumption, IEEE Transactions on Engineering Management, IEEE Engineering Management Review, and Business Strategy and Development.

Richard Evans (Senior Member, IEEE) received the Ph.D. degree in enterprise social software from the University of Greenwich, London, U.K., in 2013. He is Co-Director of the College of Digital Transformation and Associate Professor in Digital Innovation within the Faculty of Computer Science at Dalhousie University, Canada. He is an established academic with research, teaching, and supervision experience in the fields of digital innovation and transformation, design and engineering management, and entrepreneurship. He has authored/co-authored numerous papers in peer-reviewed journals, including IEEE Transactions on Engineering Management, Journal of Business Research, Technological Forecasting and Social Change, and the International Journal of Production Research.

Sajid Nazir is a Junior researcher and Ph.D. student at Lappeenranta-Lahti University Technology (LUT), Finland. He is also associated with the Institute of Business Management (IoBM), Karachi-Pakistan, as a Senior Lecturer at the Department of Logistics and Supply Chain Management. He joined academia right after completing his master's in supply chain management from Coventry University, UK in 2018. Sajid Nazir has more than 10 years of experience working in the Academia as well as in the corporate sector on national as well as international levels such as Banking, Aviation, Pharmaceutical, and other service industries as a supply chain professional. His work has been published in journals and conferences in the fields of supply chain management and innovation management. His areas of interest are blockchain technologies, Resilient Supply Chain, Technology and innovation management, Industry 5.0, Sustainable Supply Chain Performance, and innovations in Supply Chain.

Khuram Shahzad is an assistant professor of digital innovation management in the School of Technology and Innovations and the Innovation and Entrepreneurship InnoLab research platform at the University of Vaasa, Finland. His current research interests concern digital technologies and digital transformation, open innovation, R&D and innovation, innovation ecosystem, blockchain, and supply chain management. Dr. Shahzad's work has been published in several journals of international repute, including Industrial Marketing Management, International Business Review, R&D Management, IEEE Transactions on Engineering Management, Journal of Business& Industrial Marketing, Journal of Change Management, etc.

Giedrius Jucevicius is a professor at the Faculty of Economics and Management, Vytautas Magnus University. He holds a PhD in business administration. He is also the Head of Research and Management PhD study program. His areas of scientific interest include innovation management, inter-organizational relations, entrepreneurial and innovation ecosystems, industrial clusters, and international comparative management. Dr. Giedrius Jurevicius is the author of numerous scientific papers and monographs on regional innovation ecosystems, management under uncertainty, and institutional and cultural dimensions of management systems. He is also an active participant of the international scientific events and associations, such as EURAM, ISPIM, ECKM, and ECIE, as well as the leader of research projects on the complexity aspects of management research, smart development, and knowledge/innovation ecosystems.

Artificial Humans and Innovation in Industry 5.0

MinHye Lee, Mir Dost, and Jude Bennett

Introduction

Now, it is more common than before to see robots helping doctors perform surgery or assisting restaurants by offering customers a plate of food or a cup of coffee. Scholars associate this transformative development over the past few years with emerging technologies (Kumar, 2024), which have proven to be unparalleled tools for streamlining efficiency across various industries. Collaboration between humans and technology has become commonplace, which aligns with the rise of Industry 5.0. In 2021, the European Commission (EU) announced the concept of Industry 5.0 as a new paradigm, an ideology of future industrial evolution aimed at capturing the value of human-technology partnerships to tackle the current industrial challenges and benefit industry, workers, and society (Dollija & Gura, 2022).

Before Industry 5.0, when the Industry 4.0 revolution was introduced at the 2011 Hannover Fair, the main focus was economic progress via technical advancements (Potočan et al., 2024). Industry 4.0 emphasises the use of AI-driven technologies to boost industry flexibility and efficiency through digitalisation of industrial activities and increasing automation (Xu et al., 2023). For instance, smart working and system optimisation without human supervision were the primary areas of achievement in the era of Industry 4.0. As Industry 4.0 focused too much on maximising efficiency and production, the importance of the human element in favour of a technology-driven approach was relatively ignored (Xu et al., 2023). In this sense, the heavy focus on the efficiency- and growth-driven approach to industrial transformation leads to the failure to consider sustainability, people-centred operations, and

M. Lee · M. Dost (✉) · J. Bennett
University of Winchester, Winchester, UK
e-mail: Minhye.Lee@winchester.ac.uk; Mir.Dost@winchester.ac.uk;
j.bennett1.23@unimail.winchester.ac.uk

M. Dabić et al. (eds.), *Artificial Humans*, Future of Business and Finance,
https://doi.org/10.1007/978-3-032-06604-6_9

resilient adaptation, which represents a primary shortcoming of Industry 4.0 (Liu et al., 2024).

The Industry 5.0 paradigm expands and enhances the Industry 4.0 paradigm by incorporating the altered human-intelligent system relationship (Schröder et al., 2024). Industry 5.0 refers to developing human-centred industrial processes using human cognitive capabilities (knowledge and creativity) and integrating them with intelligent system workflows (Leng et al., 2022). As seen from Table 1, the key difference between Industry 4.0 and Industry 5.0 lies in that humans and machines collaborate fully to promote synergistic human-machine integration while enhancing employment, working conditions, and production that leads to sustainable development (Leng et al., 2022).

As Industry 5.0 integrates complex systems with interconnected machines, data, and people, the fundamental idea of collaboration—literally, "co-labour", or working with others to accomplish a common goal—is fundamental in the subject of sustainable development to address challenges for economic, social, and environmental systems (Le Pennec & Raufflet, 2018). Moreover, it is crucial to understand how AI can coexist and interact with humans to create value and drive innovation, considering the goals of Industry 5.0: a value-driven approach for a sustainable, human-centric, and resilient society. In other words, Industry 5.0 actively solves these challenges and provides innovative transformations towards a more advanced and sustainable future (Dollija & Gura, 2022).

Building on the premise of the above discussion, this chapter aims to explore the collaboration between humans and machines, called "Artificial Humans", and its impact on the commercial sector. More specifically, it discusses how artificial humans can be used in marketing, examining their values and innovations through real-life case studies. It delves into the concept of innovation—how it has been understood so far and how it should be understood in the age of Industry 5.0. By doing so, the chapter makes two significant contributions: first, it may enhance understanding of the use, significance, and value creation of artificial humans and their impact on driving innovation during the era of Industry 5.0. Second, it contributes to understanding how to assess and critically evaluate the concept of innovation and propose a new conceptual understanding of innovation appropriate for the Industry 5.0 era.

Table 1 Significant differences between Industry 4.0 and Industry 5.0

Feature	Industry 4.0	Industry 5.0
Focus	Automation and digitisation	Collaboration between humans and machines
Collaboration	Limited human-AI collaboration	Extensive AI-AI and human-AI collaboration
Goals	Increased efficiency, productivity, and customisation	In addition to industry 4.0 goals: Sustainability, human-centric approach, and resilience

Methodology

This book chapter aims to provide a new conceptual understanding of the term "innovation" by reviewing and analysing real-life case studies in the era of Industry 5.0. Methodologically, it follows Huff (2009) cycle of sense-making/sense-giving (see Fig. 1). It is considered one of the valuable frameworks for understanding the study area, identifying literature gaps, and providing iterative insights.

In the sense-making stage, the authors explored previous studies examining how innovation has been understood and questioned whether this concept needs to be revisited in the context of Industry 5.0. In the sense-giving stage, the authors reviewed various studies on adopting artificial humans in the commercial sector, identifying how innovation should be interpreted.

This is a relatively new territory of investigation; therefore, the authors firmly believe that the Huff (2009) cycle of sense-making/sense-giving method is especially appropriate for this book chapter, as it allows for offering a comprehensive understanding, building a rigorous overview, and contributing new insights to a specific question (Deeb & Maddigan, 2023).

Artificial Humans

The term "artificial humans" has been used in various contexts, but it is hard to find a clear definition as its usage has evolved alongside technological advancements and narrative developments. Historically, the concept of artificial humans, which implies a symbiotic relationship between humans and machines, has existed for a long time. The idea of humans and machines working together goes back centuries. Adrienne Mayor's recent book, *Gods and Robots: Myths, Machines, and Ancient Dreams of Technology*, explores how ancient Greek myths incorporated the concept of creating lifelike artificial beings. The book highlights that, well before the advent of machine learning and self-driving cars, stories of the giant bronze robot Talos, the artificial woman Pandora, and their creator god, Hephaestus, captivated the imaginations of the ancient Greeks. Mayor also notes that while historians often credit the Middle Ages as the origin of automata, when the first self-moving devices were developed, the idea of artificial lifelike beings dates to myths and legends from

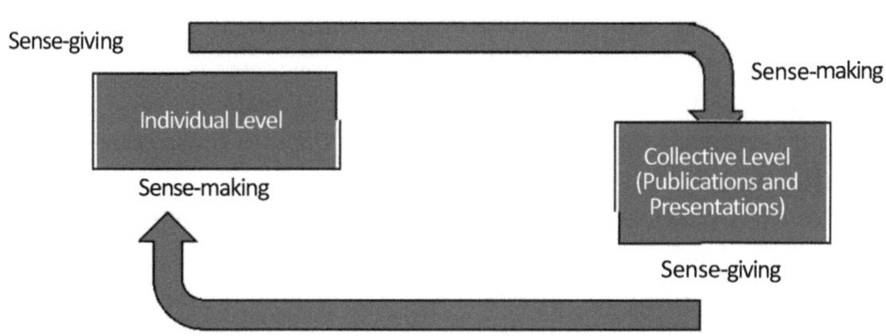

Fig. 1 Modified from Huff's (2009) sense-making and sense-giving framework

around 2700 years ago (Mayor, 2018). The longstanding collaboration between humans and machines has materialised into mixed human-robot teams during the Industry 5.0 revolution. In other words, the origin of the Industry 5.0 revolution stems from the shift in how humans interact with intelligent systems.

As AI advances, the sophistication of humanoid robots and digital human applications in many areas of modern life has correspondingly increased (Rosheim, 2006). Today, artificial humans are encountered in various aspects of daily life. The following sections outline a historical timeline of humanoid robots from the beginning to the present.

Humanoid Robots

Evidence in the literature suggests that the idea of humanoid robots dates to Leonardo da Vinci's design in 1495 (Rosheim, 2006). This assertion is supported by robot design notes found in sketchbooks that researchers rediscovered in the 1950s (Moran, 2007). These robots are believed to have been exhibited at the court of Milan in 1495. For example, the knight robot, among other capabilities, could automatically sit, stand, lift its visor, move its arms, and adjust its jaw. After the sketchbook's discovery, the robot was reconstructed, and it now functions and can express several human-like emotions (Rosheim, 2006). The statue of this robot and its operation is currently displayed in Berlin, Germany. It is believed that the potential for accelerating the development of such robots gained significant attention with the spread of the Internet. It is safe to say now that this technology enabled the creation of digital human beings.

Digital Human Beings

The spread of AI-supported robots is paving the way for the creation of digital human beings. It can be assumed that in the future, individuals might utilise digital human profiles to attend meetings, interact with clients online, and complete various tasks. For example, virtual assistants like Siri (from Apple) or Alexa (from Amazon) engage with customers through their digital personas. However, while these characters are highly functional, they may need more emotional depth for nuanced understanding and communication. Despite such limitations, these technologies are valuable alternatives to physical humans, significantly contributing to their roles (Vlahos, 2019).

The authors compare humans and artificial humans to understand their similarities and differences. They focus on three key areas: complementary strengths, enhanced decision-making, and accelerating innovation. Table 2 summarises this comparison, followed by a detailed discussion.

Complementary Strengths: Humans and AI systems possess distinct strengths and weaknesses. To fully leverage their complementary strengths, it is essential to recognise and accept each other's limitations. These strengths, though different, are

Table 2 The comparison and nexus of humans with AI/digital humans

	Humans	Digital humans/ AI	Nexus
Complementary strengths	• Flexibility and transference • Empathy and creativity • Emotions and communication • Common sense	• Pattern recognition • Consistency • Speed and efficiency • Probabilistic	Intuitive and analytic
Enhanced decision-making	• Real-life decision-making, ethical, moral and other human considerations	• Testable and corrective measures • Consistency	Focus and accuracy
Innovation acceleration	• Emotional and social intelligence • Understanding • Collaboration • Communication	• Promoting divergent thinking • Challenging expertise biases • Idea evaluation and refinement	Innovation generation and adoption

compatible and can enhance or balance one another, leading to mutual benefits and synergy. For instance, humans excel in creativity, critical thinking, and social intelligence, whereas AI systems are adept at data analysis, pattern recognition, and automation (Gorli & Kishore, 2024). By combining these strengths, we can achieve breakthroughs that surpass what we could accomplish individually. Human intelligence is primarily intuitive, while AI or digital humans are more analytical (Dellermann et al., 2019).

Enhanced Decision-Making: AI can analyse extensive datasets to detect trends and forecast outcomes, enhancing the accuracy and efficiency of human decision-making. While humans and machines approach decision-making differently (Korteling et al., 2021), machines often surpass humans in legal discovery, evaluating job candidates, and diagnosing medical conditions. However, the rise of automation also introduces new risks to society. For example, United Airlines cited an automation issue to explain a recent system shutdown. Additionally, on 19th July 2024, a software update from endpoint protection provider CrowdStrike led to a major IT outage that affected businesses, governments, and users worldwide. Despite these risks, the need for human assistance from AI tools is more significant than ever. Therefore, business leaders should involve humans in decision-making when using these tools to ensure better and more informed outcomes. This collaboration between humans and AI can lead to more precise and targeted decisions.

Innovation Acceleration: Finally, regardless of the industry's type, size, or nature, continuous innovation is essential for a business's survival. Companies must draw on diverse sources to achieve this, with knowledge being a key predictor of innovation. As a result, companies invest in internally generated knowledge and knowledge accumulated from external sources. Innovation advocates refer to these as enablers of innovation generation and adoption (Dost & Badir, 2019; Dost et al., 2020; Dost et al., 2016). However, given the significance of innovation and its increasingly short life cycle, businesses face the challenge of conducting extensive research to create knowledge for innovation. The authors suggest that it is time for companies to leverage collaboration between humans and AI tools. This human-AI partnership can cultivate a culture of innovation, as AI can uncover hidden patterns and connections that lead to new ideas and solutions. Meanwhile, humans can combine their intuition and reasoning with the vast information available to drive faster and more effective innovation. Additionally, the rapid advancements in AI present opportunities for businesses and governments to enhance human creativity and address the challenges of democratising innovation (Eapen et al., 2023).

Recently, the use of AI in research and innovation has rapidly expanded. For example, a Prosper Insights & Analytics survey revealed that over 44% of respondents regularly use AI for research purposes. In R&D, AI is an iterative tool that promotes efficient technology development and enables faster go-to-market strategies (Forbes, 2024).

Evidence also reveals that, in comparison, ideas generated by humans and AI tools that AI-generated ideas significantly outperform novelty and customer benefits. At the same time, their feasibility is comparable to ideas created by humans (Joosten et al., 2024). In the 2023 Global Innovation Survey by Boston Consulting Group (BCG), over 1000 company leaders placed product development, innovation, and R&D among their top ten priorities. Companies that implemented AI tools experienced a fivefold increase in idea generation and substantial improvements in idea validation and incubation.

Artificial Humans and Innovation in the Commercial Sector

Artificial Humans in Marketing

Businesses using AI as a supporting tool are seemingly transforming how they interact with consumers, particularly in generating, distributing, and managing content. Marketing, especially, is one of these business streams witnessing this transformation on a "very intense scale" (Chintalapati & Pandey, 2022), whereby cutting-edge AI technologies such as GPT-4, DALL-E, and Sora "mimic intelligent human behaviour" (Syam & Sharma, 2018), are increasingly being embraced, experimented with, and gradually deployed in mainstream operations. Since research identifies AI as having significant strengths in creative contexts and great innovation potential, it is plausible that the technology can automate visual advertising content to similarly high levels of innovation, quality, and persuasiveness as experts in the field.

While businesses have started experimenting with AI applications for content creation, the sustainable adoption of the technology seemingly boils down to how effectively it achieves companies' specific marketing objectives. This is a complex task, given that brands' aims, market positions, and industries can vary considerably, especially when AI does not have an innate understanding or knowledge of everything. Instead, in response to human commands, it utilises a large corpus of data (including text, images, and other information it has already learnt from experience) to apply to new situations and create new content variations. Through machine learning (Overgoor et al., 2019), the technology is essentially learning from itself based on available data, reaching conclusions and forming generalisations.

Some argue that this indicates AI is limited to creating content based on existing information it has learnt over time; thus, what it produces lacks truly original ideas. However, this continual interaction has also enabled AI to reach a more intelligent level (Davenport et al., 2020). The growth of data with which AI interacts demonstrates how it constantly learns, evolves, and improves across various human-like intellectual tasks. AI's knowledge bank expands with every input, making this argument (perhaps tenable during AI's initial stages) less significant at this more advanced point in its development. It signals that AI goes beyond (Huang & Rust, 2018) rather simplistic definition, "manifested by machines that exhibit aspects of human intelligence". After all, for AI to produce content to similarly high standards as human creativity, it needs to understand external data accurately, learn from this data, and exhibit flexible adaptability. This way, it can achieve marketing outcomes separate from generating ad content—including analysing consumer data, predicting trends, and delivering personalised results in real time and at scale.

The content AI produces also come down to the detailed instruction of the prompt—communicated via human instruction—that AI algorithms rely on to guide a specific action. However, it is important to stress that—even when a specific prompt has been instructed the data AI relies on can occasionally (though not always) be incomplete or inaccurate (Sedkaoui, 2024). Thus, it is not immune from producing visual errors or mistakes. For instance, AI cannot distinguish between what is true and false (Kumar, 2024)—and so, if the algorithm observes that a certain piece of data has a higher probability of matching the user's prompt, then it will be included in the content regardless of being accurate or not. This is why AI may occasionally present false or misleading information as a fact (Walsh et al., 2024). Inferring how AI (at this phase) is by no means perfect or fully accurate in its creations—and so, naturally bears some limitations. This means it is inevitable that AI will be used with human guidance; thus, the role of artificial humans is of paramount significance.

The Case of McDonald's

While brands could, in theory, adopt AI to automate the entire creative content process (i.e., from audience analysis or segmentation to ideation and content design), they tend to utilise the technology selectively among certain tasks—while still maintaining human oversight. Scholars assert that such usage is predominately for content design, where AI can strengthen consumer preferences by integrating artistic styles into synthetic content (Wang et al., 2023). This way, businesses could adopt the technology to emphasise imagery among posts on social media and other digital platforms. To an extent, brands in the fast-food industry (e.g., McDonald's, Burger King, KFC) have already done so—but interestingly, outside of this market, examples of AI-generated content distributed to the masses are seldom. Signalling that AI in advertising is still relatively in its infancy. It also highlights how industries embrace AI at different speeds—fast food seemingly faster than most. Therefore, through actual case studies, it is worth acknowledging how AI-generated content is utilised in this popular industry.

Visual content has emerged as a critical and influential marketing tool. More specifically, video-based advertisements (combining visual and auditory formats) are an ideal medium for the fast-food industry as individuals seek rapid information consumption. This medium often helps consumers interpret messaging faster, enhances their interest, and simplifies product understanding, yet, as consumers are no longer passive recipients of advertising and their attention spans are increasingly "challenging to maintain" (Chan & Lee, 2023). It suggests that contemporary users may seek and respond better to content that succinctly informs, entertains, and exhibits some form of value.

In line with the growth and popularity of AI's ChatGPT, McDonald's utilised the technology to launch a typographical ad—displaying the chatbot's favourable response towards the prompt: "What is the most iconic burger in the world?". Feeding into this creative novelty, fast-food competitors (including Burger King) adopted the same approach by sharing flattering answers to their prompts—outputting content related to their staple product's merits. This gained much online attention due to its comedic value and was shared widely across media platforms. While the content is very much AI-automated, from a graphic design point of view, including brand colours and bold typefaces indicates careful human oversight. Therefore, signalling how fast-food brands are utilising AI for creative content in a hybrid fashion—considering, Walsh et al. (2024) assert that while technology's vast capabilities are often the focal point and the human element is just as crucial. This suggests collaboration between AI and human creators can yield enhanced results—bringing their unique perspectives and tools to the process.

In saying that, imagery-wise, the frames from Burger King's automated campaign indicate AI's advanced ability to understand some fast-food ad conventions. For instance, although the content did not necessarily depict scenarios that resonate with average consumers, it successfully produced realistic and appetising visuals to accentuate the actual product, including the level of detail among the different ingredients and the slow-motion effects of the overflowing sauce. This indicates that visual appeal influences the effectiveness of such ads. It could be argued that—without the automated voiceover—consumers would perhaps be perplexed whether it was AI-generated or human-created, especially when some individuals have this preconceived idea that AI is substandard to human-created designs, most likely basing this off earlier AI models, which Hill and White (2020) admit, "When the tech first appeared… it was bad". It is also possible that stereotypes around AI (e.g. it is all-knowing) set unrealistic expectations and, in doing so, hinder perceptions of the technology.

It seems that fast-food brands are using AI primarily for their advancements in generating imagery, as opposed to ideation, in which human intelligence seemingly still dominates. The case above heavily spotlighted a pattern whereby artificial intelligence is consistently the narrative's focal point alongside the actual product and often in conjunction with the viral hype around its development. This way, brands can expand their creative concepts and participate in the cultural conversation.

Challenges or Limitations of Artificial Humans in Marketing

AI Scepticism

A limited understanding of AI and its potential likely fuels scepticism around what AI can and cannot accomplish, in other words, when an individual is inclined to question and have reservations. Previous research has shown it to be negatively and significantly associated with people's perceptions (Arango et al. (2023)—thereby, since negative perceptions often lead to weaker intentions to accept, it is likely to have a subsequent influence on consumers' purchase intention, advertisement evaluation, and potentially word of mouth. This correlates with Obermiller et al. (2005); in the advertising context, scepticism was found to correspond with less trust, lower perceived influence, and a more negative attitude towards the advertisements. Therefore, this factor can very much impact how consumers behave as Arango et al. (2023) uncovered similarities in the context of charitable advertising. Potential donors' adoption of AI-created images in ads negatively impacted their intentions. Consumers may feel more sceptical when conscious that the content is artificially generated. This may further signal AI aversion since knowing a piece of AI-generated content lowers their satisfaction and willingness to donate.

Lack of Trust

Distrust—regarding the level of confidence users have in algorithms to carry out actions that benefit them—is another aspect that can negatively impact perceptions. This may be related to the data being fed into AI algorithms, especially when literature has previously acknowledged that this can be flawed, biased or outdated (Davenport et al., 2020). For instance, Shin (2022) found that users with higher trust were found to attribute a higher level of credibility to chatbots and follow their recommendations. The research by Sands et al. (2022) also discovered how consumers perceived AI influencers as less trustworthy than their human counterparts, suggesting that the use of these characters is seemingly less effective for brands that are reliant on high levels of trust.

Bias Embedded Within AI

Several researchers have drawn attention to the bias that AI tools can also exhibit. While this relates to various reasons, Broussard (2023), asserts that problems are baked into our electrical systems because they are also baked into society. In other words, since it is "human universal" for individuals to have biases, the information collected in the datasets often reflects people's sentiments (i.e. potentially carrying biased ideas on race, gender, and other societal issues). For instance, Rose et al.

(2023) assert AI imagery has been shown to produce "formulaic and potentially problematic" images leaning towards certain stereotypes. This questions how well AI-generated ads connect with their target audience in ad campaigns. It can offend seriously. Especially when—despite improvements in AI—researchers could generate tropes about race, wealth, intelligence, religion, and other cultures by requesting depictions of routine activities, common personality traits or the name of another country. In some instances, they found disparities depicted to be more extreme than in the real world. While this does not represent all AI-generated imagery, there is a tendency. In such cases, this is very likely to have an immediate negative impact on consumers' perceptions.

Ultimately, computers are not sentient beings. No matter how advanced the technology becomes, though AI may be able to describe human emotions accurately (i.e. excitement or the physical sensation of being hungry), it can never empathise with humans (Sands et al., 2022). Therefore, while it fulfils a certain role, AI is likely to require significantly more development before it can connect with human beings in the same way that people respond and interact with each other.

Innovation: A Conceptual Shift from Traditional to Contemporary

Traditional Understanding of Innovation

Scholars have identified the link between innovation, improving organisational performance, and gaining a competitive advantage in the marketplace (Govindan, 2022). By and large, innovation is understood as introducing something new or a new idea, method, or device (Dost & Badir, 2019). In other words, innovation aims to create something new or to do existing things in a new way to acquire competitive advantages in a certain period (Al-Khatib & Al-Ghanem, 2022; Bashir & Verma, 2017). Kahn (2018) examined innovation from three distinct perspectives: innovation as an outcome, process, and mindset (see Table 3).

Understanding the concept of innovation is vital for achieving significant organisational competitiveness (Distanont, 2020; Al-Ajlouni, 2021). Valle and Vázquez-Bustelo (2009) also state that researchers and managers focus on identifying methods and practices that boost their effectiveness or success when addressing innovation. Innovation as an outcome is categorised into radical and incremental (Isada & Isada, 2017). Depending on the degree of novelty, radical innovation is characterised by significant improvements in products or services (Nguyen, 2018), while incremental innovation focuses on slight technological changes and adding some new value (Okuyama, 2017). Innovation is traditionally expected to have a clear outcome of either success or failure (Kahn, 2018). However, it is uncertain whether this understanding applies in the Industry 5.0 era, where robots and humans coexist and pursue values different from those of the past.

Table 3 Kahn's (2018) three perspectives on innovation

	Perspective	Focus	Examples
Innovation as an outcome	• The result or output of innovation activities	• Expected outcome or goal to achieve at the end.	• Product innovation • Process innovation • Marketing innovation • Business model innovation • Supply chain innovation • Organisational innovation
Innovation as a process	• Changes in methodology or process to improve efficiency in achieving the outcomes.	• Ways and means to achieve the goals.	• Faster processing • Greater throughput • Production systems • Service delivery systems • Organisational processes
Innovation as a mindset	• Internalisation of innovation: How individuals within an organisation embrace and internalise innovation, fostering a culture that promotes and supports innovative activities at all levels.	• Aspects to consider when achieving innovative outcomes and processes.	• Cross-functional thinking • Design thinking • A human-centred approach to innovation • Organisational culture

A New Conceptual Understanding of Innovation in the Era of Industry 5.0

The adoption of artificial humans in marketing indicates how AI is shaping the future of marketing by generating high-quality and engaging content (across text, audio, image, and video forms) with a certain level of human oversight. This marks a notable shift since what has traditionally been seen as the exclusive domain of human intelligence is now—as observed by Babatunde et al. (2024), which is the most common task that marketers use generative AI for. With AI's capacity to efficiently obtain large and diverse amounts of data, contemporary advertising is perhaps more relevant to individuals and less intrusive. This corresponds with Ford's assertion that modern marketing has seen the usage of AI as a tool for increasing the effectiveness of advertising content and enhancing ad delivery.

Consumers experience increasing ad fatigue (Smith & Yang, 2004), becoming desensitised and often disengaged due to visual ads' saturation and repetitive messaging. While there is the argument that digital spaces today remain cluttered with visual ads, the difference is seemingly how they are much more targeted based on our online search patterns and browsing consumption. In the era of Industry 5.0, we argue that innovation goes beyond simply generating new ideas; it involves implementing them in practice while considering individuals' distinctive contexts. In this vein, innovation is fundamentally a social process (Ziegler, 2017), which requires collaboration through discussions, group formation, and networking to understand individuals better.

Adopting AI and other emerging technologies provides everyone broader access to resources (Gupta et al., 2020), fostering a degree of democratisation in sharing knowledge and technology. As humans utilise AI as an additional tool depending on their purposes, ideas, ethos, and beliefs, the authors suggest that innovation in the era of Industry 5.0 is defined by less radical but more incremental advancements adapted to individual contexts or specific settings. This aligns with the argument that AI is inherently limited to generating content based on the information it has learned over time, resulting in outputs that often lack truly original ideas. Furthermore, the primary goal of innovation extends beyond merely acquiring competitive advantages; it focuses on maintaining sustainable competitive advantages (Ma, 2000) by creating distinctive values that organisations pursue.

Potential Research Areas for Consideration

Despite the numerous opportunities and outcomes of AI-human collaboration, there appear to be critical challenges in future research that require close attention. For instance, AI relies on sensors, data, algorithms, and computing power, which eventually requires businesses to place continuous monitoring and maintenance. This responsibility falls on humans, who are ethically responsible for the AI they create, deploy, and utilise (Henz, 2021). At the same time, the use of AI and other emerging technologies enhances efficacy and efficiency (Gupta et al., 2020), it is suggested that research in the social sector will benefit society. This research should consider the role of artificial humans and innovation in promoting equitable, sustainable, and human-centred approaches in the era of Industry 5.0 (Dollija & Gura, 2022).

One type of innovation that could potentially be useful in social sector research is social innovation (SI), which is created and carried out by individuals working together to address social challenges in their environment (Dawson & Daniel, 2010). SI is "the development and implementation of new products, services or models to meet social needs and create new social relationships" (Murray, 2010). Another definition of SI is the development of new solutions to social issues that are more effective, efficient, sustainable, and, crucially, fairer than existing approaches, with the primary goal of benefiting society rather than just private individuals (Agostini et al., 2017). SI develops new solutions to societal and economic challenges that benefit society rather than just a few individuals by fostering new social relationships or collaborations (Caulier-Grice, 2012). SI often addresses societal challenges such as financial and economic crises, the scarcity of non-renewable resources, energy problems, climate change, health imbalances, and other radical environmental concerns (Edwards-Schachter et al., 2012). This implies that future research could investigate which areas of social problems would most benefit from AI-human collaboration.

Artificial Humans and Innovation in Education

AI has a crucial role in education by automating administrative tasks, allowing educators to focus more on human-centred teaching (Riordan et al., 2024). There is a prevailing belief that integrating AI-supported technological tools into the classroom enhances students' overall educational experience. While there is ongoing debate about the potential threat of AI replacing teachers, it is evident that AI complements the teaching and learning process. This allows educators to focus on personalised instruction and strengthens human-led teaching methods. For example, a recent survey by the World Economic Forum found that personalised tutoring significantly improves learning outcomes, with students receiving tailored instruction outperforming 98% of their peers in traditional classroom settings. Personalisation means subjectification (Biesta, 2015). Furthermore, it aids each student in achieving their own goals through self-actualisation. This is an area where AI has limited capacities (Holmes & Tuomi, 2022); thus, the role of artificial humans is highly valued.

Considering the potential costs associated with personalised or tailored tutoring is essential. Therefore, implementing AI in education should be a collaborative effort prioritising equity. This approach ensures that all students can access these advancements regardless of their background. In other words, integrating AI into education provides a valuable means of improving teaching and learning by addressing the diverse needs of students while striving for equitable access to educational resources.

Artificial Humans in Community Development

Not long ago, researchers put their trust in the role of AI in community development due to its significant impact on society (Makridakis, 2017). Many positive AI applications provide valuable insights that aid in making informed decisions (Kumar, 2024). With its ability to process vast amounts of data at incredible speeds, AI can analyse demographic information, social trends, and economic data, offering critical insights from a community development perspective (Gupta et al., 2020). These insights help businesses and policymakers make informed decisions about resource distribution and create relevant community programmes. AI's predictive analytics also serve as a powerful tool for forecasting future trends in economic challenges (Furman & Seamans, 2019) and healthcare needs (Rong et al., 2020). The context of AI's role in community development directly ties into social innovation by demonstrating how AI can drive positive societal change (Brundage, 2016). However, it is essential to acknowledge that AI carries certain risks. For instance, misuse of AI can result in severe issues such as false information, cybersecurity risks, copyright infringements, privacy violations, loss of employment, and ethical concerns (Rességuier & Rodrigues, 2020).

Although AI technologies are valuable for education and social development, users must employ these tools responsibly. Responsible use can promote sustainable community development and encourage ethical practices. By doing this, AI can catalyse social innovation, efficient resource allocation, and the development of programmes that effectively address community needs and enhance decision-making (Kumar, 2024).

Conclusion

The chapter explores how AI can coexist with humans to create value and drive innovation in the era of Industry 5.0. The distinctive feature of Industry 5.0 is not merely maximising efficiency or productivity but developing a sustainable, human-centric, and resilient society, relying on the synergistic relationship between humans and machines. By delving deeply into the use and role of artificial humans in the commercial sector through a real-life case study, this chapter provides a valuable discussion on how AI and humans can collaborate to create value and foster innovation. Furthermore, innovation is examined, highlighting the shift from traditional views to contemporary understanding. Additionally, potential research areas are suggested, focusing on how artificial humans can be utilised in the social sector to drive social innovation.

To conclude, it is believed that advanced AI technologies are ultimately not "sentient beings" like humans. It does not understand or perceive the world similarly (e.g., real thoughts and feelings or personalities). Therefore, they might be able to emulate reactions based on human learning models cleverly—but will never feel emotions or reactions the same as a human does. In other words, it strongly fuels the argument that AI can never be as effective without human input or creativity directing it. Therefore, the role of humans in the era of Industry 5.0 should never be underestimated, especially when making decisions aimed at fostering a morally healthy society.

References

Agostini, M. R., Vieira, L. M., Tondolo, R. D. R. P., & Tondolo, V. A. G. (2017). An overview on social innovation research: Guiding future studies. *BBR. Brazilian Business Review, 14*, 385–402.

Al-Ajlouni, M. I. (2021). Can high-performance work systems (HPWS) promote organisational innovation? Employee perspective-taking, engagement and creativity in a moderated mediation model. *Employee Relations: The International Journal, 43*, 373–397.

Al-Khatib, A. W., & Al-Ghanem, E. M. (2022). Radical innovation, incremental innovation, and competitive advantage, the moderating role of technological intensity: Evidence from the manufacturing sector in Jordan. *European Business Review, 34*, 344–369.

Arango, L., Singaraju, S. P., & Niininen, O. (2023). Consumer responses to AI-generated charitable giving ads. *Journal of Advertising, 52*, 486–503.

Babatunde, S. O., Odejide, O. A., Edunjobi, T. E., & Ogundipe, D. O. (2024). The role of AI in marketing personalization: A theoretical exploration of consumer engagement strategies. *International Journal of Management & Entrepreneurship Research, 6*, 936–949.

Bashir, M., & Verma, R. (2017). Why business model innovation is the new competitive advantage. *IUP Journal of Business Strategy, 14*, 7.

Biesta, G. J. (2015). *Good education in an age of measurement: Ethics, politics, democracy*. Routledge.

Broussard, M. (2023). *More than a glitch: Confronting race, gender, and ability bias in tech*. MIT Press.

Brundage, M. (2016). Artificial intelligence and responsible innovation. Fundamental issues of artificial intelligence, 543–554.

Caulier-Grice, J. (2012). Defining social innovation. *A deliverable of the project: The theoretical, empirical and policy foundations for building social innovation in Europe (TEPSIE), European Commission 7th framework Programme/European Commission, DG Research,* 18.
Chan, C. K. Y., & Lee, K. K. (2023). The AI generation gap: Are gen Z students more interested in adopting generative AI such as ChatGPT in teaching and learning than their gen X and millennial generation teachers? *Smart Learning Environments, 10*, 60.
Chintalapati, S., & Pandey, S. K. (2022). Artificial intelligence in marketing: A systematic literature review. *International Journal of Market Research, 64*, 38–68.
Davenport, T., Guha, A., Grewal, D., & Bressgott, T. (2020). How artificial intelligence will change the future of marketing. *Journal of the Academy of Marketing Science, 48*, 24–42.
Dawson, P., & Daniel, L. (2010). Understanding social innovation: A provisional framework. *International Journal of Technology Management, 51*, 9–21.
Deeb, A. M., & Maddigan, J. (2023). Predictors of clinical deterioration of hospitalized adult medical patients: An integrative literature review protocol. *Saudi Critical Care Journal, 7*, 43–48.
Dellermann, D., Ebel, P., Söllner, M., & Leimeister, J. M. (2019). Hybrid intelligence. *Business & Information Systems Engineering, 61*, 637–643.
Distanont, A. (2020). The role of innovation in creating a competitive advantage. *Kasetsart Journal of Social Sciences, 41*, 15–21–15–21.
Dollija, E., & Gura, K. (2022). The role of humans as key enablers of industry 5.0. In *International conference on economic scientific research-theoretical, empirical and practical approaches, 2022* (pp. 39–55). Springer.
Dost, M., & Badir, Y. F. (2019). Generation or adoption? The role of social capital. *Management Decision, 57*, 1457–1471.
Dost, M., Badir, Y. F., Ali, Z., & Tariq, A. (2016). The impact of intellectual capital on innovation generation and adoption. *Journal of Intellectual Capital, 17*, 675–695.
Dost, M., Badir, Y. F., Sambasivan, M., & Umrani, W. A. (2020). Open-and-closed process innovation generation and adoption: Analyzing the effects of sources of knowledge. *Technology in Society, 62*, 101309.
Eapen, T., Finkenstadt, D. J., Folk, J., & Venkataswamy, L. (2023). How generative AI can augment human creativity. *Harvard Business Review, 101*.
Edwards-Schachter, M. E., Matti, C. E., & Alcántara, E. (2012). Fostering quality of life through social innovation: A living lab methodology study case. *Review of Policy Research, 29*, 672–692.
Furman, J., & Seamans, R. (2019). AI and the economy. *Innovation Policy and the Economy, 19*, 161–191.
Gorli, R., & Kishore, M. (2024). Automation of image processing with artificial intelligence and pattern recognition methods. In *Fusion of artificial intelligence and machine learning in advanced image processing*. Apple Academic Press.
Govindan, K. (2022). How artificial intelligence drives sustainable frugal innovation: A multitheoretical perspective. *IEEE Transactions on Engineering Management, 71*, 638–655.
Gupta, S., Kumar, V., & Karam, E. (2020). New-age technologies-driven social innovation: What, how, where, and why? *Industrial Marketing Management, 89*, 499–516.
Henz, P. (2021). Ethical and legal responsibility for artificial intelligence. *Discover Artificial Intelligence, 1*, 2.
Hill, K., & White, J. (2020). Designed to deceive: Do these people look real to you. *The New York Times, 11*, 21.
Holmes, W., & Tuomi, I. (2022). State of the art and practice in AI in education. *European Journal of Education, 57*, 542–570.
Huang, M.-H., & Rust, R. T. (2018). Artificial intelligence in service. *Journal of Service Research, 21*, 155–172.
Huff, A. S. (2009). *Designing research for publication*. Sage.
Isada, F., & Isada, Y. (2017). An empirical study regarding radical innovation, research and development management, and leadership. *Naše gospodarstvo/Our economy, 63*, 22–31.

Joosten, J., Bilgram, V., Hahn, A., & Totzek, D. (2024). Comparing the ideation quality of humans with generative artificial intelligence. *IEEE Engineering Management Review., 52*, 153.

Kahn, K. B. (2018). Understanding innovation. *Business Horizons, 61*, 453–460.

Korteling, J., Van De Boer-Visschedijk, G. C., Blankendaal, R. A., Boonekamp, R. C., & Eikelboom, A. R. (2021). Human-versus artificial intelligence. *Frontiers in Artificial Intelligence, 4*, 622364.

Kumar, W. (2024). *Artificial intelligence: A comprehensive exploration of current realities and future trajectories*, Guiding Informed Decision-Making in a Dynamic Technological Landscape. EasyChair.

Le Pennec, M., & Raufflet, E. (2018). Value creation in inter-organizational collaboration: An empirical study. *Journal of Business Ethics, 148*, 817–834.

Leng, J., Sha, W., Wang, B., Zheng, P., Zhuang, C., Liu, Q., Wuest, T., Mourtzis, D., & Wang, L. (2022). Industry 5.0: Prospect and retrospect. *Journal of Manufacturing Systems, 65*, 279–295.

Liu, Y., Zhang, Z., Jiang, S., & Ding, Y. (2024). Application of big data technology combined with clustering algorithm in manufacturing production analysis system. *Decision Making: Applications in Management and Engineering, 7*, 237–253.

Ma, H. (2000). Competitive advantage and firm performance. *Competitiveness Review: An International Business Journal, 10*, 15–32.

Makridakis, S. (2017). The forthcoming artificial intelligence (AI) revolution: Its impact on society and firms. *Futures, 90*, 46–60.

Mayor, A. (2018). *Gods and robots: Myths, machines, and ancient dreams of technology*.

Moran, M. E. (2007). Evolution of robotic arms. *Journal of Robotic Surgery, 1*, 103–111.

Murray, R. (2010). *The open book of social innovation*. National Endowment for Science, Technology and the Art.

Nguyen, T. (2018). CEO incentives and corporate innovation. *Financial Review, 53*, 255–300.

Obermiller, C., Spangenberg, E., & Maclachlan, D. L. (2005). Ad skepticism: The consequences of disbelief. *Journal of Advertising, 34*, 7–17.

Okuyama, R. (2017). Importance of tacit knowledge in incremental innovation: Implications from drug discovery cases. *Journal of Strategy and Management, 10*, 118–130.

Overgoor, G., Chica, M., Rand, W., & Weishampel, A. (2019). Letting the computers take over: Using AI to solve marketing problems. *California Management Review, 61*, 156–185.

Potočan, V., Lazányi, K., & Nedelko, Z. (2024). *Organizations and industry 4.0: Management solutions beyond technology*. Taylor & Francis.

Rességuier, A., & Rodrigues, R. (2020). AI ethics should not remain toothless! A call to bring back the teeth of ethics. *Big Data & Society, 7*, 2053951720942541.

Riordan, J.-P., Revell, L., Bowie, B., Hulbert, S., Woolley, M., & Thomas, C. (2024). Multimodal classroom interaction analysis using video-based methods of the pedagogical tactic of (un) grouping. *Pedagogies: An International Journal*, 1–18.

Rong, G., Mendez, A., Assi, E. B., Zhao, B., & Sawan, M. (2020). Artificial intelligence in healthcare: Review and prediction case studies. *Engineering, 6*, 291–301.

Rose, K., Massey, V., Marshall, B., & Cardon, P. (2023). IS professors' perspectives on AI-assisted programming. *Issues in Information Systems, 24*.

Rosheim, M. (2006). *Leonardo's lost robots*. Springer.

Sands, S., Campbell, C. L., Plangger, K., & Ferraro, C. (2022). Unreal influence: Leveraging AI in influencer marketing. *European Journal of Marketing, 56*, 1721–1747.

Schröder, A. J., Cuypers, M., & Götting, A. (2024). From industry 4.0 to industry 5.0: The triple transition digital, green and social. In *Industry 4.0 and the road to sustainable steelmaking in Europe: Recasting the future*. Springer International Publishing.

Sedkaoui, S. (2024). *Automated data analytics: Combining human creativity and AI power using ChatGPT*. John Wiley & Sons.

Shin, D. (2022). How do people judge the credibility of algorithmic sources? *AI & SOCIETY*, 1–16.

Smith, R. E., & Yang, X. (2004). Toward a general theory of creativity in advertising: Examining the role of divergence. *Marketing Theory, 4*, 31–58.

Syam, N., & Sharma, A. (2018). Waiting for a sales renaissance in the fourth industrial revolution: Machine learning and artificial intelligence in sales research and practice. *Industrial Marketing Management, 69*, 135–146.
Valle, S., & Vázquez-Bustelo, D. (2009). Concurrent engineering performance: Incremental versus radical innovation. *International Journal of Production Economics, 119*, 136–148.
Vlahos, J. (2019). *Talk to me: Amazon, Google, Apple and the race for voice-controlled AI*. Random House.
Walsh, M., Worrell, C. & Scanlon, T. (2024). *Toward use of artificial intelligence for advanced persistent threat detection.*
Wang, C., Liu, T., Zhu, Y., Wang, H., Wang, X., & Zhao, S. (2023). The influence of consumer perception on purchase intention: Evidence from cross-border E-commerce platforms. *Heliyon, 9*, e21617.
Xu, H., Pang, H., Winnink, J., Luo, R., & Wang, C. (2023). Disambiguating the definitions of the concept 'transformative innovation'. *Journal of Information Science, 49*, 932–951.
Ziegler, R. (2017). Social innovation as a collaborative concept. *Innovation: The European Journal of Social Science Research, 30*, 388–405.

Dr. MinHye Lee is a Senior Lecturer in Marketing at the University of Winchester, UK. Her research focuses on symbolic consumption, including consumer identity and consumer culture. Within the context of consumption, she is particularly passionate about ethical and sustainable practices. Recently, she has expanded her research interests to include innovation and emerging technologies.

Dr. Mir Dost is a Senior Lecturer in Innovation and Strategic Management at the University of Winchester in the UK. With over a decade of experience in teaching, research, and consultancy, Dr. Dost's expertise lies in innovation management, knowledge management, entrepreneurship, circular economy, frugal innovation, and bricolage. His research has been published in prestigious journals, including the Journal of Knowledge Management, the European Journal of Innovation Management, and Technology in Society.

Jude Bennett is an MSc Marketing graduate whose research background in sociolinguistics has shaped his interest in society's attitudes and perceptions. His work seeks to offer fresh insights into how AI is reshaping and being utilised within the marketing landscape, alongside the impact on contemporary consumers. Based in London, he has a keen interest in exploring further behavioural patterns within the dynamic world of marketing/advertising and pursuing career opportunities in this field.

Artificial Intelligence vs. Human Creativity from an Idea Management Perspective

Elina Mikelsone, Matijs Babris, Andra Marta Babre, and Anna Salnikova

Introduction

From boardrooms filled with Post-it notes to computers capable of generating, combining, and transforming familiar concepts into new ideas, idea management is significantly evolving. Where are we now, and where might we head with idea management? Are humans the only ones who can truly create new ideas? Is creativity a unique human skill that gives us an advantage over artificial intelligence? Creativity remains essential for addressing real-world challenges and is increasingly seen as a significant driver of societal advancement (Sawyer & Henriksen, 2024).

Today, many commercially available web-based idea management systems allow for continuous creativity, enabling users to generate and evaluate ideas inside and outside traditional company settings. However, with the rapid development of artificial intelligence, we may need to consider if and how we could eventually transfer certain aspects of the creative process—often labor-intensive and sometimes flawed—over to AI. And from an ethical standpoint, should we do this? This chapter raises these questions, drawing on elements of the creativity process.

Ideas are the foundation of all significant innovations—sometimes they lead to success, other times to failure, depending on the knowledge available or newly discovered. Can humans and computers manage ideas effectively together? Should AI replace the human side of creativity and idea management, or could it be used to support it? Are computers even necessary for the idea management process? Or might they diminish human creativity and our potential to generate impactful ideas?

E. Mikelsone (✉) · M. Babris · A. M. Babre
Riga Technical University, Riga, Latvia
e-mail: elina.mikelsone@rtu.lv; Matijs.Babris_1@rtu.lv; andra-marta.babre@rtu.lv

A. Salnikova
Riga Stradins University, Kurzemes Rajons, Riga, Latvia
e-mail: 044414@rsu.edu.lv

M. Dabić et al. (eds.), *Artificial Humans*, Future of Business and Finance,
https://doi.org/10.1007/978-3-032-06604-6_10

A simple folk story distinguishes pure creativity and effective idea management. In the story, a beekeeper visits a wise man, asking how to get more honey. The wise man suggests an idea, which the beekeeper immediately implements, only to return later, reporting that half his bees have died. The wise man gives another idea, and again, the beekeeper follows it straight away, but the other half of the bees die. When he returns, the wise man says, "Sad—I had so many more ideas." This story reminds us that idea management goes beyond idea generation; it includes evaluating and comparing ideas to choose the best one. Companies recognize this, and many are adopting web-based idea management systems to support this process. However, what are the advantages and drawbacks of human versus AI-generated ideas and their evaluation?

AI is reshaping innovation strategies, improving efficiency, decision-making, and sustainability, with competitive advantages and future potential in sustainability-focused AI and industrial applications. Increasingly, innovation management looks at the partnership between AI and human creativity, particularly with Generative AI (GAI), which is seen both as a collaborator in creative processes and an automation tool (Ramaul et al., 2024; Amankwah-Amoah et al., 2024). Traditional AI has been primarily used to increase productivity through process optimization and repetitive task management. Still, GAI takes this further, generating novel ideas and data that can amplify human creativity (Cooper, 2024) and it raises questions about intelectual property (Drozdal, 2021; Drozdal et al., 2021). However, since its given data and programming limit AI, it may need to produce more original, intuitive, or emotionally rich insights (Grilli & Pedota, 2024).

AI's role in innovation is increasingly viewed as complementary, enhancing human capabilities by streamlining tasks such as ideation and prototyping. This frees individuals to focus on more meaningful, creative work (Bouschery et al., 2023). The rise of generative AI offers new avenues for incorporating technology into creative tasks, raising questions about its impact on human creators and encouraging the design of AI tools that support, rather than replace, human creativity (O'Toole & Horvát, 2024). As AI evolves, it holds exciting possibilities for transforming the innovation landscape by enhancing—rather than replacing—human creativity (Roberts & Candi, 2024). Still, the relationship between AI and creativity is complex and largely unexplored, bringing both challenges and opportunities for the future of work and innovation.

Emerging research highlights AI's growing role in human creativity, particularly in knowledge management, where AI enhances knowledge creation, distribution, and innovation (Issac & William, 2021). While AI excels in data processing and close-ended problem-solving, its lack of emotional depth and originality suggests it is better suited to augmenting rather than replacing human creativity (Paesano, 2021). Studies show AI can outperform humans in question complexity and some creative tasks but still falls short in originality (Raz et al., 2024). Tools like ChatGPT improve individual creativity, especially when paired with innovation orientation and agile leadership (Thomas et al., 2024), underscoring AI's potential in collaborative creativity.

Studies have shown that while artificial intelligence can significantly boost creative thinking, it also introduces obstacles that could obstruct creativity and diminish creative confidence (Habib et al., 2024; Yang, 2020). Additionally, there are prejudices against AI. For instance, research discovered that AI-generated products, particularly those that are highly practical, often receive lower creativity ratings when labeled as AI-created. This bias is more pronounced among individuals who see AI as a substantial threat, highlighting the influence of both the characteristics of the product and the identity of the creator on creativity assessments (Hattori et al., 2024; Califano et al., 2024).

Research highlights AI's role in augmenting creativity, particularly in automated content creation, data-driven art, and innovation (Boden, 2004; Boden, 2014; McCormack et al., 2019). AI generates diverse ideas quickly, leveraging vast datasets to uncover novel patterns (Yang et al., 2020), making it valuable in brainstorming and innovation management, where speed and quantity are key (Sawyer, 2011). However, AI struggles with context, practicality, and nuance, often producing ideas lacking depth compared to human creativity, which draws on experience and emotional intelligence.

This study examines neutral and personality-driven AI configurations, revealing how AI complements human input while addressing challenges like biases and feasibility. It provides practical insights into integrating AI into creative processes, emphasizing its role as a collaborator, not a replacement.

The findings also raise policy and ethical concerns, such as intellectual property rights and inclusivity, highlighting the need for guidelines to ensure ethical AI use in creativity-driven industries. Despite progress, gaps remain in understanding how AI complements or challenges human creativity in real-world contexts. This research bridges these gaps, offering insights for innovation management, policymaking, and the design of future AI tools.

The main goal of this study was to assess the creative ability of a human team compared to artificial intelligence (AI) when set up in various ways. The focus was on examining both the number and quality of ideas generated by a neutral AI versus an AI with a more assertive personality.

Tasks to reach the aim:

1. Task 1: Facilitate two separate sessions of brainstorming activities where both the human participants and the AI engage with the same prompts. However, the AI should be set to operate under distinct configurations—one being neutral and the other having an ego-driven approach
2. Task 2: Measure the number of ideas generated by the human team and AI in each round to assess idea quantity as an indicator of divergent thinking
3. Task 3: Evaluate the quality of the ideas using a panel of expert judges based on predefined criteria such as novelty, feasibility, impact, variety, and depth
4. Task 4: Analyze the influence of AI personalities on the diversity and quality of ideas in Round 2, focusing on how different ego-driven AI traits affect the creative process
5. Task 5: Compare the human team's and AI's performance across both rounds to determine AI's strengths and limitations in creative tasks relative to human creativity

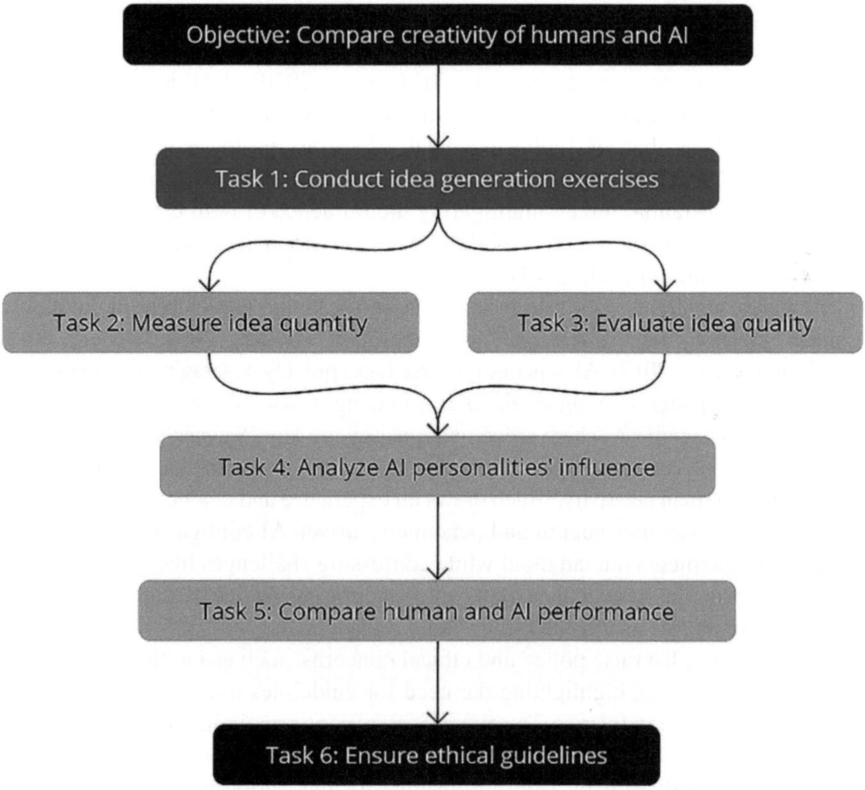

Fig. 1 Main research steps (*Source: created by authors)*

See Fig. 1. for the primary research steps.

The study adopted a within-subject framework to compare a human team with artificial intelligence over two rounds of creative brainstorming tasks. In the first round, participants evaluated a neutral AI, which lacked any ego-centric characteristics, against a human team to determine the effect of unbiased reasoning in idea generation. The second round introduced an AI with ego-driven traits, showcasing four different personalities to represent various creative approaches, and both groups tackled a new challenge. The assessment of the ideas focused on creativity research standards, which included the following:

1. Originality: The extent to which the ideas were new and differed from current solutions
2. Practicality: The feasibility and potential for real-world implementation of the ideas
3. Effectiveness: The ability of the ideas to address the problem at hand successfully
4. Diversity: The range and variation of the ideas produced
5. Detail: The comprehensiveness and sophistication of the suggested solutions

This research stands out due to its innovative method of examining the interaction between human creativity and artificial intelligence (AI) within a structured experimental framework, focusing specifically on the effects of various AI configurations on creative outcomes. Although prior research has investigated AI's role in creative endeavors, this study introduces a fresh perspective by incorporating an ego-driven AI with unique personalities to assess their impact on idea generation. The exploration of ego within AI is a relatively new field in computational creativity, highlighting the importance of this research in enhancing our understanding of AI's involvement in creative collaboration and competition with humans.

The experimental design also breaks new ground by integrating two distinct AI setups: one that is neutral and uses probabilistic reasoning to generate ideas and another that is ego-driven, mimicking human-like biases and subjective preferences. This dual setup provides a comprehensive examination of how personality traits in AI might either boost or hinder creative processes, aligning with the theories proposed by Gero and Maher (2013) concerning cognitive models of creative design thinking. Moreover, the focus on both the quantity and quality of ideas, assessed through established creativity metrics (Runco & Acar, 2012), lends a rigorous approach to the analysis, ensuring that the results contribute meaningfully to the wider research on AI and creativity. See Fig. 2 for a mind-map illustrating the originality of the research.

This study adds to the growing collection of works focused on artificial intelligence and creativity by providing a comparative evaluation of the creative processes of AI and humans. It delves into how AI personalities subtly influence creative activities, an aspect that remains largely unexamined in computational creativity research.

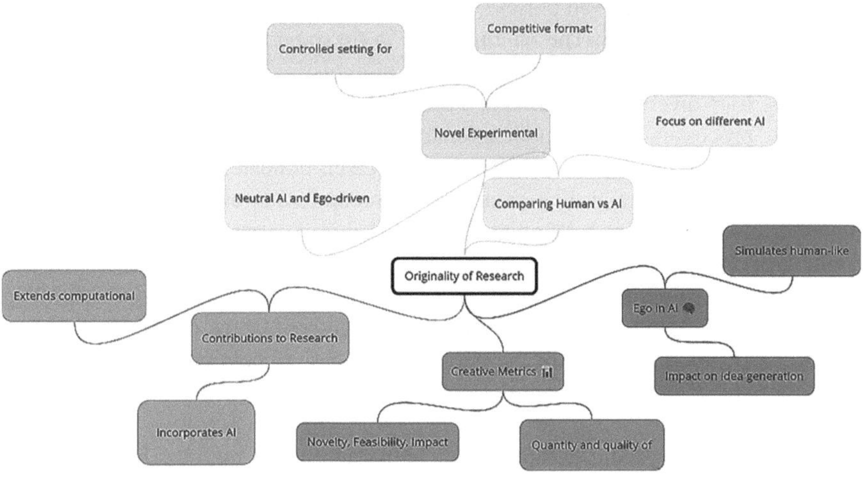

Fig. 2 Originality mind-map of the research (*Source: created by authors)*

Methods

This study was carried out as part of the "Biggest Brainstorming in the World" event in September 2023, which gathered creative individuals from all over the world to engage in a variety of innovation-centric activities. The experiment, serving as an additional feature of the event, offered a distinctive chance to evaluate human creativity against AI within a highly interactive and dynamic setting. By integrating the experiment into this large-scale brainstorming session, real-time evaluation of AI's ability to both complement and challenge human creativity during intense idea generation was made possible.

The study explored the variations in creative output between human teams and artificial intelligence (AI) under two separate setups. It primarily aimed to evaluate the number and quality of ideas produced during creative tasks and examine the influence of AI on idea generation. This section details the experimental approach, including how participants were chosen, the design of the experiment, the techniques used for measurement, and the methods of data analysis. The experiment's design and analysis are grounded in relevant research and theories related to creativity, AI, and collaboration.

Human Team: The team of human participants was carefully chosen through a purposive sampling approach, focusing on individuals from various professional and academic backgrounds in fields like design, marketing, engineering, and the arts. This selection was guided by research suggesting that diverse groups tend to produce a wider array of ideas and solutions compared to homogeneous ones (Paulus & Yang, 2000). The team comprised five members, aligning with studies that indicate smaller teams (3–6 members) are more effective in fostering creative productivity and reducing the inefficiencies associated with larger groups (Hackman & Morris, 1975). These participants had differing levels of experience in creative problem-solving but had not previously worked with AI in their professional roles to prevent any preconceived biases.

Artificial Intelligence: The AI employed in the experiment was programmed to operate in two distinct modes: a neutral, non-egoistic AI and an AI with an ego, featuring four diverse personalities. This AI system utilized sophisticated natural language processing (NLP) models, enabling it to produce coherent and context-relevant responses to creative challenges. Research indicates that AI, especially in NLP, can emulate human-like creativity by recombining established concepts in innovative ways (Colton & Wiggins, 2012). For this experiment, the publicly accessible OpenAI GPT-3.5 model was used. Besides generating standard neutral responses, three unique AI personas were created: (AI-1) "Elon Tusk," a technology enthusiast; (AI-2) "Pythagoras," inspired by the ancient Greek mathematician; and (AI-3) "PAL 9000," known for the phrase, 'I am here to help you, but I might take over the world.' The visual representations of these personas were crafted using DALL·E 2.

The study employed a within-subject approach, where both the human participants and the AI engaged in two separate sessions of creative brainstorming activities. Each session featured a distinct AI setup, enabling a comparative analysis of

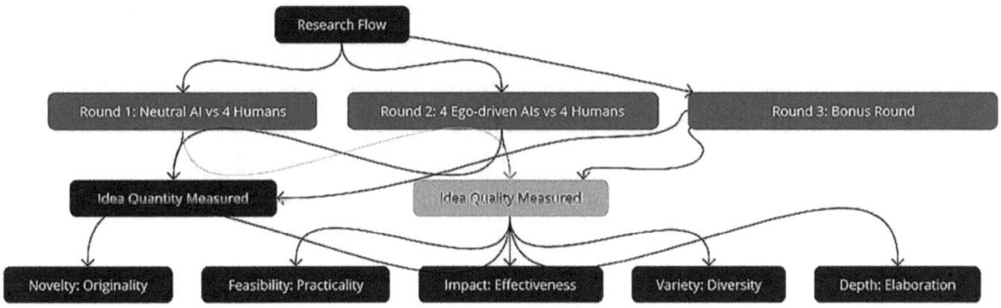

Fig. 3 Main research design elements (*Source: created by authors*)

performance across different scenarios. Key components of the experimental design are illustrated in Fig. 3.

Round 1: Neutral AI Configuration

In the initial phase of the experiment, the AI was programmed to function without attributes related to ego, focusing solely on generating ideas. It used patterns in data and probabilistic analysis to create ideas, without applying emotional or personal judgment to sort or prioritize them. Both the human team and this unbiased AI received the same set of prompts. This stage involved three questions: the classic riddle 'Why did the chicken cross the road?'; a business inquiry about 'What is the market strategy for creating the most profitable lemonade stand?'; and a futuristic concern, 'How can we prevent AI from taking over human jobs?' The purpose of this phase was to evaluate the ability of the AI and human team to produce a large number of ideas while minimizing subjective bias in the AI's reasoning. This method reflects approaches used in research concerning human-AI collaborative idea generation.

In the second phase, the AI adopted three different roles, each representing a distinct creative viewpoint: (AI-1) "Elon Tusk," embodying a tech-optimistic outlook; (AI-2) "Pythagoras," drawing inspiration from the ancient Greek mathematician's logical approach; and (AI-3) "PAL 9000," with a somewhat ominous statement, 'I am here to help you, but I might take over the world.' The same human team competed against these AI roles with a new prompt: How can technology improve education for underrepresented communities? Similar to the first phase, this exercise was conducted over 30 min, with the quantity of ideas produced by each group noted.

In this second phase, more complex questions were posed to evaluate if the AI personas could exhibit abstract thinking alongside logical reasoning. The prompts included questions such as 'How can you go 25 days without sleep?'; 'How do you make one disappear?'; and 'Name three items you would take to a deserted island.' As before, the session lasted 30 min, and the number of ideas generated by both groups was documented. This phase aimed to examine how personality and bias affected the AI's creative outputs. Previous studies indicate that incorporating personality traits into AI systems can either boost or limit creativity, depending on how these traits affect decision-making processes.

Following the main experiment, an additional round was introduced, featuring a single prompt directed at both groups. The scenario presented was: 'Imagine you are rapidly filling with water, with no windows or doors. How do you escape?' This final round was designed to assess whether the AI personas could engage in imaginative thinking, moving beyond logical, data-focused responses to devise inventive solutions in a hypothetical situation.

Throughout each session, the total count of ideas produced by both the human participants and the AI was meticulously tracked. Counting ideas is a common approach in creativity studies to gauge divergent thinking, which is the capability to come up with various possible solutions to a particular challenge (Runco & Acar, 2012).

The quality of ideas was measured using a set of criteria formulated from earlier investigations into creative problem-solving (Amabile, 1983). These criteria included the following:

- Originality: How distinct and innovative the ideas were compared to current solutions
- Practicality: The ease and likelihood of putting the ideas into practice
- Effectiveness: The potential of the ideas to address the problem at hand successfully
- Diversity: The range and variety in the ideas produced
- Complexity: The extent of detail and thoroughness in the proposed solutions.

Each idea was evaluated by a trio of independent experts skilled in creativity, innovation, and technology. They rated the ideas on a 1 to 5 scale based on the aforementioned criteria.

During the second round, an additional analysis was performed to explore the influence of different AI personalities on the variety and quality of ideas. The range of ideas produced by each AI personality was scrutinized to understand the impact on the nature of ideas generated. Past studies on AI personalities in creative contexts offered a basis for assessing this interaction (Gero & Maher, 2013).

Descriptive statistics and t-tests were employed to compare the volume of ideas produced by the human team and AI over two rounds, aiming to identify any significant disparities in their outputs. To examine whether creativity scores varied between the human team and AI across both rounds, quality scores underwent analysis of variance (ANOVA). Additionally, regression analysis was conducted to explore differences in certain quality aspects of the ideas presented.

The concepts produced underwent thematic analysis to pinpoint shared themes, patterns, and differences in creativity between the human participants and artificial intelligence. This examination was especially pertinent during the second round when AI personas demonstrated varied thinking influenced by their inherent biases. Thematic coding adhered to recognized models for classifying innovative ideas within problem-solving studies, as outlined by Sawyer in 2011.

The study followed ethical guidelines, ensuring informed consent, anonymity, and transparency about AI features and the experiment. Independent assessments and blind scoring minimized bias in evaluating AI creativity. By analyzing various AI personas and using established creativity metrics, the research provided structured insights into AI's strengths and limitations in idea generation and creative problem-solving.

Results

Key Results

A study comparing how AI and humans generate ideas revealed notable differences in both the number and quality of ideas produced during two phases of evaluation. Refer to Table 1 for details.

A notable difference between AI and human participants was the substantial number of ideas each produced. In both phases of the study, AI consistently surpassed humans in generating ideas. In the first phase, AI came up with an impressive total of 42 ideas, while human participants managed to produce 22. This pattern was similar in the second phase, as AI generated 32 ideas, compared to the 21 ideas from humans. In the Bonus round, AI produced six ideas, whereas the humans had just one. These findings show that AI is inherently capable of producing a much larger volume of ideas than humans within the same period. However, this discovery brings up significant questions regarding the balance between the quantity and quality of ideas, which becomes clear when assessing the ideas using various quality standards.

A group of five specialists in idea management assessed the quality of ideas using five critical criteria: originality, practicality, potential impact, diversity, and

Table 1 Key results

			Idea quality* (average evaluation by five idea management experts)				
		Idea quantity	Novelty: the ideas were unique and original compared to existing solutions.	Feasibility: the practicality and likelihood of the ideas being implemented	Impact: the potential of the ideas to solve the given problem effectively	Variety: the diversity and range of ideas generated	Depth: the level of detail and elaboration present in the proposed solutions
Round 1	Humans	22	5	4	5	4	4
	AI	42	2	3	3	2	2
Round 2	Humans	21	5	4	5	4	4
	AI	32	4	3	3	4	3
Bonus round	Humans	1	5	4	5	4	4
	AI	6	2	3	3	2	3

Source: created by authors

level of detail. These criteria provided a more comprehensive evaluation beyond just the number of ideas generated.

1. Originality (the uniqueness and creativity of the ideas).

Originality, which measures how unique and creative the ideas are, was an area where human contributors consistently excelled, achieving a perfect score in every round. This demonstrates their ability to harness creativity for innovative ideas. On the other hand, AI struggled with originality in the first round, scoring a 2, but showed improvement in the second round with a score of 4. However, in the bonus round, the AI's score dropped back to 2. These findings indicate that while AI showed some progress in creating original ideas, it still lags behind humans in consistently generating unique and creative concepts.

2. Practicality (the likelihood of ideas being implemented).

Practicality assesses how feasible and implementable the ideas are in reality. Humans consistently scored 4 out of 5 in all rounds, reflecting their capability to consider real-world limitations and propose viable solutions. In comparison, the AI's score remained at 3 across all rounds. Although the difference is slight, it highlights a small advantage for humans in evaluating practicality. The results suggest that AI, while having some understanding of practical considerations, is less effective than humans in assessing the feasibility of ideas in various contexts.

3. Potential impact (the ability of ideas to effectively address the problem).

Potential impact evaluates how well ideas can address a given problem. Human participants consistently received the highest score of 5 in all rounds, indicating their ideas were perceived as highly effective. Conversely, the AI's impact score was lower at 3 in every round, suggesting that despite generating numerous ideas, they were less aligned with the problem and less effective compared to human ideas.

4. Diversity (the range and variety of ideas generated).

Diversity refers to the extent of different ideas produced. Human participants consistently scored 4 in all rounds, showing a strong ability to generate a range of solutions. In contrast, the AI started with a score of 2 in the first round, improved to 4 in the second round, but fell back to 2 in the bonus round. This pattern indicates that while the AI could diversify its ideas in the second round, it was less consistent than humans in maintaining diversity.

5. Level of detail (the detail and elaboration in proposed solutions).

Level of detail assesses how thoroughly ideas are developed. Human participants consistently scored 4 across all rounds, indicating their greater ability to elaborate on ideas, providing deeper insights and more comprehensive proposals. In contrast, the AI started with a score of 2 in the first round and improved to 3 in the second and bonus rounds. These results suggest that although the AI generated many ideas, their depth and elaboration were less frequent than those produced by humans.

This study highlights the strengths and limitations of AI in idea generation. While AI consistently produced more ideas, human-generated ideas outperformed AI in originality, practicality, potential impact, diversity, and detail. AI's tendency toward "quantity over quality" often resulted in ideas lacking depth and feasibility. However, improvements in AI's originality, diversity, and detail over successive rounds suggest its potential to enhance idea quality with further development. The findings emphasize AI's value as a complementary tool in collaborative creativity, with room for growth in producing impactful and actionable solutions.

Statistical Analysis

ANOVA Results

A statistical analysis employing ANOVA (analysis of variance) was performed to measure the variation in idea quality between AI and human participants. This technique assessed whether there were statistically significant differences in the scores across five main dimensions: novelty, feasibility, impact, variety, and depth. The comprehensive results and their interpretations for each of these metrics are provided below. Refer to Table 2 for the ANOVA test analysis.

To understand the differences in idea quality between AI and human participants, an ANOVA (analysis of variance) was conducted. This analysis focused on five dimensions—novelty, feasibility, impact, variety, and depth—to assess the statistical significance of the differences observed. For novelty, F value is 4.0, and P value is 0.184. While human participants consistently scored higher in novelty, this difference between human and AI-generated ideas was insignificant. The P value of 0.184, above the conventional significance threshold of 0.05, suggests that the observed gap in novelty could be due to random variation rather than an actual systematic difference. Therefore, although human ideas generally appear more novel, this trend cannot be confidently attributed to a fundamental distinction between the two groups.

For feasibility F value is 4.0 and P value is 0.184. Similar to the results for novelty, the analysis found no statistically significant difference in the feasibility of ideas generated by humans versus AI. While humans received consistently higher

Table 2 ANOVA

	F value	P value
Novelty	4	0.183503419
Feasibility	4	0.183503419
Impact	Inf	0
Variety	4	0.183503419
Depth	9	0.095465966

Source: created by authors

scores for feasibility, the P value of 0.184 indicates that this difference may not be meaningful, as it could be attributed to random variation. Thus, this difference needs solid statistical support despite the perception that human ideas were more practical.

For impact F value is infinite and P value is 0.000. Interpretation: The impact scores revealed a statistically significant difference between human and AI-generated ideas. The infinite F value was due to the consistent impact scores received by human participants across both rounds. With a P value of 0.000, the analysis confirms that human-generated ideas had a significantly higher impact, with no overlap in variance between the two groups. This suggests that humans consistently produce ideas with more potential to solve problems effectively.

For variety F value is 4.0 and P value is 0.184. The variety metric, which measures the diversity of ideas, did not indicate a statistically significant difference between humans and AI. Although humans scored higher on average, the P value of 0.184 suggests that this difference is likely due to random chance rather than a meaningful variation. As a result, while humans demonstrated a broader range of ideas, this finding needs to be backed by strong statistical evidence.

For depth F value is 9.0 and P value is 0.095. In the depth category, which assesses the level of detail and elaboration, the F value of 9.0 indicates a more considerable variance between human and AI-generated ideas. However, the P value of 0.095 is still above the 0.05 threshold for statistical significance. This suggests that, while there is a trend toward more detailed human ideas, the difference could be more statistically significant at the conventional level. However, this metric is approaching significance, implying that further analysis with a larger sample size might reveal a more pronounced difference.

The statistical analysis of idea quality across the five dimensions—novelty, feasibility, impact, variety, and depth—yielded mixed results.

Impact was the only dimension in which a statistically significant difference was identified. Humans consistently produced ideas with higher impact, supported by the infinite F value and a P value of 0.000, indicating a substantial and undeniable difference between the two groups.

The differences between AI and human performance were not statistically significant regarding novelty, feasibility, variety, and depth. Although observable trends favored human ideas, particularly in novelty and depth, the P values suggest that these differences could be due to random variation rather than meaningful distinctions between the groups.

Notably, the depth metric showed a P value approaching significance, suggesting that the gap between human and AI performance in this dimension might become more evident with further data.

Regression Analysis: Impact of Idea Quality on Quantity

A regression model further explored the relationship between the number of ideas generated (idea quantity) and the five idea quality metrics (novelty, feasibility, impact, variety, and depth). The analysis provided the following key insights:

Model Fit R-squared: 0.998. This exceptionally high R-squared value suggests that the model explains 99.8% of the variance in idea quantity, indicating a solid fit.

Adjusted R-squared: 0.995. The adjusted value, while slightly lower, still confirms that the model accounts for the vast majority of the variance in idea quantity, even after considering the number of predictors in the model.

Intercept (const): 56.55. This value represents the theoretical baseline number of ideas when all quality metrics are zero. Although this is not practical in this context, it sets the foundation for understanding how the other variables influence idea quantity.

Novelty, Feasibility, Variety: Each metric had a positive coefficient 2.32. This indicates that a one-unit increase in these metrics is associated with an approximate rise of 2.32 ideas. However, the P values for these metrics (0.091) suggest that these relationships are not statistically significant at the conventional 0.05 level, meaning these positive relationships could be due to chance.

Impact: The coefficient for impact was 6.45. This indicates that a one-unit increase in the impact score is associated with a significant rise in idea quantity. The P value for effects (0.066) is closer to significance but slightly above the 0.05 threshold.

Depth: The coefficient for depth was −23.89. This negative coefficient indicates that higher depth scores are associated with reducing the number of ideas generated. This relationship is statistically significant, with a P value of 0.033, meaning that depth has a clear inverse relationship with idea quantity.

Impact and Depth emerged as the most influential variables in the model. The impact was positively correlated with idea quantity, suggesting that more impactful ideas drive higher output. Conversely, depth was negatively correlated with idea quantity, indicating that ideas with more elaboration and detail tend to reduce overall output, possibly due to the increased cognitive focus required.

Novelty, Feasibility, and Variety also showed positive relationships with idea quantity, but these associations were not statistically significant, meaning they could be driven by random variation in this sample.

This regression analysis reveals a nuanced relationship between idea quality and quantity. Depth reduces the number of ideas generated, while impact is the most potent positive predictor of idea quantity. These findings suggest that while depth and elaboration require more focused thinking, leading to fewer ideas, the impact can fuel more prolific idea generation. The firm fit of the model highlights that these quality metrics collectively explain much of the variance in idea quantity.

Thematic Analysis of Ideas Created

Round 1 (Neutral)

Patterns of AI Creativity: In this round, the neutral AI likely produced an extensive array of broad and varied ideas, potentially lacking in context or detailed explanation. Meanwhile, the human participants probably came up with fewer ideas but with more practicality and insight, focusing on feasibility and depth.

Variety: AI quickly proposes numerous potential solutions without ranking them by priority. Realism: Human-generated concepts are rooted in real-world applicability and informed by experience and context.

Round 2 (Ego-Driven):

AI Personalities: AI-1 is "Elon Tusk," representing a tech optimist's view; AI-2 is "Pythagoras," channeling the approach of the ancient Greek mathematician; and AI-3 is "PAL 9000," characterized by the notion, 'I am here to assist you, but I might take over the world.' The AI demonstrates divergent thinking, especially in its ego-driven forms, with each personality offering a distinct creative angle. In contrast, human participants provide outputs that are more balanced and aware of context.

Impact of Bias: The inherent biases in AI personalities manifest in the range of ideas they produce—some may be visionary yet impractical, while others are cautious but achievable.

The thematic analysis of the video illustrates how AI, in both neutral and ego-driven modes, enriches the creative process by generating a high volume of ideas with varying levels of innovation and applicability. The human team acts as a stabilizing influence, stressing feasibility and depth, especially in intricate real-world scenarios.

Discussion and Implications

The results of this study add to the expanding research on artificial intelligence's creative abilities, especially when compared to human groups. They emphasize the complex ways AI can either support or hinder creative problem-solving, depending on how it is set up. The AI's strong performance in generating a large number of ideas supports earlier research showing AI's capacity to handle large data sets and quickly produce numerous ideas using extensive datasets and probabilistic reasoning (Boden, 2004; Colton & Wiggins, 2012; Yang et al., 2020). This ability to generate diverse ideas efficiently is a significant advantage of AI, particularly in brainstorming sessions where the focus is on the quantity of ideas (Sawyer, 2011).

In contrast, the consistent ability of human teams to produce higher-quality ideas, especially regarding feasibility and depth, aligns with established findings that suggest human creativity is based on contextual understanding, experiential knowledge, and practical application (Amabile, 1983; Lubart, 2005). Human participants can incorporate complex real-world elements, emotional intelligence, and specific expertise in their creative work, areas where AI currently faces challenges. This underscores a crucial limitation of AI in creativity: while it excels in quantity, it often struggles with the depth and applicability necessary for practical problem-solving (Smith et al., 1995; Song et al., 2020; Song, 2022, Gero, 2022).

The addition of ego-driven AI personalities in the second phase of the study increased the diversity of ideas, demonstrating AI's potential to mimic different creative thinking styles. This mirrors the concept of cognitive diversity in human teams, where diverse viewpoints can boost innovation (Gero & Maher, 2013; Sawyer, 2011). However, this also affected feasibility, as some AI personalities introduced biases that limited the practicality of ideas. This observation reflects

Lubart's (2005) point that AI's innovative contributions need careful guidance to align with desired outcomes.

The human team's capability to produce more contextually relevant and actionable ideas, especially in tasks like improving education for marginalized communities, highlights the value of human insight in creativity. These findings suggest that AI can complement human creativity by providing a wide array of ideas, particularly in its neutral form, but cannot yet replace humans in making nuanced decisions and understanding the context of creative tasks (Runco & Acar, 2012; Lubart, 2005). Bringing in AI personalities emphasizes the need to balance AI's capabilities with human oversight, as AI-driven creativity alone might not consistently produce practical solutions without proper configuration.

Research increasingly recognizes AI as a valuable creative partner, particularly for generating diverse ideas, aligning with studies on human-AI co-creativity (McCormack et al., 2019; Besold & Schorlemmer, 2021). However, AI's limitations in feasibility and real-world understanding make human input crucial. Balancing AI's rapid idea generation with human refinement is essential, and further research should optimize AI personalities to enhance creativity without sacrificing practicality.

The study assessed idea quality solely through human evaluations, raising concerns about subjectivity and consistency, as biases and personal perspectives may have influenced ratings. It used a limited set of criteria—novelty, feasibility, impact, variety, and depth—which, while standard in creativity research, may overlook important aspects like emotional resonance, cultural relevance, and sustainability, potentially missing key dimensions of practical and effective creative solutions.

The study may have limited its understanding of AI's creative capabilities by focusing solely on human evaluations and a narrow set of quality metrics. The absence of automated or data-driven evaluation methods also restricted the potential for uncovering patterns through a more extensive, objective analysis. This highlights the need for future research to include a broader range of criteria and possibly hybrid evaluation methods (combining human and AI assessments) to gain a more nuanced understanding of creativity generated by both humans and AI (Carvalho & Görür, 2021).

The results of this experiment add to the expanding research on AI's creative abilities, especially when compared to human teams, and emphasize the complex ways AI can either boost or hinder creative problem-solving, depending on its setup. AI's exceptional performance in generating a large number of ideas is consistent with previous research showing AI's capacity to handle vast data sets and quickly produce numerous ideas through extensive datasets and probabilistic reasoning. This ability to efficiently generate diverse ideas is a primary strength of AI, providing an advantage in brainstorming situations where idea volume is prioritized.

Conversely, the human team's consistent production of higher-quality ideas, particularly in terms of feasibility and depth, aligns with existing research indicating that human creativity is deeply rooted in contextual understanding, experiential knowledge, and practical application. Humans can incorporate complex real-world factors, emotional intelligence, and specialized knowledge into their creative outputs, areas where AI currently falls short. This points to a significant limitation in AI's creative potential: while AI excels in generating quantity, it often struggles with the depth and applicability necessary for real-world problem-solving.

In Round 2, the introduction of ego-driven AI personalities broadened the diversity of ideas, demonstrating AI's potential to mimic different creative thinking styles. This reflects theories of cognitive diversity in human teams, where varied perspectives can enhance innovation. However, this also affected feasibility, as some AI personalities introduced biases that reduced the practicality of their outputs. This suggests that while personality traits can enrich AI's creative output, they may also introduce biases that limit the practicality of the ideas.

The human team's capacity to produce more contextually relevant and actionable ideas, especially in complex tasks like improving education for underrepresented communities, highlights the importance of human insight in creativity. These findings suggest that AI can complement human creativity by providing a wide range of ideas, particularly in its neutral form. However, AI cannot yet replace humans' nuanced decision-making and contextual awareness in creative tasks. The inclusion of AI personalities underscores the need to balance AI's abilities with human oversight, as AI-driven creativity alone may not consistently lead to practical solutions without proper configuration.

The findings also support the increasing recognition of AI as a valuable creative partner, especially in generating diverse and novel ideas. This aligns with recent studies exploring human-AI co-creativity, indicating that AI can significantly enhance creative processes by broadening the possibilities considered by humans. However, its limitations in understanding feasibility, depth, and real-world constraints mean that human intervention remains crucial. The balance between AI's rapid, divergent thinking and human ability to critically assess and refine ideas suggests that future research should explore how AI personalities can be fine-tuned to maximize creative output without sacrificing practicality.

Furthermore, AI's potential to significantly impact creative equity is being acknowledged, as it can democratize access to innovative resources and empower underrepresented groups to innovate. This aligns with emerging perspectives that view AI as a tool for fostering diversity in innovation, enabling a broader range of individuals to contribute meaningfully to creative endeavors. Future research could investigate how AI could further enhance creative equity, especially in educational and community-based settings, ensuring that these technologies empower rather than marginalize.

Based on the findings, several recommendations emerge for organizations, researchers, and AI developers interested in leveraging AI for creative processes. Firstly, organizations aiming to improve ideation sessions can benefit from using neutral AI systems to generate a high volume of diverse ideas, particularly useful in the early stages of brainstorming where quantity and divergent thinking are prioritized. However, to ensure these ideas are feasible and contextually relevant, involving human experts in the subsequent stages of idea refinement is crucial. This approach leverages AI's strengths in volume while utilizing human expertise for depth, practicality, and implementation.

This study emphasizes the potential of ego-driven AI to enhance creativity while highlighting the need to mitigate biases through careful design. Future development should refine AI models to balance creative diversity with practicality and tailor AI tools for industry-specific needs. The findings underscore AI's role in promoting creative equity, particularly in education and community development, by democratizing idea generation and empowering underrepresented groups. Businesses, educators, and non-profit organizations can leverage AI to drive innovation and inclusivity, while developers and policymakers should focus on ethical, adaptive models that support human-AI collaboration responsibly.

Conclusions and Future Research

The study revealed that artificial intelligence created a significantly higher number of ideas compared to the human team. While AI showed exceptional performance in generating a large volume of ideas, it fell short in terms of depth and practicality. Conversely, although humans generated fewer ideas, their solutions were more practical and contextually appropriate, underscoring the value of human insight in complex situations. In the second phase of the experiment, introducing AI personalities with distinct egos led to a greater variety of ideas. However, it also resulted in biases, as some personalities tended to favor ambitious concepts, while others opted for more cautious and practical solutions. These results indicate that AI is useful for producing a diverse range of ideas, but human involvement is crucial for ensuring depth, practicality, and contextual relevance in creative endeavors.

The study highlighted the complementary strengths of humans and AI in creative problem-solving and the potential to enhance AI outputs through carefully designed personalities. The findings suggest several promising directions for future research, particularly in human-AI collaboration in creative endeavors. A primary area for further investigation is the development of advanced AI personalities and cognitive models that can more closely mimic human creativity's complexity. Future research could focus on improving AI's ability to balance innovation with feasibility by incorporating a deeper contextual understanding and practical applicability into its creative process. Building on existing models, such as those of computational creativity, researchers should explore how AI can be designed to adapt its creative styles dynamically based on the task.

Another key area is examining the long-term effects of human-AI co-creativity across various fields, including design, art, and problem-solving. Studies could assess the sustainability of human-AI collaborations over time and whether AI's creative abilities evolve with feedback from human collaborators. This could help clarify how AI can continuously learn and enhance its creative contributions through interaction with humans. Future research could delve into the ethical aspects of AI creativity, particularly regarding the attribution of creative authorship and intellectual property rights when AI plays a significant role in innovative outcomes.

Declaration statement: AI was used to edit and improve the language of the final submission.

References

Amabile, T. M. (1983). The social psychology of creativity: A componential conceptualization. *Journal of Personality and Social Psychology, 45*(2), 357–376. https://doi.org/10.1037/0022-3514.45.2.357

Amankwah-Amoah, J., Abdalla, S., Mogaji, E., Elbanna, A., & Dwivedi, Y. K. (2024). The impending disruption of creative industries by generative AI: Opportunities, challenges, and research agenda. *International Journal of Information Management, 102759*. https://doi.org/10.1016/j.ijinfomgt.2024.102759

Besold, T. R., & Schorlemmer, M. (2021). *Attributing creativity in AI: From tools to agents. Artificial Intelligence and Law*.

Boden, M. A. (2004). *The creative mind: Myths and mechanisms*. Psychology Press.

Boden, M. A. (2014). Creativity and artificial intelligence. In *Oxford University Press eBooks* (pp. 224–244). https://doi.org/10.1093/acprof:oso/9780199836963.003.0012.

Bouschery, S. G., Blazevic, V., & Piller, F. T. (2023). Augmenting human innovation teams with artificial intelligence: Exploring transformer-based language models. *Journal of Product Innovation Management, 40*(2), 139–153. https://doi.org/10.1111/jpim.12656

Califano, G., Zhang, T., & Spence, C. (2024). Would you trust an AI chef? Examining what people think when AI becomes creative with food. *International Journal of Gastronomy and Food Science, 100973*. https://doi.org/10.1016/j.ijgfs.2024.100973

Carvalho, F., & Görür, O. (2021). Co-creativity in human-AI collaboration: A mixed-initiative approach. *International Journal of Human-Computer Studies, 150, 102613.*

Colton, S., & Wiggins, G. A. (2012). Computational creativity: The final frontier? *European Conference on Artificial Intelligence*, 21–26. https://doi.org/10.3233/978-1-61499-098-7-21

Cooper, R. G. (2024). The AI transformation of product innovation. *Industrial Marketing Management, 119*, 62–74. https://doi.org/10.1016/j.indmarman.2024.03.008

Drozdal, J. (2021). *Intellectual property and AI creativity: A legal framework. Harvard Law Review*.

Drozdal, J., Diakopoulos, N., & Park, S. (2021). AI-generated art: Attribution, ownership, and copyright. *ACM Symposium on Applied Computing*.

Gero, J. S. (2022). *Design computing and cognition'20*. Springer Nature.

Grilli, L., & Pedota, M. (2024). Creativity and artificial intelligence: A multilevel perspective. *Creativity and Innovation Management, 33*(2), 234–247. https://doi.org/10.1111/caim.12580

Habib, S., Vogel, T., Anli, X., & Thorne, E. (2024). How does generative artificial intelligence impact student creativity? *Journal of Creativity, 34*(1), 100072. https://doi.org/10.1016/j.yjoc.2023.100072

Hackman, J., & Morris, C. G. (1975). Group tasks, group interaction process, and group performance effectiveness: A review and proposed integration. *Advances in Experimental Social Psychology*, 45–99. https://doi.org/10.1016/s0065-2601(08)60248-8

Hattori, E. A., Yamakawa, M., & Miwa, K. (2024). Human bias in evaluating AI product creativity. *Journal of Creativity, 34*(2), 100087. https://doi.org/10.1016/j.yjoc.2024.100087

Issac, W., & William, S. (2021). AI and organizational knowledge creation. *Journal of Knowledge Management, 28*(7).

Lubart, T. (2005). How can computers be partners in the creative process: Classification and commentary on the special issue. *International Journal of Human-Computer Studies, 63*(4–5), 365–369. https://doi.org/10.1016/j.ijhcs.2005.04.002

McCormack, J., Gifford, T., & Hutchings, P. (2019). Autonomy, authenticity, authorship, and intention in computer-generated art. In *Tenth International Conference on Computational Creativity (ICCC)* (pp. 304–311).

O'Toole, K., & Horvát, E. (2024). Extending human creativity with AI. *Journal of Creativity, 34*(2), 100080. https://doi.org/10.1016/j.yjoc.2024.100080

Paesano, A. (2021). Artificial intelligence and creative activities inside organizational behavior. *International Journal of Organizational Analysis, 31*(5), 1694–1723. https://doi.org/10.1108/ijoa-09-2020-2421

Paulus, P. B., & Yang, H. (2000). Idea generation in groups: A basis for creativity in organizations. *Organizational Behavior and Human Decision Processes, 82*(1), 76–87. https://doi.org/10.1006/obhd.2000.2888

Ramaul, L., Ritala, P., & Ruokonen, M. (2024). Creational and conversational AI affordances: How the new breed of chatbots are revolutionizing the knowledge industries. *Business Horizons.* https://doi.org/10.1016/j.bushor.2024.05.006

Raz, T., Reiter Palmon, R., & Kennett, Y. N. (2024). Open and closed-ended problem-solving in humans and AI: The influence of question asking complexity. *Thinking Skills and Creativity, 53*, 101598. https://doi.org/10.1016/j.tsc.2024.101598

Roberts, D. L., & Candi, M. (2024). Artificial intelligence and innovation management: Charting the evolving landscape. *Technovation, 136*, 103081. https://doi.org/10.1016/j.technovation.2024.103081

Runco, M. A., & Acar, S. (2012). Divergent thinking as an indicator of creative potential. *Creativity Research Journal, 24*(1), 66–75. https://doi.org/10.1080/10400419.2012.652929

Gero, J. S., & Maher, M. L. (2013). Computational and cognitive models of creative design thinking. *International Journal of Computational Creativity*, 1–22.

Sawyer, R. K. (2011). *Explaining creativity: The science of human innovation.* Oxford University Press.

Sawyer, R. K., & Henriksen, D. (2024). *Explaining creativity: The science of human innovation* (3rd ed.). Oxford University Press.

Smith, S. M., Ward, T. B., & Finke, R. A. (1995). *The creative cognition approach.* MIT Press.

Song, D., Hu, C., & Wang, Q. (2020). A hybrid approach to AI-generated art: Integrating computational creativity with human expertise. *Journal of Computational Creativity, 2*(4), 145–156.

Song, H. (2022). Human-AI collaboration and creative cognition. *Cognitive Science.*

Thomas, A., Duggal, H. K., Khatri, P., & Corvello, V. (2024). ChatGPT appropriation: A catalyst for creative performance, innovation orientation, and agile leadership. *Technology in Society, 78*, 102619. https://doi.org/10.1016/j.techsoc.2024.102619

Yang, W., Zhang, Z., & Yu, H. (2020). Harnessing AI to support human creativity: Theoretical foundations and practical insights. *AI & Society, 35*(3), 485–498.

Yang, Y. (2020). Creativity and artificial intelligence: A survey of computational creativity. *Journal of Artificial Intelligence Research.*

PhD Elina Mikelsone, Riga Technical University Head of Design Factory and professor. She is the founder of the Idea Innovation Institute, an innovation expert, and a lecturer at five universities. Her work centers on innovation and idea management, combining academic research with professional practice. Elina has consulted over 400 enterprises, authored 30+ scientific articles, and developed the "Fitness of Ideas" learning module for 2000+ participants. She contributed to international projects like Horizon2020 "Cities2030" and is an expert for the Latvian Council of Science.

PhD Matijs Babris is the Deputy Director for Innovation at the Architecture and Design Institute of Riga Technical University. He is a lecturer and researcher specializing in community-centered co-creation, urban development, and sustainable practices, including nature tourism. Matijs coordinates industry collaborations, manages applied research projects, and oversees RTU's participation initiatives such as INTERREG and Horizon2020. As a co-founder of Acoustic Technologies, he develops sustainable 3D-printed acoustic solutions. His academic contributions include publications on creative districts and user-centered design. Matijs also promotes youth innovation through events like hackathons, fostering advancements in road safety and technology-driven solutions.

Andra Marta Babre is a researcher and project manager at organizations like Riga Technical University and the Latvian Nature Tourism Association, specializing in Interreg projects. As an expert in creative thinking and co-creation, Andra has delivered seminars and workshops, empowering participants with problem-solving skills. With an academic background in architecture and urban planning, she has contributed to projects and publications focusing on urban development, creative hubs, and sustainable practices. Andra excels at fostering innovation through interdisciplinary collaboration, mentoring, and interactive sessions, inspiring transformative ideas and practical solutions for diverse challenges.

Anna Salnikova is a student at Riga Stradins University, specializing in Health and Sports Sciences. She is a co-founder of Acoustic Technologies, contributing to the development of sustainable 3D-printed acoustic solutions. Her experience includes managing projects under Interreg programs and organizing academic events such as online workshops, hackathons, and ideation sessions. She has also engaged in startup acceleration programs, focusing on early-stage innovation and business development.

Effective Human AI-Collaboration for the Boost in Productivity

Mazhar Mohsin, Tapani Honkanen, Muhammad Imran, and Sarah Zafar

Introduction

Human-AI collaboration (HAC) is the process by which one or more humans and one or more AI systems function as team members, each with unique and complementary capabilities work to achieve some shared goal (Tahaei et al., 2023). This allows HAC to leverage the strengths of human cognition and creativity in synergy with AI's efficient data processing and complex pattern recognition capabilities (Dashti et al., 2010; Shaikh Mohd Azhar Mohd Abrar, 2024). For instance, AI applications applied within human-AI collaboration (HAC) can comprise use cases such as chatbots for communication, virtual assistants for task management, and recommender systems for decision support. HAC has become a hot topic of study dating from fields of information science to cybersecurity with the ability to revolutionize these areas through the complementarities of expert human knowledge with precision of AI (Bruni, 2024; Olla et al., 2024; Tag et al., 2023). Human-AI collaboration comes with many benefits, but adoption comes with challenges. A central concern is the aspect of trust and interpretability, since many AI models are "black boxes," and users cannot understand and validate outputs generated by an

M. Mohsin (✉) · T. Honkanen
School of Business, Design and Technology, Häme University of Applied Sciences, Hämeenlinna, Finland
e-mail: mazhar.mohsin@hamk.fi; tapani.honkanen@hamk.fi

M. Imran
KIMEP University, Almaty, Kazakhstan
e-mail: m.imran@kimep.kz

S. Zafar
NUST Business School, National University of Sciences and Technology, Islamabad, Pakistan
e-mail: sarah.phd24nbs@student.nust.edu.pk

M. Dabić et al. (eds.), *Artificial Humans*, Future of Business and Finance,
https://doi.org/10.1007/978-3-032-06604-6_11

AI (Molina et al., 2024). Various explainable AI (XAI) approaches have recently been developed to enhance interpretability and user trust. A further pressing issue is around bias and fairness in AI decision-making. AI models are built on large amounts of historical data, which can introduce human biases and result in decision-making that is unfair or discriminatory. Human-in-the-loop (HITL) frameworks try to remedy these problems by embedding human oversight, but they can ironically infuse human biases into the system themselves (Kumar et al., 2024). From a technical perspective, high-quality training data is necessary for building robust AI models, but weaknesses in human feedback loops can adversely influence AI learning (Lysaght et al., 2019).

Moreover, human intuition needs to complement AI decision-making augmentation, and the recommendation of AI should be used to increase rather than replace human expertise (Askarisichani et al., 2022). User acceptance and cognitive load management are other challenges. ML tools must delicately balance the amount of guidance they provide and the influence they exert over their human counterparts. Research shows that users may not adopt AI systems that go against human intuition or generate non-intuitive recommendations (Schraagen, 2023).

The objective of this paper is to analyze these challenges and propose frameworks for human-AI collaboration in different segments. To achieve the objective, this chapter deals with the following research questions:

How human-AI collaboration impacts the decision-making process?

How are collaborative reinforcement and AI models used in different walks of life?

What are the different frameworks available to explore the relationship between human and AI collaboration?

How human-AI collaborations improve the productivity and performance of a business?

Moreover, the study explores how decision-making augmentation, collaborative reinforcement learning, and human oversight mechanisms can enhance AI integration across multiple sectors. By addressing these challenges, this research aims to contribute to the development of more effective, ethical, and sustainable human-AI collaboration models.

Frameworks and Theories of Human-AI Collaboration

Human-in-the-Loop Systems

Human-in-the-loop (HITL) and human-on-the-loop (HOTL) are essential paradigms in human-AI collaboration, involving human oversight and intervention within AI decision-making processes (Hao et al., 2024; Park et al., 2024). HITL systems necessitate human intervention, whereby human feedback directly affects AI action in real time. Such systems are practiced in training AI and validating models and aid in decision support in high-stakes domains like healthcare and autonomous driving (Kumar et al., 2024). In contrast, HOTL systems are designed to work independently while providing humans oversight with the option to intervene when needed. It is therefore more efficient, yet maintains a level of control, as with AI-based cybersecurity and military defenses (Van Den Bosch & Bronkhorst, 2018). Systems integrating human-machine collaboration provide avenues for AI decisions to be interpretable by human operators, preventing ethical guidelines from being overlooked without human supervision, addressing issues inherent to autonomous decision-making (Reis, 2024; Tiziana et al., 2024). One of the recurring challenges in HITL and HOTL systems is the balance between cognitive load and AI performance. Explainable artificial intelligence (XAI) techniques, including model visualization and natural language rationales, can help illuminate trust in these algorithms. Future studies will develop powerful adaptive learning algorithms that utilize system quiescence to modulate human engagement according to context and levels of confidence by implementing HITL and HOTL in optimized workflows (Paul et al., 2024).

Decision-Making Augmentation

Decision-making augmentation uses AI's computational methods to assist human decision-making rather than replace it. AI analyzes extensive datasets, recognizes patterns, and produces recommendations, enhancing human decision-making. Such systems are common in areas like business analytics, finance, and medical diagnosis where AI helps professionals make better decisions (Askarisichani et al., 2022). Artificial intelligence (AI)-driven decision support is represented in this capacity by applications such as healthcare, wherein AI models analyze medical images, predict patient outcomes, and recommend treatment (Wang et al., 2024). Likewise, in the military context, AI increases awareness of the situation through processing more data from battlefields and enabling commanders to make strategic decisions effectively (Adams et al., 2024). But AI use in decision-making presents challenges in bias, accountability, and explainability. Such systems require augmentation with the ethical consequences of AI outputs so human-AI teams are able to ensure that decisions put forward remain therefore feasible and fair (Schraagen, 2023). Innovation and creativity have been amplified with human-AI collocation; however, AI models need to be trained to consider ethics and psychological factors before employing them in decision making process. Vinchon et al. (2023) presented a manifesto to evaluate the multiple possibilities of human-AI collaboration for ethical use of AI in the field of innovation and creativity. Osamor et al. (2023) examined the use of chatbots and AI in education and emphasized the development of ethical frameworks to avoid the unethical use of AI in education. Choudhary et al. (2025) considered the social aspects of human-AI collaboration with the inspiration from the division of labor and evaluated the possibilities of using AI along with human collaboration to get a competitive advantage in specialized jobs. Zirar et al. (2023) also explored the social aspects of human-AI collaboration in the workplace and suggested ways for the co-existence of workers and AI to achieve the organizational objectives. AI-human decision-making in the future will most likely be done through hybrid intelligence, where AI integrates itself with human knowledge to enhance collaborative decision-making processes (Lauer & Wieland, 2021).

Collaborative Reinforcement Learning

Collaborative reinforcement learning (CRL) is an extension of traditional reinforcement learning (RL) that supplements RL with human input during training. In contrast to regular RL, where we expect agents to learn via self-exploration, CRL integrates auxiliary-designed human feedback to accelerate learning and steer agents' alignment with human preferences (Ho et al., 2022). CRL is particularly powerful in arenas where real-time or near real-time complex decisions must be made with many variables, e.g., robotics, industrial automation, and gaming. In the context of human-AI collaboration, CRL allows AI systems to learn in real time from human preferences regarding actions and decisions (Luebbers et al., 2023). In smart manufacturing, CRL is utilized for production processes, integrating AI-enabled automation and human expertise to provide flexible and adaptive manufacturing systems (Haindl et al., 2022).

CRL not only improves the learning time of AI agents to reach optimal performance but also helps save a lot of time by using human experience. On the other hand, CRL also suffers from human variability and inconsistency in the feedback provided to these systems, leading to noise in the training phase (Dubey et al., 2020). Building on CReL Luebbers et al. (2022) describe future work.

On more advanced CRL frameworks that integrate uncertainty modeling, confidence-aware AI agents, and adaptive human-AI feedback loops. Leveraging the dynamism of CRL in human-AI collaboration allows AI systems to reach unprecedented levels of adaptability, personalization, and efficiency in a variety of application areas ranging from healthcare to autonomous systems (Schleiger et al., 2024).

Existing Tools and Technologies

Existing Tools

A rapid change in technology has changed the way of doing work with a team. Due to AI, there is a transition from human-human teaming to human-AI collaboration resulting in high productivity, efficiency, and more transparency in the outcomes. AI uses the set of instructions and follows the dedicated frameworks to understand the situation for which it is trained. However, analyzing new situations and events with reasoning is a challenge for AI. On another hand, humans have a capability to analyze new complex situations without training and have better capabilities for reasoning. HAC takes advantage of the capabilities of humans as well as AI which not only boosts productivity but ensures transparency, even though there are various ways of effective collaboration of human and AI for the performance improvement. Collaboration between human and AI assists in different ways. Schmutz et al. (2024) studied team management and suggested the use of AI agents as team members improves the level of communication, reduces the response time, and brings the transparency. The use of human-AI collaboration is effective in feedback systems such as its use in educational and government organizations. The feedback improves the accuracy of information and communications (Y. Li et al., 2024a, 2024b). Similarly, human-AI collaboration has exponentially increased interpretation skills; AI assists humans in generating reports, graphics, and animation to speed up the new product or model development (H. Li et al., 2024a, 2024b). Due to rapid evolution in AI, now it can be used in the decision-making process because of its analytical reasoning and critical thinking power. Booyse and Scheepers (2024) explored the barriers in adopting an AI for the decision-making and found its use is effective in combination with human reasoning and discussion. A lot of forms of human-AI collaboration have been discussed in the literature; however, in the last 5 years, most of the research in human-AI collaboration addressed the communication, feedback system, collaboration, interpretation, and decision-making/analytics (Brusilovsky, 2024; Hou et al., 2023; Jiang et al., 2023; Vössing et al., 2022; Westphal et al., 2023). Therefore, these chapters focus on these capabilities because of their applicability in expediting human productivity and efficiency. It is important to note that these

capabilities have been analyzed with respect to human-AI collaboration and relationship among them not explored in this chapter. Figure 1 shows the effective capabilities of HAC.

This chapter will explore the tools and technologies for each capability of the HAC in practice. The use of AI to solve business and societal problems is very high, and many startups and companies are developing AI apps focused on human-AI collaboration. The development of AI-based apps has been rising since the availability of ChatGPT to the public. Now, companies are integrating AI using APIs to customize their business needs. As many companies are working with AI-human teaming and it would be difficult to cover all of them, this chapter explores two leading IT companies, Google and Microsoft, as both companies, along with AWS, have a combined share of $84 billion in 2024 (Cloud Market Share, 2024).

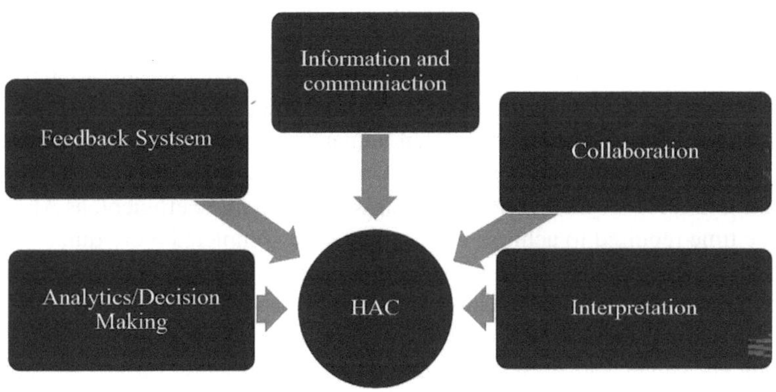

Fig. 1 Effective capabilities of human-AI collaboration

Information and Communication

The information and communication involve a one-way or two-way flow of information. Advertisements, announcements, blogs, stories, news, online stores, and companies' websites are examples of one-way flow of information. Unlike the traditional hawkers' system, this new means of source assist humans in promoting their products, messages, or opinion to the masses. In addition, communication involves flow of information in two or more directions. The examples of HAC in communication are social media, messaging apps, emails, video conferencing, and audio apps.

Collaboration

Human-AI collaboration has assisted collaboration among the teams working remotely. Due to globalization companies are operating virtually and hiring employees worldwide and using their expertise using HAC which enables collaboration among team members. There are various platforms used for collaboration such as cloud storage/sharing, workflow automation, meetings, audio/video conference, communication, and project management tools.

Interpretation

Due to expansion of businesses and their reach worldwide, a large amount of data is being generated requiring a smarter way of dealing with it using human-AI teaming. The visualization and graphical representation of data assist humans to identify the potential challenges in the businesses. Therefore, the use of dashboards which sometimes use real data streaming from different sources such as the web, individuals, and machines is then further analyzed using AI model, and it helps human in interpretation and decision-making. Moreover, the visuals and dashboard assist humans in managing the troubleshooting and other measures which boost the productivity of business.

Before the invention of AI, humans collaborated with each other to accomplish tasks. However, with the emergence of AI-powered chatbots, collaboration has shifted from being exclusively between humans to a partnership between humans and AI. This shift has significantly impacted the way tasks are completed. When humans utilize AI for their work, the process becomes more efficient, as AI accelerates the time required to achieve results. Tasks are completed more quickly, easily, and with greater accuracy, enhancing overall productivity. Moreover, AI minimizes human errors, offers valuable data-driven insights, and streamlines repetitive tasks, allowing individuals to focus on more complex and creative endeavors. AI chatbots can quickly gather and present a wide range of information on any subject from across the web within seconds, making navigation significantly easier for users. If a human were to perform this task manually, it would take considerably more time.

Therefore, AI intervention greatly enhances efficiency by saving time and simplifying information retrieval. Tables 1 and 2 show the HAC tools developed by Microsoft and Google.

Analytics/Decision-making

Industry 4.0 evolution changed the production configurations from manual to highly automated systems requiring minimum involvement of humans. However, due to the complexity of operation, involvement of human cannot be fully avoided. Data generated through the sensor of machines, ERP systems, point of sales, and online transaction is being analyzed for decision-making using AI and machine learning/deep learning models such as clustering, predictions, and optimization.

Feedback System

Research and development, academia, and medical industries are extensively using the human-AI collaboration feedback apps. Teachers use feedback systems to manage the students' assessments and give them feedback. Doctors can see the medical reports directly from the lab and give prescriptions to the patients using the HAC feedback systems.

Existing Technologies

HAC mainly relies on machine learning, deep learning, and other AI technologies such as data mining, clustering, metaheuristics, and data-driven models. Mahmud et al. (2023) investigated the human-AI collaboration for the creative work by employing the machine learning models which significantly improved the performance of overall business; their findings suggest AI can't replace human completely; instead it may work as team to deal the complex and creative problems. Luebbers et al. (2022) employed augmented reality in human-robot teaming in which robots used AI techniques such as predictable planning, justification generated by robots, and visual counter factual explanation to collaborate with human in AR environment.

Haindl et al. (2022) evaluated the smart manufacturing system to assess the impact of human-AI collaboration for the collaboration, runtime monitoring, and validation using machine learning models having the capacity to graph, produce, and process data from smart manufacturing system. Gaming industry is the perfect usage of human-AI collaboration. Kickmeier-Rust and Holzinger (2019) analyzed the pathfinding algorithm in the games with and without human involvement, analyzed travelling salesman problem, and found that human teaming with AI generates better results than without human involvement. Table 3 shows the use of different technologies being employed for each capability of human-AI collaboration.

Table 1 Human-AI collaboration tools from Microsoft

Capabilities of human-AI collaboration						
Teaming tool and communication	Information & Communication	Collaboration	Interpretation	Analytics/ decision-making	Feedback system	Functionality
Calendar	✓					Manages the schedules
Class Notebook		✓				Digital notebook for collaboration
Connections			✓			Customized news and resources
Delve	✓		✓			Workplace and work type insights
Engage	✓	✓				Information sharing among teams
Excel			✓	✓		Calculation, analysis, and reporting
Forms			✓	✓	✓	Getting insights from surveys
Kaizala	✓					Workplace communication
Learning	✓					Online learning platform
Lists			✓	✓		Create tables and database
Loop	✓	✓				Project management
One Drive		✓				Data storage and data sharing
Outlook	✓				✓	Email and task scheduling
Planner	✓	✓			✓	Project management
Power Apps	✓	✓	✓	✓	✓	Low code application development
Power Automate		✓			✓	Synchronization of information

Capabilities of human-AI collaboration						
Teaming tool and communication	Information & Communication	Collaboration	Interpretation	Analytics/ decision-making	Feedback system	Functionality
Power BI	✓		✓	✓		Visualization and data interpretation
Project	✓	✓		✓	✓	Project management
Reading Coach	✓					AI-based reading practice
Reflect					✓	Well-being and emotions
SharePoint	✓					Sharing of content
Stream	✓		✓			Video recording, editing, and sharing
Teams	✓	✓			✓	Meetings and collaboration
Visio			✓			Drawing
Whiteboard	✓		✓			Teaching and briefing
Word		✓	✓			Writing and collaboration

Table 2 Human-AI collaboration tools from Google

Capabilities of human-AI collaboration						
Teaming tool and communication	Information & Communication	Collaboration	Interpretation	Analytics/ decision-making	Feedback system	Functionality
Gmail		✓			✓	Email and task scheduling
Drive		✓				Data storage and data sharing
Classroom	✓	✓	✓		✓	Teaching and training
Docs	✓		✓			Writing
Gemini	✓		✓	✓		Multi-purpose AI tool
Sheets	✓		✓	✓		Calculations and data analysis
Slides	✓		✓			Presentation/visualization
Calendar	✓					Create and schedule events
Meet	✓	✓			✓	Video conference and meeting
Forms			✓	✓	✓	Survey design and feedback
Sites	✓		✓			Customized website
YouTube	✓		✓			Video streaming
Maps	✓			✓		Creates routes and directions
News	✓		✓			Customized news and updates
Google ads	✓		✓		✓	Creates ads to attract customers
Photos			✓			Saves images and videos
Translate	✓	✓	✓		✓	Translates multiple languages
Vault	✓				✓	Reviews the matter shared with You
Keep			✓			Records notes
Cloud search	✓	✓	✓	✓		Data sharing and storage

Table 3 AI techniques employed in human-AI collaboration (HAC) with application

Capabilities	Technique	Application	Source
Information and communication	JS Warm Machine education and bi-directional communication Multi-agent team simulation learning model	Human-AI collaboration Language Integration of ethics and moral in AI Goal and belief communication between human and AI	(H. A. Abbass et al., 2022) (H. Abbass et al., 2021) (van Zoelen et al., 2020)
Collaboration	Neural network and meta learning JADE (Java Agent Development Framework): HACO Maturity model	Collaboration among machines, AI, and humans Human-AI teaming in virtual environments Urban energy efficiency	(X. Li et al., 2022) (Dubey et al., 2020) (Mulder & Meyer-Vitali, 2023)
Interpretation	LineageD+ (machine learning model) Generative algorithms with VR AI-based medical chart coding	Visualization of biological data Situation awareness visuals Medical Chart analysis	(Hong et al., 2024) (Tabrez et al., 2022) (Wang et al., 2024)
Analytics/decision-making	AI-based prediction model with behavioral analysis Predicting model of human-AI decision-making	Demand forecast Group decision-making	(Lauer & Wieland, 2021) (Askarisichani et al., 2022)
Feedback system	HAILEY (an AI loop agent) INT (human-AI integration testing)	AI-in-the-loop writing systems to empower humans Behavior analysis	(Sharma et al., 2023) (Chen et al., 2022)

Case Studies and Applications in HAC

The use of human-AI teaming has been on the rise since the last few years; businesses are using HAC to improve their productivity, performance, transparency, and visibility. This section of the chapter provides the cases and application of HAC in different areas. The use of human AI collaboration is useful for every walk of life. However, practice and literature have exhibited the extensive use of human-AI in different areas such as healthcare, manufacturing, retail industry, and defense which is due to their macroeconomic scale and their substantial impact on the overall economy.

Healthcare

Healthcare systems involve humans making quick and faster decisions, especially during emergencies. However, longer working hours, complex medical procedures, and administrative issues put additional burden on humans resulting in errors. However, the collaboration of humans with AI can avoid such issues, and humans together with AI can manage unforeseen situations in healthcare systems. Traditionally, literature depicted the usage of HAC in healthcare systems. Aadil and Maaz (2024) explored the teaming of human and AI in healthcare systems to assess the performance of healthcare workers with and without AI; findings suggested the improvement in the performance when human and AI work together in team taking care of each other's job and ensuring trust.

There are various avenues such as patient facing, vaccines, ambulance service triage, surgeries, and radiology where AI can be coupled with human to get competitive advantage (Sujan, 2023). The use of robots in the surgery is increasing worldwide which uses pattern recognition, machine learning, and deep learning models to ensure accuracy and safety during the surgery. The UAE has recently adopted robotic surgery, and interviews with the healthcare experts revealed positive impact of robotic surgeries especially urology, brain surgery, and gynecology (Barkati et al., 2023). AI may assist physicians to overcome their human deficiency to deal with the complex situations rising during medical procedures (Agarwal et al., 2024). However, there is a need to develop a framework that will ensure the trust and behavioral aspect of teaming between human and AI.

Manufacturing

There is extensive use of HAC in manufacturing especially in robotic manufacturing facilities. The flexible manufacturing system utilizes the HAC for reconfiguration, schedule changes, and maintenance. AI assists machine and human to improve the productivity and accuracy of manufacturing facilities. Haindl et al. (2022) studied HAC in smart manufacturing settings and used knowledge graphs to gather the data about product and process in the manufacturing system and then utilized the machine learning model to make a smart proactive system dealing with flexibility of products and process.

Industry 4.0 requires a highly automated smart manufacturing system with dynamic capabilities in which AI is the integral part ensuring high level of accuracy and design conformance of the products. AI along with robots, machines, and human forms a human-machine-AI teaming which combines the capabilities of man, machine, and AI (Javaid et al., 2022). Digital twin is a digital replica of any manufacturing system which behaves like a real system and uses the AI tools for the synchronization of digital twin with the real systems (Biller & Biller, 2023). There is an increased investment in AI and robotics to achieve flexibility and accuracy in the manufacturing processes in which HAC plays a pivotal role such as human can configure robots according to product characteristics and robot can provide higher level of accuracy in complex products (Zhang & Doyle, 2023).

Retail Industry

Due to globalization, there is a paradigm shift from brick-and-mortar stores to online e-commerce. Online stores use HAC to attract customers, manage orders, respond to queries/return, and optimize the inventory level (Pillai et al., 2020). The use of chatbots is at peak in e-commerce which assists consumers with their queries or concerns instantly. The use of AI chatbots helps managers to manage the inventory and shelf life of products in store. The use of robots, human, and AI in fulfillment centers facilitates the order management from the receiving to the delivery. According to an interview with an Amazon robotic team, around 750,000 robots are working in fulfillment centers along with humans, and they use AI to collaborate with human and other logistics fleet (The Amazing Ways Amazon Is Using AI Robots, 2024). The use of voice bots is on the rise, and now AI callers work with human agents at call centers for retail and other services. Klaus and Zaichkowsky (2020) analyzed the bot services and their benefits to the customers. Bots use algorithms to respond to the specific questions raised by customers. Unlike humans, bots quickly respond to the relevant questions and assist human decision-making in a shorter period of time.

Defense

As compared to the other sectors, the defense sector is more critical and involves careful decision-making at different levels of operations. Due to its volatile nature, relying entirely on AI may lead to disasters; however, taking advantage of HAC in defense can utilize the human decision-making power along with the efficiency of AI. Van Den Bosch and Bronkhorst (2018) addressed the cooperation between human and AI for better decision-making and suggested the interactive explanatory dialogues can be achieved through the analysis of situations and their judgments. Historically, the military is the first sector utilizing emerging technologies to gain competitive advantage.

AI is still using human instruction, and its cognitive and situation assessment capabilities are limited which means they can process the information and queries for which they are trained. In case of some unforeseen situations, the output of AI model might not be accurate. A limitation of AI is that it is trained on a specific dataset. When presented with new information outside of that dataset, it lacks the capacity to process or respond effectively. Additionally, AI struggles with contextual understanding, creativity, and human emotions, which can impact its ability to generate highly intuitive responses (Morosan & Dursun-Cengizci, 2024; Selwyn, 2022; Vo et al., 2022). Therefore, AI alone cannot work in defense. According to John Boyd, "Machines don't fight wars. People do, and they use their minds" (UK Development Concepts and Doctrine Centre, 2018).

Adams et al. (2024) provided a review of challenges faced by the human military and using the robot as team member to combat.

It has been found that integration of humans with robots will improve the overall performance leaving the concerns of robots with fixed and well-defined instruction ignoring the unforeseen situation in the war. Schraagen (2023) analyzed the adoption of AI in military as team member of human in ergonomic context and highlighted the challenges in the future such as ethical risk assessment, verification, and validation of objects. Moreover, moral factors such as trust, collaboration, teaming, and integrity traits should be kept in mind in HAC.

Challenges in Human-AI Collaboration

There are substantial ethical, technical, safety, and user-acceptance difficulties within the implementation of artificial intelligence in human-AI teams (Schecter et al., 2023). Attempting to ensure fairness and transparency in AI decision-making systems poses challenges, especially in the sensitive fields of finance and health care. Systems with human oversight, such as human-in-the-loop (HITL) systems, address these challenges, but can lead to discriminatory biases if not managed correctly, owing to the biases of the human annotators (Kumar et al., 2024). Moreover, addressing AI's interpretability and explainability is another key hurdle. Many machine learning systems work as "black boxes" whereby it becomes challenging for human associates to ever trust or check the accuracy of the generated outputs. Recently, there has been increasing focus towards explainable AI (XAI) which includes model visualization and natural language explanations and is believed to greatly enhance user trust and responsibility in AI monocular decisions. Even though this thesis sounds attractive at first, there still lies a major challenge in balancing the level of explainability against performance as better, more interpretable models invariably result in poor accuracy than their opaquer interpreted models (Anthony et al., 2023).

One of the most pressing technical challenges is the need for robust training data, as human feedback loops can introduce inconsistencies that negatively impact AI performance (Kumar et al., 2024). Moreover, AI safety concerns arise when autonomous systems operate without sufficient human oversight, especially in mission-critical applications such as autonomous driving or medical diagnostics. HITL frameworks attempt to address these issues by incorporating domain experts into the AI training and validation process, ensuring that the system remains aligned with real-world expectations and ethical standards (Beede et al., 2020). However, user acceptance remains a challenge, as many users struggle to trust AI recommendations, particularly when explanations are not intuitive or when AI systems contradict human expertise. To enhance user trust and acceptance, AI systems must be designed with user-friendly interfaces that offer clear, justifiable, and context- aware explanations for their decisions. Addressing these challenges is crucial for the successful implementation of human-AI teams across various industries.

Future Research Directions and Implications

AI is evolving day by day, and new tools and technologies of AI are teaming up with humans to facilitate them in their lives. One of the challenges in HAC is in the jobs involving decision-making and critical thinking along with innovation. In the future HAC will boost the human-AI collaboration to speed up the product/service development process. Scientists are working on AI-brain integration to get the advantage of human-AI collaboration using brain AI Mind Map which has the capability to collaborate in real time. In terms of AI tools, in the future more robust and optimized machine learning and deep learning models having self-reconfiguration according to the situation will help humans in critical jobs involving human decision-making such as courts, designers, and physician. Moreover, integration of AI tools with automation and robots in hardware industry such as electronic, automotive, textile, manufacturing, and agriculture will improve the quality of products at cost of minimum engagement of human. Moreover, adoption and use of AI create also new inequalities and divides. In the future, the frameworks combining social, technological, and economical aspects of human-AI collaboration can be developed.

Recently, most of the research work focuses on the frameworks addressing the development of human-AI teaming; however, there is limited work on fully functional human-AI models in real life. Future research may explore the possibilities of deploying HAC models into businesses and evaluating their behavior over time especially during the unforeseen or new circumstances. As the applications of human-AI collaboration are increasing in different businesses, so in the future in addition to robotics and healthcare, its applications can be extended to law, agriculture, and hospitality industries. Human-AI collaboration engaging virtual reality and augmented reality can be adopted in research and development, professional training, and medical education. Therefore, technical, social, and legal challenges for integration and these technologies can be explored too. Human-AI collaboration can be effective only when AI is capable to analyze the situation and decoding it into its language itself which require experts to develop mode advance and real models with human-like capabilities.

Conclusion

In this paper we have explored the various aspects of human-AI collaboration (HAC), its frameworks, tools, challenges, and future avenues. Through a review of human-in-the-loop (HITL) and human-on-the-loop (HOTL) systems, decision-making augmentation, and collaborative reinforcement learning (CRL), this research contributes to an understanding of how AI can provide support to enhance productivity, precision, and creativity in various sectors, ranging from healthcare and manufacturing to retail and defense. An important strength of this investigation is its systematic consideration of how the role of technological, ethical, and cognitive factors in HAC conditions interact, allowing the finding of measures to create more adaptive and human-centered AI systems gained.

While this study provides a broad overview of HAC, several areas would benefit from further investigation. Much of the discussion relies on the current body of literature, and while we believe that these ideas hold promise, they need to be empirically validated in real-world case studies and experiment implementations as well. Also, as AI technologies develop further, new challenges around ethical AI, workforce adaptation, or regulatory frameworks might arise, which would require continuous interdisciplinary research. Further demonstrations of HAC applications in different industries outside of the four we cover here, like law, education, agriculture, and public services, could broaden mainstream understandings of its real-world potential.

The future of HAC will require developing smarter, more adaptive, context-aware AI systems that work together with human expertise and decision-making that relies on ethical and transparent practices. Breakthroughs in explainable AI (XAI), cognitive load management, and reduction of bias will be critical to increasing trust and acceptance of AI-assisted decisions. In addition, hybrid intelligence models in which AIs actively collaborate with humans based on the relative expertise and context of each stakeholder may help facilitate more seamless and effective collaboration with humans.

To sum up, trust, collaboration, and responsible AI deployment are essential for the effective adoption of HAC. To responsibly keep to overcome existing challenges and harness AI's potential, HAC can play a role in shaping a future where AI augments human intelligence, not replaces it, resulting in more effective, ethical, and human-centered technologies.

References

Aadil, G. M., & Maaz, S. M. (2024). Human-AI-collaboration in healthcare. *International Journal for Research in Applied Science and Engineering Technology, 12*(1). https://doi.org/10.22214/ijraset.2024.57939

Abbass, H. A., Petraki, E., & Hunjet, R. (2022). JSwarm: A Jingulu-inspired human-AI-teaming language for context-aware Swarm guidance. *Frontiers in Physics, 10*. https://doi.org/10.3389/fphy.2022.944064

Abbass, H., Petraki, E., Hussein, A., McCall, F., & Elsawah, S. (2021). A model of symbiomemesis: Machine education and communication as pillars for human-autonomy symbiosis.

Philosophical Transactions of the Royal Society A: Mathematical, Physical and Engineering Sciences, 379(2207). https://doi.org/10.1098/rsta.2020.0364

Adams, J. A., Scholtz, J., & Sciarretta, A. (2024). Human–robot teaming challenges for the military and first response. In *Annual review of control, robotics, and autonomous systems* (Vol. 7). https://doi.org/10.1146/annurev-control-061223-124431

Agarwal, R., Dugas, M., & Gao, G. (2024). Augmenting physicians with artificial intelligence to transform healthcare: Challenges and opportunities. *Journal of Economics and Management Strategy, 33*(2). https://doi.org/10.1111/jems.12555

Anthony, C., Bechky, B. A., & Fayard, A.-L. (2023). "Collaborating" with AI: Taking a system view to explore the future of work. *Organization Science, 34*(5), 1672–1694. https://doi.org/10.1287/orsc.2022.1651

Askarisichani, O., Bullo, F., Friedkin, N. E., & Singh, A. K. (2022). Predictive models for human–AI nexus in group decision making. *Annals of the New York Academy of Sciences, 1514*(1), 70–81. https://doi.org/10.1111/nyas.14783

Barkati, N., Ntefeh, N., Okasha, A., Takshe, A. A., ElKhatib, R., & Chelli, S. (2023). Robotic assisted surgery in the United Arab Emirates: healthcare experts' perceptions. *Journal of Robotic Surgery, 17*(6). https://doi.org/10.1007/s11701-023-01716-6

Beede, E., Baylor, E., Hersch, F., Iurchenko, A., Wilcox, L., Ruamviboonsuk, P., Vardoulakis, L. M. (2020). A Human-Centered Evaluation of a Deep Learning System Deployed in Clinics for the Detection of Diabetic Retinopathy. In Proceedings of the 2020 CHI Conference on Human Factors in Computing Systems (CHI '20). Association for Computing Machinery, New York, NY, USA, 1–12. https://doi.org/10.1145/3313831.3376718

Biller, B., & Biller, S. (2023). Implementing digital twins that learn: AI and simulation are at the core. *Machines, 11*(4). https://doi.org/10.3390/machines11040425

Booyse, D., & Scheepers, C. B. (2024). Barriers to adopting automated organisational decision-making through the use of artificial intelligence. *Management Research Review, 47*(1). https://doi.org/10.1108/MRR-09-2021-0701

Bruni, S. (2024). A retrospective engineering analysis of human-AI teams using the Sidekick principles. *SoutheastCon, 2024*, 1368–1369. https://doi.org/10.1109/SoutheastCon52093.2024.10500218

Brusilovsky, P. (2024). AI in education, learner control, and human-AI collaboration. *International Journal of Artificial Intelligence in Education, 34*(1). https://doi.org/10.1007/s40593-023-00356-z

Chen, Q. Z., Schnabel, T., Nushi, B., & Amershi, S. (2022). HINT: Integration testing for AI-based features with humans in the loop. International conference on intelligent user interfaces, proceedings IUI. https://doi.org/10.1145/3490099.3511141

Choudhary, V., Marchetti, A., Shrestha, Y. R., & Puranam, P. (2025). Human-AI ensembles: When can they work? *Journal of Management, 51*(2), 536–569. https://doi.org/10.1177/01492063231194968

Cloud Market Share For $84B Q3 (2024) AWS, Microsoft, Google cloud lead. Retrieved February 16, 2025, from https://www.crn.com/news/cloud/2024/cloud-market-share-for-84b- q3-2024-aws-microsoft-google-lead.

Dashti, H. T., Ardalan, A., Siahpirani, A. F., Tonejc, J., Uilecan, I. V., Simas, T., Miranda, B., Ribeiro, R., Wang, L., & Assadi, A. H. (2010). Pattern recognition in collective cognitive systems: Hybrid human-machine learning (HHML) by heterogeneous ensembles. Proceedings of the 2010 international conference on artificial intelligence, ICAI 2010, 1.

Dubey, A., Abhinav, K., Jain, S., Arora, V., & Puttaveerana, A. (2020). HACO: A framework for developing human-AI teaming. *ACM International Conference Proceeding Series*. https://doi.org/10.1145/3385032.3385044

Haindl, P., Buchgeher, G., Khan, M., & Moser, B. (2022). *Towards a reference software human-architecture for AI teaming in smart manufacturing*. https://doi.org/10.1145/3510455.3512788

Hao, X., Demir, E., & Eyers, D. (2024). Exploring collaborative decision-making: A quasi-experimental study of human and Generative AI interaction. *Technology in Society, 78*(102662). https://doi.org/10.1016/j.techsoc.2024.102662

Ho, J., Wang, C.-M., Chuang, C.-H., King, C.-T., Feng, C.-W., Chou, T.-H., Chen, Y.-M., Yang, Y.-H., & Hsiao, Y.-C. (2022). Bootstrapping human-autonomy collaborations by using brain-computer interface of SSVEP for multi-agent deep reinforcement learning. 2022 IEEE 3rd international conference on human-machine systems (ICHMS). (pp. 1–6). https://doi.org/10.1109/ICHMS56717.2022.9980765

Hong, J., Maciejewski, R., Trubuil, A., & Isenberg, T. (2024). Visualizing and comparing machine learning predictions to improve human-AI teaming on the example of cell lineage. *IEEE Transactions on Visualization and Computer Graphics, 30*(4). https://doi.org/10.1109/TVCG.2023.3302308

Hou, K., Hou, T., & Cai, L. (2023). Exploring trust in human–AI collaboration in the context of multiplayer online games. *Systems, 11*(5). https://doi.org/10.3390/systems11050217

Javaid, M., Haleem, A., Singh, R. P., & Suman, R. (2022). Artificial intelligence applications for industry 4.0: A literature-based study. *Journal of Industrial Integration and Management, 7*(1). https://doi.org/10.1142/S2424862221300040

Jiang, N., Liu, X., Liu, H., Lim, E. T. K., Tan, C. W., & Gu, J. (2023). Beyond AI-powered context-aware services: the role of human–AI collaboration. *Industrial Management and Data Systems, 123*(11). https://doi.org/10.1108/IMDS-03-2022-0152

Kickmeier-Rust, M. D., & Holzinger, A. (2019). Teaming up with artificial intelligence: The human in the loop of serious game pathfinding algorithms. *Lecture notes in computer science (including subseries lecture notes in artificial intelligence and lecture notes in bioinformatics), 11385 LNCS*. https://doi.org/10.1007/978-3-030-11548-73_3.

Klaus, P., & Zaichkowsky, J. (2020). AI voice bots: a services marketing research agenda. *Journal of Services Marketing, 34*(3). https://doi.org/10.1108/JSM-01-2019-0043

Kumar, S., Datta, S., Singh, V., Datta, D., Kumar Singh, S., & Sharma, R. (2024). Applications, challenges, and future directions of human-in-the-loop learning. *IEEE Access, 12*, 75735–75760. https://doi.org/10.1109/ACCESS.2024.3401547

Lauer, T., & Wieland, S. (2021). Human-AI-collaboration in the context of information asymmetry—a behavioral analysis of demand forecasting. *Lecture Notes in Networks and Systems, 271*. https://doi.org/10.1007/978-3-030-80624-8_1

Li, H., Xue, T., Zhang, A., Luo, X., Kong, L., & Huang, G. (2024a). The application and impact of artificial intelligence technology in graphic design: A critical interpretive synthesis. *Heliyon, 10*(21), e40037. https://doi.org/10.1016/j.heliyon.2024.e40037

Li, X., Koren, Y., & Epureanu, B. I. (2022). Complementary learning-team machines to enlighten and exploit human expertise. *CIRP Annals, 71*(1). https://doi.org/10.1016/j.cirp.2022.04.019

Li, Y., Li, Y., Chen, Q., & Chang, Y. (2024b). Humans as teammates: The signal of human–AI teaming enhances consumer acceptance of chatbots. *International Journal of Information Management, 76*, 102771. https://doi.org/10.1016/j.ijinfomgt.2024.102771

Luebbers, M. B., Tabrez, A., & Hayes, B. (2023). Augmented reality-based explainable AI strategies for establishing appropriate reliance and trust in human-robot teaming.

Lysaght, T., Lim, H. Y., Xafis, V., & Ngiam, K. Y. (2019). AI-assisted decision-making in healthcare. *Asian Bioethics Review, 11*(3), 299–314. https://doi.org/10.1007/s41649-019-00096-0

Mahmud, B., Hong, G., & Fong, B. (2023). A study of human-AI symbiosis for creative work: Recent developments and future directions in deep learning. *ACM Transactions on Multimedia Computing, Communications and Applications, 20*(2). https://doi.org/10.1145/3542698

Molina, D. A., Kharlov, V., & Chen, J.-S. (2024). Towards effective human-AI collaboration in decision-making: A comprehensive review and conceptual framework. *2024 Portland international conference on management of engineering and technology (PICMET)*. (pp. 1–6). https://doi.org/10.23919/PICMET64035.2024.10653303.

Morosan, C., & Dursun-Cengizci, A. (2024). Letting AI make decisions for me: an empirical examination of hotel guests' acceptance of technology agency. *International Journal of Contemporary Hospitality Management, 36*(3). https://doi.org/10.1108/IJCHM-08-2022-1041

Mulder, W., & Meyer-Vitali, A. (2023). A maturity model for collaborative agents in human-AI ecosystems. *IFIP advances in information and communication technology, 688 AICT*. https://doi.org/10.1007/978-3-031-42622-323.

Olla, R., Hand, E., Louis, S. J., Houmanfar, R., & Sengupta, S. (2024). A cybersecurity game to probe human-AI teaming. 2024 IEEE conference on games (CoG), (pp. 1–5). https://doi.org/10.1109/CoG60054.2024.10645666

Osamor, A., Ifelebuegu, K. P., & Cherukut, P. (2023). Chatbots and AI in education (AIEd) tools: The good, the bad, and the ugly. *Journal of Applied Learning and Teaching, 6*(2). https://doi.org/10.37074/jalt.2023.6.2.29

Paul, T. S., Lafond, D., Sanches, F. C., Thivierge, J.-S., & Fagette, A. (2024). AI agents learning human decision policies for collaborative situation assessment in NORAD C2 operations. 2024 IEEE 4th international conference on human-machine systems (ICHMS), 1–6. https://doi.org/10.1109/ICHMS59971.2024.10555797

Park, J., Oh, C., & Kim, H. Y. (2024). AI vs. Human-generated content and accounts on Instagram: User preferences, evaluations, and ethical considerations. 79(102705). https://doi.org/10.1016/j.techsoc.2024.102705

Pillai, R., Sivathanu, B., & Dwivedi, Y. K. (2020). Shopping intention at AI-powered automated retail stores (AIPARS). *Journal of Retailing and Consumer Services, 57*. https://doi.org/10.1016/j.jretconser.2020.102207

Reis, J. (2024). *Customer service through AI-powered human-robot relationships: Where are we now? The case of Hennna cafe, Japan.* (Vol. 77). https://doi.org/10.1016/j.techsoc.2024.102570

Schecter, A., Hohenstein, J., Larson, L., Harris, A., Hou, T.-Y., Lee, W.-Y., Lauharatanahirun, N., DeChurch, L., Contractor, N., & Jung, M. (2023). Vero: An accessible method for studying human–AI teamwork. *Computers in Human Behavior, 141*, 107606. https://doi.org/10.1016/j.chb.2022.107606

Schleiger, E., Mason, C., Naughtin, C., Reeson, A., & Paris, C. (2024). Collaborative intelligence: A scoping review of current applications. *Applied Artificial Intelligence, 38*(1). https://doi.org/10.1080/08839514.2024.2327890

Schmutz, J. B., Outland, N., Kerstan, S., Georganta, E., & Ulfert, A.-S. (2024). AI-teaming: Redefining collaboration in the digital era. *Current Opinion in Psychology, 58*, 101837. https://doi.org/10.1016/j.copsyc.2024.101837

Schraagen, J. M. (2023). Responsible use of AI in military systems: Prospects and challenges. *Ergonomics, 66*(11). https://doi.org/10.1080/00140139.2023.2278394

Selwyn, N. (2022). The future of AI and education: Some cautionary notes. *European Journal of Education, 57*(4). https://doi.org/10.1111/ejed.12532

Shaikh Mohd Azhar Mohd Abrar. (2024). Integrating Artificial Intelligence with Human Psychology. *International Journal of Advanced Research in Science, Communication and Technology.* https://doi.org/10.48175/ijarsct-15250

Sharma, A., Lin, I. W., Miner, A. S., Atkins, D. C., & Althoff, T. (2023). Human–AI collaboration enables more empathic conversations in text-based peer-to-peer mental health support. *Nature Machine Intelligence, 5*(1). https://doi.org/10.1038/s42256-022-00593-2

Sujan, M. A. (2023). Looking at the safety of AI from a systems perspective: Two healthcare examples. In *SpringerBriefs in applied sciences and technology: Vol. Part F1246.* https://doi.org/10.1007/978-3-031-32633-28.

Tabrez, A., Luebbers, M. B., & Hayes, B. (2022). Descriptive and prescriptive visual guidance to improve shared situational awareness in human-robot teaming. *Proceedings of the international joint conference on autonomous agents and multiagent systems, AAMAS, 2.*

Tag, B., van Berkel, N., Verma, S., Zhao, B. Z. H., Berkovsky, S., Kaafar, D., Kostakos, V., & Ohrimenko, O. (2023). DDoD: Dual Denial of decision attacks on human-AI teams. *IEEE Pervasive Computing, 22*(1), 77–84. https://doi.org/10.1109/MPRV.2022.3218773

Tahaei, M., Constantinides, M., Quercia, D., Kennedy, S., Muller, M., Stumpf, S., Liao, Q. V., Baeza-Yates, R., Aroyo, L., Holbrook, J., Luger, E., Madaio, M., Blumenfeld, I. G., De-Arteaga, M., Vitak, J., & Olteanu, A. (2023). Human-centered responsible artificial intelligence: Current & future trends. Conference on human factors in computing systems -proceedings. https://doi.org/10.1145/3544549.3583178

Tiziana, C. C., Riccardo, S. V., Hubbard, E.-M., Daly, A., & Lohse, N. (2024). An ethical framework for human-robot collaboration for the future people-centric manufacturing: A collaborative endeavour with European subject-matter experts in ethics. *78*(102680). https://doi.org/10.1016/j.techsoc.2024.102680

TheAmazingWaysAmazonIsUsingAIRobots.(2024).RetrievedFebruary16,2025,fromhttps://www.forbes.com/sites/bernardmarr/2024/09/20/the-amazing-ways-amazon-is-using- ai-robots/.

UK Development Concepts And Doctrine Centre. (2018). Joint concept note 1/18 human-machine teaming. Joint Concept Note 1/18, 38(993).

Van Den Bosch, K., & Bronkhorst, A. (2018). Human-AI cooperation to benefit military decision making. NATO Science & Technology Organization, June.

van Zoelen, E. M., Cremers, A., Dignum, F. P. M., van Diggelen, J., & Peeters, M. M. (2020). Learning to communicate proactively in human-agent teaming. *Communications in Computer and Information Science, 1233*. https://doi.org/10.1007/978-3-030-51999-520

Vinchon, F., Lubart, T., Bartolotta, S., Gironnay, V., Botella, M., Bourgeois-Bougrine, S., Burkhardt, J. M., Bonnardel, N., Corazza, G. E., Glăveanu, V., Hanchett Hanson, M., Ivcevic, Z., Karwowski, M., Kaufman, J. C., Okada, T., Reiter-Palmon, R., & Gaggioli, A. (2023). Artificial intelligence & creativity: A manifesto for collaboration. *Journal of Creative Behavior, 57*(4). https://doi.org/10.1002/jocb.597

Vo, T. H., Nguyen, N. T. K., Kha, Q. H., & Le, N. Q. K. (2022). On the road to explainable AI in drug-drug interactions prediction: A systematic review. *Computational and Structural Biotechnology Journal, 20*. https://doi.org/10.1016/j.csbj.2022.04.021

Vössing, M., Kühl, N., Lind, M., & Satzger, G. (2022). Designing transparency for effective human-AI collaboration. *Information Systems Frontiers, 24*(3). https://doi.org/10.1007/s10796-022-10284-3

Wang, W., Gao, G., & Agarwal, R. (2024). Friend or Foe? Teaming between artificial intelligence and workers with variation in experience. *Management Science, 70*(9). https://doi.org/10.1287/mnsc.2021.00588

Westphal, M., Vössing, M., Satzger, G., Yom-Tov, G. B., & Rafaeli, A. (2023). Decision control and explanations in human-AI collaboration: Improving user perceptions and compliance. *Computers in Human Behavior, 144*. https://doi.org/10.1016/j.chb.2023.107714

Zhang, Y., & Doyle, T. (2023). Integrating intention-based systems in human-robot interaction: A scoping review of sensors, algorithms, and trust. *Frontiers in Robotics and AI, 10*. https://doi.org/10.3389/frobt.2023.1233328

Zirar, A., Ali, S. I., & Islam, N. (2023). Worker and workplace Artificial Intelligence (AI) coexistence: Emerging themes and research agenda. *Technovation, 124*, 102747. https://doi.org/10.1016/j.technovation.2023.102747

Mazhar Mohsin received his PhD in Computer Science from the School of Computing, University of Eastern Finland. He is currently a Senior Lecturer at Häme University of Applied Sciences, Finland. His research interests include artificial intelligence, computer vision, deep learning, and machine learning.

Tapani Honkanen works as a Head of Degree at Häme University of Applied Sciences, Finland. He is currently working on his PhD at the Technological University of The Shannon: Midlands Midwest in Business Computing. His main research interests include machine learning operations and data stream mining.

Muhammad Imran Earned his PhD in Industrial and Management Engineering from Hanyang University, South Korea, specializing in operations and supply chain management. He has expertise in business modeling and simulation, optimization, healthcare supply chain management, and humanitarian supply chain management. Currently, Muhammad Imran is a faculty member at KIMEP University, Almaty, Kazakhstan.

Sarah Zafar is a doctoral student at NUST Business School, NUST, Islamabad. She is currently doing her coursework. Her research interests include artificial intelligence and its implementation at the workplace and organizational behavior.

AI-Driven Collaborative Maintenance Strategies for Repairable Parts: A Cost-Effective Solution for Pakistan's Aviation Sector

Sajid Nazir

Introduction

The emergence of digital technologies has enabled companies to establish diverse forms of partnerships, alliances, acquisitions, and mergers to promote collaborative environment (Yan et al., 2023; Shen et al., 2021). This collaborative approach enables companies to enhance value generation by minimizing waste in processes, reducing transaction costs, and mitigating risks (Abdi et al., 2022; Pereira et al., 2021). Consequently, firms who involve in collaboration with external entities are more effectively positioned to innovate (Swink, 2006) as these partnerships enhance their access to the strategic resources necessary for the development of novel goods and practices (Najafi-Tavani et al., 2018; Chesbrough, 2007). According to Olson et al. (2001), increased levels of cooperation result in better innovative product performance than when levels of cooperation are lower. This demonstrates that businesses that collaboratively work together have a greater capacity to modify their products, operations, and services in order to meet the market demands. While those businesses who do not rely solely on the internal resource and knowledge developments (Hameed et al., 2021; Swaminathan & Moorman, 2009) have less ability to forecast strategic outcomes, limited resources and high knowledge acquisition costs make it challenging for businesses to succeed independently (González-Benito et al., 2016; Wilkinson & Young, 2002). However, on the other hand, collaborative partnerships can enhance skills, alleviate resource constraints, facilitate knowledge integration, stimulate creativity, and encourage the exploration and utilization of new business avenues. As a result of these, inter-organizational relationship leads to economic growth and enhanced competitiveness (Daghar et al., 2021; Najafi-Tavani

S. Nazir (✉)
Lappeenranta-Lahti University Technology, Kouvola Unit, Finland
e-mail: sajid.nazir@lut.fi

M. Dabić et al. (eds.), *Artificial Humans*, Future of Business and Finance, https://doi.org/10.1007/978-3-032-06604-6_12

et al., 2018; Daugherty et al., 2006), while facilitating innovative business practices leads to sustainable growth (Shan et al., 2020; Ries & Euchner, 2013).

The global aviation sector exhibits a similarity in the functionality and design of its products and services, thereby determining the potential for new value creation (Pereira et al., 2021; Wang et al., 2017; Franke, 2007). However, collaborative innovative relationships in the aviation industry have the potential to significantly contribute to support sustainability, particularly through streamlining the processes of inventory acquisition and maintenance of un-serviceable (U/S) or repairable rotable parts. This collaboration in aviation industry seeks to minimize transport as well as its associated costs and enhance sustainability through the application of artificial intelligence (AI) for monitoring the life cycle of rotable components. As a result utilizing AI enables airlines to more accurately predict the maintenance requirements of components, thereby avoiding unnecessary repairs and extending their usability. Furthermore, this initiative also introduces a collaborative order and shipment system, which consolidates U/S or repairable rotable parts from all five major airlines into a single shipment for repair. As a result consolidated order offers logistics efficacy while simultaneously reducing transportation costs and carbon emissions. This collaboration demonstrates a strategic approach that effectively addresses operational challenges while simultaneously in line with global efforts aimed at enhancing the sustainability of aviation.

In Pakistan's aviation sector, all five airline operators maintain separate contracts with various repair agencies for unserviceable (U/S) or repairable rotable parts, despite operating similar fleets. An un-serviceable (U/S) or repairable rotable parts refers to an aircraft component that can undergo multiple repairs or overhauls, allowing it to be returned to service throughout its life cycle instead of being disposed of after one use (Greenwood Aerospace, 2023). This fragmented approach results in increased transportation expenses, lower bargaining leverage, and inefficiencies in the operations. However, through the implementation of a collaborative or centralized contract with repair agencies, airlines can achieve substantial cost reductions and enhance operational efficiencies. A collaborative approach would allow airlines to negotiate improved terms, benefit from economies of scale, and consolidate shipments for repairs, thus decreasing transportation costs. Furthermore, using artificial intelligence to track and forecast rotable part life will improve maintenance planning and help to reduce unplanned breakdowns. This collaboration enhances operational efficiency and fosters sustainability by minimizing carbon emissions through reduced and optimized shipments. In doing so, this study aims to investigate the advantages of a collaborative and centralized contract model for the repair of unserviceable (U/S) rotable parts among airline operators in Pakistan, by utilizing artificial intelligence (AI) to improve cost efficiency, optimize transportation process, and offers sustainable operations. This research enhances the understanding of how collaboration among competing airlines generates shared value while benefiting all stakeholders involved. Furthermore, it develops a model for future collaborative activities in the aviation industry by opening the ways for improved supply chain operations, increased negotiation power, and economies of scale. Additionally, this study aligns with the global aims of lowering carbon emissions and optimizing resource utilization by promoting sustainability and operational efficiency in the aviation sector while positioning Pakistan's aviation industry as an environmentally responsible and forward-thinking sector. The following paragraph explains the structure of the chapter.

This chapter is structured as follows: subsequent to the brief introduction, the literature review thoroughly explores prior research related to the role of procurement in the supply chain, by focusing on critical concepts such as cost-efficiency, supplier relationship management, and sustainability within a collaborative procurement practice, utilizing recent studies to explain its benefits and associated challenges. Following that, the research methodology section highlights the methodology of the study, which includes the research strategy, data gathering techniques, and analytical tools that have been utilized in this research. Furthermore, the case study part presents the existing process and proposes how collaborative procurement could alleviate the industry inefficiencies through AI-enabled digital platform. The subsequent section presents the managerial implications of collaborative procurement in enhancing Pakistan's aviation sector, focusing on cost savings, operational efficiency, and sustainability. Finally, the conclusions and future recommendations section summarizes the key results and potential challenges.

Literature Review

Collaborative Innovative Practices in Supply Chain

The importance of collaborative innovation in both product and process development cannot be overstated in this era of digital innovations (Matarneh et al., 2024; Najafi-Tavani et al., 2018; Wang et al., 2017; Swink, 2006). According to recent studies (Wan et al., 2024; Nazir et al., 2023; Nilsson & Göransson, 2021; Tariq et al., 2017; Zimmermann et al., 2016), innovation plays a crucial role in modern supply chains in terms of creating value, increasing competitiveness, attracting consumers, and promoting sustainability. Innovations in the supply chain encompass both new products and new processes innovations (Nazir et al., 2024; Shen et al., 2021; Najafi-Tavani et al., 2018; Tariq et al., 2017). The term "product innovation" is used to describe the process of adding new features to existing products or their designs (Wan et al., 2024), while the process innovation involves novel methods for the production and delivery of products (Najafi-Tavani et al., 2018), resulting in improvements in cost and performance attributes (Henríquez-Calvo et al., 2024; Sari et al., 2020). The objective is to reassess the existing process and incorporate innovative features to enhance efficiency, such as through process integration and mutual trust; a supply chain can gain a collaborative advantage that lowers both the opportunity and monitoring cost, improving the SC performance and offering sustainable development (Zhang et al., 2023; Cao & Zhang, 2010), while collaborative innovation during the product design phase can mitigate the environmental effects of product life cycle resources (Shen et al., 2021; Mangun & Thurston, 2002). Consequently, collaborative innovation in supply chain involves upstream supplier and mid-stream manufacturer collaborating to co-develop a product incorporating multiple innovative elements, in which the manufacturer is in charge of product innovation, while the supplier is in charge of process innovation to streamline the manufacturing system and lower unit production costs (Chaouni Benabdellah et al., 2024; Shen et al., 2021). According to Shan et al. (2020), collaborative innovation in supply chains has not only been the primary way by which global firms are able to deal with the numerous disruptions, but it has also been the driving force behind the expansion of supply chain dynamic capabilities as well as achievement of sustainable development. In light of market diversity, intense competition, and shortened product life cycles, many enterprises within the supply chain are building collaborative relationships to promote sustainability and resilience (Ali et al., 2023; Shen et al., 2021; Scholten & Schilder, 2015). Collaborative relationship refers to when two or more organizations develop a synergistic connection, they commit to working together to address challenges, accomplish common objectives, and share knowledge, social responsibility, and financial rewards (Shan et al., 2020). According to Lambert et al. (1998), one of the most important aspects of supply chain cooperative innovation is the use of modern technological tools to achieve the integration of information and other diverse resources along the supply chain. The objective is to establish a unifying link and attain the shared aim of both parties.

Collaborative Innovation in Aviation Industry

Collaboration is essential for driving innovation and generating value within the aviation sector (Pereira et al., 2021) and has been regulated by diverse frameworks based on its aims, participating entities, and timeframes (Kamel, 2006). However, in the aviation sector, both the products and services share similarities in terms of functionality or design, which restricts the potential for the creation of new value (Franke, 2007), while this sector has the potential to establish new business models through collaborations to optimize operations by minimizing complexities, reduce maintenance repair and overhaul (MRO) costs, and facilitates sustainable growth (Abdi et al., 2022; Pereira et al., 2021; Ries & Euchner, 2013). As the collaborative innovation is effective for addressing complex and critical issues, it expands the innovation cycle to include additional stakeholders and leverages resources and opportunities across the organizational boundaries (Trivellato et al., 2020). According to Jolink and Niesten (2016), companies work in several partnerships such as mergers, acquisitions, and strategic alliances in order to stimulate innovation. Nevertheless, strategic alliances have the potential to investigate collaborative innovations and generate value through partnerships, where participants work together to reduce transaction costs and minimize risks (Pereira et al., 2021; Chesbrough, 2007). The strategic alliances often possess a defined duration, are designated for a certain initiative, and engage particular divisions of the participating firms (Kamel, 2006). Consequently, companies that engage with external entities are more adept at innovation, as these partnerships enhance their access to the strategic resources necessary for the development of new product and processes (Najafi-Tavani et al., 2018).

Challenges in Driving Collaborative Innovation in Pakistan's Aviation Sector

Collaboration is essential for businesses to create and capture value (Yan et al., 2023; Wang et al., 2017; Swink, 2006). However, on the other hand, it fails for many reasons, such as not having enough money, not being clear on who is responsible for what, resistance to change or not having enough commitment, and bureaucratic delays (Asghar & Mohsin, 2023; Demirkesen & Tezel, 2022; Porter & Birdi, 2018) are the key challenges in achieving effective collaboration among the parties involved (Pereira et al., 2021). For example, Pakistan International Airline (PIA) is run by the government, so it has to follow different rules than other four private companies (Asghar & Mohsin, 2023). This can cause differences and make private players not want to work together because of distinct approval processes. Another challenge is employing resistance as people who are used to doing things in the traditional old ways may be against technology or digital solutions because they are afraid of losing their jobs. According to Guo et al. (2012), sometimes, people struggle with giving up their habits, ideas, and beliefs, along with the stress that comes with embracing new technology. However, these challenges can be addressed through effective leadership, building trust, streamlining regulatory processes, boosting technological capabilities, and encouraging collaboration via public-private partnerships and a dedication to common objectives (Mokogwu et al., 2024; Pereira et al., 2021; Najafi-Tavani et al., 2018).

Research Methodology

This research study utilizes a qualitative approach, focusing on a single case study design to evaluate the feasibility and possible benefits of creating a collaborative innovative platform for repairing of unserviceable (U/S) rotable parts in the aviation industry in Pakistan. In doing so, the case study method is suitable for this type of research because its exploration has a deep understanding of the particular challenges and opportunities associated with building a collaborative innovative platform for the repair of rotable parts. According to Creswell and Creswell (2017), case study research allows for flexible data gathering methods that align with the research aims. In doing so, this study primarily investigates the impact of collaborative supply chain practices for the repair of unserviceable (U/S) or repairable rotable parts among five airline operators in Pakistan such as Pakistan International Airlines, Airblue, Serene Air, Fly Jinnah, and AirSial by utilizing artificial intelligence (AI) to improve cost efficiency, reducing repair costs, enhancing collaborative relationships, and promoting sustainability. This case study method enables a comprehensive examination of the current practices of rotable parts repairing among the five prominent airlines in Pakistan. It highlights the inefficiencies present in existing processes and explore the advantages of collaborative practices for rotable parts repairing. For this reason, semi-structured interviews have been organized and executed with procurement specialists, managers, executives overseeing supply chain operations, and maintenance staff in Pakistan's aviation sector. The primary objective of the interviews is to ascertain the existing processes of rotable parts repairing of each airline and the challenges associated with this particular process. Therefore, the interview questions are designed to identify the existing process of (U/S) or repairable rotable parts repairing and associated challenges as well as the advantages of centralized or collaborative contract with the repair agencies.

Case Study of Aviation Industry

Identifying the Existing Unserviceable Parts Repairing Process

Currently, all the five major airline operators such as Pakistan International Airlines, Airblue, Serene Air, Fly Jinnah, and AirSial as shown in Figs. 1, 2, 3, 4, and 5 accordingly use a fragmented approach for the repairing and maintenance of unserviceable (U/S) rotable components. Each carrier contracts with a different repair agency globally on an individual basis for the maintenance or repairing of these parts, despite utilizing the same parts across various airlines with identical fleets, i.e., Boeing or Airbus. As a result of individual agreements with several repair agencies, each carrier has to comprise with the contract pricing and service delivery while lacking the negotiating terms of bulk discounts. Furthermore, each carrier handles the shipment and clearance of U/S parts individually which leads to increase the transportation costs and carbon emissions due to multiple shipments. However, on the other hand, collaborative consolidated order leads to a single bulk order with reduced transportation costs and better terms with the repair agencies in a

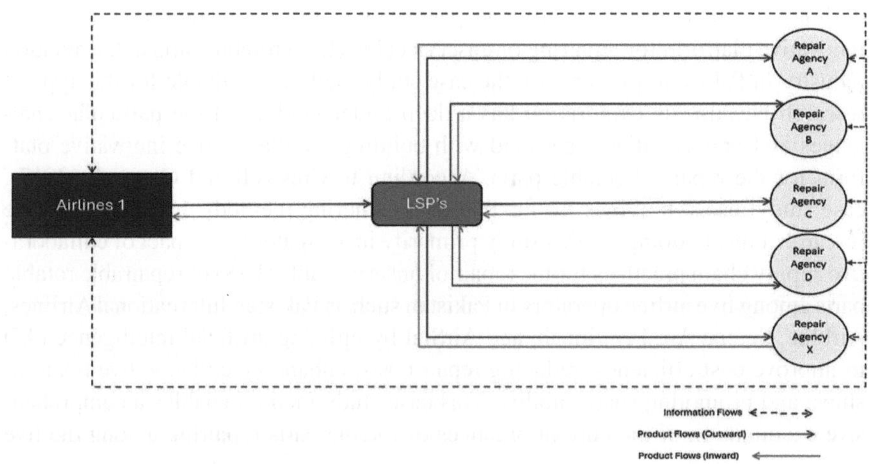

Fig. 1 Existing process of Airline 1

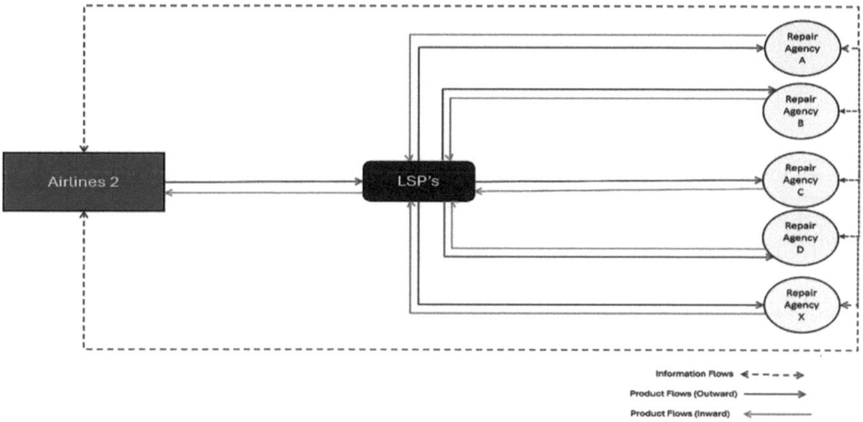

Fig. 2 Existing process of Airline 2

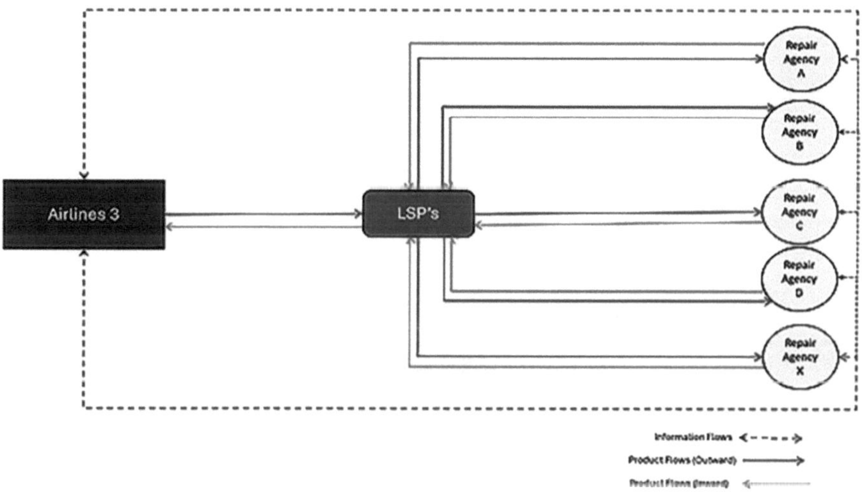

Fig. 3 Existing process of Airline 3

sustainable manner due to low number of shipments. While these airlines employ basic inventory management systems, the industry has not completely incorporated modern technology like AI to estimate rotable part life cycles. Consequently, the airlines could face unforeseen breakdowns or repair requirements, resulting in unscheduled maintenance, heightened expenses, and operational downtime. Additionally, the collaboration and data sharing among airlines concerning repair schedules, parts usage, and maintenance cycles are quite restricted. Therefore, this results in unnecessary duplication in handling U/S parts leading to inefficiencies and lost chances for cost savings. Addressing these challenges requires a more centralized and collaborative strategy for repair and maintenance of U/S parts, which could enhance resource optimization, lower costs, and foster sustainability in the aviation industry. Here are the (Figs. 1, 2, 3, 4, and 5) presenting the existing processes of all five airlines.

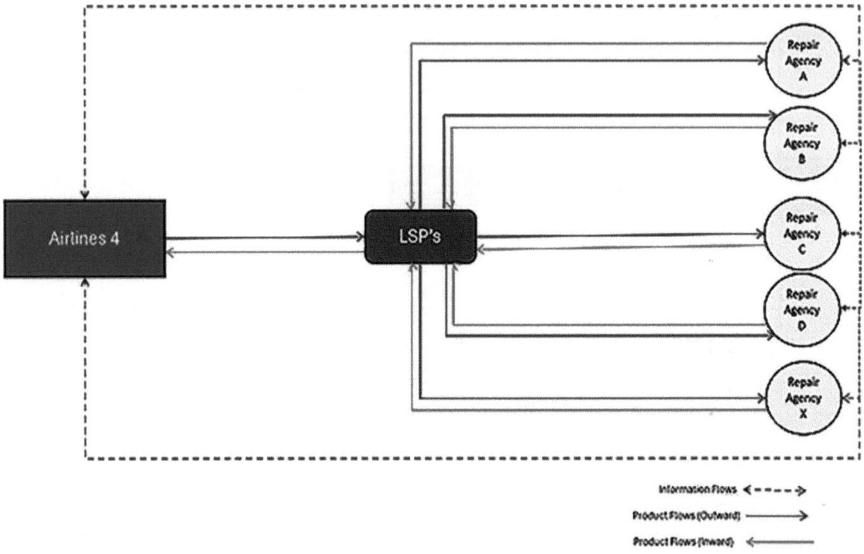

Fig. 4 Existing process of Airline 4

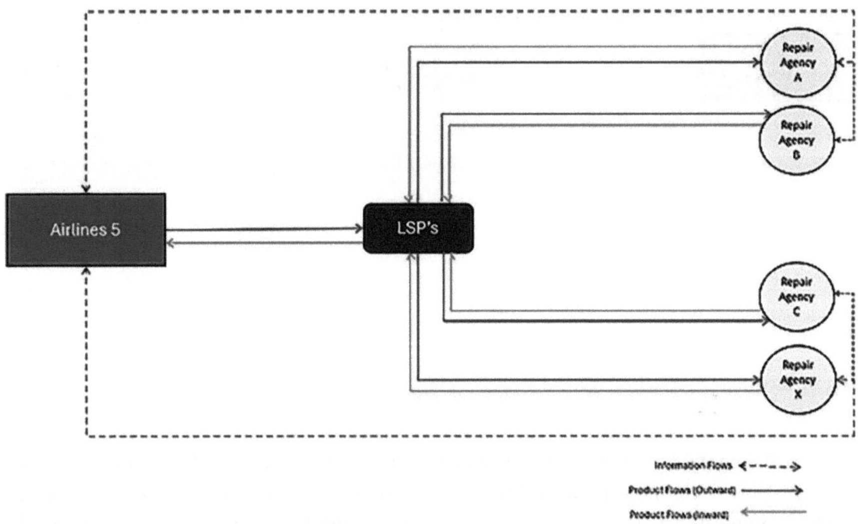

Fig. 5 Existing process of Airline 5

Proposed Model for Collaboration Through AI-Enabled System

In order to address the inefficiencies, present in the existing dispersed approach, the following practices are proposed for developing a collaborative, AI-enabled system for the repair and maintenance of unserviceable (U/S) rotable parts. These practices highlight the cost reduction, operational efficiency, and sustainability while promoting integration among the five airline operators in Pakistan. Firstly, a centralized AI-driven digital system is designed to oversee the maintenance and repair of rotable components for all five airlines. This platform serves as a foundational element for collaboration, enabling airlines to consolidate their repair orders and integrate effectively with the repair agencies. For example, each airline representative or concerned person will put information into the shared system about their rotable parts, such as their current condition, history of repairs, and expected life cycle to clarify the things for repair agencies. In doing so, by consolidating their maintenance needs into one consolidated order, airlines can cut down the operational redundancies, such as if multiple airlines operate similar fleets, such as the Airbus A320, and requires the repairs of the same components (i.e., landing gear). The system will consolidate these requests into a single centralized order for repairs, which will be sent to a single repair agency. Secondly, this collaborative digital platform will integrate with designated repair agencies via AI-enabled digital model, creating an effective communication channel among airlines and the service providers. The system will evaluate the performance of repair agencies by monitoring processing times, response time, and costs to ensure accountability and facilitate the continuous improvement. Furthermore, the proposed model focusses on consolidated shipments for U/S rotable parts to deal with high transportation costs and inefficiencies in the existing system, such as the AI-enabled digital platform will consolidate repair orders from all carriers into one consolidated shipment. For instance, rather than having each airline dispatch individual shipments to a repair agency, a unified, consolidated shipment will be organized and dispatched via logistics service providers (LSPS's). The AI algorithms will enhance shipment schedules and routes to reduce transportation costs and adverse environmental impact.

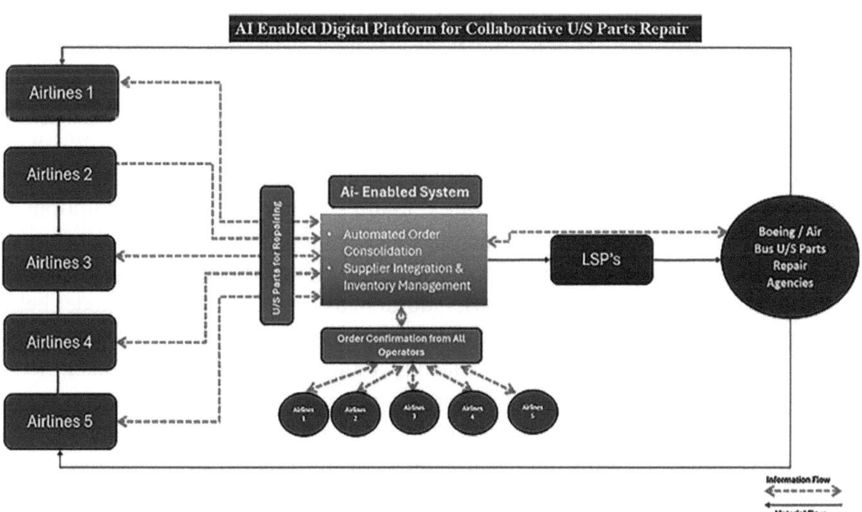

Fig. 6 AI-enabled digital platform for collaborative repairs

Additionally, this collaborative model enables airlines to negotiate improved terms with the repair agencies by positioning themselves as an integrated, unified company, such as the airlines will engage in collective negotiations with the repair agencies, utilizing their collected volume to obtain bulk discounts and better terms. In doing so, this leads to better supplier relationship management by developing mutually beneficial partnerships with the repair agencies. Consequently, the implementation of AI-driven collaborative practices in Pakistan's aviation industry has the potential to facilitate a transition toward digitalization that is more efficient, sustainable, and cost-effective, thereby establishing a benchmark for collaborative innovation within the global aviation sector. The proposed practices could serve as a basis for future collaborative initiatives, including shared inventory management and joint procurement activities (Fig. 6).

Managerial Implications

The suggested collaborative framework for the repair of U/S rotable components, driven by artificial intelligence and centralized agreements, presents a considerable managerial implication for airline operators, repair agencies, and industry authorities. The outcomes may contribute to decision-making processes, resource allocation strategies, cost management approaches, and sustainability initiatives. Centralized contracts with the repair agencies and combined shipments allow the managers to accomplish substantial cost savings through bulk negotiating and economies of scale. For example, a collective or collaborative contract for all five airlines, rather than individual negotiations by each operator, could potentially yield to avail higher discount from repair agencies due to increased repair volumes. This leads to a decrease in total maintenance costs, enabling managers to direct additional resources toward other operational priorities, including fleet enhancements or employee training. Furthermore, the managers may utilize the AI-generated information to switch from reactive to proactive repair strategies, thereby optimizing resource utilization and minimizing unplanned downtimes. Predictive AI suggests that a particular rotable part within the fleet will soon reach the end of its life cycle across all airlines, thus enabling the maintenance managers to proactively schedule repairs, thereby preventing mid-operation failures that could lead to disruptions in the planned schedules. In doing so, maintenance managers enhance control of repair schedules, hence reducing urgent repairs and operational downtime that frequently result in flight delays or cancellations. Additionally, this collaborative model helps managers in achieving sustainability objectives by minimizing the number of shipments and emissions through order consolidations. A consolidated shipment from all five airlines decreases the frequency of shipments by 50 to 70 percent, rather than individual shipments or dispatching U/S rotable parts to repair agencies. This has a direct impact on reducing the amount of fuel consumed as well as the carbon emissions. This collaborative approach will allow the airline managers to transitioning from a competitive position to a cooperative environment, in order to capitalize the mutual benefits of shared data and resources.

Conclusion and Future Recommendations

This study highlights the importance of a collaborative and AI-driven strategy for the management of unserviceable (U/S) rotable parts within Pakistan's aviation industry. Currently, the decentralized approach of having separate contracts with repair agencies causes inefficiencies in the process and higher costs and minimizes the sustainability opportunities. However, on the other hand, the proposed collaborative system, supported by a centralized AI-driven platform, could transform the aviation industry of Pakistan by streamlining the repair orders, incorporating predictive maintenance technologies, and enhancing transportation via consolidated shipments. This collaborative strategy sets a basis for building trust and cooperation among all competitive parties and creating opportunities for further joint initiatives. This research findings and framework provide a potential model for various industries or regions aiming to enhance operations via collaborative efforts and digital innovation. In the future, it is better to initiate a pilot program with two or three airlines to evaluate the practicality of the centralized repairing system and the AI-enabled platform and to assess its effectiveness regarding cost reduction, operational productivity, and environmental sustainability prior to expanding to all five airlines. Furthermore, it is mandatory to continuously optimize and improve the AI-enabled platform to integrate advanced machine learning algorithms, maintaining enhanced accuracy in predictive maintenance and the life cycle assessment of rotable parts and, also, creating a uniform procedure for repair workflows, data structures, and reporting standards to facilitate the seamless collaboration among all involved airlines and repair agencies. Upon the successful implementation of the collaborative repair system, broaden the collaboration to encompass more domains, like cooperative procurement of airplane parts, inventory sharing, or even collaborative training programs for maintenance personnel.

Acknowledgements During the preparation of this work, the author(s) used Grammarly for language editing and proofreading the manuscript. After using this tool/service, the author(s) reviewed and edited the content as needed and take(s) full responsibility for the content of the publication.

References

Abdi, Y., Li, X., & Càmara-Turull, X. (2022). Exploring the impact of sustainability (ESG) disclosure on firm value and financial performance (FP) in airline industry: The moderating role of size and age. *Environment, Development and Sustainability, 24*(4), 5052–5079. https://doi.org/10.1007/s10668-021-01649-w

Ali, M., Nazir, S., & Junaid, M. (2023). Blockchain driven supply chain management and supply chain resilience: Role of intellectual capital. *Management for Professionals*, 239–254. https://doi.org/10.1007/978-981-99-0699-4_14

Asghar, S., & Mohsin, H. (2023). Pakistan air lines (PIA)–a case study. *ISSRA Papers, 15*(1), 111–125.

Cao, M., & Zhang, Q. (2010). Supply chain collaboration: Impact on collaborative advantage and firm performance. *Journal of Operations Management, 29*(3), 163–180. https://doi.org/10.1016/j.jom.2010.12.008

Chaouni Benabdellah, A., et al. (2024). Designing a collaborative product development process from a knowledge management perspective. *Journal of Knowledge Management, 28*(8), 2383–2412. https://doi.org/10.1108/jkm-05-2023-0384

Chesbrough, H. (2007). Business model innovation: It's not just about technology anymore. *Strategy & Leadership, 35*(6), 12–17. https://doi.org/10.1108/10878570710833714

Creswell, J. W., & Creswell, J. D. (2017). *Research design: Qualitative, quantitative, and mixed methods approaches*. SAGE Publications, Inc.

Daghar, A., Alinaghian, L., & Turner, N. (2021). The role of collaborative interorganizational relationships in supply chain risks: A systematic review using a social capital perspective. *Supply Chain Management: An International Journal, 26*(2), 279–296. https://doi.org/10.1108/scm-04-2020-0177

Daugherty, P. J., et al. (2006). Is collaboration paying off for firms? *Business Horizons, 49*(1), 61–70. https://doi.org/10.1016/j.bushor.2005.06.002

Demirkesen, S., & Tezel, A. (2022). Investigating major challenges for industry 4.0 adoption among construction companies. *Engineering, Construction and Architectural Management.* Preprint. https://doi.org/10.1108/ecam-12-2020-1059

Franke, M. (2007). Innovation: The winning formula to regain profitability in aviation? *Journal of Air Transport Management, 13*(1), 23–30. https://doi.org/10.1016/j.jairtraman.2006.11.003

González-Benito, Ó., Muñoz-Gallego, P. A., & García-Zamora, E. (2016). Role of collaboration in innovation success: Differences for large and small businesses. *Journal of Business Economics and Management, 17*(4), 645–662. https://doi.org/10.3846/16111699.2013.823103

Greenwood Aerospace. (2023). *What are rotable parts and how to manage them, defense and military contracting for aerospace parts*. Available at: https://www.governmentprocurement.com/news/what-are-rotable-parts-and-how-to-manage-them. Accessed January 7, 2025.

Guo, X. *et al.* (2012) 'The dark side of elderly acceptance of preventive mobile health services in China', *Electronic Markets*, 23(1), pp. 49–61. doi:10.1007/s12525-012-0112-4.

Hameed, W. U., Nisar, Q. A., & Wu, H.-C. (2021). Relationships between external knowledge, internal innovation, firms' open innovation performance, Service Innovation and Business Performance in the Pakistani Hotel Industry. *International Journal of Hospitality Management, 92*, 102745. https://doi.org/10.1016/j.ijhm.2020.102745

Henríquez-Calvo, L., et al. (2024). Analysis of the impact process innovation and collaboration on competitiveness in small and medium-sized enterprises: A case study in Colombia. *Procedia Computer Science, 231*, 636–641. https://doi.org/10.1016/j.procs.2023.12.171

Jolink, A., & Niesten, E. (2016). The impact of venture capital on governance decisions in collaborations with start-ups. *Small Business Economics, 47*(2), 331–344. https://doi.org/10.1007/s11187-016-9719-8

Kamel, M. (2006). Collaboration for innovation in closed system industries: The case of the aviation industry. *Engineering Management Journal, 18*(4), 16–22. https://doi.org/10.1080/10429247.2006.11431709

Lambert, D. M., Cooper, M. C., & Pagh, J. D. (1998). Supply chain management: Implementation issues and research opportunities. *The International Journal of Logistics Management, 9*(2), 1–20. https://doi.org/10.1108/09574099810805807

Mangun, D., & Thurston, D. L. (2002). Incorporating component reuse, remanufacture, and recycle into product portfolio design. *IEEE Transactions on Engineering Management, 49*(4), 479–490. https://doi.org/10.1109/tem.2002.807292

Matarneh, S., et al. (2024). Industry 4.0 technologies and circular economy synergies: Enhancing corporate sustainability through sustainable supply chain integration and flexibility. *Environmental Technology & Innovation, 35*, 103723. https://doi.org/10.1016/j.eti.2024.103723

Mokogwu, C., Achumie, G. O., Adeleke, A. G., Okeke, I. C., & Ewim, C. P. (2024). A leadership and policy development model for driving operational success in tech companies. *International Journal of Frontline Research in Multidisciplinary Studies, 4*(1), 1–14.

Najafi-Tavani, S., et al. (2018). How collaborative innovation networks affect new product performance: Product innovation capability, process innovation capability, and absorptive capacity. *Industrial Marketing Management, 73*, 193–205. https://doi.org/10.1016/j.indmarman.2018.02.009

Nazir, S., et al. (2023). Role of intellectual capital in implementing blockchain technology-driven sustainable supply chain: A proposed framework. *Management for Professionals*, 201–218. https://doi.org/10.1007/978-981-99-0699-4_12

Nazir, S., et al. (2024). Sustainable performance and disaster management in the oil and gas industry: An Intellectual Capital Perspective. *Resources Policy, 92*, 105042. https://doi.org/10.1016/j.resourpol.2024.105042

Nilsson, F., & Göransson, M. (2021). Critical factors for the realization of sustainable supply chain innovations—model development based on a systematic literature review. *Journal of Cleaner Production, 296*, 126471. https://doi.org/10.1016/j.jclepro.2021.126471

Olson, E. M., Walker, O. C., Ruekerf, R. W., & Bonnerd, J. M. (2001). Patterns of cooperation during new product development among marketing, operations and R&D: Implications for project performance. *Journal of Product Innovation Management, 18*(4), 258–271. https://doi.org/10.1111/1540-5885.1840258

Pereira, B., Lohmann, G., & Houghton, L. (2021). The role of collaboration in innovation and value creation in the aviation industry. *Journal of Creating Value, 7*(1), 44–59. https://doi.org/10.1177/23949643211010588

Porter, J. J., & Birdi, K. (2018). 22 reasons why collaborations fail: Lessons from water innovation research. *Environmental Science & Policy, 89*, 100–108. https://doi.org/10.1016/j.envsci.2018.07.004

Ries, E., & Euchner, J. (2013). What large companies can learn from start-ups. *Research-Technology Management, 56*(4), 12–16. https://doi.org/10.5437/08956308x5604003

Sari, R. N., et al. (2020). Effect of environmental management accounting practices on organizational performance: Role of Process Innovation as a mediating variable. *Business Process Management Journal, 27*(4), 1296–1314. https://doi.org/10.1108/bpmj-06-2020-0264

Scholten, K., & Schilder, S. (2015). The role of collaboration in supply chain resilience. *Supply Chain Management: An International Journal, 20*(4), 471–484. https://doi.org/10.1108/scm-11-2014-0386

Shan, H., Li, Y., & Shi, J. (2020). Influence of supply chain collaborative innovation on sustainable development of supply chain: A study on Chinese enterprises. *Sustainability, 12*(7), 2978. https://doi.org/10.3390/su12072978

Shen, B., et al. (2021). Collaborative innovation in supply chain systems: Value creation and leadership structure. *International Journal of Production Economics, 235*, 108068. https://doi.org/10.1016/j.ijpe.2021.108068

Swaminathan, V., & Moorman, C. (2009). Marketing alliances, firm networks, and f i rm V a l u e Cr e a t i on. *Journal of Marketing, 73*(5), 52–69. https://doi.org/10.1509/jmkg.73.5.52

Swink, M. (2006). Building collaborative innovation capability. *Research-Technology Management, 49*(2), 37–47. https://doi.org/10.1080/08956308.2006.11657367

Tariq, A., et al. (2017). Drivers and consequences of green product and process innovation: Asystematic review, conceptual framework, and future outlook. *Technology in Society, 51*, 8–23. https://doi.org/10.1016/j.techsoc.2017.06.002

Trivellato, B., Martini, M., & Cavenago, D. (2020). How do organizational capabilities sustain continuous innovation in a public setting? *The American Review of Public Administration, 51*(1), 57–71. https://doi.org/10.1177/0275074020939263

Wan, M., et al. (2024). Dynamic path for green product development: A game-theoretic analysis of product-process innovation with supply chain collaboration. *Computers & Industrial Engineering, 195*, 110428. https://doi.org/10.1016/j.cie.2024.110428

Wang, F., et al. (2017). Collaborative innovation capability in IT-enabled inter-firm collaboration. *Industrial Management & Data Systems, 117*(10), 2364–2380. https://doi.org/10.1108/imds-09-2016-0392

Wilkinson, I., & Young, L. (2002). On cooperating: Firms, relations and networks. *Journal of Business Research, 55*(2), 123–132. https://doi.org/10.1016/s0148-2963(00)00147-8

Yan, F., et al. (2023). Building supply chain resilience through collaborative innovation: An information processing theory perspective. *Journal of Digital Economy, 2*, 233–243. https://doi.org/10.1016/j.jdec.2024.01.004

Zhang, Y., et al. (2023). Blockchain technology and sustainable supply chain practices: Leading towards organizational performance. *Journal of Advanced Manufacturing Systems, 22*(03), 549–569. https://doi.org/10.1142/s0219686723500257

Zimmermann, R., Ferreira, L. M. D. F., & Carrizo Moreira, A. (2016). The influence of supply chain on the innovation process: A systematic literature review. *Supply Chain Management: An International Journal, 21*(3), 289–304. https://doi.org/10.1108/scm-07-2015-0266

Sajid Nazir is a Junior researcher and Ph.D. student at Lappeenranta-Lahti University Technology (LUT), Finland. He is also associated with the Institute of Business Management (IoBM), Karachi-Pakistan, as a Senior Lecturer at the Department of Logistics and Supply Chain Management. He joined academia right after completing his master's in supply chain management from Coventry University, UK, in 2018. Sajid Nazir has more than 10 years of experience working in the Academia as well as in the corporate sector on national as well as international levels such as banking, aviation, pharmaceutical, and other service industries as a supply chain professional. His work has been published in journals and conferences in the fields of supply chain management and innovation management. His areas of interest are blockchain technologies, resilient supply chain, technology and innovation management, Industry 5.0, sustainable supply chain performance, and innovations in supply chain.

Sociomaterial Perspectives of AI and Procurement

Luciana Blaha, David M. Brown, Krishan Chandarana, and Amber Devin

Introduction

The exponential rise of AI adoption and development within organizations has been well-documented in management literature. It is widely accepted that AI applications impact profoundly upon business functions, such as decision-making processes and role design (Faraj et al., 2018), and both public- and private-sector procurement (Dor & Coglianese, 2021; Westphal & Wang, 2023, Guida et al., 2023). However, despite growing knowledge of AI's contribution to procurement, numerous human-AI interactions and their algorithmic characteristics remain partially unexplored, particularly in terms of the decision-making which underpins such interactions (Zhu et al., 2016; Kosmol et al., 2019; Bienhaus & Haddud; 2018; Schoenherr & Speier-Pero, 2015; Franck et al., cited in Guida et al., 2023). Studies of human interactions with technology have proliferated since the early 2010s, but now with particular growth in studies exploring relationships between humans and technology from a sociotechnical assemblage perspective.[1]

This sociomaterial frame facilitates analysis of how AI, its related technologies (e.g., robotics), and its interactions with humans enable or constrain human

[1] According to Kinkaid (2020), the term "assemblage" describes processes through which different entities come together, form relations, and operate as provisional "wholes." "Assemblage" can refer to processes in a variety of settings—for instance, in urban regeneration (McGuirk et al., cited in Kinkaid, 2020), neighborhood change (Grossmann and Haase, cited in Kinkaid, 2020), or participatory development (Grove and Pugh, cited in Kinkaid, 2020).

L. Blaha (✉) · D. M. Brown · K. Chandarana
University of Edinburgh, Edinburgh, UK
e-mail: M.Blaha@hw.ac.uk; David.Brown@hw.ac.uk; kc2005@hw.ac.uk

A. Devin
Heriot Watt University, Edinburgh, Scotland
e-mail: A.Devin@hw.ac.uk

M. Dabić et al. (eds.), *Artificial Humans*, Future of Business and Finance,
https://doi.org/10.1007/978-3-032-06604-6_13

behavior. It also enables an understanding of their impacts upon regulation, organizational performance (Chedrawi & Haddad, 2022; Johri, 2022), and broader digital business ecosystems (Zhao & Yang, 2022; van Rijmenam, 2019). Additionally, it helps to construct "biographies" of adopted algorithms (Glaser et al., 2021), which explore how AI's non-congruence with certain human goals, decisions, behaviors, and understandings shapes it over time.

In this chapter, we adopt Glaser et al.'s (2021) algorithmic biography perspective of sociomateriality, thereby understanding procurement as a key moment in this "biography" of AI algorithms, where the integration of AI instigates organizational changes and innovations (Roy et al., 2025). This framework emphasizes the entanglement of social, material, and technological elements, acknowledging the co-constitution of technological innovations with human practices (Orlikowski & Scott, 2008), and exploring that AI may amplify or perpetuate human biases and understandings (Johri, 2022) while simultaneously disrupting and accelerating knowledge work (Coombs et al., 2020).

This chapter also reflects the duality of AI in procurement: AI not only optimizes procurement activities but also transforms organizational boundaries and social practices. Indeed, AI challenges established perspectives of expertise and decision-making (Faraj et al., 2018; Coombs et al., 2020), supplier selection, contract development (Chai et al., 2013), and organizational workflow change (Orlikowski & Scott, 2008). Understanding this duality enables a more comprehensive and nuanced exploration of AI's broader implications for procurement, particularly in terms of ethical challenges and organizational change. Given the acceleration of knowledge creation in this area, we have performed a systematic review of academic and policy literature to identify the broader implications and ethical challenges faced by organizations as they procure AI. Following a review of 694 papers and policy documents, we identified six research gaps, which we will address from a sociomaterial perspective. Finally, we discuss key technological and ethical dimensions of AI procurement and demonstrate the need for AI research to adopt holistic perspectives which consider human oversight and social accountability. This chapter therefore contributes to broader discourses on AI's role in shaping organizational futures, in which the fusion of human and artificial intelligence plays an increasingly central role.

Methodology: Systematic Literature Review

We undertook our literature review in accordance with Page et al.'s (2021) PRISMA approach, which provides guidance on reviewing extant sources to understand social interventions, as illustrated in Fig. 1 below.

The initial search strategy used keywords and search terms such as "Artificial Intelligence," "Procurement," "Supply Chain Management," and "Organizations." As Google Scholar alone yielded 156,000 results for "Procurement of Artificial Intelligence," the search was refined by combining search terms and using multiple academic search engines, yielding 15,400 results from Google Scholar, 74 from Discovery, 12 from Scopus, and 8 from Web of Science. Furthermore, we applied

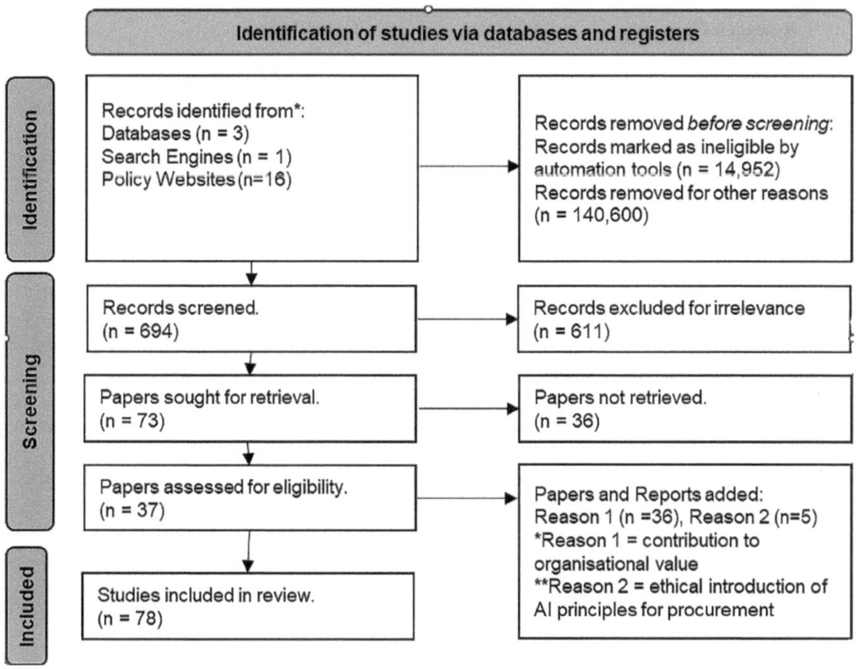

Fig. 1 Literature review flow diagram

filters such as "peer-reviewed," "English language," and "literature reviews" to explore the prevalence of different types of sources and to condense and categorize results. This produced 676, 2, 3, and 2 results, respectively – a combined total of 683 articles. Relevance checks reduced this to 37 articles. Additionally, 16 policy documents were screened, of which 5 were deemed sufficiently relevant to a study of organizational AI use in the context of procurement, and were added to the 37 articles, resulting in a total of 42 sources.

Due to the narrowness of sources identified by the initial search phase, keywords such as "sustainability" and "outsourcing" were introduced to verify potential research gaps, garnering an additional 130 results from Google Scholar and 2 results from each of the remaining three databases, providing a total of 136 results. These were also subjected to relevance checks, and the remaining sources were added to the first wave of 42 results, giving a total of 78 sources.

Selected sources were split into two groups: (i) sources concerned with organizational value (i.e., contributions to the supply chain, management of the procurement of AI, or AI's contribution to the management of procurement) and (ii) ethical considerations on AI usage for these purposes. The sources were then reviewed for quality and their potential contribution to our analysis, which identified key foci – and gaps in knowledge—of how AI is understood and approached by organizations. These foci and gaps are shown in Fig. 2, which also summarizes our observations on the literature.

Research Gaps	Focus Areas
I. Procurement of AI, and AI Technologies	Despite discussion of AI, and of AI in procurement processes, the empirical exploration of technology procurement is limited, particularly in terms of the decisions, practices, and negotiations which complement such processes from both supplier and client perspectives.
II. Measuring the Impact of AI on Procurement	The literature suggests that metrics surrounding the quality, effectiveness, and efficiency of procurement require improvements. There is a requirement for more context-aware research on (i) how to accurately and quantitatively measure AI impacts upon procurement processes, and (ii) on a longitudinal scale.
III. Role of AI in Auditing	Auditing of procured technologies remains an emergent research area, particularly within public sector contexts. Additionally, discussions of the potential of AI to refine auditing, and whether it can address the issues associated with manual auditing, are underdeveloped.
IV. Adoption in Developing Countries	The potential of digital supply chain principles, including AI, is being explored in emerging economies such as India. However, further research is required to understand challenges and opportunities specific to significantly different socioeconomic contexts.
V. Government Initiatives and Policies	Literature exists on the role of government initiatives in advancing digitalized manufacturing. However, there is a dearth of empirical studies to complement policy documents, white papers and systematic literature reviews of how government policies can influence AI adoption for procurement.
VI. Sustainability	Further empirical data is required on organizations' sustainability practices and how AI procurement can align with them.

Fig. 2 Literature review observations

The first phase of our review reveals that studies of AI in organizations, and of AI's roles in shaping organizations – particularly through procurement—remain fragmented despite increased data availability. Moreover, our review suggests that, by neglecting holistic perspectives which reflect the interconnected nature of AI's usage and influence within organizations, extant studies contribute insufficiently to addressing the challenges of performance metric relevance, technology adoption, and power imbalances.

These initial findings supported our interest in exploring AI's impacts upon stakeholders more cohesively by adopting a sociomaterial lens, which we will later explain in more detail. Furthermore, the findings confirmed the importance of ascertaining the influence upon organizations of current approaches to AI usage. This prompted the review of 16 further policy documents regulating, proposing specific approaches to AI. Of these, 5 were chosen for their direct relevance to procurement and will be discussed in Sect. 4.

Augmented Human Procurement Systems

Procurement contributes to organizational growth by acquiring technologies which drive digitalization and augment organizational capabilities (Porter, cited in Bienhaus & Haddud, 2018). AI automation can enhance customer engagement (Brown & Thompson, 2023), automate routine processes (Shams et al., 2025), and facilitate data-driven decision-making (Davenport & Ronanki, 2018).

For instance, AI can improve operational capability within the procurement process by augmenting supplier and product screening, through comparing features such as affordability and quality (Guida et al., 2023). This arguably affects transactions between procurement teams and potential suppliers (Kosmol et al., 2019). An example of this is IBM's D&B Ask Procurement, an AI assistant designed to help procurement professionals *"accelerate the discovery of supply chain risks and opportunities, including financial risk and critical supplier insights"* (IBM, 2025). While the AI assistant provides technical information through its screening, its influence upon the process is recognized and mitigated by IBM through the training of procurement teams to *"instill optimistic attitudes"* toward its use (ibid.)

Moreover, AI was presented as supporting decision-making where goals had been clearly set, and decisions followed a predetermined flow within the organization. As an example, Microsoft's Open AI supply-chain services were designed to decide which demand patterns would be most likely and to streamline product distribution by companies such as Zara and H & M (AIX, 2023).

However, aligning these algorithmic and automation technologies with strategic goals often presents challenges, particularly in responsible sourcing and system compliance (Engstrom et al., 2020; Hickok, 2022). Moreover, the organizational, human "assemblages" in which the various AI applications are procured receive no overt consideration. In fact, they are often disjointed from the systemic view of how AI is integrated within wider automation systems, despite them having aggregate effects upon service and knowledge work (Coombs et al., 2020; Ng et al., 2021; Blaha, 2021).

Within this digitalization narrative, internal operations improvements are often presented as the main driver of the procurement of AI. This often focuses on performance gains, knowledge development, and operational excellence (Guida et al., 2023). More specifically, the motivations for integrating AI into work most often include a recognition of the efficiency of algorithms, and a desire to support senior-level strategic decision-making (Santhi & Muthuswamy, 2023), and the elevated expectations and costs which accompany these aspirations (Glas & Kleeman, 2016). These are in turn related to procurement professionals and other employees who may consequently benefit by being freed to focus on more meaningful work (Guida et al., 2023).

The supplier-client relationship was also highlighted as critical to the successful integration of AI to augment human work (Barrad et al., 2020), in particular when related to the readiness of the purchasing organization and its AI supplier. Barrad et al. (2020) suggest that, if the human function is to be augmented optimally, consideration must be given to the environmental, technological, organizational, humanistic, financial, and data aspects of the integration—especially when the AI supplier and AI-using organization collaborate for this purpose (Kosmol et al., 2019; Handfield et al., 2019; Handfield, 2019). Doing this effectively is predicated upon communication, context-focus (Lorentz et al., 2021; Bag et al., 2020), and power balance (Bienhaus & Haddud, 2018; Bag et al., 2020) between these two stakeholders, particularly when clarifying the use of AI for both suppliers and customers (Glas & Kleeman, 2016).

In the literature review, in which we observed this initial state of procurement perspectives on AI, another prevalent theme was the significant transformation of procurement due to the contributing technologies (Abolbashari et al., 2018; Rajeb & Appolloni, 2022), although this was acknowledged while also noting that the AI which contributes is also evolving (Guida et al., 2023; Glas & Kleeman, 2016). Supply-chain management articles framed this within the context of industry-wide advancements accelerating the need for procurement to respond to the increased use of AI, and the desire to improve internal organization operations (Rajeb & Appolloni, 2022; Bag et al., 2020, Lasi et al., 2014; Herold et al., 2023), while simultaneously questioning how the effectiveness of AI is measured when faced with the increasing volatility of supply chains (Helo & Hao, 2022; Narwane et al., 2021; Liu et al., 2011). In this context, the establishment of product requirements, the search for suppliers, the selection of suppliers, contract negotiation, and re-designing processes are still considered fundamental to procurement (Bienhaus & Haddud, 2018; Stange et al., 2022), with cross-departmental collaboration considered particularly influential (Herold et al., 2023). In terms of AI's augmentation of procurement, extant studies were heavily oriented toward exploring the internal drivers for e-procurement—especially financial situation, resources, data architecture, and strategic goals (e.g., Ronchi et al., 2010) – which through AI can augment supplier selection (Bifulco et al., 2021), internal auditing (Wang et al., 2020), data sourcing, data maintenance, and data management (Bifulco et al., 2021). This was shown to increase supplier confidence in the client (Kosmol et al., 2019) and the likelihood of the overall intelligent automation system increasing the organization's adaptability (Liu et al., 2011).

Given this approach, it is unsurprising that AI procurement has therefore developed as a strategic priority (Bienhaus & Haddud, 2018; Herold et al., 2023) for organizations seeking to increase control, transparency, and decentralization (Ronchi et al., 2010; Lorentz et al., 2021). This strategic, cross-function prioritization can direct performance metrics (Abolbashari et al., 2018). However, many of the challenges facing the augmentation of purchasing processes were process-related, such as establishing appropriate structures for procedures, capacities, capabilities, and processes (Bienhaus & Haddud, 2018). Other sources focused either on concrete moments within supplier selection or, subsequent to acquisition, the measurement of impact beyond project-specific algorithmic performance measures (Liu et al., 2011), while other capabilities deemed to be contingent upon employees' digital skills (Gholizadeh et al., 2020).

This complex and yet emergent view of AI in the procurement function of organizations highlights the importance of human understanding, behaviors, decisions, and processes—at least within purchasing and supplying organizations – in relation to how AI augments human work and whether AI may be considered an artificial worker.

Artificial Humans: The Sociomaterial Perspective

Earlier in this chapter, we highlighted the role of humans in implementing AI into working life and the workplace impacts of AI technologies—especially in relation to how the AI had been procured. To account for these complex influences, we propose a view connecting human drivers and experience with algorithmic influences and features: sociomateriality.

The sociomaterial perspective offers a nuanced lens for examining the integration of new technologies – particularly AI and automation – into organizational processes in a way which does discriminate against the human, not the machine. In the context of procurement, this approach helps us to identify the complex interplay between technology, organizational processes, and human actors, which are often approached in literature in a fragmented, case-by-case manner. At its core, sociomateriality advises that the social and the material are inseparable and mutually constitutive (Orlikowski & Scott, 2008), recognizing the need to account for both organizational dynamics and technologies and the ways in which they are intertwined and continuously shape each other.

This entanglement becomes particularly evident in the realm of AI and automation procurement. The procurement process changes from a prescribed acquisition decision, shaped solely by humans, to a complex dance of algorithms, data, human decision-making, and organizational policies. As Glaser et al. (2021) point out, this creates a tension between the human "assemblage" of organizational dynamics and the new features of the algorithm and the practices they encourage. Overall, these tensions must lead to new human decisions and their translation into technology, leading to a balanced configuration where the organization's stakeholders can interact with the technologies in a stable, accepted way over time. These conflicts are important to study not just due to their complex nature but due to their questioning of power, expertise, and organizational identity in the area where the algorithms are introduced (Rajeb & Appolloni, 2022; Bag et al., 2020).

This is an important shift in understanding, as it enables us to move beyond the debate of "humans versus machines" towards a more organizationally integrated perspective (Mauthner & Kazimierczak, 2018), which can help management scholars to capture emerging knowledge on the technology, the humans involved in the process, and interaction between humans and technologies (Orlikowski, 2010).

The sociomaterial perspective therefore proposes algorithms as non-human actors in organizational processes, which can create new practices and knowledge (Orlikowski, 2010; Symon & Pritchard, 2015). In the context of procurement, this could include not just AI systems but also the data which they process, the algorithms which they use, and the physical infrastructures which support them. These non-human actors are not passive tools but active participants in shaping organizational outcomes, as they directly impact upon decisions just as they impact upon organizational knowledge (Coombs et al., 2020).

For instance, the choice of data used to train an AI procurement system can have significant impacts upon supplier selection (Bienhaus & Haddud, 2018), potentially reinforcing or challenging existing biases in the procurement process without direct intervention from human workers (Johri, 2022). Moreover, certain AI applications can augment human decision-making by processing vast amounts of data and identifying patterns which might be invisible to human actors (Bifulco et al., 2021), leading to new or unforeseen decisions. Consequently, AI can also reshape work boundaries and coordination activities (Faraj et al., 2018). As systems integrating applications like machine learning and natural language processing become more sophisticated in interpreting and learning from external data, they necessitate new forms of human expertise. Procurement professionals, for example, may need to develop skills in data analysis and algorithm management alongside their traditional negotiation and supplier relationship management skills (Bienhaus & Haddud, 2018; Stange et al., 2022), leading to knowledge and capacity changes within the organization. This transformation therefore extends beyond the procurement process itself, permeating throughout the organization and reshaping human capabilities and interactions. However, this enhancement is not a unidirectional phenomenon. Human actors, in turn, shape how the AI is used, interpreted, and integrated into organizational practices – for instance, through the shaping of the associated data architecture (Ronchi et al., 2010), the redesigning of processes, and even in negotiations with suppliers (Bienhaus & Haddud, 2018; Stange et al., 2022). Transformations enacted by AI-human partnerships can therefore be understood as dialogical, reciprocal, iterative, and self-perpetuating.

Procurement is therefore important as a biographical moment, because AI's integration into procurement processes represents a transformative shift, where algorithms enter organizational ecosystems, shaping decision-making and determining the trajectory of AI deployment as they are used over time. As Glaser et al. (2021) suggest, as AI applications become embedded within organizational structures, they influence how processes are undertaken and decisions made. This redefines human-technology relations and reshapes work practices, decision methods, roles, and expertise within organizations (Orlikowski & Scott, 2008; Faraj et al., 2018; Guida et al., 2023).

Back to the Humans

So how can this increasingly common sociomaterial interaction inform humans within organizations? Haider and Sundin (2019) argue that the increasing prevalence of AI-driven search engines and recommendation systems in day-to-day activities necessitates a new understanding of information literacy. They propose an approach which accounts for the invisible algorithmic processes which shape our information environments, offering the concept of *infrastructural meaning-making* to describe how users must learn to interpret and navigate these complex sociotechnical systems.

This approach aligns with the work of Priharsari and Abedin (2021), who examine how sociomateriality can help us to understand value co-creation in online communities. They highlight how the material aspects of digital platforms, such as their interfaces and algorithms, are inextricably linked with social practices of information sharing and knowledge creation, suggesting instead that human technology literacy emerges from the complex interplay between users, technologies, and social contexts.

AI-enhanced procurement processes and information environments therefore function in a complex web of trust and relationship-building which emerges when such technologies are procured (Dor & Coglianese, 2021; Rice, 2024; Coglianese, 2024). As Akter et al. (2023) highlight, the learning, management, and infrastructure management capabilities of organizational actors play a crucial role in this context. Trust is no longer just about interpersonal relationships between procurement professionals and suppliers or between information seekers and sources. Trust therefore extends to the AI systems themselves, the data they use, and in the organization's ability to manage these complex sociotechnical systems (Coglianese, 2024).

This expanded notion of trust and relationship-building is further explored by scholars such as Coglianese (2024), who emphasize the importance of understanding the intricate connections between customers, suppliers, and technological systems. From the sociomaterial perspective, these relationships are not considered separate from technology, but as co-constituted with it. For example, a supplier's reliability might be judged not solely on their past performance but on how well their systems integrate with the buying organization's IT infrastructure, creating supplier dependencies and potential software ecosystems restricted by the client's procured technologies.

This perspective is particularly evident in the way AI technologies are reshaping the procurement processes themselves. The use of predictive analytics, chatbots, and machine learning algorithms in procurement (Burger et al., 2023) integrate AI as an active participant within decision-making processes. This participation blurs the traditional boundaries between human and machine agency, creating what Van der Aalst (2021) describes as a *hybrid intelligence approach* or what may be conceptualized as ***artificial human workers,*** in procurement practices.

As AI systems become more sophisticated, they become increasingly capable of handling complex tasks which were traditionally performed by humans (Faraj et al.,

2018), thereby leading to the refocusing of human roles toward strategic thinking, ethical oversight, and interpersonal skills which complement AI capabilities.

Artificial Humans in the System

To observe these interactions in a more coherent way, it may be useful to adopt an assemblage-wide or systemic view. According to scholars such as Henman (2020), a systemic approach can help identify the farther-reaching effects of the implementation of AI, such as the emergent knowledge creation (Orlikowski & Scott, 2008) and the development of new practices within the organization.

The sociomaterial perspective may therefore help us to trace these interconnections and understand their implications. As the boundaries between human and machine decision-making become more blurred, this influences the boundaries between the development and use of AI (Waardenburg & Huysman, 2022). This is due to the interaction and adaptation of AI to the information supplied by humans and the knowledge and practices of workers through the interaction with AI and leads to the creation of new understandings of roles within the organization's system, in which terms such as "user" and "developer" become more nuanced in the procurement of AI.

However, as AI becomes more autonomous and influential in decision-making processes, questions arise about accountability, transparency, fairness (Henman, 2020), and the underlying challenges which new working practices and their conceptualizations bring (Faraj et al., 2018).

As Haider and Sundin (2019) point out, the rapidly evolving nature of digital technologies can make it difficult to pin down the specific material configurations which shape information practices at any given moment, meaning that the assemblages in which humans are becoming artificial are difficult to capture. At the same time, such scholars advise an approach which still strives to understand these different role-technology configurations by gaining visibility into the exact roles and processes involved – for example, ascertaining where employees may protect their roles or reconfigure their professional activities (Faulconbridge et al., 2023).

Due to difficulties in undertaking this, some scholars have criticized sociomateriality for potentially obscuring important distinctions between human and non-human actors. Leonardi (2013), for instance, argues for a critical realist approach which maintains an analytical separation between the social and the material while acknowledging their mutual influence. Moreover, methodologically, sociomateriality presents both opportunities and challenges for researchers in its ability to capture the complex, dynamic nature of sociomaterial entanglements. Hultin (2019), for instance, calls for more innovative approaches, such as ethnographic methods, to identify material aspects of organizational practices or to trace the flows of algorithms in real time.

By rejecting the notion of technology as a separate entity which impacts organizations from the outside, the sociomaterialist perspective allows for the empirical investigation of how technologies and social practices are mutually constitute, constantly shaping and reshaping each other. While it may remain limited in specific investigation instruments, this view not only enhances our understanding of current practices but may support future developments in technology design and adoption. As organizations and individuals continue to grapple with rapid advancements in AI and automation, the sociomaterial perspective allows scholars to move beyond simplistic notions of technological determinism or social constructivism, toward a more nuanced understanding of the complex, dynamic, and mutually influential relationship between the social and the material in organizational life. However, this view is constrained to the organization itself, with a limited overview of the regulatory impact held by outside actors. In the next section, we review a series of documents showcasing how AI procurement is regulated and understood, before reflecting upon the latest implications of these organizational dynamics on the journey of humans converging with AI in the workplace.

Regulating the Artificial

As previously discussed, procurement represents a key algorithmic biographical moment for organizations. Within this, it provides many valuable examples of how procurement mediates the relationship between humans and AI technologies, especially in the light of current global changes to the regulation of AI used by organizations. This regulatory transformation has become particularly evident in the focus on how procurement affects human decision-makers and the use of AI systems, in some of the policy documents we reviewed below. Additionally, there is a recognition of the importance of the sociomaterial, or sociotechnical, perspective influencing the implementation of AI in key areas of society, such as government services and citizens' lives.

An example of this can be found in the OECD's AI principles (OECD, 2021), which emphasize transparency, accountability, and human oversight. The OECD's value-based principles stress the importance of *inclusive growth, sustainable development, and well-being* while advocating for AI systems that *respect human rights, democratic values and diversity* (OECD, 2021). This suggests that the procurement process should not merely focus on technological capabilities but also consider the impact upon stakeholders from how data is processed, sourced, and controlled from the inception of the AI product, throughout its life cycle in the company. The concept of *transparency and explainability* in the OECD guidelines (OECD, 2021) is particularly relevant to guarding the ability to question the systems by understanding their decisions. This principle requires the selection of AI systems which can provide clear explanations for their decisions, thus preserving human oversight.

The European Union AI Act (European Commission, 2024) further illustrates how procurement can shape the human-AI interaction. The Act focuses on ensuring *safety, [protecting] fundamental human rights and fostering innovation* by introducing rules for high-risk AI applications. This regulatory approach requires organizations to evaluate the ethical implications of AI systems before implementation, effectively pushing the boundary of human oversight earlier within the AI lifecycle and, in fact, toward procurement. The Act's prohibition of certain AI practices, such as those *exploiting vulnerabilities or using subliminal techniques* (European Commission, 2024), sets clear boundaries for what is acceptable in AI procurement.

In the context of using AI for procurement, the NIST AI Risk Management Framework (NIST, 2024) looks at managing the risks associated with AI in decision-making processes. The framework identifies key areas of concern such as *confabulation, dangerous recommendations, data privacy, and information integrity* (NIST, 2024). These considerations require organizations to anticipate and mitigate potential risks which could blur the line between human and machine decision-making from the outset, potentially influencing the procurement supplier selection and contract negotiation stages (scrutiny for *automation bias* and *emotional entanglement between humans and AI systems* is most clearly required).

The Alan Turing Institute's work on AI ethics and governance (The Alan Turing Institute, 2024) offers further key considerations for more clearly defining the human-technology boundaries in AI procurement. The focus on *fairness, technical safety, accountability, explainability, and data stewardship* suggests enhanced screening of technical requirements while also prioritizing [AI] *systems that work effectively together with humans, maintaining appropriate human control and preventing undue influence*.

In the context of using AI for procurement, the NIST Cybersecurity Framework (NIST, 2024) provides valuable insights into managing cybersecurity risks. The frameworks look at understanding and assessing risks, prioritizing actions, and communicating effectively about them early on, to maintain robust security measures and protecting against cyber threats.

Throughout these key regulatory policies on AI and AI procurement, we can identify a focus on the risks implied by both the selection of specific AI products for an organizational system and the consideration of where knowledge, expertise, and responsibility boundaries are drawn between human workers and AI systems.

By revisiting the sociomaterial perspective in the context of AI procurement and use, we can see how the human-technology boundary is not fixed but is constantly being negotiated and redefined through procurement decisions and subsequent implementation practices in each case. This is evidenced both through the case studies in academic and grey literature and the regulatory documents screened for procurement implications. Case studies from public procurement illustrate how AI is being used to enhance transparency, accountability, and innovation, while raising important ethical considerations as the algorithms are adopted throughout the business processes (Hickok, 2022). Therefore, the procurement process is not just a technical endeavor, but one which involves complex sociotechnical negotiations and their long-term impacts upon organizational structure and human capabilities as well (Rajeb & Appolloni, 2022). The procurement process can thus be recognized as a crucial moment, determining the integration of AI into organizations and the consequences of how they navigate between the need for innovation and guarding human trust (Hardcastle et al., 2025).

Implications for Organizational Practice

In the previous sections, we explored how the continuous interactions between humans and AI systems shape the development and utilization of these technologies, influencing organizational outcomes and innovation trajectories (Faraj et al., 2018). However, the concrete implications of these for organizations are still being explored. The long-term impacts of blurring boundaries between humans and technology in procurement and AI are multifaceted and profound, and this convergence is reshaping organizational structures, decision-making processes, and the very nature of work itself.

One significant impact is the evolution of human roles within procurement. As AI systems become more sophisticated, they are increasingly capable of handling complex tasks traditionally performed by humans (Faraj et al., 2018). This shift is leading to a hybrid intelligence approach within procurement practices, in which standard activities like cost determination are automated while also integrating human expertise for empathy and nuanced judgement, such as in supplier negotiations (Van der Aalst, 2021; Ostheimer et al., 2021).

The integration of AI within procurement is also transforming decision-making processes. Predictive analytics and machine learning algorithms are enhancing the accuracy and efficiency of procurement decisions, but this raises concerns about the potential for automation bias, where humans may rely excessively upon AI recommendations without sufficient critical evaluation (NIST, 2024). This emphasizes the need for a balanced approach which leverages AI capabilities while maintaining human oversight and judgement. Moreover, as procurement processes become increasingly data-driven, the risk of data breaches and misuse of sensitive information grows (OECD, 2021). This necessitates robust cybersecurity measures and ethical guidelines for data handling in AI-driven procurement systems (NIST, 2024).

The ethical implications of AI in procurement are significant and long-lasting. Issues of fairness, transparency, and accountability become paramount as AI systems play a larger role in supplier selection and contract negotiations (European Commission, 2024). There is a growing need for explainable AI in procurement to ensure that decisions can be understood and justified, maintaining trust in the procurement process (The Alan Turing Institute, 2023). The blurring of human-technology boundaries also impacts the skills required in the procurement profession. There is an increasing demand for professionals who can effectively work alongside AI systems, interpreting their outputs and making strategic decisions (Coombs et al., 2020). This shift necessitates continuous learning and adaptation within the workforce. Furthermore, AI's ability to process vast amounts of data can enable more sophisticated supplier relationship management and risk assessment (Helo & Hao, 2022).

Lastly, as AI becomes more prevalent in procurement, it will likely influence organizational values, communication patterns, and power structures. This cultural shift may lead to new forms of collaboration between humans and AI systems, potentially fostering innovation but also requiring careful management to maintain human-centric values. However, this increased complexity brings new vulnerabilities and dependencies which need to be managed carefully. While the blurring of boundaries between humans and technology in procurement and AI offers significant opportunities for efficiency and innovation, it also presents challenges which need to be addressed proactively to produce ethical, secure, and effective procurement practices and to ensure that human work is shaped and augmented in a manner which is beneficial to all parties.

Conclusion

In this chapter, we have identified procurement as a key biographical moment in AI integration, emphasizing its role in mediating the relationship between humans and AI technologies. We have also contributed to theory by analyzing how extant sources depict the relationship between humans and AI and presenting insights from this analysis in the context of regulatory developments. The sociomaterial perspective reveals that AI procurement influences not only organizational structures but also how it reshapes human interactions and decision-making processes. Our findings underscore the need for a holistic research approach to address research gaps and leverage AI for organizational innovation, as highlighted by both existing and emerging guidelines. These guidelines underscore the importance of ethical considerations in AI procurement, ensuring that the selected technologies align with organizational values and societal norms. Like the new OECD principles (published in 2021 but reviewed in 2024), the EU AI Act (European Commission, 2024) now reinforces the significance of this moment of procurement by setting clear boundaries for acceptable AI practices, influencing procurement decisions to prioritize systems which respect human autonomy and decision-making capacity.

While significant progress has been made in understanding the role of AI in procurement, several research gaps remain. We suggest that future areas of research can include developing more robust methods for measuring AI's impact on procurement processes, including both quantitative metrics and qualitative assessments of organizational change. Similarly, research into AI auditing practices specific to procurement, ensuring that AI systems remain aligned with organizational goals and ethical standards over time, would have significant impact upon practice. Sustainability considerations in AI procurement represent an additional, crucial area for future research which remains underexplored. As organizations increasingly prioritize environmental and social responsibility, understanding how AI can support sustainable procurement practices becomes paramount, especially given the energy requirements presented by using such technologies.

When reflecting upon the emerging but still distant "artificial humans," we observe the concept of artificially augmented human workers. The blurring of boundaries between humans and technology in procurement processes supports the conceptualization of augmented human intelligence in professional contexts, where human judgement and AI capabilities work in tandem to drive organizational innovation and efficiency. As organizations continue to navigate the complex landscape of AI integration, understanding the sociomaterial dynamics at play in procurement processes not only enables strategy formulation for successful AI adoption but also helps in maintaining an appropriate balance between human agency and technological capability. By continuing to explore these dynamics, we can work toward a future where AI technologies are not just tools, but integral components of new, augmented organizational intelligence.

References

Abolbashari, M. H., Chang, E., Hussain, O. K., & Saberi, M. (2018). Smart buyer: A Bayesian network modelling approach for measuring and improving procurement performance in organizations. *Knowledge-Based Systems, 142*, 127–148.

AIX. (2023). Case study: Zara's comprehensive approach to AI and supply chain management, AI case studies, 23 September 2023, AI Expert Available at: https://aiexpert.network/case-study-zaras-comprehensive-approach-to-ai-and-supply-chain-management/.

Akter, S., Hossain, M. A., Sajib, S., Sultana, S., Rahman, M., Vrontis, D., & McCarthy, G. (2023). A framework for AI-powered service innovation capability: Review and agenda for future research. *Technovation, 125*, 102768.

Bag, S., Wood, L. C., Mangla, S. K., & Luthra, S. (2020). Procurement 4.0 and its implications on business process performance in a circular economy. *Resources, Conservation and Recycling, 152*, 104502.

Barrad, S., Gagnon, S., & Valverde, R. (2020). An analytics architecture for procurement. *International Journal of Information Technologies and Systems Approach (IJITSA), 13*(2), 73–98.

Bienhaus, F., & Haddud, A. (2018). Procurement 4.0: Factors influencing the digitisation of procurement and supply chains. *Business Process Management Journal, 24*(4), 965–984.

Bifulco, I., et al. (2021). An intelligent system for focused crawling from big data sources. *Expert Systems with Applications., 184*, 115560.

Blaha, L. (2021). Reconceptualizing intelligent automation: A Scottish case study. Doctoral Thesis, University of Aberdeen.

Brown, D. M., & Thompson, A. (2023). *Essentials of marketing: Theory and practice for a marketing career*. Routledge.

Burger, M., Nitsche, A. M., & Arlinghaus, J. (2023). Hybrid intelligence in procurement: Disillusionment with AI's superiority? *Computers in Industry, 150*, 103946.

Chai, J., Liu, J. N., & Ngai, E. W. (2013). Application of decision-making techniques in supplier selection: A systematic review of literature. *Expert Systems With Applications, 40*(10), 3872–3885.

Chedrawi, C., & Haddad, G. (2022). The rise of quasi-humans in AI fueled organizations, an ultimate socio-materiality approach to the lens of Michel Serres. *Pacific Asia Journal of the Association for Information Systems, 14*(2), 2.

Coglianese, C. (2024). Procurement and artificial intelligence. In *Handbook on public policy and artificial intelligence* (pp. 235–248). Edward Elgar Publishing.

Coombs, C., Hislop, D., Taneva, S. K., & Barnard, S. (2020). The strategic impacts of intelligent automation for knowledge and service work: An interdisciplinary review. *The Journal of Strategic Information Systems, 29*(4), 101600.

Davenport, T. H., & Ronanki, R. (2018). Artificial intelligence for the real world. *Harvard Business Review, 96*(1), 108–116.

Dor, L. M. B., & Coglianese, C. (2021). Procurement as AI governance. *IEEE Transactions on Technology and Society, 2*(4), 192–199.

Engstrom, D. F., Ho, D. E., Sharkey, C. M., & Cuéllar, M. F. (2020). Government by algorithm: Artificial intelligence in federal administrative agencies. NYU School of Law, Public Law Research Paper, (pp. 20–54).

European Commission. (2024). Artificial Intelligence Act Explorer. https://artificialintelligence-act.eu/ai-act-explorer/.

Faraj, S., Pachidi, S., & Sayegh, K. (2018). Working and organizing in the age of the learning algorithm. *Information and Organization, 28*(1), 62–70.

Faulconbridge, J., Sarwar, A., & Spring, M. (2023). How professionals adapt to artificial intelligence: The role of intertwined boundary work. *Journal of Management Studies*.

Gholizadeh, H., et al. (2020). A robust fuzzy stochastic programming for sustainable procurement and logistics under hybrid uncertainty using big data. *Journal of Cleaner Production, 258*, 120640.

Glas, A. H., & Kleeman, F. C. (2016). The impact of industry 4.0 on procurement and supply management: A conceptual and qualitative analysis. *International Journal of Business and Management Invention, 5*(6), 55–66.

Glaser, V. L., Pollock, N., & D'Adderio, L. (2021). The biography of an algorithm: Performing algorithmic technologies in organizations. *Organization Theory, 2*(2), 26317877211004609.

Guida, M., Caniato, F., Moretto, A., & Ronchi, S. (2023). The role of artificial intelligence in the procurement process: State of the art and research agenda. *Journal of Purchasing and Supply Management, 29*(2), 100823.

Haider, J., & Sundin, O. (2019). *Invisible search and online search engines: The ubiquity of search in everyday life* (p. 160). Taylor and Francis.

Handfield, R. (2019). Shifts in buyer-seller relationships: A retrospective on. *Industrial Marketing Management, 83*, 194–206.

Handfield, R., Jeong, S., & Choi, T. (2019). Emerging procurement technology: Data analytics and cognitive analytics. *International Journal of Physical Distribution and Logistics Management, 49*(10), 972–1002.

Hardcastle, K., Vorster, L., & Brown, D. M. (2025). Is AI annihilating affordances of autonomy and advertising? *Journal of Advertising*. ahead of press.

Helo, P., & Hao, Y. (2022). Artificial intelligence in operations management and supply chain management: An exploratory case study. *Production Planning and Control, 33*(16), 1573–1590.

Henman, P. (2020). Improving public services using artificial intelligence: Possibilities, pitfalls, governance. *Asia Pacific Journal of Public Administration, 42*(4), 209–221.

Herold, S., et al. (2023). Dynamic capabilities for digital procurement transformation: A systematic literature review. *International Journal of Physical Distribution and Logistics Management., 53*(4), 424–447.

Hickok, M. (2022). Public procurement of artificial intelligence systems: New risks and future proof. *AI and Society, 39*(3), 1213–1227.

Hultin, L. (2019). On becoming a sociomaterial researcher: Exploring epistemological practices grounded in a relational, performative ontology. *Information and Organization, 29*(2), 91–104.

IBM. (2025). Accelerate procurement processes to boost productivity. Available at: https://www.ibm.com/products/watsonx-orchestrate/procurement.

Johri, A. (2022). Augmented sociomateriality: Implications of artificial intelligence for the field of learning technology. *Research in Learning Technology, 30*.

Kinkaid, E. (2020). Can assemblage think difference? A feminist critique of assemblage geographies. *Progress in Human Geography, 44*(3), 457–472.

Kosmol, T., Reimann, F., & Kaufmann, L. (2019). You'll never walk alone: Why we need a supply chain practice view on digital procurement. *Journal of Purchasing and Supply Management, 25*(4), 100553.

Lasi, H., Fettke, P., Kemper, H. G., Feld, T., & Hoffmann, M. (2014). Industry 4.0. *Business and Information Systems Engineering, 6*, 239–242.

Leonardi, P. M. (2013). Theoretical foundations for the study of sociomateriality. *Information and Organization, 23*(2), 59–76.

Liu, Q., et al. (2011). A multi-agent based system of E-procurement exception management. *Knowledge-Based Systems, 24*, 49–57.

Lorentz, H., Aminoff, A., Kaipia, R., & Srai, J. S. (2021). Structuring the phenomenon of procurement digitalisation: Contexts, interventions and mechanisms. *International Journal of Operations and Production Management, 41*(2), 157–192.
Mauthner, N. S., & Kazimierczak, K. A. (2018). Theoretical perspectives on technology and society: Implications for understanding the relationship between ICTs and family life. In *Connecting families?* (pp. 21–40). Policy Press.
Narwane, V. S., Raut, R. D., Yadav, V. S., Cheikhrouhou, N., Narkhede, B. E., & Priyadarshinee, P. (2021). The role of big data for supply chain 4.0 in manufacturing organisations of developing countries. *Journal of Enterprise Information Management, 34*(5), 1452–1480.
Ng, K. K., Chen, C. H., Lee, C. K., Jiao, J. R., & Yang, Z. X. (2021). A systematic literature review on intelligent automation: Aligning concepts from theory, practice, and future perspectives. *Advanced Engineering Informatics, 47*, 101246.
NIST. (2024). AI risk management framework. National Institute of Standards and Technology. https://www.nist.gov/itl/ai-risk-management-framework.
OECD. (2021). Recommendation of the Council on Artificial Intelligence. https://oecd.ai/en/ai-principles.
Orlikowski, W. J. (2010). The sociomateriality of organisational life: Considering technology in management research. *Cambridge Journal of Economics, 34*(1), 125–141.
Orlikowski, W. J., & Scott, S. V. (2008). The entanglement of technology and work in organizations.
Ostheimer, J., Chowdhury, S., & Iqbal, S. (2021). An alliance of humans and machines for machine learning: Hybrid intelligent systems and their design principles. *Technology in Society, 66*, 101647.
Page, M. J., McKenzie, J. E., Bossuyt, P. M., Boutron, I., Hoffmann, T. C., Mulrow, C. D., et al. (2021). The PRISMA 2020 statement: An updated guideline for reporting systematic reviews. *Systematic Reviews, 10*, 89.
Priharsari, D., & Abedin, B. (2021). What facilitates and constrains value co creation in online communities: A sociomateriality perspective. *Information and Management, 58*(6), 103433.
Raja Santhi, A., & Muthuswamy, P. (2023). Industry 5.0 or industry 4.0 S? Introduction to industry 4.0 and a peek into the prospective industry 5.0 technologies. *International Journal on Interactive Design and Manufacturing (IJIDeM), 17*(2), 947–979.
Rajeb, A., & Appolloni, A. (2022). The nexus of industry 4.0 and circular procurement: A systematic literature review and research agenda. *Sustainability., 14*, 15633.
Rice, A. J. (2024). The rise of intelligent procurement: Embracing AI and data analytics for cross-functional synergy. *Journal of Supply Chain Management, Logistics and Procurement, 6*(4), 319–329.
Ronchi, S., Brun, A., Golini, R., & Fan, X. (2010). What is the value of an IT e-procurement system? *Journal of Purchasing and Supply Management, 16*(2), 131–140.
Roy, S. K., Dey, B. L., Brown, D. M., Abid, A., Apostolidis, C., Christofi, M., & Tarba, S. (2025). Business model innovation through AI adaptation: The role of strategic human resources management. *British Journal of Management*. ahead of press.
Shams, S. M. R., Brown, D. M., & Hardcastle, K. (2025). *Sustainable marketing: Marketing strategy for people, planet and profit*. Springer.
Stange, R., Schiele, H., & Henseler, J. (2022). Advancing purchasing as a design science: Publication guidelines to shift towards more relevant purchasing research. *Journal of Purchasing and Supply Management, 28*(1), 100750.
Symon, G., & Pritchard, K. (2015). Performing the responsive and committed employee through the sociomaterial mangle of connection. *Organization Studies, 36*(2), 241–263.
Schoenherr, T., & Speier-Pero, C. (2015). Data science, predictive analytics, and big data in supply chain management: current state and future potential. *Journal of Business Logistics, 36*(1), 120–132.
Turing Institute. (2024). AI ethics and governance in practice. The Alan Turing Institute. https://www.turing.ac.uk/research/research-projects/ai-ethics- and-governance-practice.
Van Der Aalst, W. M. (2021). Hybrid intelligence: To automate or not to automate, that is the question. *International Journal of Information Systems and Project Management, 9*(2), 5–20.

van Rijmenam, M. (2019). Sociomateriality in the age of emerging information technologies: How big data analytics, blockchain and artificial intelligence affect organisations (Doctoral dissertation, University of Technology Sydney (Australia)).

Waardenburg, L., & Huysman, M. (2022). From coexistence to co-creation: Blurring boundaries in the age of AI. *Information and Organization, 32*(4), 100432.

Wang, K., et al. (2020). An AI-based automated continuous compliance awareness framework (CoCAF) for procurement auditing. *Big Data and Cognitive Computing, 4*(23), 1–14.

Westphal, T., & Wang, R. (2023). Artificial intelligence with Chinese characteristics: National strategy, security and authoritarian governance.

Zhu, Y., Xie, C., Sun, B. W., & Yan, X. G. (2016). Predicting China's SME credit risk in supply chain financing by logistic regression, artificial neural network and hybrid models. *Sustainability, 8*(5), 433. https://doi.org/10.3390/su8050433

Zhao, W. W., & Yang, Y. (2022). Artificial intelligence meets onto-epistemologies: Distinctive sociomaterial perspectives for organizational research at the intersection of digital business ecosystems and robotics. In *Handbook on digital business ecosystems* (pp. 424–437). Edward Elgar Publishing.

Luciana Blaha is an Assistant Professor in Intelligent Automation and Management Operations at Heriot-Watt University, Edinburgh, where she leads the Intelligent Automation Systems Lab in the Edinburgh Business School. Her research investigates intelligent automation systems (including AI, digital twins, RPA, and chatbots) and their impact on organizational behavior, reuniting findings from science and technology studies, business management, and computing science to improve system and organizational outcomes. Her work explores emerging behaviors and understandings of technology from the perspective of stakeholders within and outside the organization to inform practitioners on procurement, design, and adoption.

David M. Brown is an Associate Professor of Marketing at Heriot-Watt University, Edinburgh. His main research foci are internal marketing, social entrepreneurship, the role of marketing in social and environmental sustainability, and the adaptation and appropriation of technology. His work has been published in journals such as the *Journal of World Business*, *British Journal of Management*, *Journal of Business Research*, and *Industrial Marketing Management*. He has also authored three major textbooks, including Routledge's *Essentials of Marketing* and Springer's *Sustainable Marketing*.

Krishan Chandarana is currently an MSc Human Resource Management student at Edinburgh Business School and Research Assistant at Heriot Watt University. He is preparing to pursue a PhD following his postgraduate studies inspired by successfully undertaking an EPSRC-funded research internship in 2023 looking at how AI-augmented procurement. His research activity includes looking at AI adoption in organizations, with a focus on human resource management.

Amber Devin is a final-year Philosophy (MA Hons) student at the University of Edinburgh and an MSc candidate in AI Ethics and Policy. She is a successful graduate of the EPSRC summer vacation internship scheme. Her project at Heriot-Watt University project involved investigating AI and financial ethics and drafting an AI ethics framework for fraud prevention in the financial sector. Her research interests include algorithmic bias, black-box problems, and data privacy concerns, alongside regulatory and implementation considerations. She also has a keen interest in exploring the intersection of AI ethics with social justice issues.

Human-Artificial Intelligence (HAI) Teaming in STEM Education: A Conceptual Framework for Skill Development in Industry 5.0

Baibhaw Kumar and Csaba Deák

Introduction

The usage of artificial intelligence (AI) in classrooms has ascended in recent years, especially in the last 5 years. This has had an impact on the education sector globally generally and on STEM education, in particular at schools and universities. Pretty soon, it will be possible to picture a classroom where every student has their own private instructor who helps them study at their own pace. The rapid improvement in the efficiency of instruments driven by artificial intelligence and other developments in this field are making such fantasies a reality. With these resources, schools may quickly and easily tailor lessons to each student's individual requirements in terms of content, speed, and delivery (Popenici & Kerr, 2017; Owoc et al., 2021; Ferreira Mello et al., 2023).

AI can offer real-time, personalized assistance by utilizing complex algorithms of large language models. This enables learners to go at their own pace and receive focused feedback, resulting in a considerable increase in engagement and an improvement in learning outcomes (Sifat & Bhattacharya, 2023). It will not be so far when we see AI as a very perceptive mentor who is always adapting new methods with the latest data and information to fit the learner's preferred speed and style. In addition to maintaining student engagement, this personalized touch makes it easier for them to overcome challenges. Personalized learning systems driven by AI are very good at meeting students' varied learning needs. These systems examine enormous volumes of student's data to find learning trends, areas of strength, and opportunities for development. This data-driven approach allows AI to create highly personalized learning pathways that cater to individual student profiles. For instance, Intelligent Tutoring Systems (ITS) can deliver real-time, individualized guidance

B. Kumar (✉) · C. Deák
University of Miskolc, Miskolc, Hungary
e-mail: baibhaw.kumar@uni-miskolc.hu; csaba.deak@uni-miskolc.hu

M. Dabić et al. (eds.), *Artificial Humans*, Future of Business and Finance,
https://doi.org/10.1007/978-3-032-06604-6_14

and support, helping students navigate their specific challenges (Ferreira Mello et al., 2023). These technologies enable a more effective and efficient learning experience by diagnosing learning gaps and providing customized pedagogy lessons. Studies show that students using personalized learning systems do better academically and show more interest than students in standard classroom environments (Fariani et al., 2023). Let's not overlook the ethical problems, as they are the big issue with tremendous power with a deal of responsibility. To guarantee that the technology is used responsibly and fairly, concerns including data privacy, algorithmic bias, and the transparency of AI systems must be properly controlled (Atchley et al., 2024). Because AI systems frequently require large datasets of students to operate efficiently, data privacy could be a serious concern for policymakers. It is essential to make sure that the collection, storage, and use of this data respect the privacy of the students. Algorithmic bias can also result in unfair outcomes, especially for students who belong to marginalized groups. As a result, it is crucial to create and put into place policies and procedures that support equity and openness in AI- driven learning resources (Baker & Hawn, 2022).

As STEM (Science, Technology, Engineering, and Mathematics) education evolves, a new chapter also transforms the pedagogy principles, telling the growth of how humans and artificial intelligence are collaborating to realize the full potential of learning (Deák et al., 2021). The era of human-AI (HAI) is constantly developing around us, combining the precision of data and algorithms with the wisdom of experience to create a collaborative symphony that is revolutionizing education (Atchley et al., 2024). The chart shown in Fig. 1 was gathered in order to examine current patterns in scholarly literature about the use of AI in STEM education. We hope to better understand the interdisciplinary nature of AI research within STEM education by classifying the topics covered in these papers from 2014 to 2024 and determining which areas have attracted the greatest attention.

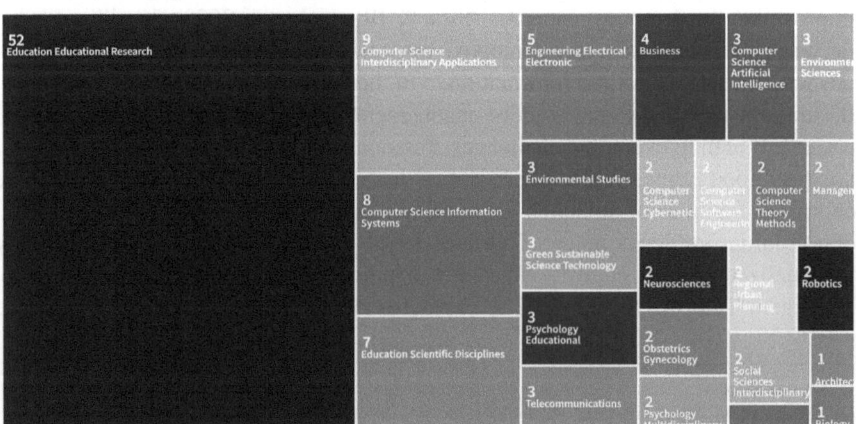

Fig. 1 Categories of subjects the AI in STEM papers majorly dealt in the time frame (2014–2024) (Source: https://www.webofscience.com/)

The figure distinctly shows that the majority of AI-related STEM research falls under the category of Educational Research, indicating a strong focus on how AI can be integrated into educational practices to enhance learning outcomes. This suggests that the academic community is particularly interested in exploring how AI can transform teaching methodologies, student engagement, and learning environments.

This book chapter invites readers to explore the remarkable tools that are reshaping education, tools designed not just to assist but to partner with teachers and students in their educational journey. From intelligent tutors that adapt to a student's unique pace to platforms that personalize every lesson, we assess how these innovations are enhancing the human touch in education, making learning more intuitive and engaging than ever before. Before diving into these breakthroughs, we take a moment to think things through and perform a SWOT analysis that helps us see where we need to go. While recognizing the positive aspects of this new partnership, such as customization, effectiveness, and the depth of data-driven insights, we equally acknowledge its negative aspects, like implementation difficulties and moral conundrums.

Methodology

Throughout history, industrial revolutions have transformed the skills required by workers in a variety of industries. Steam-powered devices necessitated advanced mechanical abilities during Industry 1.0. With the introduction of Industry 2.0, electricity became the standard, demanding electrical and manufacturing skills. Industry 3.0 introduced automation via computers, necessitating an understanding of electronics and information technology. Since 2000, Industry 4.0 has been focused on smart manufacturing, where robotics and data analysis abilities are required for optimization. Now, in Industry 5.0, the emphasis is on integrating AI with sustainability and human values, necessitating AI competence, sustainability, and collaboration with intelligent robots (Ahmad et al., 2022). Similarly, education has progressed simultaneously. From traditional lecture-based learning in Education 1.0 to Internet-based Education 2.0 and knowledge-based Education 3.0, each stage has prepared students for the industrial skill demands (Supriya et al., 2024). Moving forward, Education 4.0 emphasizes innovation and problem-solving, mirroring Industry 4.0's requirements, whereas Education 5.0 incorporates human-AI collaboration, sustainability, and ethics to prepare students for the linked world of tomorrow.

In other words, Industry 5.0 requires fresh graduates to work closely with AI. This opens the possible discussion on the collaboration between humans and technology to create tailored and environmentally friendly products instead of relying solely on automation. This means that upcoming students will focus on being creative, solving problems, and making decisions, while machines handle challenging and monotonous tasks. Here comes the need to shift in skill development through pedagogy (Deák & Kumar, 2024). The aftermath of the 2020 pandemic marks a considerable improvement over Industry 4.0, emphasizing collaboration between humans and intelligent systems rather than depending entirely on automation and digitization. Employers are now seeking critical soft skills such as creativity, emotional intelligence, and sophisticated problem-solving abilities, as well as technical competency in areas like artificial intelligence, data analysis, machine learning, robotics, etc. in order to succeed in this recent industrial shift toward more sustainable solutions. Figure 2 illustrates the evolution of industries from Industry 1.0 to Industry 5.0 and the corresponding evolution in education from Education 1.0 to Education 5.0. It demonstrates how the skills required by each industrial phase have shaped the way we approach education and why a new pedagogical framework is necessary for Industry 5.0.

In order to evaluate AI's impact on STEM education, this chapter uses a holistic approach, with a particular emphasis on the changing demands of Industry 5.0. Gathering and analyzing the many AI-powered methods and resources used by STEM teachers today is the first order of business. Some examples of these tools are ITSs, ALPs, AI-powered data analytics, and automated assessment tools.

The authors did a SWOT (strengths, weaknesses, opportunities, and threats) analysis to evaluate the efficacy of these tools in the STEM pedagogy spectrum. Further, this study presents a comprehensive review of the competencies needed for Industry 5.0, which include skills such as creative thinking, advanced data analysis, and ethical decision-making. In order to determine what skills and knowledge future workers will need to succeed in an Industry 5.0 setting, this analysis assessed the latest scientific publications, industrial developments, and the latest available AI-based digital tools. Lastly, a framework for the human-AI (HAI) model is

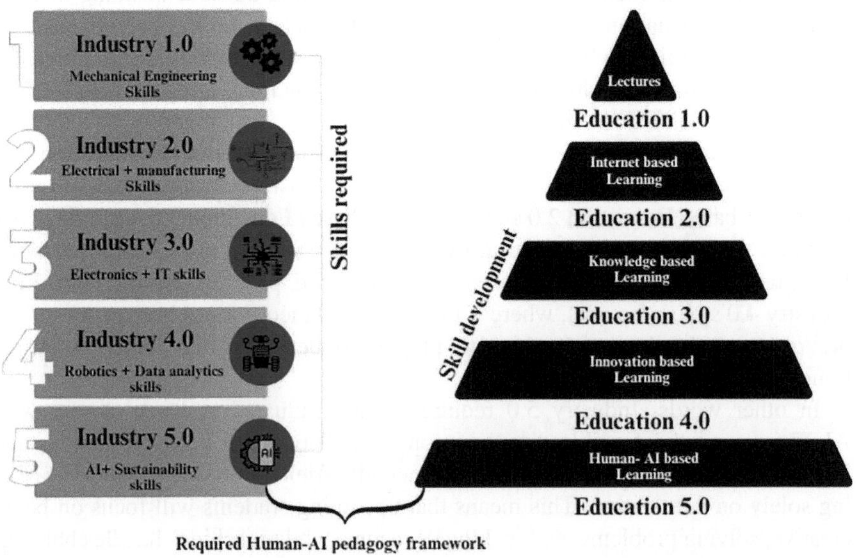

Fig. 2 Evolution of industrial skill requirements and complementary educational models

proposed by synthesizing these findings. This framework integrates the benefits of AI with more traditional forms of education and tool preparation to foster the development of critical skills needed for Industry 5.0. The goal of the framework is to provide educators, educational management, and legislators with the tools they need to effectively incorporate AI into STEM education in order to better prepare students for the challenges and possibilities of the workforce of the future.

Role of AI in STEM Pedagogy

Students' perspectives on STEM courses are shifting as a result of a groundbreaking technological development, i.e., the incorporation of (AI-based) digital technologies into STEM education. In this section, we evaluate the recent advancements in AI integration in STEM education, along with some real-world examples and applications. We will focus on how AI is influencing STEM education in terms of personalized learning, assessment, tutoring, immersive learning, computational thinking, interdisciplinary learning, and ethical considerations at different points in STEM pedagogy.

Customized and Adaptive Education

Recently, AI-powered adaptive learning platforms, which tailor the curriculum to each individual student's needs, have revolutionized personalized education to a great extent (Gligorea et al., 2023). These systems employ advanced algorithms to evaluate data on student performance and make dynamic modifications to the content, tempo, and level of difficulty. By guaranteeing that every student gets the right amount of challenge and assistance, personalization greatly improves student engagement and comprehension of STEM topics (Khan et al., 2022). For example, DreamBox (Foster, 2024), Carnegie Learning, developers of the widely deployed Cognitive Tutor (Ritter et al., 2015), and Knewton (Conklin, 2016) use AI to build personalized learning paths so that students can study subjects more efficiently at their own speed. The benefits of such tools are still less discussed; some of these are mentioned in Table 1. They offer the potential to bridge learning gaps more effectively than traditional methods by providing immediate feedback and customized learning paths, thereby optimizing the learning process and improving academic outcomes. These AI platforms also have the potential to free up teachers' time so they may concentrate more on interactive, higher-order teaching activities rather than repetitive assessment chores. However, the implementation of adaptive or personalized AI in STEM education is not without challenges. Data privacy and security concerns are paramount, as these systems require extensive data on student performance to function effectively. Moreover, the complexity of AI systems can pose a barrier to adoption, particularly in under-resourced schools where technical support may be limited for educators and learners.

Table 1 Recent tools developed with AI for adaptive and customized learning in STEM

Program name	Tools	Remarks	References
DreamBox learning	AI algorithms, data analytics	DreamBox learning uses AI to create personalized learning paths in mathematics, adjusting content in real time based on student performance. This enhances engagement and comprehension by catering to individual learning needs	(Foster, 2024)
Knewton	Adaptive learning technology, machine learning	Knewton offers personalized learning experiences by adapting instructional content to the student's pace and understanding level. The platform aims to improve efficiency in learning STEM subjects by providing the right challenges and support	(Conklin, 2016)
Carnegie learning	Cognitive models, machine learning	Carnegie learning integrates AI to offer customized tutoring in mathematics, using cognitive models to predict student performance and adapt the learning material accordingly	(Ritter et al., 2015)
Smart sparrow	Adaptive learning platform data analytics	Smart sparrow allows educators to create adaptive lessons tailored to student needs, enabling a personalized learning experience. The platform's flexibility supports various STEM subjects and adjusts based on student interactions and feedback	(Weltman et al., 2019)
Century K12	AI-powered insights learning analytics	Century K12 Tech utilizes AI to provide personalized learning recommendations and insights, helping students progress at their own pace. The platform focuses on identifying knowledge gaps and offering targeted content to bridge them	Century intelligent learning
Microsoft power BI	Entrepreneurial mindset	Uses Microsoft Power BI Desktop to incorporate evidence-based decision-making into engineering and technology classes, which helps students develop an entrepreneurial attitude	(Bosman et al., 2022)

Automated Assessment and Predictive Analytics

Automated assessment tools powered by AI provide immediate feedback, helping students identify and rectify their mistakes immediately. These tools also enable educators to efficiently monitor student progress and their respective learning gaps. Additionally, AI-driven predictive analytics can forecast future learning outcomes based on current performance data, guiding educators in making data-informed instructional decisions (Phil Long & Siemens, 2011; Baker & Inventado, 2014). Systems such as Gradescope and Coursera leverage AI to streamline grading processes and offer personalized recommendations, thereby enhancing the overall learning experience. As shown in Table 2, Edmentum and Knewton Alta, for example, use predictive analytics technologies that guarantee personalized learning by projecting future learning results based on present performance data. These methods and tools enable educators to customize to cater to each student's specific requirements by making data-driven evaluations. Real-time feedback and personal mentorship are offered by automated tutoring platforms such as ASSISTments, which may close learning gaps more successfully than conventional pedagogical approaches (Feng & Heffernan, 2005).

However, the feasibility of implementing these technologies in practical classroom pedagogy raises several critical questions. For instance, how can schools ensure the fairness in assessment/prediction when deploying AI-driven systems that require extensive student data? The complexity and cost of these technologies may also pose significant barriers to adoption, particularly in under-resourced schools. Moreover, the effectiveness of these tools heavily relies on robust AI algorithms and substantial teacher training. Are educators adequately prepared to integrate these AI assessment/prediction tools into their teaching practices, and do they trust these systems to deliver fair and unbiased assessments? Although predictive analytics can help inform instructional practices, there is a chance that an excessive dependence on data-driven judgements could obscure the sophisticated knowledge that seasoned

Table 2 AI tools for automated assessments and predictive analytics in STEM pedagogy

Program name	Tools	Remarks	References
Gradescope	AI-powered grading, machine learning	Gradescope helps automate the grading processes, providing immediate feedback to students. This tool helps educators efficiently monitor student progress, identify learning gaps, and streamline the grading process	(Singh et al., 2017)
Coursera	Predictive analytics, data analytics, AI algorithms	Coursera leverages AI to offer personalized learning recommendations and predict future learning outcomes based on current performance data. This helps guide educators in making data-informed instructional decisions and enhances the overall learning experience	(Urban, 2023)
ASSISTments	Automated tutoring, data analytics	ASSISTments provides automated assessment and tutoring for math, offering real-time feedback and analytics on student performance. It helps teachers identify areas where students struggle and provides targeted interventions	(Feng et al., 2023)
Edmentum	AI-driven learning platform, predictive analytics	Edmentum uses AI to deliver personalized learning experiences and predictive analytics to forecast student performance. The platform helps educators adjust instructional strategies based on data-driven insights	
Knewton Alta	Adaptive learning, predictive analytics	Knewton Alta combines adaptive learning technology with predictive analytics to provide personalized recommendations and predict student outcomes. This approach enhances learning efficiency and helps educators track progress effectively	(Jones & Bomash, 2018)

teachers bring to the classroom. In education, striking a balance between human interaction and technical efficiency is still crucial.

Intelligent Tutoring Systems (ITS)

Intelligent Tutoring Systems (ITS) work with AI tools to deliver personalized, one-on-one tutoring, simulating the benefits of human tutors through large language models (LLM) (Stamper et al., 2024). These systems diagnose student difficulties, provide customized feedback, and adapt learning experiences to meet individual needs. Few a times, students are shy to ask questions in classrooms being afraid of their peers. In this regard, research shows that ITS can significantly improve student learning outcomes and engagement by offering tailored instructional strategies and support (Alam, 2023). Among many, a few examples of ITS include Carnegie Learning's MATHia and Pearson's MyLab, both of which use AI to personalize mathematics instruction and practice (Guo et al., 2021). A few ITS programs are presented in Table 3.

Applications for virtual and augmented reality driven by AI are very new and aid immersive learning environments that improve comprehension of challenging STEM subjects. With the aid of these technologies, students can engage in more natural and intuitive visualization and interaction with scientific phenomena and engineering concepts. For example, programs like Labster (Reen et al., n.d.) and Google Cardboards (Laseinde & Dada, 2023) make abstract ideas more concrete and approachable by utilizing AR and VR to create interactive virtual labs and simulations (Kumar et al., 2023).

Table 3 Recent programs developed and used in ITS

Program name	Tools	Remarks	References
Carnegie learning's MATHia	AI algorithms, cognitive models	Provides personalized math instruction, diagnosing difficulties, and offering customized feedback	(Almoubayyed et al., 2023)
Pearson's MyLab	AI-driven assessments in communication and language learning	Personalizes math practice by adapting to student performance, providing tailored support	(Aitken et al., 2014)
ALEKS	Knowledge space theory, AI algorithms	Identifies knowledge gaps and offers targeted instruction, personalizing the learning path	(Cosyn et al., 2021)
Korbit	Personalized learning paths, interactive feedback	Uses AI to tailor learning materials and paths based on learner's performance, enhancing active learning	(Serban et al., 2020)
BLS tutoring	Dynamic mobile based AI tutoring for language	Provides opportunity for homework, examination, and exercises which are self-directed	(Ni & Cheung, 2023)

Coding and Computational Thinking

The necessity of providing students with the necessary abilities for the digital age is the driving force behind the increasing emphasis on incorporating computational thinking and coding into STEM curricula. Yilmaz and Karaoglan Yilmaz (2023) study's conclusions showed that the experimental group students had considerably higher levels of computational thinking abilities, programming self-efficacy, and lesson motivation than the control group. One could argue that utilizing ChatGPT and other AI technologies in programming instruction could be beneficial. AI facilitates this integration by offering students individualized feedback and interactive coding environments, which aid in the development of their problem-solving and programming abilities. AI is used by websites like https://code.org/ and https://scratch.mit.edu/ to provide learners with customized tasks and real-time support, encouraging computational thinking in young learners (Grover & Pea, 2013). Empirical studies indicate that computational thinking is significantly and favorably predicted by the digital divide in terms of access to and use of different technologies (Celik, 2023). Additionally, developers should take into account individuals' motivation, skill level, and availability while creating AI-based experiences for them. Most engineering and coding education resources use screen-based technology, which aren't necessarily developmentally suitable for very young students. Nevertheless, others (Sullivan & Strawhacker, 2021) are also offering low-cost, screen-free methods of teaching engineering and coding that prioritize STEAM, a more interdisciplinary approach which is further discussed in the next section.

Interdisciplinary Education

The STEAM approach is a new pedagogy form, which stands for Science, Technology, Engineering, Arts, and Mathematics, and pushes the boundaries of STEM by emphasizing the significance of integrating multiple disciplines to stimulate innovation and creativity (Kumar & Deák, 2023). AI can support interdisciplinary or even multidisciplinary learning by creating links between topics that don't initially seem connected and encouraging comprehensive approaches to problem-solving. Videos for STEAM-based learning enhance what kids already know about supportive activities before they play. Project-Based Learning (PBL) provides educational resources and supplies for kids' play activities learning about young children's learning processes (Mufarihah et al., 2023).

AI-driven initiatives, for instance, have the potential to blend technology and art, inspiring students to apply engineering concepts to artistic pursuits on a broader level of interdisciplinarity (Relmasira et al., 2023). Students can explore the connections between engineering, design, and art with the use of tools like Tinkercad (Erdogan et al., 2023) and Makey Makeys (Turcotte, 2024), which helps them develop both technically and creatively. Also, students explore creative art platforms such as DALLE (https://openai.com/index/dall-e/) for text-to-image, SUNO (https://suno.com/) for text-to-song and SORA for text-to-music generation. This will change the dynamics of Arts integration to STEM resulting in a dynamic STEAM pedagogy expanding the HAI model with arts.

Ethical and Social Consequences

As AI becomes more ingrained in STEM education, it is imperative to consider the ethical and societal implications of this development. To guarantee the appropriate application of AI, issues like data privacy, algorithmic bias, and the effect on equity and accessibility must be addressed. The current state of divides perpetuates structural biases in teaching and learning by creating a vicious cycle that is not broken by continuous reflection and action from learners, educators, educational leaders, designers, scholars, and policymakers (Dieterle et al., 2024).

AI in education is understood and applied in three ways. It serves as a research approach for academics to improve understanding of learning and strengthen real-world educational outcomes. It functions as a commercial opportunity for business. It also appears as political rhetoric used to argue for changes in education systems (Eynon & Young, 2020). The way "AI" is framed in these three contexts will produce radically different results. Frameworks that protect student data and advance equity in AI applications must be created by educators and legislators. The curriculum should also include talks about the moral application of AI, enabling students to assess AI technologies critically and interact with them in an ethical manner.

Role of HAI in Skill Development for Industry 5.0

Today the industrial age is in its fifth generation, i.e., Industry 5.0, which represents a major shift in the manufacturing sector, focusing on creativity through teamwork between humans and machines, as well as highlighting the importance of sustainability and innovation. But how far are we ready to adopt this shift? Cutting-edge technologies such as artificial intelligence, robotics, and the Internet of Things (IoT) can be seamlessly integrated these days into our daily activities, resulting in an innovation process that is both more flexible and tailored to individual needs or is rather smart (Özdemir & Hekim, 2018). Natural user interfaces, such as gestures, are used to capture attention because they allow humans to manage technology using intuitive and natural behaviors. It is the future direction for Industry 5.0 because it keeps humans at the core of the system and allows for the integration of new technologies, but these innovations need new skills (Adel, 2022).

One of the biggest challenges in the skill sector is a lack of trainers and cost constraints in providing proper training to humans who work with AI (Maddikunta et al., 2022). By the time Industry 5.0 is completely implemented, the demand for a competent workforce will increase, as will the use of new technologies, necessitating adequate training for both trainees and prospective trainers. Hence, universities must realize this pattern and change their teaching techniques to encourage the development of these skill sets as students prepare to enter the new employment

Table 4 Identified skills that could benefit from the HAI pedagogy and aid the skill requirements of Industry 5.0

Skill identified	AI tools	Remarks
Complex problem-solving	(ITS), Knewton Alta	ITS tools offer personalized scenarios and problem-solving exercises, helping students develop analytical skills
Creativity and innovation	AI-powered simulation software, AI-based design tools	AI tools like simulation software foster creative thinking by allowing students to experiment with innovative designs
Emotional intelligence	AI-driven emotional recognition tools	These tools help students understand and manage emotions, crucial for leadership roles in Industry 5.0
Data analysis and interpretation	Data analytics platforms, AI-powered learning analytics	Platforms like Tableau and AI-driven analytics tools help students gain insights from large datasets
Digital literacy	Adaptive learning systems, Coursera	Adaptive learning tools help students become proficient with digital tools, essential for Industry 5.0 readiness
Interdisciplinary collaboration	Collaborative AI platforms (e.g., GitHub, Slack)	AI tools facilitate teamwork across different disciplines, promoting collaborative problem-solving skills
Critical thinking	AI-based debate and decision-making tools	These tools encourage students to engage in debates and complex decision-making processes, enhancing critical thinking
Sustainability and ethical awareness	AI-powered environmental simulators, ethical AI platforms	AI simulators help students understand the impact of their decisions on sustainability and ethical considerations

market. Some of the skills which are relevant for the Industry 5.0 that can make the educators think of the HAI to upgrade skills are listed in Table 4.

In this chapter, further, we discuss this challenge and introduce our proposed structure for human-AI (HAI) teaming. The structure fosters a learning atmosphere where students can enhance both their technical and interpersonal abilities through the collaborative integration of AI tools in STEM. To make a robust framework, the consecutive section presents a SWOT analysis for the assessment of various dimensions discussed in the previous section.

SWOT Analysis of HAI and STEM

In this section, the authors present a comprehensive SWOT analysis of (HAI) approaches within educational settings, as illustrated in Fig. 3. This SWOT analysis highlights the benefits, drawbacks, opportunities, and threats associated with HAI teaming, which helps to clarify the multifaceted impacts of AI on education. Artificial intelligence (AI) has the power to revolutionize education by tailoring teachings to the specific requirements of students and providing valuable data to educators. Personalization and data-driven insights are two of these identified strengths for the HAI. The potential biases and high implementation costs are just

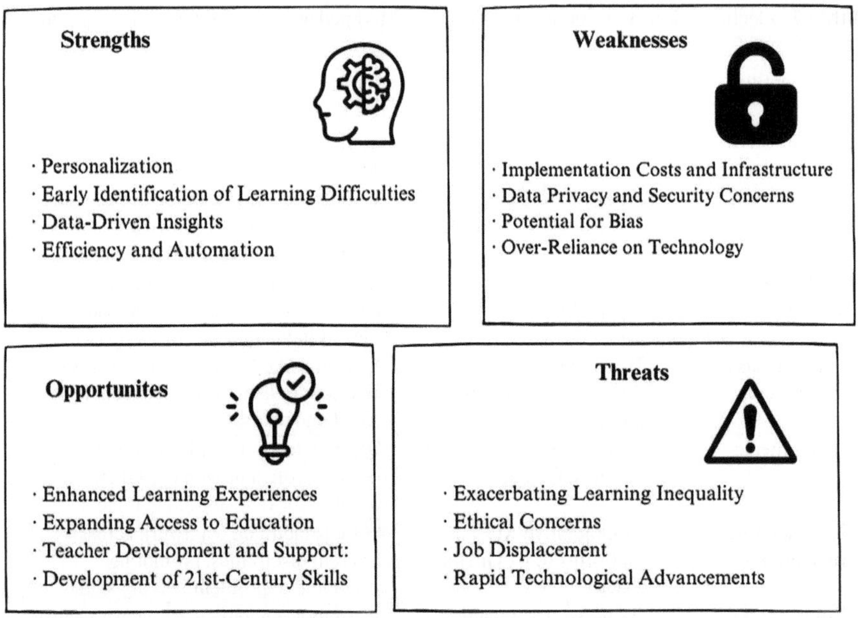

Fig. 3 Pictorial representation of the identified SWOT parameters

two of the downsides that should be considered before committing to widespread HAI use. Particularly for students in underprivileged or rural regions, the highlighted potential, such as improving learning experiences and increasing access to education, shows the encouraging doors that AI may open in sooner times. Policymakers and institutions should be careful in their implementation techniques to safeguard HAI teaming together for the benefit of all students, especially those with special educational needs, considering the challenges it poses, including increased learning inequity and possible ethical biases.

Strengths

Personalization or Customization: The AI is usually found to be good in customized requirements of the learners, and it adjusts its pace accordingly. More engaged students and more successful learning can be achieved with HAI implementation.

Difficulty in Diagnosis: Sometimes it gets difficult for teachers to diagnose the learning difficulty of poor performing students; it might happen due to exceeding capacity of classrooms, but AI smartly identifies the reasons why the student underperforms. This early diagnosis helps in the quick attention of the teacher.

Data Insights: A deeper comprehension of learning patterns and trends is made possible by HAI's capacity to process and analyze large-scale datasets. As a result, teachers are more equipped to decide on curriculum revisions or new designs.

Efficiency and Automation: AI can automate administrative, instructional, and grading tasks. Consequently, educators can dedicate additional time to offering personalized instruction and taking extra care on students who need more efforts.

Weaknesses

Infrastructure and Implementation Costs: Including AI in education necessitates a large financial outlay for training, hardware, software, and continuing maintenance. This can be a significant obstacle, especially for schools/universities with limited funding.

Data Security and Privacy Issues: AI tools gather and examine a lot of student data. Strong policies are necessary to avoid illegal breaches and unethical usage, and ensuring the privacy and security of sensitive data is of utmost importance.

Bias Potential: The quality of AI algorithms depends on the quality of the data they are trained on its a known fact. AI systems have the potential to reinforce and magnify preexisting biases in educational environments if the data they use reflects such biases on cultural, historical, regional, and some other such dimensions.

Over-reliance on Technology: Relying overtly on AI-powered technologies may impede the growth of human abilities or sensitivities for learners at different levels such as creativity, critical thinking, and social-emotional intelligence.

Opportunities

Personalized content: Virtual reality (VR), simulations, and ITS can all be used together to create immersive and captivating learning experiences.Increasing Access to Education: AI-powered platforms and tools have the ability to remove geographi cal boundaries and give students in underserved or rural places access to high-quality education at their doorstep.

Teacher Development and Help: By delivering subject-based data-driven insights into student performance, recommending tailored interventions, and encouraging collaboration among educators, AI can offer teachers invaluable help.

Development of Industry 5.0 Skills: By utilizing HAI, educators may help kids develop critical twenty-first-century abilities like data analysis, computational thinking, and problem-solving, which will equip them for the employment of the future in Industry 5.0, which is different from the last decade's requirements.

Threats

Learning Inequality: It's known that students of marginalized community due to financial or regional constraints have drawbacks in learning, and they might not be able to afford high subscription charges for these AI tools.

Ethical Concerns: Data privacy of the participants and teachers is at stake. The algorithm biases also need to be checked for fair practices.

Job Displacement: There are worries about possible job displacement in the education industry of STEM educators as AI gets better and better.

Quick Technical Advancements: It's difficult to stay up with the rapid development of AI technologies and keep the classrooms updated.

This SWOT analysis serves as a strategic tool to guide the effective analysis for the integration of AI in STEM education, ensuring that its adoption is both inclusive and impactful, ultimately leading to empowerment in skill development that contributes to a wholesome growth of learners and empower them for the skills required in Industry 5.0.

Proposed Framework

A conceptual framework for human-artificial intelligence (HAI) that provides a systematic way to understand and manage the difficulties involved with using AI tools and approaches at various levels of pedagogy in STEM education for both learners and teachers is inevitable. Figure 4 is a concept representation that offers students and educators choices in how they comprehend their knowledge and skills. HAI learning needs to be contextually relevant and personalized

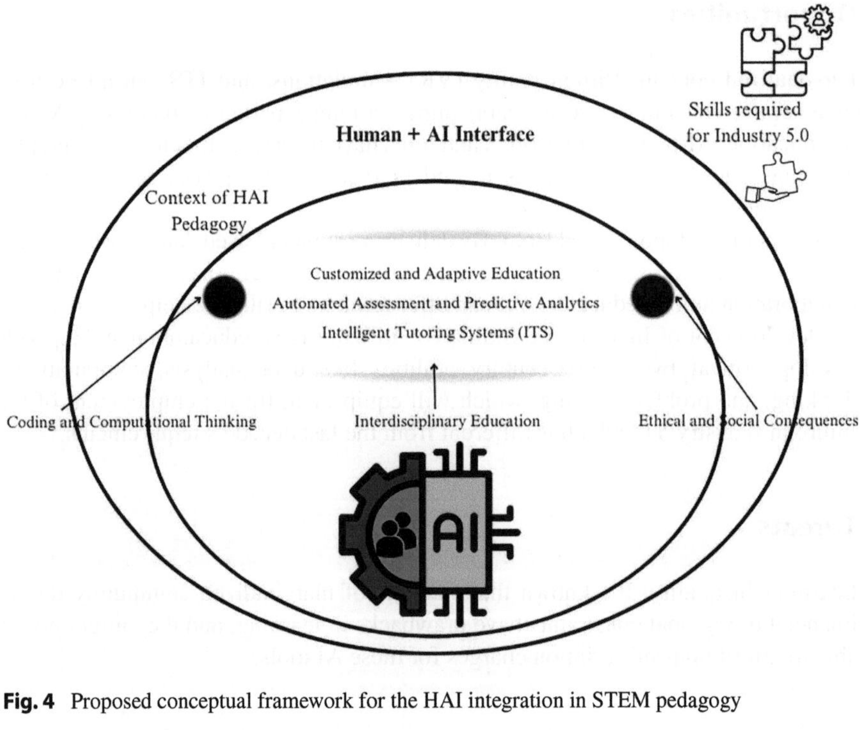

Fig. 4 Proposed conceptual framework for the HAI integration in STEM pedagogy

while also improving engagement and results. The framework does this by taking into account each student's strengths, interests, and past experiences with AI tools.

The framework is centered around the HAI interface, which represents the core interaction between educators, students, and AI tools in the educational process. This interface is where the collaborative potential of HAI teaming is realized, allowing for a dynamic exchange of knowledge, feedback, and instructional strategies. Surrounding this central interface are the key elements that constitute the primary dimensions of HAI in STEM education. Customized and Adaptive Education, Automated Assessment and Predictive Analytics, and Intelligent Tutoring Systems (ITS) are key internal components that directly interact with the human-AI interface. Externally, the framework incorporates broader dimensions that influence and are influenced by the central HAI interface: Coding and Computational Thinking, Interdisciplinary Education, and Ethical and Social Consequences. These external dimensions influence and are influenced by the HAI interface. The HAI framework is visually represented as a series of interconnected elements, with the HAI interface at its core. Arrows connect the central interface to the surrounding dimensions, symbolizing the flow of influence and interaction. The outer frame represents the broader context and dynamics of HAI pedagogy, which encompasses the socio- cultural, ethical, and practical considerations that shape the implementation of AI in education and skill development for Industry 5.0. The HAI interface is positioned at the center of the framework, which emphasizes the value of cooperation and mutual improvement between teachers, students, and AI.

Discussion

The HAI+ STEM framework provides a choice of flexibility to educators on a broader perspective of pedagogy. The framework also yields practical and ethical challenges possible with the framework. To mitigate them, policymakers must think of laws that safeguard data privacy with a top-down approach. AI-based pedagogy platforms in the future will become more data-driven, collecting information that might be sensitive. The proposed framework addresses this by including components that emphasize morality, interdisciplinary linkages, and fundamental abilities like coding and computational thinking in STEM. However, there also lies a few financial constraints in implementing AI platforms or tools in classrooms on a large scale in the educational sector. The less developed regions of the world might struggle to adopt this just transition. At the same time, the AI platform builders or big conglomerates such as Google or Microsoft must think of innovative platforms that can be adopted on a large scale with less investment costs or maybe by offering subscription-based payment to the needy. Cooperative training models from AI companies for educators will not only enhance educator's teaching skills but will also provide a chance for the underprivileged section of students with fair and equal opportunities to foster.

Conclusion

An investigation into the changing field of human-AI (HAI) teaming in STEM education was investigated in this chapter, with a focus on the revolutionary potential of AI technologies to improve learning and teaching. We have critically evaluated how AI-driven technologies, like (ITS), Automated Assessment and Predictive Analytics, and Customized and Adaptive Education, are changing educational scenarios through a thorough evaluation of recent advancements. These tools offer chances for momentum, personalization, and data-driven insights that haven't been seen before.

As a result, teachers may adjust their teaching approaches, and students can interact with the material in ways that best suit their particular requirements and environments. Our thorough SWOT analysis supports the main claim of this chapter, which is that successful human-AI collaboration in education holds the key to opening up new pedagogical possibilities. This assessment found drawbacks, such as the possibility of bias and the requirement for strong ethical frameworks, in addition to pros, such as AI's capacity to personalize learning and offer real-time feedback. Our suggested conceptual framework acts as a tactical manual for incorporating AI in a way that is impactful and inclusive, guaranteeing that the advantages of AI are dispersed fairly among various learning groups. In the future, researchers can utilize this framework to direct the development of moral and inclusive AI frameworks in pedagogy, and educators can gain from knowing how to integrate AI tools into their teaching practices. Additionally, they can investigate which crucial areas AI can be further improved and modified to match the changing needs of Industry 5.0. We believe that HAI teaming is important in STEM education. HAI is not merely a technological upgrade but also a paradigm shift that changes the roles of teachers and students in the STEM/STEAM pedagogy. We can build a future where learning is more egalitarian and effective by carefully integrating AI into classrooms, enabling students to flourish in a world that is becoming more complicated and driven by AI. Thus, this chapter serves both as a guide and a call to action for utilizing AI in education to its greatest potential.DeclarationDuring the preparation of this chapter, the authors used Grammarly and ChatGPT-4o for language editing.

References

Adel, A. (2022). Future of industry 5.0 in society: Human-centric solutions, challenges and prospective research areas. *Journal of Cloud Computing, 11*(1), 40. https://doi.org/10.1186/s13677-022-00314-5

Ahmad, I., et al. (2022). MOOC 5.0: A roadmap to the future of learning. *Sustainability*. https://doi.org/10.3390/su141811199

Aitken, J.E., Andrew D. Wolvin and Roy M. Berko (2014) 'Listening Tests: Pearson's MyLab in Teaching Communication and Spanish.' In Cases on communication technology for second language acquisition and cultural learning, in.

Alam, A. (2023). Harnessing the power of AI to create intelligent tutoring systems for enhanced classroom experience and improved learning outcomes. In G. Rajakumar, K.-L. Du, & Á. Rocha

(Eds.), *Intelligent communication technologies and virtual mobile networks* (pp. 571–591). Springer Nature.

Almoubayyed, H. et al. (2023). Rewriting math word problems to improve learning outcomes for emerging readers: A randomized field trial in Carnegie learning's MATHia. N. Wang et al. (Eds.), *Artificial intelligence in education. Posters and late breaking results, workshops and tutorials, industry and innovation tracks, practitioners, doctoral consortium and blue sky.* (pp. 200–205). Cham: Springer Nature.

Atchley, P., et al. (2024). Human and AI collaboration in the higher education environment: Opportunities and concerns. *Cognitive Research: Principles and Implications, 9*(1), 20. https://doi.org/10.1186/s41235-024-00547-9

Baker, R. S., & Hawn, A. (2022). Algorithmic bias in education. *International Journal of Artificial Intelligence in Education, 32*(4), 1052–1092. https://doi.org/10.1007/s40593-021-00285

Baker, R. S., & Inventado, P. S. (2014). Educational data mining and learning analytics. In J. A. Larusson & B. White (Eds.), *Learning analytics: From research to practice* (pp. 61–75). Springer. https://doi.org/10.1007/978-1-4614-3305-74

Bosman, L., Magana, A., & Kotla, B. (2022). Promoting evidence-based decision making practices to develop the entrepreneurial mindset enabled by Microsoft Power BI Desktop. In *2022 IEEE Frontiers in education conference (FIE)* (pp. 1–6). https://doi.org/10.1109/FIE56618.2022.9962585

Celik, I. (2023). Exploring the determinants of artificial intelligence (AI) literacy: Digital divide, computational thinking, cognitive absorption. *Telematics and Informatics, 83*, 102026. https://doi.org/10.1016/j.tele.2023.102026

Conklin, T. A. (2016). Knewton (An adaptive learning platform available at https://www.knewton.com/). *Academy of Management Learning & Education, 15*(3):635–639. https://doi.org/10.5465/amle.2016.0206.

Cosyn, E., et al. (2021). A practical perspective on knowledge space theory: ALEKS and its data. *Journal of Mathematical Psychology, 101*, 102512. https://doi.org/10.1016/j.jmp.2021.102512

Deák, C., et al. (2021). Evolution of new approaches in pedagogy and STEM with inquiry-based learning and post-pandemic scenarios. *Education Sciences*. https://doi.org/10.3390/educsci11070319

Deák, C., & Kumar, B. (2024). A systematic review of STEAM education's role in nurturing digital competencies for sustainable innovations. *Education Sciences.*. Multidisciplinary Digital Publishing Institute (MDPI). https://doi.org/10.3390/educsci14030226

Dieterle, E., Dede, C., & Walker, M. (2024). The cyclical ethical effects of using artificial intelligence in education. *AI & Society, 39*(2), 633–643. https://doi.org/10.1007/s00146-022-01497-w

Erdogan, R., et al. (2023). Examination of the usability of Tinkercad application in educational robotics teaching by eye tracking technique. *Smart Learning Environments, 10*(1), 27. https://doi.org/10.1186/s40561-023-00242-0

Eynon, R., & Young, E. (2020). Methodology, legend, and rhetoric: The constructions of AI by academia, industry, and policy groups for lifelong learning. *Science, Technology, & Human Values, 46*(1), 166–191. https://doi.org/10.1177/0162243920906475

Fariani, R. I., Junus, K., & Santoso, H. B. (2023). A systematic literature review on personalised learning in the higher education context. *Technology, Knowledge and Learning, 28*(2), 449–476. https://doi.org/10.1007/s10758-022-09628-4

Feng, M. et al. (2023). Implementing and evaluating ASSISTments online math homework support at large scale over two years: Findings and lessons learned. In N. Wang et al. (Eds.), *Artificial intelligence in education.* (pp. 28–40). Cham: Springer Nature.

Feng, M., & Heffernan, N. T. (2005) *Informing teachers live about student learning: Reporting in the assistment system.* Available at: www.assistment.org.

Ferreira Mello, R. et al. (2023) *Education in the age of generative AI context and recent developments.* Available at: https://doi.org/10.48550/arXiv.2309.12332.

Foster, M. E. (2024). Evaluating the impact of supplemental computer-assisted math instruction in elementary school: A conceptual replication. *Journal of Research on Educational Effectiveness, 17*(1), 94–118. https://doi.org/10.1080/19345747.2023.2174919

Gligorea, I., et al. (2023). Adaptive learning using artificial intelligence in e-learning: A literature review. *Education Sciences*. Multidisciplinary Digital Publishing Institute (MDPI). https://doi.org/10.3390/educsci13121216

Grover, S., & Pea, R. (2013). Computational thinking in K–12: A review of the state of the field. *Educational Researcher, 42*(1), 38–43. https://doi.org/10.3102/0013189X12463051

Guo, L., et al. (2021). Evolution and trends in intelligent tutoring systems research: A multidisciplinary and scientometric view. *Asia Pacific Education Review, 22*(3), 441–461. https://doi.org/10.1007/s12564-021-09697-7

Jones, A., & Bomash, I. (2018). Validating mastery learning: Assessing the impact of adaptive learning objective mastery in Knewton Alta. In C. Penstein Rosé et al. (Eds.), *Artificial intelligence in education* (pp. 433–437). Springer.

Khan, N., et al. (2022). Connecting digital literacy in higher education to the 21st century workforce. *Knowledge Management and E-Learning, 14*(1), 46–61. https://doi.org/10.34105/j.kmel.2022.14.004

Kumar, A., et al. (2023). Gamified learning and assessment using ARCS with next-generation AIoMT integrated 3D animation and virtual reality simulation. *Electronics, 12*(4). https://doi.org/10.3390/electronics12040835

Kumar, B., & Deák, C. (2023). Evolving minds: A literature-driven and empirical exploration of STEAM skill development and learning approaches. *Journal of Innovation Management, 11*(4), 71–96. https://doi.org/10.24840/2183-0606011.0040004

Laseinde, O. T., & Dada, D. (2023). Enhancing teaching and learning in STEM Labs: The development of an android-based virtual reality platform. *Materials Today: Proceedings*. https://doi.org/10.1016/j.matpr.2023.09.020

Maddikunta, P. K. R., et al. (2022). Industry 5.0: A survey on enabling technologies and potential applications. *Journal of Industrial Information Integration, 26*, 100257. https://doi.org/10.1016/j.jii.2021.100257

Mufarihah et al. (2023). Learning videos as support media before playing children on STEAM learning contents at PAUD Nurul Hidayah. (pp. 713–718). https://doi.org/10.2991/978-2-38476-022-076.

Ni, A., & Cheung, A. (2023). Understanding secondary students' continuance intention to adopt AI-powered intelligent tutoring system for English learning. *Education and Information Technologies, 28*(3), 3191–3216. https://doi.org/10.1007/s10639-022-11305-z

Owoc, M. L., Sawicka, A., & Weichbroth, P. (2021). Artificial intelligence technologies in education: Benefits, challenges and strategies of implementation. In M. L. Owoc & M. Pondel (Eds.), *Artificial intelligence for knowledge management* (pp. 37–58). Springer.

Özdemir, V., & Hekim, N. (2018). Birth of industry 5.0: Making sense of big data with artificial intelligence, "the Internet of Things" and next-generation technology policy. *OMICS A Journal of Integrative Biology, 22*(1), 65–76. https://doi.org/10.1089/omi.2017.0194

Phil Long, B., & Siemens, G. (2011). Penetrating the fog: Analytics in learning and education.

Popenici, S. A. D., & Kerr, S. (2017). Exploring the impact of artificial intelligence on teaching and learning in higher education. *Research and Practice in Technology Enhanced Learning, 12*(1), 22. https://doi.org/10.1186/s41039-017-0062-8

Reen, F. J., et al. (n.d.). Student informed development of virtual reality simulations for teaching and learning in the molecular sciences. *Journal of Biological Education*, 1–17. https://doi.org/10.1080/00219266.2024.2386250

Relmasira, S. C., Lai, Y. C., & Donaldson, J. P. (2023). Fostering AI literacy in elementary science, technology, engineering, art, and mathematics (STEAM) education in the age of generative AI. *Sustainability, 15*(18). https://doi.org/10.3390/su151813595

Ritter, S. et al. (2015) *Carnegie learning's adaptive learning products*. Available at: https://www.educationaldatamining.org/EDM2015/proceedings/demo633-634.pdf. Accessed August 22, 2024.

Serban, I. V. et al. (2020). A large-scale, open-domain, mixed-interface dialogue-based ITS for STEM, In I. I. Bittencourt et al. (Eds.), *Artificial intelligence in education*. (pp. 387–392). Cham: Springer.

Sifat, R. I., & Bhattacharya, U. (2023). Transformative potential of artificial intelligence in global health policy. *Journal of Market Access & Health Policy, 11*(1), 2230660. https://doi.org/10.1080/20016689.2023.2230660

Singh, A. et al. (2017). Gradescope: A fast, flexible, and fair system for scalable assessment of handwritten work. In *L@S 2017—Proceedings of the 4th (2017) ACM conference on learning at scale*. Association for Computing Machinery, Inc, (pp. 81–88). Available at: https://doi.org/10.1145/3051457.3051466

Stamper, J., Xiao, R., & Hou, X. (2024). Enhancing LLM-based feedback: Insights from intelligent tutoring systems and the learning sciences. In A. M. Olney et al. (Eds.), *Artificial intelligence in education. Posters and late breaking results, workshops and tutorials, industry and innovation tracks, practitioners, doctoral consortium and blue sky* (pp. 32–43). Springer Nature.

Sullivan, A., & Strawhacker, A. (2021). Screen-free STEAM: Low-cost and hands-on approaches to teaching coding and engineering to young children. In C. Cohrssen & S. Garvis (Eds.), *Embedding STEAM in early childhood education and care* (pp. 87–113). Springer. https://doi.org/10.1007/978-3-030-65624-95

Supriya, Y., et al. (2024). Industry 5.0 in smart education: Concepts, applications, challenges, opportunities, and future directions. *IEEE Access, 12*, 81938–81967. https://doi.org/10.1109/ACCESS.2024.3401473

Turcotte, N. (2024). Designing collaborative tech-rich learning: building a multi-player game controller with Makey Makeys. *Journal of Technology-Integrated Lessons and Teaching, 2*(2), 68–74. https://doi.org/10.13001/jtilt.v2i2.8281

Urban, A. (2023). How hands-on assessments can boost retention, satisfaction, skill development, and career outcomes in online courses. *AI, Computer Science and Robotics Technology*. https://doi.org/10.5772/acrt.23

Weltman, H. R., et al. (2019). Evaluation of an adaptive tutorial supporting the teaching of mathematics. *European Journal of Engineering Education, 44*(5), 787–804. https://doi.org/10.1080/03043797.2018.1513993

Yilmaz, R., & Karaoglan Yilmaz, F. G. (2023). The effect of generative artificial intelligence (AI)-based tool use on students' computational thinking skills, programming self-efficacy and motivation. *Computers and Education: Artificial Intelligence, 4*, 100147. https://doi.org/10.1016/j.caeai.2023.100147

Baibhaw Kumar is a lecturer at the University of Miskolc, Hungary, specializing in Renewable Energy. He holds a PhD in Mechanical Engineering. His research focuses on renewable energy, energy storage, innovation management, and STEM/STEAM pedagogy. His work in renewable energy, innovation, and pedagogy approaches reflects his commitment to theoretical advancements and practical solutions for a sustainable future. At present, he lectures on Environmental Management at the Faculty of Mechanical Engineering and Informatics, University of Miskolc.

Csaba Deák is a professor at the University of Miskolc, Hungary, and an innovation management consultant. Between 2012 and 2014, he was the deputy chairman of the National Innovation Office (NIH) of Hungary. He is a guest lecturer at Universitatea Babes-Bolyai, Romania, and a graduate faculty member at Florida Agricultural and Mechanical University. He is also the founder and honorary chairman of the North Hungarian ICT Cluster. He is also working as a management consultant for several transnational companies. His main fields of research and training are Innovation Management, Project Management, and Strategic Management. He is also a fellow of ISPIM.

Ethical Considerations of Human-AI Collaboration: A Normative Perspective for Organizational Practice

Keze Zhang, Majid Khan, and Sajid Khan

Introduction

Artificial intelligence (AI) is defined as the ability of machines to perform human-like cognitive tasks (Benbya et al., 2020); its applications have become an emerging but crucial element in the current workplace. Particularly, the early 2020s has witnessed the mass adoption of large language models (LLMs), such as the series of GPT models by OpenAI. Prior studies have identified the wide application of AI applications for professional uses in different settings, such as research and development (Sundberg & Holmström, 2024), human resource management (Aguinis et al., 2024), marketing (Huang & Rust, 2021), and supply chain management (Toorajipour et al., 2021).

The wide adoption of AI applications has sparked debates about their double-edged sword effect. There is no doubt that these applications, such as ChatGPT, Bing Chat, and Gemini, have revolutionized the way individuals interact with technology. Existing literature has revealed that those applications can enhance work efficiency by enabling users to access vast amounts of information, automate routine tasks, organizing information into reports, and even assisting in decision-making processes (Huang & Rust, 2021; Toorajipour et al., 2021). Bill Gates, a

K. Zhang
Department of Science and Technology Studies, Faculty of Science, University of Malaya, Kuala Lumpur, Malaysia
e-mail: s2001206@siswa.um.edu.my

M. Khan (✉)
Lecturer of Management and Sustainable Business at the School of Management, Massey University, Palmerston North, New Zealand
e-mail: M.Khan@massey.ac.nz

S. Khan
Ghulam Ishaq Khan Institute of Engineering Sciences and Technology, Topi, Pakistan
e-mail: dr.sajidkhan@giki.edu.pk

M. Dabić et al. (eds.), *Artificial Humans*, Future of Business and Finance,
https://doi.org/10.1007/978-3-032-06604-6_15

leading figure in business and technology fields, also once remarked that "improvements in artificial intelligence are the *most important* innovation at the moment...the applications of generative AI like OpenAI's ChatGPT could improve office efficiency, drafting invoices and letters."[1]

However, alongside these benefits, ethical concerns have emerged regarding the potential risks associated with widespread AI-based application use. Privacy issues are at the forefront, as AI-based applications often require access to large datasets, which may include sensitive or personal information (Zhang et al., 2022). The potential for data breaches or misuse of this information raises significant ethical questions. Additionally, the ability of AI-based applications to generate information has led to worries about misinformation (Chen & Shu, 2024), as these models can be used to create convincing but entirely false narratives. Furthermore, concerns have been raised about the threat to work and employment due to the wide application of AI technology (Mirbabaie et al., 2022). Similar to the Luddites, the members of English textile workers were against the use of automated machinery in the nineteenth century; the automation in work empowered by AI-based applications also has fostered job insecurity among workers in organizations, especially those with routine-intensive jobs (Domini et al., 2021).

Rather than the general ethical dilemmas on AI application, an emerging interest arises in the ethical debates in human-AI interaction, especially human-AI collaboration. Human-AI collaboration refers to problem-solving in which "two or more agents work together to achieve shared goals [...] involving at least one human and at least one computational agent" (Terveen, 1995), which the role of AI is to "augment what people want to do rather than substitutes it" (Harper, 2019). Siemon (2022) constructed four team roles of AI-based teammates, namely, the coordinator, creator, perfectionist, and doer. Each of these skills and behaviors can contribute to the more effective design of human-AI collaborated teams and enhance the understanding of the team dynamics and processes. This type of collaboration in work settings has started to be explored by scholars, with a number of positive outcomes identified (Hitsuwari et al., 2023; Simón et al., 2024; Sowa et al., 2021). However, there remain issues around human-AI interaction. Traditionally, there has been issues of data privacy and general moral issues; human-AI collaboration poses contemporary issues including violation of ethical principles such as rights, justice, responsibility, autonomy, and accountability (Heyder et al., 2023).

Therefore, it is important to expand existing literature on ethics of human-AI interaction, responding to the recent calls for deeper ethical exploration (e.g., Golgeci et al., 2025; Aubert & Chan, 2024). As a corollary, our chapter explores these issues in the workplace through the framework of traditional theories of morality – that provide foundation for moral reasoning and guide ethical decision-making in day-to-day life. Particularly, our chapter discusses human-AI interaction in relation to theories such as egoism, utilitarianism, ethics of duty, rights, and justice.

The chapter is organized as follows. Section 2 presents an introduction to the five ethical theories. Section 3 introduces the recent studies on human-AI collaboration

[1] See https://www.cnbc.com/2023/02/10/bill-gates-says-ai-like-chatgpt-is-the-most-important-innovation.html.

in the workplace, highlighting its benefits and drawbacks for organizations. Section 4 will provide a comprehensive and critical analysis of human-AI collaboration by applying ethical theories, followed by the implications for organizational research and practices in Sect. 5. Finally, Sect. 6 concludes the chapter by identifying gaps in current research on human-AI interaction and suggestions for future empirical studies to explore ethical considerations further.

Normative Ethical Theories

Egoism

Egoism is among the oldest philosophical perspectives, with roots tracing back to ancient Greek thinkers, including Plato. Egoism continues to hold significant influence in contemporary economic thought, particularly in connection to Adam Smith's (1723–1790) foundational work on the development of modern liberal economies.

Egoism posits that an action is morally right when the decision-maker freely choses to pursue their short-term or long-term self-interest. In other words, the perspective that aligns morality with self-interest is known as egoism. Moral philosophers distinguish between two types of egoism: personal and impersonal. Personal egoists suggest that individuals must pursue their own long-term interests but refrain from prescribing what others should do. In contrast, impersonal egoists assert that everyone ought to act in accordance with their own long-term interests. Adam Smith argued that within an economic system, the pursuit of individual self-interest is acceptable because it leads to morally desirable outcomes for society, facilitated by the "invisible hand" of the marketplace. For example, while a seller might benefit in the short term from offering substandard products, consumers will eventually recognize the poor quality and shift to better alternatives in the market.

However, this theory has faced criticism for its inherent weaknesses. First, it assumes that a societal mechanism exists to prevent individual egoists from pursuing their interests at the expense of others. In Smith's work, this mechanism is the market itself. Yet, numerous instances reveal that markets do not always function equitably, leading to outcomes that individual interests harm others. This is particularly evident in the rise of anti-globalization movements, which are driven by the reality that global markets do not operate perfectly, resulting in stark inequalities in wealth distribution worldwide. Furthermore, egoism is criticized from a sustainability perspective. Critics argue that if individuals relentlessly pursue their own self-interest, it raises the question of what will happen to future generations and the long-term well-being of the planet.

Utilitarianism

Utilitarian logic is closely associated with the work of British philosophers Jeremy Bentham and John Stuart Mill (1806–1873) and has significantly influenced modern economics. Bentham and Mill's contributions to the development of utilitarianism have shaped economic theories that prioritize maximizing overall welfare and societal benefit, aligning with broader consequentialist principles. Utilitarianism is a moral philosophy that advocates for actions that produce the greatest possible good over harm for all those affected. "Good" in this context is understood as happiness or pleasure, which is why this principle is often referred to as the "greatest happiness principle." Utilitarianism, as a consequentialist theory, focuses merely on the outcomes of an action and seeks to maximize positive outcomes against the negative ones. It suggests that humans try to maximize pleasures and minimize pains – thus the action that results from such a perspective will result in greatest amount of good for largest number of people. Utilitarianism emphasizes collective welfare and the overall well-being of society, unlike egoism, which centers on individual self-interest. Utilitarian logic relies on cost-benefit analysis – and any action that has most benefits and least costs is considered as the optimal choice.

Over time, utilitarianism has been subjected to intense criticism. These concerns include subjectivity, quantification, and the distribution of utility. To start, the judgment of what causes pleasures or pains in an individual life is an inherently subjective exercise when performing the cost-benefit analysis, given that the "party" doing the analysis is generally doing it from a subjective perspective. This subjectivity complicates evaluation of goodness or otherwise in a given context. Second, there are perils in assessing the costs and benefits of each scenario. The evaluation of issues involving life and death may be especially fraught, since they are tied to intrinsic values that are difficult to measure. It serves as a strong argument for questioning whether utilitarianism can be a guiding principle for making decisions due to the challenge in accounting for human life alone and its intrinsic value. Lastly, one main issue with utilitarianism is that it often ignores minority interests, as the theory claims that the greatest good for the greatest number must be prioritized. Utilitarianism has a large critique: suitable considerations for the vulnerable ones or minorities (in most cases) could be lost in this, since these individuals may be beneficial for society as a whole.

Ethics of Duty

German philosopher Immanuel Kant fundamentally rejected utilitarianism and, instead, argued that all individuals are rational and autonomous beings. From her perspective, morality is rooted in certain, abstract, and unchangeable principles, which are known as priori moral laws and argued to become the guidelines for all ethical dilemmas.

Kant developed a theoretical framework for deriving these principles, termed the categorical imperative, which he regarded as the supreme principle of morality. This framework should be applied to every moral issue uniformly, regardless of individuals involved in specific situations, their interests, or the outcomes of applying these principles.

The categorical imperative has three main maxims:

Maxim of Universalizability: Act only according to that maxim whereby you can, at the same time, will that it should become a universal law.

Maxim of Human Dignity: Act only so that you use humanity, both in yourself and in others, as an end in itself, never as merely a means to an end.

Maxim of Autonomy: Act according to that maxim by which you can at the same time will that it should become a universal law, determined by your own rational ity rather than external forces.

Through these maxims, Kant highlights the critical role of moral duty and the inherent worth of every individual, asserting that ethical decisions must transcend mere outcomes.

There are also a number of issues with the ethics of duty. The first is its undervaluation of outcomes. While Kant would say that decision-makers are free to form the same decision considering the outcomes, there lies the inefficiency: others making the same decision do not help to efficiently assess the outcome. In short, this theory places almost no weight on the consequences of one's actions, instead favoring ideas of duty, which can lead to a disinterest in the practical consequences. The second issue is the complexity of the theory. The Ethics of Duty has a clear rule for how to determine if an action is ethical, dependent on if it is the actor's duty to do it. In practice, this judgement can be fairly complicated in terms of particular frameworks, like Kant's categorical imperative. The third is the optimism built into this theory. Kant's way of thinking has an optimism built in, since it takes for granted that people are rational autonomous agents who do the right thing for the right reasons. This assumption is quite naive (if not idealistic) particularly in the world of business, where self-interest, competition, and external pressures may be stronger motivators for decision-making than moral obligation.

Ethics of Rights

The notion of "natural rights," moral claims to which all humans have in their nature and that need to be honored and protected, especially by the state, was proposed by the British philosopher John Locke (1632–1714). Locke and other rights theorists then listed life, liberty, and property as among the most basic of these rights. Over the years, that idea has extended to claims of rights like freedom of speech, freedom of consent, freedom of conscience, freedom of privacy, and the right to a fair legal process. These are now often called "human rights," with the stipulation that these rights of universal human dignity should apply to everyone, without distinction on the basis of gender, race, religion, nationality, or other markers of difference.

The state of nature, according to Locke, is an absence of government but not an absence of mutual obligations from one person to another. Other than self-preservation, the law of nature – according to reason – teaches "all mankind, who will but consult it, that being all equal and independent, no one ought to harm another in their lives, liberty, or possessions." Unlike Thomas Hobbes, who saw the state of nature as a state of confusion and danger, Locke held that humans had natural rights to life, liberty, and property, and the state of nature could be relatively peaceful. However, men must agree to form a commonwealth, thereby leaving the state of nature, in order to create an arbitral body for settling disputes and remedying injustices.

Locke's assertion that these natural rights to life, liberty, and property precede the establishment of civil society profoundly influenced the American Revolution and laid the foundation for modern liberalism, emphasizing the protection of individual rights through the rule of law.

The ethical significance of the notion of rights lies in the fact that rights often impose corresponding duties on others to respect, protect, or facilitate them. In this sense, rights are closely linked to duties, as the rights of one individual create obligations for others. For instance, ownership right imposes a burden on every other person that dissuades one from causing any interference with or taking unlawfully the owner's property. So also is the right to privacy, which obliges others from dealing in terms of gathering one's personal information without his/her consent. Rights and duties are thus viewed as often coin faces; every right typically has on the flip side a corresponding duty to uphold it.

Ethics of Justice

The idea of a "state of nature," whether real or hypothetical, came to dominate political thought in the seventeenth and eighteenth centuries. Nevertheless, it has shaped what is today the most respected effort to glean objective principles of justice and fairness – that of the American philosopher John Rawls. In theory of justice (1971), Rawls proposed not a pre-social or pre- political state of nature, but a thought experiment to discover the basis for a just society. He contended that the basic elements of justice could most appropriately be determined by imagining a group of rational persons selecting the rules of governance without knowledge of their own social standings, advantages, or disadvantages – a device he dubbed the "veil of ignorance." In doing so, Rawls, like previous philosophers such as Hobbes, Locke, and Rousseau, argued that the best way to appraise the justice of social institutions is to consider their absence and assess the principles that would come into place in an unbiased setting.

In *A Theory of Justice*, John Rawls proposes two key principles—or "tests"—to determine whether an action can be considered just. According to Rawls, justice is achieved when:

Each individual has an equal right to the most extensive system of basic liberties, compatible with a similar system of liberty for all.

Social and economic inequalities are arranged so that they: a) provide the greatest benefit to the least advantaged; and b) are linked to positions and roles that are open to everyone under conditions of fair equality of opportunity.

The first principle is paramount: before permitting any form of inequality, it must be ensured that basic liberties are equally distributed to everyone affected by the decision. This principle thus prioritizes the realization of fundamental human rights for all, which must be satisfied before moving to considerations of inequality.

The second principle acknowledges that inequalities are inevitable in a free and competitive society. However, two conditions must be met to ensure their justice. First, inequalities are just if even the least advantaged in society are better off than they would be without them. For instance, high executive salaries could be justified if they lead to improved corporate performance that results in better wages or working conditions for lower-level employees. Second, these inequalities are only justifiable if access to positions of power, like corporate leadership roles, is open to all individuals under conditions of fair equality of opportunity, ensuring that success is not restricted to a privileged few.

Human-AI Collaboration in the Workplace

Positive Outcomes at Work

Even though human-AI collaboration has become an emerging research topic in the recent few years; some of its positive outcomes have been revealed in work settings. Scholars have widely discussed its positive influence on work performance. AI-human collaboration addresses key challenges while transforming workplace practices to enhance efficiency and productivity.

AI-human collaboration can transform the way people work and benefit us in the workplace in terms of efficiency. Sowa et al. (2021) discuss different levels of proximity between AI and humans and to use human-AI collaboration to improve overall working productivity. So, it can be useful to collaborate with AI to increase productivity by automating repetitive and tedious tasks (Wang et al., 2019). AI-enabled systems help employees move on to higher-value activities that require creativity and critical thinking skills by automating routine tasks like data entry, scheduling, and document management. Hitsuwari et al. (2023) explored human-AI interactions in the context of creative artwork – and demonstrated that such collaborations have better creativity in haiku production, manifested in the production of beautiful poetry. The study of Simón et al. (2024) assessed how human-AI collaboration plays its role in organizational value creation, and their evidence supported its positive impact on organizational dynamic capability.

AI also contributes to personal growth by providing resources for self-education and personal enhancement (Ou et al., 2024). AI-powered tools, such as language improvement tools and AI-based decision-support systems, can provide workers with real-time feedback and insights that help them make well-informed decisions and react effectively to complex problems. Since AI tools are trained on large training datasets, they could at some time gain more experience in decision-making than a human's lifetime (Graßmann & Schermuly, 2021). Moreover, in terms of job satisfaction, AI-human collaboration can reduce the burden of mundane tasks, making work more engaging (La Sala et al., 2024; Lai & Rau, 2024). For instance, through partnering with AI, employees may gain more satisfaction and engagement by reducing the strains on repetitive tasks that can be automated by AI. AI's instrumental, informative, caring, and intimate role in human-AI partnership is also found to be beneficial for mitigating stress among employees (Le & Cayrat, 2024), which can enhance their job satisfaction.

Ethical Challenges in Human-AI Collaboration

Transparency is one critical issue in human-AI collaboration, as the opacity of many AI systems (often referred to as the "black box" problem (Wadden, 2022)) can obscure how decisions are made, complicating efforts to assign responsibility for outcomes. Without clear explanations of how AI models function, individuals at work may struggle to fully understand or trust the decisions and recommendations their AI partners provide. This lack of transparency can lead to the under-reliance of AI due to incomplete information (Vössing et al., 2022). Beyond the "black box" problem, Andrada et al. (2023) synthesized the three types of transparency in AI, namely, (1) information transparency, (2) material transparency, and (3) transformational transparency. Information transparency is a major concern in transparency and entails the information shared on an AI system, generally to aid in assessments of its fairness, trustworthiness, safety, effectiveness, accountability, compliance with regulations, and legality (Andrada et al., 2023). Transparency about AI systems' materiality also matters, including the hardware used to realize some AI applications, its production or maintenance demands, and the relations between labor that are implicated in operations (Andrada et al., 2023). For instance, data centers and other sources of large-scale computation supporting AI applications are frequently involved in greenhouse gas emissions (Lannelongue et al., 2021), yet little is disclosed on their environmental impact by the developers. Finally, neural and bodily transformations may happen when individuals are excessively engaged in collaboration with AI, such as weakened wayfinding abilities and skills due to pervasive GPS use (Gillett & Heersmink, 2019). Hence, transformational transparency, i.e., the disclosure of how hidden changes may happen to the human partners of AI, is crucial, especially on the important effects on the agent's cognitive, epistemic, or ethical capacities.

Another concern lies in the bias of human-AI collaboration. Noticeably, Alon-Barkat and Busuioc (2023) explored the bias from the human-AI interactions in public sector decision-making from the perspectives of social psychology and information processing. Their empirical studies revealed two major types of biases, namely, automation bias and selective adherence, among the decision-makers engaged in human-AI collaboration. Automation bias refers to "the use of automation as a heuristic replacement for vigilant information seeking and processing" (Mosier et al., 1998). When collaborating with AI-based applications, human users are likely to believe in the outputs or suggestions from them rather than the situation-based judgment from human decision-makers, including bureaucratic discretion and professional judgment (Alon-Barkat and Busuioc 2023). This bias has become a particular concern given the well-documented failures and malfunctioning of AI-based systems. As remarked by Jiang et al. (2023), AI-based systems learn discrimination from humans, since the systems are developed based on the training dataset that possibly involves discriminative information. As a result, automation bias may cause human discrimination to be imposed on human-AI teams. For instance, recruitment decisions suggested by the AI-based system may be unfavorable toward job candidates from marginalized groups if it is trained on historical hiring data that already skews toward these groups. This not only perpetuates unfairness but also masks discrimination under the guise of objectivity, as AI decisions can seem neutral despite being influenced by biased data. Even if the AI-based systems provide unbiased suggestions, selective adherence to algorithmic advice is also found to introduce bias into the human-AI collaboration (Alon-Barkat & Busuioc, 2023). Specifically, human decision-makers are more likely to follow the algorithmic prediction that accords with a group stereotype, which provides expectancy confirmation. Some studies on the use of algorithmic tools found the existence of this selective adherence in risk assessment by criminal courts (Green & Chen, 2019; Stevenson, 2018).

In organization settings, human-AI collaboration also brings in ethical concerns in job security for human employees. As a critical group of internal stakeholders, employees are the driver of organizational success. Yet, they are subject to various concerns from the arising human-AI collaboration, even if they are not in jobs with route tasks that are likely to be replaced with AI. Job insecurity arises from the required efforts to adapt and master new AI-related skills, without which some negative work-life-related outcomes (e.g., creative performance, well-being, and psychological health) may appear (Wu et al., 2024). In addition, the presence of AI tends to prompt negative outcomes from employees with tasks requiring thinking skills, especially when they compare their skills to the AI (Vorobeva et al., 2022). Similarly, Yin et al. (2024) identified the double-edged sword effect of AI assistants on employees' innovation behavior, and the negative effect is prevailing in organizations low in AI readiness.

Ethical Theories Applied to Human-AI Collaboration

Egoism

From the perspective of egoism, which emphasizes self-interest as the foundation of moral decision-making, the ethical implications of human-AI collaboration can be analyzed through the lens of individual or organizational benefit. Individuals or organizations might collaborate with AI to enhance their personal or competitive advantage. As discussed, AI can increase efficiency, reduce labor costs, and optimize decision-making, aligning with the egoistic goal of maximizing self-interest. However, there is the risk of exploitation, i.e., using AI to gain an unfair advantage, manipulate markets, or sideline human workers. If AI is used solely for personal gain without considering the broader societal or ethical impact, this could lead to social inequality or the erosion of jobs. In addition, an egoist might endorse creating highly autonomous AI systems that serve their interests. However, over-reliance on AI for selfish purposes could introduce unintended risks, including reduced human oversight or even harmful decision-making if AI systems prioritize profit over ethics.

Utilitarianism

As a consequentialist ethical theory, utilitarianism attends to the maximization of collective welfare when deciding whether an action is ethical or not. The concern over human-AI collaboration therefore lies in whether this arrangement maximizes benefits for the largest number of people while minimizing harm. Cost-benefit analysis becomes a necessary step for identifying the consequences through assessing the potential impact of AI-based systems on different stakeholders. If certain human-AI collaboration arrangements introduce more costs but fewer benefits, it is considered as not ethical to conduct them from the perspective of utilitarianism. For instance, some organizations consider the introduction of AI-based systems in animation production as an augmentation of the productivity of human employees, but this decision deserves caution under the principle of utilitarianism. It comes with a cost of losing confidence in creativity among human employees, especially the low-skilled ones (Magni et al., 2024), and the benefits may be limited due to the public's negative bias toward AI creative work (Magni et al., 2024).

Ethics of Duty

Ethics of duty calls for adherence to moral rules and principles, meaning whether the adoption of AI-based systems for collaboration is ethical or not should be evaluated against the three key principles, such as consistency, human dignity, and universality. Consistency implies that there should be necessary organizational guidelines for human-AI collaborations followed by everyone with no exception. When engaging in human-AI collaboration, human dignity also becomes a vital ethical aspect, which includes employees' autonomy and rationality. Specifically, ethics may be violated when employees are prompted to have their own needs, choices, and expectations withheld when collaborating with AI. Moreover, the human-AI collaboration needs to be conducted in a way that is acceptable to the organizational stakeholders, not only employees, so that this novel type of collaboration can be accepted and adhered to the principle of universality.

Ethics of Rights

Human-AI collaboration interacts with fundamental human rights, in particular the right to privacy, which has become a common threat in human-AI collaboration

(Razmerita et al., 2022). AI applications frequently require personal data as the input for completing the tasks, raising concerns about the potential violations of privacy. For example, unauthorized access to sensitive personal data, algorithmic profiling, and intrusive surveillance practices could endanger the privacy of human collaborators by creating a climate of constant monitoring. In addition, though AI can be a collaborator for dangerous and repetitive work tasks to potentially improve workplace safety and efficiency and create more job opportunities for emerging business needs, human-AI collaboration can, meanwhile, threaten the right to work since it may lead to significant unemployment in society, particularly for low-skilled workers (Domini et al., 2021). If this AI-linked job opportunity decline in the labor market is not addressed properly through governmental intervention, the deepening integration of AI in business could contribute to social issues that violate the right to work and economic security.

Ethics of Justice

From the perspective of justice, the ethical implications of human-AI collaboration can be developed based on the principles of fairness and equity and the distribution of benefits and drawbacks in organizations. Justice emphasizes that AI systems should be developed and adopted in a way that avoids biases that could lead to discriminatory outcomes so that there can be fair treatment to all individuals. A key concern is that AI algorithms may be trained based on biased data, and the outputs generated by such algorithms can reinforce the existing social inequality and cause unfairness in some functions, including recruitment, criminal justice, and healthcare. Moreover, justice implies that the benefits from collaborating with AI, such as increased efficiency and access to opportunities, should be distributed equitably across different social groups, rather than within the individuals from privileged groups. Meanwhile, AI systems may also cause harmful outcomes, drawing the need for establishing an accountability framework to determine the responsibility and rectify injustices among human collaborators.

Implications for Practices and Research

Ethical Guidelines for Human-AI Collaboration

Egoism prioritizes individual benefit without harming others. In human-AI collaborations, employees may prioritize their own self-interest, but they need to ensure that the actions taken do not cause undue harm to others. In AI applications where personal benefit is a priority (e.g., personalized AI systems), the system should optimize outcomes that benefit individuals. However, it should also include safeguards that prevent this pursuit of personal advantage from causing harm or infringing on the well-being of other individuals or groups.

Utilitarianism addresses the maximization of collective goods in human-AI collaboration. Thus, AI should be used to ensure that collective benefit is maximized in various settings, such as healthcare, education, or environmental management. In collaborative settings, this means the human-AI collaboration should serve as an approach to maximize the benefits of organizational stakeholders. Practically, organizational managers need to consider and inform them of the costs and benefits of the introduction of certain human-AI collaborations, and some costs outweighing benefits should be avoided.

Ethics of duty emphasizes adhesion to ethical principles and rules, such as consistency, human dignity, and universality. Thus, AI systems should be designed to strictly adhere to ethical guidelines, such as respecting privacy, justice, and honesty. AI systems should not break ethical rules for efficiency or to meet personal or organizational objectives. For example, AI systems deployed for internal decision-making should enable people to hold their own beliefs and expectations, even if that entails a greater cost for organizations or delay in the process. It is a focus on doing what is right, regardless of the consequences.

The ethics of rights focuses on protecting individual rights in human-AI interaction, meaning AI systems must respect the rights of all people in the collaboration and protect people from abuse or adverse effects during human-AI collaboration. The final aim of providing individual rights shall be desired in human-AI collaboration. AI systems must also be designed and deployed in ways that respect fundamental human rights, including data privacy, freedom from discrimination, and the right to informed consent. For instance, when utilized for surveillance, AI systems should respect individuals' rights to privacy and freedom of movement while also ensuring that individuals are aware of how their data is being used, thereby providing transparency and control over personal information.

Justice ethics urge making sure that AI decisions are fair and equitable. The design and use of such systems should be done in a manner that is fair and ensures benefits and risks are borne in a balanced way by all parties involved in the collaboration. Justice in the context of AI-human collaboration means avoiding the over-benefit of a certain demographic group or socioeconomic class, which can be often seen as an "elevation" of the AI over the average human, so that they are not left behind. All stakeholders should be considered before the AI system is deemed fully functional and is then deployed, to ensure that AI systems are fair, protecting the rights, needs, and vulnerabilities of all stakeholders. In particular, AI needs to ensure equal resource distribution, underrepresented groups.

IncludingAvoiding Bias that Disadvantages Ethical Considerations in AI Development and Deployment

The emergence of ethical uses of AI will need organizations to have ethical principles put in place throughout the AI life cycle, from design to deployment. This means establishing ethical review gateways during critical stages such as system design, data collection, model training, and testing. For example, organizations can establish internal ethics review committees that periodically review AI projects, ensuring that ethical standards are upheld across the life cycle. These committees would include not just AI developers but also ethicists, legal experts, and outsiders, who would help provide a wide range of perspectives in ethics evaluations.

There is a need to put in place clear accountability mechanisms to ensure the responsible use of AI systems. Establishing this requires defining various roles and responsibilities across the organization to oversee the upholding of ethical standards in AI development and deployment. One approach is the formation of an ethics officer role or an interdisciplinary team responsible for monitoring the ethical dimensions of AI systems. These persons or units would be responsible for reviewing AI results, handling ethical issues, and making sure that AI methods meet internal and external rules. Additionally, organizations can implement protocols for addressing unintended consequences, like when an AI system produces biased results or breaching data privacy laws. Contracts with any third-party AI solutions should also include accountability mechanisms to ensure that those solutions and their products meet the ethical standards set by the organization.

One major ethical issue is bias in AI systems, especially in cases where AI is used in decision-making processes such as hiring, lending, or criminal justice. Organizations must implement measures to reduce bias by identifying potential sources of bias at every stage of the AI development process. This includes auditing training data for diversity and representation of all user groups. They should, in addition, be tested regularly to ensure fair outcomes across demographic categories. There exist various techniques such as fairness metrics, which can assess how different groups are being treated by an AI model and whether any corrective actions are required. Organizations should be fair by promoting the case for consideration, such as the impact of AI on underprivileged populations, making sure that the systems are not increasing the existing inequalities. This is why if companies audit for bias and iterate on their model continuously, the bias in their AI will go down over time.

Data governance practices are essential for ethical AI development. They must protect user data and comply with data privacy laws like the General Data Protection Regulation (GDPR). Ethical data governance ensures that data is used as originally intended by the data provider and collected only once permission is received from individuals. Data must be protected by strong encryption, anonymization, and strictly controlled access, to minimize the risk of data breaches or misuse. In addition, organizations must tell users how they handle their data and allow them to manage its usage or even opt out of an AI system if they want to. Protecting data privacy also helps organizations to earn their users trust and can help avoid the often-discussed ethical pitfalls involving data misuse.

Finally, stakeholder engagement is another consideration, as accountability in AI development/effective integration of ethics requires input from a variety of stakeholders. That means reaching beyond AI developers and technologists to include ethicists, end-users, regulators, and affected communities. Engaging with stakeholders helps to ensure that diverse perspectives are taken into account and that AI systems are designed with the needs and expectations of those affected in mind.

Engaging with a diverse set of stakeholders ensures that AI systems are designed and deployed in ways that are consistent with the values and ethical norms of society. April: You will need to work with other bodies, which may include regulatory agencies, academic institutions, and non-governmental organizations (NGOs), to understand the timely guidelines and best practices. Partnerships outside of companies can offer organizations expert insights, resources, and tools that strengthen their internal ethical frameworks. By joining forces with other stakeholders and industry consortiums or AI ethics research centers, organizations can shape broader conversations and help inform the development of industry-wide standards around AI ethics and transparency.

Future Research Directions

Based on the traditional ethics theories and the topic of emerging ethical problems in human-AI collaboration, some research works can also be allocated to understand this phenomenon better. Referring to an egoistic view of ethics, we can examine how an individual's self-interest in human-AI collaboration, including achievement orientation or Dark Triad personality traits, Machiavellianism, narcissism, and psychopathy—may promote unethical use of AI-based systems. Additionally, some studies can also be conducted to identify the unintended consequences of introducing AI partners to work teams, particularly how to predict and mitigate harm to vulnerable employees. As suggested by utilitarianism, it remains a question of how future AI models can better account for the potential negative impacts on minorities while still prioritizing the overall majority benefit.

There are also some potential research gaps in the ethics of duty, rights, and justice in human-AI collaboration. It becomes a concern how the ethicality of human-AI collaboration can be universally agreed upon and obeyed by all, which requires input from organizations' stakeholders to establish more strategic insights. Meanwhile, the human rights impact of human-AI collaboration has been addressed by previous studies, but it remains to be seen how this work arrangement may influence some more implicit rights in work settings. For instance, whether human-AI collaboration hinders or enables the right to disconnect can be addressed by future research. Furthermore, procedural and distributive justice in the design, implementation, and monitoring of AI for collaboration can be explored further as well, which may be linked to the well-being of employees from marginalized groups.

Conclusion

The increasing adoption of AI applications such as ChatGPT, Bing Chat, and Gemini fosters human-AI collaboration in organizational settings, bringing both opportunities and ethical challenges that demand careful consideration. By applying normative ethical theories, egoism, utilitarianism, ethics of duty, rights, and justice, this chapter has explored the diverse moral dimensions of human-AI collaboration, offering a structured analysis of the benefits, risks, and responsibilities associated with AI integration. Each theory provides a unique lens through which to assess the implications of AI in enhancing productivity while ensuring fairness, transparency, respect for individual rights, and other ethical considerations. As organizations continue to integrate AI technologies, developing comprehensive ethical guidelines and strategies is crucial to navigating these complexities. The chapter also highlights the need for future research to address emerging ethical dilemmas, ensuring that human-AI collaboration fosters both performance and moral responsibility in the workplace.

References

Aubert, B., & Chan, Y. (2024). Evolving strategic IS themes. *The Journal of Strategic Information Systems, 33*(1), 101821. https://doi.org/10.1016/j.jsis.2024.101821

Aguinis, H., Beltran, J. R., & Cope, A. (2024). How to use generative AI as a human resource management assistant. *Organizational Dynamics, 53*(1), 101029. https://doi.org/10.1016/j.orgdyn.2024.101029

Alon-Barkat, S., & Busuioc, M. (2023). Human–ai interactions in public sector decision making: "Automation bias" and "selective adherence" to algorithmic advice. *Journal of Public Administration Research and Theory, 33*(1), 153–169. https://doi.org/10.1093/jopart/muac007

Andrada, G., Clowes, R. W., & Smart, P. R. (2023). Varieties of transparency: Exploring agency within AI systems. *AI & Society, 38*(4), 1321–1331. https://doi.org/10.1007/s00146-021-01326-6

Benbya, H., Davenport, T. H., & Pachidi, S. (2020). Artificial intelligence in organizations: Current state and future opportunities. *MIS Quarterly Executive, 19*(4).

Chen, C., & Shu, K. (2024). Combating misinformation in the age of LLMs: Opportunities and challenges. *AI Magazine*, 1–15. https://doi.org/10.1002/aaai.12188

Domini, G., Grazzi, M., Moschella, D., & Treibich, T. (2021). Threats and opportunities in the digital era: Automation spikes and employment dynamics. *Research Policy, 50*(7), 104137. https://doi.org/10.1016/j.respol.2020.104137

Gillett, A. J., & Heersmink, R. (2019). How navigation systems transform epistemic virtues: Knowledge, issues and solutions. *Cognitive Systems Research, 56*, 36–49. https://doi.org/10.1016/j.cogsys.2019.03.004

Golgeci, I., Ritala, P., Arslan, A., McKenna, B., & Ali, I. (2025). Confronting and alleviating AI resistance in the workplace: An integrative review and a process framework. *Human Resource Management Review, 35*(2), 101075. https://doi.org/10.1016/j.hrmr.2024.101075

Graßmann, C., & Schermuly, C. C. (2021). Coaching with artificial intelligence: Concepts and capabilities. *Human Resource Development Review, 20*(1), 106–126. https://doi.org/10.1177/1534484320982891

Green, B., & Chen, Y. (2019). Disparate interactions: An algorithm-in-the-loop analysis of fairness in risk assessments. Paper presented at the proceedings of the conference on fairness, accountability, and transparency, Atlanta, GA, USA.

Harper, R. H. R. (2019). The role of HCI in the age of AI. *International Journal of Human Computer Interaction, 35*(15), 1331–1344. https://doi.org/10.1080/10447318.2019.1631527

Heyder, T., Passlack, N., & Posegga, O. (2023). Ethical management of human-AI interaction: Theory development review. *The Journal of Strategic Information Systems, 32*(3), 101772. https://doi.org/10.1016/j.jsis.2023.101772

Hitsuwari, J., Ueda, Y., Yun, W., & Nomura, M. (2023). Does human–AI collaboration lead to more creative art? Aesthetic evaluation of human-made and AI-generated haiku poetry. *Computers in Human Behavior, 139*, 107502. https://doi.org/10.1016/j.chb.2022.107502

Huang, M.-H., & Rust, R. T. (2021). A strategic framework for artificial intelligence in marketing. *Journal of the Academy of Marketing Science, 49*(1), 30–50. https://doi.org/10.1007/s11747-020-00749-9

Jiang, N., Liu, X., Liu, H., Lim, E. T. K., Tan, C.-W., & Gu, J. (2023). Beyond AI-powered context-aware services: The role of human–AI collaboration. *Industrial Management & Data Systems, 123*(11), 2771–2802. https://doi.org/10.1108/IMDS-03-2022-0152

La Sala, A., Fuller, R., Riolli, L., & Temperini, V. (2024). The rise of hybrids: Plastic knowledge in human–AI interaction. *Journal of Knowledge Management*. https://doi.org/10.1108/JKM-10-2023-1024

Lai, X., & Rau, P.-L. P. (2024). AI as co-leader: Effects of human consideration and AI structure behaviors on leadership effectiveness and neural activation. *International Journal of Human–Computer Interaction*, 1–19. https://doi.org/10.1080/10447318.2024.2365029

Lannelongue, L., Grealey, J., & Inouye, M. (2021). Green algorithms: Quantifying the carbon footprint of computation. *Advanced Science, 8*(12), 2100707. https://doi.org/10.1002/advs.202100707

Le, K. B. Q., & Cayrat, C. (2024). Howdy, Robo-partner: Exploring artificial companionship and its stress-alleviating potential for service employees. *Journal of Service*. Management ahead-of-print (ahead-of-print). https://doi.org/10.1108/JOSM-09-2023-0408

Magni, F., Park, J., & Chao, M. M. (2024). Humans as creativity gatekeepers: Are we biased against ai creativity? *Journal of Business and Psychology, 39*(3), 643–656. https://doi.org/10.1007/s10869-023-09910-x

Mirbabaie, M., Brinker, F., Möllmann Frick, N. R. J., & Stieglitz, S. (2022). The rise of artificial intelligence—understanding the AI identity threat at the workplace. *Electronic Markets, 32*(1), 73–99. https://doi.org/10.1007/s12525-021-00496-x

Mosier, K. L., Dunbar, M., McDonnell, L., Skitka, L. J., Burdick, M., & Rosenblatt, B. (1998). Automation bias and errors: Are teams better than individuals? *Proceedings of the Human Factors and Ergonomics Society Annual Meeting, 42*(3), 201–205. https://doi.org/10.1177/154193129804200304

Ou, A. W., Stöhr, C., & Malmström, H. (2024). Academic communication with AI-powered language tools in higher education: From a post-humanist perspective. *System, 121*, 103225. https://doi.org/10.1016/j.system.2024.103225

Razmerita, L., Brun, A., & Nabeth, T. (2022). Collaboration in the machine age: Trustworthy human-AI collaboration. In M. Virvou, G. A. Tsihrintzis, & L. C. Jain (Eds.), *Advances in selected artificial intelligence areas: World outstanding women in artificial Intelligence* (pp. 333–356). Springer. https://doi.org/10.1007/978-3-030-93052-31_4

Siemon, D. (2022). Elaborating team roles for artificial intelligence-based teammates in human-AI collaboration. *Group Decision and Negotiation, 31*(5), 871–912. https://doi.org/10.1007/s10726-022-09792-z

Simón, C., Revilla, E., & Jesús Sáenz, M. (2024). Integrating AI in organizations for value creation through human-AI teaming: A dynamic-capabilities approach. *Journal of Business Research, 182*, 114783. https://doi.org/10.1016/j.jbusres.2024.114783

Sowa, K., Przegalinska, A., & Ciechanowski, L. (2021). Cobots in knowledge work: Human—AI collaboration in managerial professions. *Journal of Business Research, 125*, 135–142. https://doi.org/10.1016/j.jbusres.2020.11.038

Stevenson, M. (2018). Assessing risk assessment in action. *Minnesota Law Review, 103*, 303.

Sundberg, L., & Holmström, J. (2024). Innovating by prompting: How to facilitate innovation in the age of generative AI. *Business Horizons, 67*(5), 561–570. https://doi.org/10.1016/j.bushor.2024.04.014

Terveen, L. G. (1995). Overview of human-computer collaboration. *Knowledge-Based Systems, 8*(2), 67–81. https://doi.org/10.1016/0950-7051(95)98369-H

Toorajipour, R., Sohrabpour, V., Nazarpour, A., Oghazi, P., & Fischl, M. (2021). Artificial intelligence in supply chain management: A systematic literature review. *Journal of Business Research, 122*, 502–517. https://doi.org/10.1016/j.jbusres.2020.09.009

Vorobeva, D., El Fassi, Y., Costa Pinto, D., Hildebrand, D., Herter, M. M., & Mattila, A. S. (2022). Thinking skills don't protect service workers from replacement by artificial intelligence. *Journal of Service Research, 25*(4), 601–613. https://doi.org/10.1177/10946705221104312

Vössing, M., Kahl, N., Lind, M., & Satzger, G. (2022). Designing transparency for effective human-AI collaboration. *Information Systems Frontiers, 24*(3), 877–895. https://doi.org/10.1007/s10796-022-10284-3

Wadden, J. J. (2022). Defining the undefinable: The black box problem in healthcare artificial intelligence. *Journal of Medical Ethics, 48*(10), 764–768. https://doi.org/10.1136/medethics-2021-107529

Wang, D., Weisz, J. D., Muller, M., Ram, P., Geyer, W., Dugan, C., Tausczik, Y., Samulowitz, H., & Gray, A. (2019) Human-AI collaboration in data science: Exploring data scientists' perceptions of automated AI. Proceedings of the ACM on human-computer interaction 3 (CSCW):Article 211. doi:https://doi.org/10.1145/3359313.

Wu, T.-J., Liang, Y., & Wang, Y. (2024). The buffering role of workplace mindfulness: How job insecurity of human-artificial intelligence collaboration impacts employees' work-life-related outcomes. *Journal of Business and Psychology*. https://doi.org/10.1007/s10869-024-09963-6

Yin, M., Jiang, S., & Niu, X. (2024). Can AI really help? The double-edged sword effect of AI assistant on employees' innovation behavior. *Computers in Human Behavior, 150*, 107987. https://doi.org/10.1016/j.chb.2023.107987

Zhang, X., Chan, F. T. S., Yan, C., & Bose, I. (2022). Towards risk-aware artificial intelligence and machine learning systems: An overview. *Decision Support Systems, 159*, 113800. https://doi.org/10.1016/j.dss.2022.113800

Keze Zhang is a master's degree holder by research candidate from Department of Science and Technology Studies, Faculty of Science, University of Malaya. He received his Bachelor of Management degree with distinction from Xiamen University. His research interests lie in business ethics and human resource management, in particular Diversity, Equity, and Inclusion (DEI). His ongoing research projects attend to the intersectionality between organizational migrant inclusion and social structures.

Majid Khan is a Lecturer of Management and Sustainable Business at the School of Management, Massey University. His research interests focus on corporate social responsibility, sustainability communication and praxis, forced labor, leadership, and ethical issues in business. His research seeks to explore the intersection of business and society, with an emphasis on generating both theoretical insights and empirical evidence that can inform practical applications.

Sajid Khan is working as Assistant Professor of Entrepreneurship and Innovation at GIKI, Pakistan. He has earned his PhD in Management from Massey University, New Zealand. Sajid's research interest includes pedagogic theory, training evaluation, responsible innovation, dilemma management, and creativity.

MIX
Papier aus verantwortungsvollen Quellen
Paper from responsible sources
FSC® C105338

If you have any concerns about our products,
you can contact us on
ProductSafety@springernature.com

In case Publisher is established outside the EU,
the EU authorized representative is:
Springer Nature Customer Service Center GmbH
Europaplatz 3, 69115 Heidelberg, Germany

Printed by Libri Plureos GmbH
in Hamburg, Germany